Designing Enterprise Applications
with the J2EE™ Platform, Second Edition

The Java™ Series

Lisa Friendly, Series Editor
Tim Lindholm, Technical Editor
Ken Arnold, Technical Editor of The Jini™ Technology Series
Jim Inscore, Technical Editor of The Java™ Series, Enterprise Edition

http://www.javaseries.com

Eric Armstrong, Stephanie Bodoff, Debbie Carson, Maydene Fisher, Dale Green, Kim Haase
The Java™ Web Services Tutorial

Ken Arnold, James Gosling, David Holmes
The Java™ Programming Language, Third Edition

Joshua Bloch
Effective Java™ Programming Language Guide

Mary Campione, Kathy Walrath, Alison Huml
The Java™ Tutorial, Third Edition:
A Short Course on the Basics

Mary Campione, Kathy Walrath, Alison Huml,Tutorial Team
The Java™ Tutorial Continued:
The Rest of the JDK™

Patrick Chan
The Java™ Developers Almanac 1.4, Volume 1

Patrick Chan
The Java™ Developers Almanac 1.4, Volume 2

Patrick Chan, Rosanna Lee
The Java™ Class Libraries, Second Edition, Volume 2:
java.applet, java.awt, java.beans

Patrick Chan, Rosanna Lee, Doug Kramer
The Java™ Class Libraries, Second Edition, Volume 1:
java.io, java.lang, java.math, java.net, java.text, java.util

Patrick Chan, Rosanna Lee, Doug Kramer
The Java˜ Class Libraries, Second Edition, Volume 1:
Supplement for the Java™ 2 Platform,
Standard Edition, v1.2

Kirk Chen, Li Gong
Programming Open Service Gateways with Java™
Embedded Server

Zhiqun Chen
Java Card™ Technology for Smart Cards:
Architecture and Programmer's Guide

Li Gong
Inside Java™ 2 Platform Security:
Architecture, API Design, and Implementation

James Gosling, Bill Joy, Guy Steele, Gilad Bracha
The Java™ Language Specification, Second Edition

Doug Lea
Concurrent Programming in Java™ , Second Edition:
Design Principles and Patterns

Rosanna Lee, Scott Seligman
JNDI API Tutorial and Reference:
Building Directory-Enabled Java™ Applications

Sheng Liang
The Java™ Native Interface:
Programmer's Guide and Specification

Tim Lindholm, Frank Yellin
The Java™ Virtual Machine Specification, Second Edition

Roger Riggs, Antero Taivalsaari, Mark VandenBrink
Programming Wireless Devices with the Java™ 2
Platform, Micro Edition

Henry Sowizral, Kevin Rushforth, Michael Deering
The Java 3D™ API Specification, Second Edition

Sun Microsystems, Inc.
Java™ Look and Feel Design Guidelines: Advanced Topics

Kathy Walrath, Mary Campione
The JFC Swing Tutorial:
A Guide to Constructing GUIs

Seth White, Maydene Fisher, Rick Cattell, Graham Hamilton, Mark Hapner
JDBC™ API Tutorial and Reference, Second Edition:
Universal Data Access for the Java™ 2 Platform

Steve Wilson, Jeff Kesselman
Java™ Platform Performance:
Strategies and Tactics

The Jini™ Technology Series

Eric Freeman, Susanne Hupfer, Ken Arnold
JavaSpaces™ Principles, Patterns, and Practice

Jim Waldo/Jini™ Technology Team
The Jini™ Specifications, Second Edition,
edited by Ken Arnold

The Java™ Series, Enterprise Edition

Stephanie Bodoff, Dale Green, Kim Haase, Eric Jendrock, Monica Pawlan, Beth Stearns
The J2EE™ Tutorial

Rick Cattell, Jim Inscore, Enterprise Partners
J2EE™ Technology in Practice:
Building Business Applications with the Java™ 2 Platform,
Enterprise Edition

Mark Hapner, Rich Burridge, Rahul Sharma, Joseph Fialli, Kim Haase
Java™ Message Service API Tutorial and Reference:
Messaging for the J2EE™ Platform

Inderjeet Singh, Beth Stearns, Mark Johnson, Enterprise Team
Designing Enterprise Applications with the Java™ 2
Platform, Enterprise Edition

Vlada Matena and Beth Stearns
Applying Enterprise JavaBeans™ :
Component-Based Development for the J2EE™ Platform

Bill Shannon, Mark Hapner, Vlada Matena, James Davidson, Eduardo Pelegri-Llopart, Larry Cable, Enterprise Team
Java™ 2 Platform, Enterprise Edition:
Platform and Component Specifications

Rahul Sharma, Beth Stearns, Tony Ng
J2EE™ Connector Architecture and Enterprise Application
Integration ´

Designing Enterprise Applications

with the J2EE™ Platform, Second Edition

Inderjeet Singh, Beth Stearns,
Mark Johnson, and the Enterprise Team

✦ Addison-Wesley

Boston • San Francisco • New York • Toronto • Montreal
London • Munich • Paris • Madrid
Capetown • Sydney • Tokyo • Singapore • Mexico City

The publisher offers discounts on this book when ordered in quantity for special sales. For more information, please contact:

Pearson Education Corporate Sales Division
One Lake Street
Upper Saddle River, NJ 07458
(800) 382-3419
corpsales@pearsontechgroup.com

Visit Addison-Wesley on the Web: www.aw.com/cseng/

Library of Congress Control Number: 2002102513

ISBN 0-201-78790-3
Text printed on recycled paper
1 2 3 4 5 6 7 8 9 10—CRS—0605040302
First printing, March 2002

Contents

Foreword

$\mathbf{Y}$OU'RE holding one part of a truly stellar phenomenon in the computing industry: the Java 2 Platform, Enterprise Edition. This book is a key piece of a visionary effort that began more than two years ago with the introduction of the J2EE platform. In that time, the J2EE engineering team has defined a new ecosystem for networked computing and taught the world a new way to develop distributed applications.

This team has changed the computing world on many levels. They've reinforced the core values of Java technology: portability, scalability, security, and community. They've redefined the model for developing big, industrial-strength enterprise applications. They've invented new licensing models, driven a new compatibility model, and invigorated a new adoption model. Through the Java Community Process, they've taught intense competitors that working together—and building smarter—can be the key to successfully growing a marketplace that offers more for everyone.

With the release of the J2EE 1.3 platform, the momentum continues. Six months after the initial release of the J2EE 1.3 platform, the introduction of compatible products is running 56% over the rate for the previous version.

Part of the reason for this phenomenal uptake is, of course, the range of new features in the J2EE 1.3 platform. These include improved container-managed persistence, the new EJB Query Language, message-driven EJBs, support for the J2EE Connector architecture, as well as enhancements such as servlet filters and improved JSP tag library support. Our J2EE licensees have been eager to introduce these features to the platform, and J2EE developers have been anxious to begin taking advantage of them.

In this regard, the Java BluePrints team truly stands alone—first out of the box with real solutions and tested guidelines to help you use these features to best advantage. Because of the quality of their efforts, Java BluePrints has also been a phenomenal success during the past two years. More than a half million developers have downloaded the BluePrints book and demo application code. A dozen application server vendors now redistribute J2EE BluePrints with their J2EE compatible products. Four vendors have even introduced commercial products based on J2EE BluePrints. Elsewhere, BluePrints is recognized, written about, and praised by every major Java technology-focused publication. A number of technical institutes even use BluePrints to train the next generation of Java application developers.

The Java software organization focuses on efforts like these because we see the net effect: a huge win for software developers everywhere, at all levels of the software development food chain. By fostering Java technology standards like the J2EE platform and providing content like BluePrints, we're working to ensure that the Java software development community continues to grow, flourish, and mature.

This book is central to that effort. The enterprise team who brought it together are thought leaders who can help you build the skill sets you need to be ready for new opportunities. Like you, they stay awake nights thinking about how to build applications that are more flexible, more portable, higher performance, and easier to develop. They're tuned into solving the problems that you face day to day. Working alongside the folks who define and implement the technologies they are using, they explore the "what-if" scenarios that this rich platform suggests and sift through design options to come up with clear guidelines for the what and how of software design on the J2EE platform.

The future holds great things for Java technology and the BluePrints program. During the coming months, our Java Web Services Developer Pack, The Java Web Services Tutorial, and Java BluePrints for Web Services will help developers build applications that take advantage of the services-on-demand promised by the Sun ONE architecture. Building on what's already available, these offerings will enhance the phenomenal success of the J2EE platform and the Java application marketplace.

By taking advantage of the gold mine of advice you'll find in this book, you too can be part of the phenomenal success that is the J2EE platform.

Rich Green
Vice President and General Manager
Java and XML Software, Sun Microsystems
Santa Clara, California
February, 2002

Preface

THIS book, now in its second edition, describes standard approaches to designing multitier enterprise applications with the Java™ 2 Platform, Enterprise Edition. This book, and the accompanying Java Pet Store sample application, are part of the successful Java BluePrints program created by Sun Microsystems with the introduction of the J2EE platform. This program has been used by thousands of application architects, developers, and students to attain better understanding of the programming model inherent in the J2EE platform.

This book and the Java BluePrints program don't provide information on how to use individual Java technologies to write applications—that's the role of the companion Java Tutorial program. Instead, Java BluePrints focuses on guidelines for application architecture, such as distributing J2EE application functionality across tiers and choosing among design options within each tier. This book assumes that the reader already has basic knowledge of the J2EE platform. We recommend that readers without this knowledge familiarize themselves with the J2EE Tutorial either before or while reading this volume. See "Related Information" later in the Preface for details.

This book describes the architecture and design principles employed in building J2EE applications, and explores of the specific approach adopted by the sample application. Striking a balance between specific details and broad principles is never easy. The hope behind this effort is that the principles presented here are both consistent with and a useful complement to the implementation provided by the sample applications documented in this book.

This book is intended primarily for system architects and enterprise application developers engaged in or considering a transition to the J2EE platform. It is also useful for product vendors interested in developing applications consistent with the J2EE standard.

Obtaining the Sample Application

You can download the Java Pet Store sample application, version 1.3, which is described in this book, from:

```
http://java.sun.com/blueprints/code/
```

The sample application requires a J2EE v1.3-compliant platform on which to run. You can download J2EE SDK™, which is a freely available implementation of that platform, from:

`http://java.sun.com/j2ee/download.html`

Related Information

Pointers to J2EE documentation can be found at:

`http://java.sun.com/j2ee/docs.html`

For information on how to use the J2EE SDK to construct multitier enterprise applications, refer to the *J2EE Tutorial*, available at:

`http://java.sun.com/j2ee/tutorial/`

The J2EE technologies cited in this book are described in their specifications:

- *Java™ 2 Platform, Enterprise Edition Specification, Version 1.3* (J2EE specification). Available at <`http://java.sun.com/j2ee/download.html`>

- *Java™ 2 Platform, Standard Edition Specification, Version 1.3* (J2SE specification). Available at <`http://java.sun.com/j2se/1.3/docs/`>

- *Java™ Servlet Specification, Version 2.3* (Servlet specification). Available at <`http://java.sun.com/products/servlet/`>

- *JavaServer Pages™ Specification, Version 1.2* (JSP specification). Available at <`http://java.sun.com/products/jsp/`>

- *Enterprise JavaBeans™ Specification, Version 2.0* (EJB specification). Available at <`http://java.sun.com/products/ejb/`>

- *Java™ API for XML Processing Specification, Version 1.1 (JAXP* specification). Available at <`http://java.sun.com/xml/jaxp/`>

- *J2EE™ Connector Architecture Specification, Version 1.0 (Connector* specification). Available at <`http://java.sun.com/j2ee/connector/`>

- *JDBC™ API Specification, Version 2.0* (JDBC specification). Available at <`http://java.sun.com/products/jdbc/`>

- *JDBC™ Standard Extension API Specification, Version 2.0* (JDBC extension specification). Available at <http://java.sun.com/products/jdbc/>

- *Java™ Transaction API Specification, Version 1.0.1* (JTA specification). Available at <http://java.sun.com/products/jta/>

- *Java Naming and Directory Interface™ Specification, Version 1.2* (JNDI specification). Available at <http://java.sun.com/products/jndi/>

- *Java IDL.* Available at <http://java.sun.com/j2se/1.3/docs/guide/idl/>

- *RMI over IIOP.* Available at <http://java.sun.com/products/rmi-iiop/>

- *Java™ Message Service Specification, Version 1.0.2* (JMS specification). Available at <http://java.sun.com/products/jms/>

- *Java™ Authentication and Authorization Service Specification, Version 1.0* (JAAS specification). Available at <http://java.sun.com/products/jaas/>

- *JavaMail™ API Specification, Version 1.2* (JavaMail specification). Available at <http://java.sun.com/products/javamail/>

- *JavaBeans™ Activation Framework Specification, Version 1.0.1* (JAF specification). Available at <http://java.sun.com/products/javabeans/glasgow/jaf.html>

Typographic Conventions

Table 0.1 describes the typographic conventions used in this book.

Table 0.1   Typographic Conventions

Typeface or Symbol	Meaning	Example
AaBbCc123	The names of commands, files, and directories; interface, class, method, and deployment descriptor element names; programming language keywords	Edit the file `Main.jsp`. How to retrieve a `UserTransaction` object. Specify the `resource-ref` element.
AaBbCc123	Variable name	The files are named *XYZ*`file`.
AaBbCc123	Book titles, new words or terms, or words to be emphasized	Read Chapter 6 in *User's Guide*. These are called *class* options. You *must* be root to do this.

Acknowledgments

This book is the result of many people's efforts.

The authors listed for each chapter had primary responsibility for the content provided there and also made significant contributions to other chapters. In addition, Abhishek Chauhan, Vinita Khanna, and Stephanie Bodoff contributed significantly to the chapters in the first edition of this book. Liz Blair was instrumental in developing the initial drafts of the EJB-tier chapter.

We are indebted to Thierry Violleau, Umit Yalcinalp, Kate Stout, Norbert Lindenberg, and Danny Coward for their comprehensive reviews and thoughtful comments on many chapters. We would also like to thank Eduardo Pelegri-Llopart, Jon Ellis, David Bowen, Monica Pawlan, Tim Lindholm, Tom Kast, Mark Hapner, Bill Shannon, John Crupi, Sanjeev Krishnan, Stephanie Bodoff, Dale Green, Mark Roth, Martin Flynn, Brian Beck, Andrey Dikanskiy, and Craig McClanahan for their input.

Our special thanks go to our management, Larry Freeman, Cori Kaylor, Vivek Nagar, and Jeff Jackson, for their whole-hearted support and commitment to the BluePrints program and to this book in particular.

We would never have made it to the end of this project without the support of Suzy Pelouch who did an excellent job at pulling together all the pieces.

The authors of the J2EE specifications and the developers of the reference implementation provided useful input at various points during the development of the J2EE programming model.

About the Authors

Authors listed in alphabetical order by first name:

BETH STEARNS is the principal partner of ComputerEase Publishing, a computer consulting firm she founded in 1982. Her client list includes Sun Microsystems, Inc., Silicon Graphics, Inc., Oracle Corporation, and Xerox Corporation. Among her publications are the "Java Native Interface" chapter in *The Java Tutorial Continued* book in the Addison-Wesley Java Series, "The EJB Programming Guide" for Inprise Corporation, and "Understanding EDT," a guide to Digital Equipment Corporation's text editor. She co-authored with Vlada Matena the book, *Applying Enterprise JavaBeans: Component-Based Development for the J2EE Platform*, which is part of the Addison-Wesley Java Series. She is also a co-author with Rahul Sharma and Tony Ng of another book in the Addison-Wesley Java Series, *J2EE Connector Architecture and Enterprise Application Integration*.

GREG MURRAY is a member of the Java BluePrints team at Sun Microsystems. He is a contributing author to the first edition of this book. Greg contributed to the design of the Java Pet Store sample application with an emphasis on the Web tier. Prior to working on the Java BluePrints team, Greg was a member of the Global Products Engineering group of Sun Microsystems, where he developed internationalization tools.

INDERJEET SINGH is the lead architect on the Java BluePrints team at Sun Microsystems, where he investigates the best uses of J2EE technologies for enterprise application design. Inderjeet has been involved with the Java BluePrints program since its inception. He is a regular speaker on enterprise application design. In the past, Inderjeet has also designed fault-tolerance software for large-scale distributed telecommunications switching systems. Inderjeet holds an M.S. in computer science from Washington University in Saint Louis, and a B.Tech. in computer science and engineering from Indian Institute of Technology, Delhi.

JIM INSCORE manages technical publications for the Java 2 Platform, Enterprise Edition, in the Java Software Group of Sun Microsystems. His roles include overseeing developer documentation, such as the J2EE Tutorial and J2EE BluePrints, providing developer content for the java.sun.com Web site. Jim serves as technical editor on the Java Series, Enterprise Edition, from Addison-Wesley and is a coauthor, with Rick Cattel, of the Java Series book, *J2EE Technology in Practice*. Jim has been involved with object-oriented and enterprise-related technologies for more than 15 years, working with developer documentation and marketing programs for organizations that include Oracle, Ingres, NeXT, Kaleida, and Macromedia. Prior to that, he spent 10 years writing marketing communications materials for the technical marketplace.

LINDA DEMICHIEL is the specification lead of the Expert Group for the Enterprise JavaBeans™ specification, under the Java Community Process program, and a Senior Staff Engineer in the J2EE platform group at Sun Microsystems. She has over 15 years of industry experience in the areas of databases, distributed computing, and OO. She has a Ph.D. in computer science from Stanford University.

MARK JOHNSON is a software developer, trainer, writer, and speaker living in Fort Collins, Colorado. He is President of Elucify Technical Communications, a Colorado corporation dedicated to making accessible difficult or novel topics in science and technology through clear explanation and example. He has been a columnist at *JavaWorld* since 1997 and is a member of the National Association of Science Writers. He is currently a consultant with the Java BluePrints group at Sun. Mark completed a B. S. in computer and electrical engineering at Purdue University in 1986, followed by two years of graduate work at Purdue, concentrating in signal processing and computer systems.

NICHOLAS KASSEM is a Senior Staff Engineer with Sun Microsystems and has influenced and had responsibility for a number of technologies and initiatives within Java Software, including the Java Web Server, Java Embedded Server, the Servlet API, JavaServer Pages, Java Message Queuing, and the J2EE programming model. He is currently leading the Java API for XML Messaging (JAXM) initiative. Nicholas has more than twenty years of industry experience and has held senior engineering and management positions at Philips (Data Systems) and the Santa Cruz Operation. He has had direct responsibility for a wide variety of engineering projects, including the development of Data Communications Gateway Hardware (DISOSS), Novell and Lan Manager protocol stacks, and an implementation of OSF

DCE on SCO UNIX. He is an engineering graduate of Birmingham University in the United Kingdom.

RAHUL SHARMA is the lead architect and specification lead of J2EE Connector Architecture 1.0 and JAX-RPC specifications. He works as an architect in the J2EE platform group of Sun Microsystems, Inc. Rahul has also worked on exploring how the Java platform can be used for building carrier-grade applications. Rahul has an MBA from Haas School of Business, University of California at Berkeley, and a B.E. in computer engineering from Delhi University.

RAY ORTIGAS is an engineer with the Java BluePrints group at Sun Microsystems, where he works on wireless and enterprise applications using Java technology. A former intern with the Java Tutorial, where he authored the "First Cup of Java" trail, Ray earned his B.Sc. in computer science from the University of Toronto in Canada.

RON MONZILLO is a Senior Staff Engineer at Sun Microsystems, where he is the J2EE security specification lead. Ron was responsible for the design and standardization of the EJB secure interoperability protocol, CSIv2. Prior to joining Sun, Ron worked for the Open Group where he contributed to the evolution of the Distributed Computing Environment. Ron has also worked for BBN, where he developed Network Management systems, and as a Principal Investigator for the MITRE Corporation where he researched fault-tolerant distributed database systems and multiprocessor architectures. Ron received an M.S. in computer science from the University of Connecticut and a B.S. in biology from Bates College.

SEAN BRYDON is a member of the Java BluePrints team at Sun Microsystems. Sean contributed to the design of the Java Pet Store sample application with an emphasis on the application and the tiers for EIS and the EJB component architecture. In the past, Sean has worked on the JavaLoad™ team and has spent a summer as an intern at SunLabs. Sean holds an M.S. in computer science from the University of California at Santa Barbara and also a B.S. in computer science from the University of California at Santa Barbara.

TONY NG is the technical lead of the J2EE SDK and Reference Implementation at Sun Microsystems, Inc. Previously, he was the implementation lead of the J2EE Connector Architecture. He is a contributing author to the first edition of *Designing Enterprise Applications with the Java 2 Platform, Enterprise Edition,* and *J2EE*

Connector Architecture and Enterprise Application Integration in the Addison-Wesley Java Series. Tony has an M.S. in electrical engineering and computer science from Massachusetts Institute of Technology and a B.S. in computer science from the University of Illinois, Urbana-Champaign.

VIJAY RAMACHANDRAN is a member of the technical staff at Sun Microsystems, where he works as the Team Lead of the Java BluePrints team. His major contributions include guidelines on best practices when developing business solutions using enterprise beans. Before joining the BluePrints team, Vijay was a member of the Enterprise Server Products Group of Sun Microsystems working on Sun's enterprise server products line. Vijay holds an M.S. in computer science from Santa Clara University, California, and a B.E. in electrical engineering from Madras University, India.

CHAPTER 1

Introduction

by Jim Inscore and Nicholas Kassem

SINCE its introduction more than two years ago, the Java 2 Platform, Enterprise Edition (J2EE), has rapidly established a new model for developing distributed applications. This model is based on well-defined components that can automatically take advantage of sophisticated platform services. These components can be developed according to standard guidelines, combined into applications, deployed on a variety of compatible server products, and reused for maximum programmer productivity. This model is intended to both standardize and simplify the kind of distributed applications required for today's networked information economy. The success of the J2EE platform is in large part due to the success of this model.

Today, all leading application server and enterprise information system vendors have adopted the J2EE standard and introduced products based on the J2EE platform specification. Application architects and developers have come to rely on the J2EE standard to help them solve the various design challenges that face them day to day.

While the fundamentals of the J2EE platform are relatively easy to describe, mapping these features to architectural issues in the design of distributed applications requires deeper understanding and careful decision making. Although the J2EE standard offers a simplified programming model compared to previous alternatives, the platform isn't monolithic. Certain features require that architects and developers weigh their options before making design decisions and be prepared to re-think those decisions as they uncover new challenges. That, in turn, requires some understanding of the design motivations behind the platform and of the trade-offs involved in applying specific design features to a specific architectural problem.

Different implementations of the J2EE platform may provide distinguishing characteristics that improve their performance or development ease in particular areas. However, the level of abstraction provided by the J2EE standard enables common themes to be developed, explained, and explored and certain common design guidelines to be developed. That's what Java BluePrints is all about. It answers questions like:

- What's the best way to apply each type of J2EE component?

- Where does it make sense to use Java servlets and where to use JavaServer Pages?

- What's the best way to factor business logic between entity beans and session beans?

- How do you choose between container-managed and bean-managed persistence when using entity beans?

- What are the design and performance trade-offs between choosing a distributed architecture and one based on local interfaces?

- In this increasingly security-conscious world, how do you design distributed applications to be accessible to users who need them and secure from unwanted intrusion?

Before the remainder of this book takes you more deeply into these and other details of J2EE application architectures, this chapter gives you a look at some of the design motivations behind the J2EE platform. It describes the high-level benefits of the J2EE platform and discusses ways that using it as the underlying architecture for distributed applications makes sense for a variety of application requirements.

1.1   Challenges of Enterprise Application Development

Timing has always been a critical factor when organizations adopt new technologies, and the accelerated pace of the information-driven business model puts greater emphasis on response times. Organizations need to be able to project enterprise systems into various client channels, and to do so in a way that's reliable, productive, and capable of sustaining frequent updates to both information and services. The principal issue is how to keep up with today's business challenges—whatever they may be—while maintaining and leveraging the value of existing information assets. In this environment, timeliness, productivity, security, and predictability are all absolutely critical to building and maintaining momentum. A number of factors can enhance or impede an organization's ability to deliver custom enterprise applications quickly and to maximize their value over their lifetime.

1.1.1 Programming Productivity

The ability to develop and deploy applications is key to success in the information economy. Applications must go quickly from prototype to production and must continue to evolve even after they are deployed.

Productivity is thus vital to responsive application development. Providing application development teams with standard means to access the services required by multitier applications and standard ways to support a variety of clients can contribute to both responsiveness and flexibility.

The current divergence of technologies and programming models is a destabilizing factor in Internet and other distributed computing applications. Traditional Web technologies such as HTML and Common Gateway Interface (CGI) have provided a mechanism for distributing dynamic content, while back-end systems such as transaction processors and database management systems have provided controlled access to the data to be presented and manipulated. These technologies present a diversity of programming models: some based on well-defined standards; others on more ad-hoc standards; and others still on proprietary architectures.

With no single application model, it can be difficult for teams to communicate application requirements effectively and productively. As a result, architecting applications becomes more complex. What's more, the skill sets required to integrate these technologies aren't well organized for effective division of labor. For example, CGI development requires coders to define both content and layout of a dynamic Web page.

Another complicating factor in application development time is the choice of clients. While many applications can be distributed to Web browser clients through static or dynamically generated HTML, others may need to support a specific type of client or to support several types of clients simultaneously. The programming model needs to support a variety of client configurations, with minimum effect on basic application architecture and on the application's core business logic.

1.1.2   Integration with Existing Systems

Much of the data of value to organizations has been collected over the years by existing enterprise information systems. Much of the programming investment resides in applications on those same systems. The challenge for developers of enterprise applications is how to reuse and commoditize these existing information assets.

To achieve this goal, application developers need standard ways to access middle-tier and back-end services such as database management systems and transaction monitors. They also need systems that provide these services consistently, so that new programming models or styles aren't required as integration expands to encompass various systems within an enterprise.

1.1.3   Freedom of Choice

Application development responsiveness requires the ability to mix and match solutions to come up with the optimum configuration for the task at hand. Freedom of choice in enterprise application development should extend from servers to tools to components. The wide range of J2EE compatible solutions available today and in the future ensures the maximum freedom of choice.

The availability of choices among server products gives an organization the ability to select configurations tailored to their application requirements. It also provides the ability to move quickly and easily from one configuration to another as internal and external demand requires.

Access to the appropriate tools for the job is another important choice. Development teams should be able to adopt new tools as new needs arise, including tools from server vendors and third-party tool developers. What's more, each member of a development team should have access to tools that are most appropriate to their skill set and contribution.

Finally, developers should be able to choose from a ready market of off-the-shelf application components to take advantage of external expertise and to enhance development productivity.

1.1.4   Response to Demand

When designing large-scale distributed applications, both availability and scalability are key considerations. The more easily and automatically that an application can handle changes in use patterns and system configurations, the better. Systems that require any redesign, recoding, or redeployment to achieve either availability or scalability will limit flexibility and diminish expected performance.

To scale effectively, systems need to be designed to handle multiple client interactions with ease. They need mechanisms for efficient management of system resources and services such as database connections and transactions. For highest availability, they need access to features such as automatic load balancing and failover, without any effort on the part of the application developer. Applications should be able to run on any server configuration appropriate to anticipated client volumes and to easily switch configurations when the need arises. Support for clustered application deployment environments contributes to achieving many of these goals.

1.1.5   Maintaining Security

More than ever, information systems security is on the minds of IT managers and system architects. That's because protecting information assets to maximize their value can jeopardize that very value. Traditionally, IT departments have been able to maintain a relatively high level of control over the environment of both servers and clients. When information assets are exposed in less-protected environments, it becomes increasingly important to maintain tight security over the most sensitive assets, while allowing seemingly unencumbered access to others.

One of the difficulties in integrating disparate systems is providing a unified security model. Single sign on across internal application and asset boundaries is important to creating a positive user experience with the applications. Security needs to be compatible with existing mechanisms. In cases where customers need to access secure information, the mechanisms need to maintain high security (and user confidence) while remaining as unobtrusive and transparent as possible.

1.2   The Platform for Enterprise Solutions

The J2EE platform represents a single standard for implementing and deploying enterprise applications. During its first two years, the J2EE standard's success has transformed the marketplace for distributed computing products. This success is largely due to the fact that the J2EE platform has been designed through an open process, engaging a range of enterprise computing vendors to ensure that it meets the widest possible range of enterprise application requirements. As a result, the J2EE platform addresses the core issues that impede organizations' efforts to maintain a competitive pace in the information economy. Organizations have recognized this and quickly adopted the new platform standard.

1.2.1   J2EE Platform Overview

The J2EE platform is designed to provide server-side and client-side support for developing distributed, multitier applications. Such applications are typically configured as a client tier to provide the user interface, one or more middle-tier modules that provide client services and business logic for an application, and back-end enterprise information systems providing data management. Figure 1.1 illustrates the various components and services that make up a typical J2EE environment.

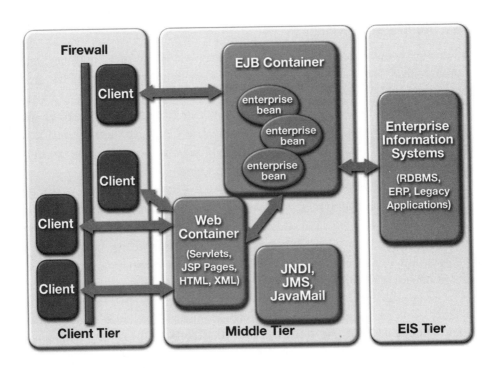

Figure 1.1   J2EE Environment

1.2.1.1   Multitier Model

As illustrated, the J2EE platform provides a multitier distributed application model. This means that the various parts of an application can run on different devices. The

J2EE architecture defines a *client tier*, a *middle tier* (consisting of one or more sub-tiers), and a *back-end tier*. The client tier supports a variety of client types, both outside and inside of corporate firewalls. The middle tier supports client services through Web containers in the *Web tier* and supports business logic component services through Enterprise JavaBeans™ (EJB™) containers in the *EJB tier*. On the back end, the enterprise information systems in the *EIS tier* are accessible by way of standard APIs.

1.2.1.2   Container-Based Component Management

Central to the J2EE component-based development model is the notion of containers. Containers are standardized runtime environments that provide specific services to components. Components can expect these services to be available on any J2EE platform from any vendor. For example, all J2EE Web containers provide runtime support for responding to client requests, performing request-time processing (such as invoking JSP pages or servlet behavior), and returning results to the client. In addition, they provide APIs to support user session management. All EJB containers provide automated support for transaction and life cycle management of EJB components, as well as bean lookup and other services. Containers also provide standardized access to enterprise information systems; for example, providing access to relational data through the JDBC API.

In addition, containers provide a mechanism for selecting application behaviors at assembly or deployment time. Through the use of deployment descriptors (XML files that specify component and container behavior), components can be configured to a specific container's environment when deployed, rather than in component code. Features that can be configured at deployment time include security checks, transaction control, and other management responsibilities.

While the J2EE specification defines the component containers that a platform implementation must support, it doesn't specify or restrict the containers' configurations. Thus, both container types can run on a single platform, Web containers can live on one platform and EJB containers on another, or a J2EE platform can be made up of multiple containers on multiple platforms.

1.2.1.3   Support for Client Components

The J2EE client tier provides support for a variety of client types, both within the enterprise firewall and outside. Clients can be offered through Web browsers by using plain HTML pages, HTML generated dynamically by JavaServer Pages™

(JSP™) technology, or Java applets. Clients can also be offered as stand-alone Java language applications. J2EE clients are assumed to access the middle tier primarily using Web standards, namely HTTP, HTML, and XML. Because of its flexible programming model, the J2EE platform can support a number of simple application models implemented primarily on the strengths of its Web tier component technologies.

To support more complex user interactions, it may be necessary to provide functionality directly in the client tier. This functionality is typically implemented as JavaBeans™ components that interact with the service in the middle tier via servlets. Client-tier JavaBeans components would typically be provided by the service as an applet that is downloaded automatically into a user's browser. To eliminate problems caused by old or non-standard versions of the Java Virtual Machine in a user's browser, the J2EE application model provides special support for automatically downloading and installing the Java Plug-in. In addition, the J2EE platform is flexible enough to support alternate client models easily, including wireless phones and handheld devices that use programming models provided by the Java 2 Platform, Micro Edition.

Client-tier beans can also be contained in a stand-alone application client written in the Java programming language. In this case, the enterprise typically would make the client available for users to download from a browser using Java Web Start technology. Java Web Start technology makes application deployment portable by providing browser-based download and installation mechanisms. With both application and deployment portability, this ensures that users can always access and work with the latest versions of stand-alone application clients.

If desired, non-Java clients such as Visual Basic programs can present J2EE services to users. Since the service is presented by servlets in the middle tier to first-tier clients using the standard HTTP protocol, it is easy to access it from practically any program running on any operating system.

1.2.1.4   Support for Business Logic Components

While simple J2EE applications may be built largely in the client tier, business logic is often implemented on the J2EE platform in the middle tier as Enterprise JavaBeans components (also known as enterprise beans). Enterprise beans allow the component or application developer to concentrate on the business logic while the complexities of delivering a reliable, scalable service are handled by the EJB container.

In many ways, the J2EE platform and EJB architecture have complementary goals. The EJB component model is the backbone of industrial-strength application architectures in the J2EE programming model. The J2EE platform complements the EJB specification by:

- Fully specifying the APIs that an enterprise bean developer can use to implement enterprise beans

- Defining the larger, distributed programming environment in which enterprise beans are used as business logic components

1.2.1.5 Support for the J2EE Standard

The J2EE standard is defined through a set of related specifications. Key among these are the J2EE specification, the Enterprise JavaBeans specification, the Java Servlet specification, and the JavaServer Pages specification. Together, these specifications define the architecture described in this book. In addition to the specifications, several other technology deliverables support the J2EE standard, including the J2EE Compatibility Test Suite, the J2EE reference implementation, and the J2EE SDK.

The J2EE Compatibility Test Suite (CTS) helps maximize the portability of applications by validating the specification compliance of a J2EE platform product. This test suite begins where the basic Java Conformance Kit (JCK) leaves off. The CTS tests conformance to the Java standard extension APIs that are not covered by a JCK. In addition, it tests a J2EE platform's ability to run standard end-to-end applications.

The J2EE reference implementation, a complete implementation of the J2EE standard provided by Sun Microsystems, represents an operational definition of the J2EE platform. It is used by licensees as the "gold standard" to determine what their product must do under a particular set of application circumstances. It is the standard platform for running the J2EE Compatibility Test Suite, and it can be used by developers to verify the portability of an application. The J2EE reference implementation is available in both binary and source code form.

The J2EE SDK, based on the J2EE reference implementation binary, is provided freely to the developer community to help expedite developer adoption of the J2EE standard. Although not a commercial product and not available for commercial use, the J2EE SDK is useful for developing application demos and prototypes, such as the Java Pet Store sample application described in this book. The J2EE SDK also includes application verification and deployment tools to simplify development, and the J2EE Tutorial, which provides step-by-step examples and information that developers need to begin working with the platform.

Another word on J2EE standards and portability: The J2EE specifications have, by design, set the platform-compatibility bar at a level that's relatively easy to clear. Because the platform specifications are developed collaboratively, platform vendors must have plenty of opportunity to supply J2EE platform implementations. Obvious and unreasonable implementation hurdles were avoided. For example, there are no restrictions on vendors adding value to J2EE products by supporting services not defined in the specifications.

While the J2EE standard is designed to encourage component portability, specific results are primarily a function of how a component uses services provided by its container. Vendor-specific features limit component portability. The J2EE specifications spell out a base set of capabilities that a component can count on, providing components with a level of cross-container portability. Needless to say, an application developer expecting to deploy on a specific vendor implementation of the J2EE platform should be able to do so across a wide range of operating systems and hardware architectures.

1.2.2   J2EE Platform Benefits

With features designed to expedite the process of developing distributed applications, the J2EE platform offers several benefits:

- Simplified architecture and development

- Freedom of choice in servers, tools, and components

- Integration with existing information systems

- Scalability to meet demand variations

- Flexible security model

1.2.2.1   Simplified Architecture and Development

The J2EE platform supports a simplified, component-based development model. Because it is based on the Java programming language and the Java 2 Platform, Standard Edition (J2SE™ platform), this model offers "Write-Once-Run-Any-where™" portability, supported by any server product that conforms to the J2EE standard.

The component-based J2EE development model can enhance application development productivity in a number of ways:

- **Maps easily to application functionality**—Component-based application models map easily and flexibly to the functionality desired from an application. As the examples presented throughout this book illustrate, the J2EE platform provides a variety of ways to configure the architecture of an application, depending on such things as client types required, level of access required to data sources, and other considerations. Component-based design also simplifies application maintenance, since components can be updated and replaced independently—new functionality can be shimmed into existing applications simply by updating selected components.

- **Enables assembly- and deploy-time behaviors**—Because of the high level of service standardization, much of the code of a J2EE application can be generated automatically by tools, with minimal developer intervention. In addition, components can expect standard services to be available in the runtime environment and can dynamically connect to other components by means of consistent interfaces. As a result, many application behaviors can be configured at application assembly or deployment time, without recoding. Component developers can communicate requirements to application deployers through specific deployment descriptors and settings. Tools can automate this process to further expedite development.

- **Supports division of labor**—Components help divide the labor of application development among specific skill sets, enabling each member of a development team to focus on his or her ability. Web page authors can create JSP templates, Java programming language coders can implement application behavior, domain experts can develop business logic, and application developers and integrators can assemble and deploy applications. This division of labor also expedites application maintenance. For example, the user interface is the most dynamic part of many applications, particularly on the Web. With the J2EE platform, Web page authors can tweak the look and feel of JSP pages without programmer intervention.

The J2EE specifications define a number of roles, including application component provider, application assembler, and application deployer. On some development teams, one or two people may perform all these roles, while on others these tasks may be further subdivided into more specific skill sets (such as user interface designers, programmers, and so on).

1.2.2.2   Integrating Existing Enterprise Information Systems

The J2EE platform, together with the J2SE platform, includes a number of industry standard APIs for accessing existing enterprise information systems. Basic access to these systems is provided by the following APIs:

- The J2EE Connector architecture is the infrastructure for interacting with a variety of Enterprise Information System types, including ERP, CRM, and other legacy systems.

- The JDBC™ API is used for accessing relational data from the Java programming language.

- The Java Transaction API (JTA) is the API for managing and coordinating transactions across heterogeneous enterprise information systems.

- The Java Naming and Directory Interface™ (JNDI) is the API for accessing information in enterprise name and directory services.

- The Java Message Service (JMS) is the API for sending and receiving messages via enterprise messaging systems such as IBM MQ Series and TIBCO Rendezvous. In the J2EE platform version 1.3, message-driven beans provide a component-based approach to encapsulating messaging functionality.

- The JavaMail™ API is used for sending and receiving e-mail.

- Java IDL provides the mechanism for calling CORBA services.

- Java APIs for XML provide support for integration with legacy systems and applications, and for implementing Web services in the J2EE platform.

In addition, specialized access to enterprise resource planning and mainframe systems such as IBM's CICS and IMS is provided through the J2EE Connector architecture. Since each of these systems is highly complex and specialized, they require unique tools and support to ensure utmost simplicity to application developers. Thanks to new integration features in the platform, enterprise beans can combine the use of connector access objects and service APIs with middle-tier business logic to accomplish their business functions.

1.2.2.3   Choice of Servers, Tools, and Components

The J2EE standard and J2EE brand have created a huge marketplace for servers, tools, and components. The J2EE brand on a server product ensures the consistent level of service that is fundamental to the goals of the J2EE platform. At the same time, J2EE standards ensure a lively marketplace for tools and components. Based on past experience and industry momentum, all leading enterprise software vendors are expected to provide the marketplace for J2EE 1.3 products.

The standardization and branding of the J2EE platform provides many benefits, including:

- **A range of server choices**—Application development organizations can expect J2EE branded platforms from a variety of vendors, providing a range of choices in hardware platforms, operating systems, and server configurations. This ensures that businesses get a choice of servers appropriate to their needs.

- **Designed for tool support**—Both enterprise beans and JSP page components are designed to be manipulated by graphical development tools and to allow automating many of the application development tasks traditionally requiring the ability to write and debug code. Both J2EE server providers and third-party tool developers have developed tools that conform to J2EE standards and support various application development tasks and styles. Application developers have a choice of tools to manipulate and assemble components, and individual team members may choose tools that best suit their specific requirements.

- **A marketplace for components**—Component-based design ensures that many types of behavior can be standardized, packaged, and reused by any J2EE application. Component vendors will provide a variety of off-the-shelf component solutions, including accounting beans, user interface templates, and even vertical market functionality of interest in specific industries. Application architects get a choice of standardized components to handle common or specialized tasks.

The J2EE standard and associated branding program ensure that solutions are compatible. By setting the stage for freedom of choice, the J2EE platform makes it possible to develop with confidence that the value of your investment will be protected.

1.2.2.4   Scales Easily

J2EE containers provide a mechanism that supports simplified scaling of distributed applications, with no application development effort.

Because J2EE containers provide components with transaction support, database connections, life cycle management, and other features that influence performance, they can be designed to provide scalability in these areas. For example, containers may pool database connections, providing clients with quick, efficient access to data.

Because containers may run on multiple systems, Web containers can automatically balance load in response to fluctuating demand.

1.2.2.5   Simplified, Unified Security Model

The J2EE security model is designed to support single sign on access to application services. Component developers can specify the security requirements of a component at the method level to ensure that only users with appropriate permissions can access specific data operations. While both Enterprise JavaBeans technology and Java Servlet APIs provide programmatic security control, the basic role-based security mechanism (where groups of users share specific permissions) is specified entirely at application deployment time. This provides both greater flexibility and better security control.

1.3   J2EE Application Scenarios

The following sections present a number of application scenarios, setting the stage for a detailed discussion of the sample application. The J2EE specifications encourage architectural diversity. The J2EE specifications and technologies make few assumptions about the details of API implementations. The application-level decisions and choices are ultimately a trade-off between functional richness and complexity.

The J2EE programming model is flexible enough for applications that support a variety of client types, with both the Web container and EJB container as optional. Figure 1.2 reflects a range of possible application configurations, including cases where clients interact solely with the Web container, where clients interact directly with the EJB container, and full-blown multitier applications with stand-alone clients, Web-tier components, middle-tier EJB components, and EIS-tier access to resources and data. While the J2EE platform has no implicit bias favoring one application scenario over another, a J2EE product should be able to support any and all of these scenarios.

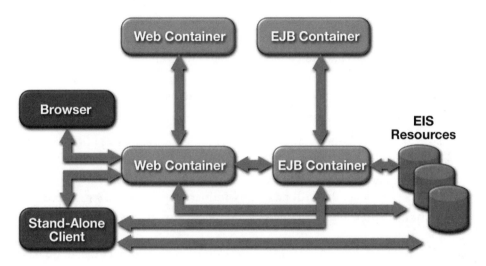

Figure 1.2   J2EE Application Scenarios

The sample application is a multitier application that uses both a Web container and an EJB container. The following enterprise requirements heavily influenced the choices made in developing the sample application:

- The need to make rapid and frequent changes to the "look" of the application

- The need to partition the application along the lines of presentation and business logic so as to increase modularity

- The need to simplify the process of assigning suitably trained human resources to accomplish the development task such that work can proceed along relatively independent but cooperating tracks

- The need to have developers familiar with back-office applications unburdened from GUI and graphic design work, for which they may not be ideally qualified

- The need to have the necessary vocabulary to communicate the business logic to teams concerned with human factors and the aesthetics of the application

- The ability to assemble back-office applications using components from a variety of sources, including off-the-shelf business logic components

- The ability to deploy transactional components across multiple hardware and software platforms independently of the underlying database technology

- The ability to externalize internal data without having to make many assumptions about the consumer of the data and to accomplish this in a loosely coupled manner

Clearly, relaxing any or all of these requirements would influence some of the application-level decisions and choices that a designer would make. Although it is reasonable to speak of "throw-away" presentation logic (that is, applications with a look and feel that ages rapidly), there is still significant inertia associated with business logic. This is even more true in the case of database schemas and data in general. It is fair to say that as one moves further away from EIS resources, the volatility of the application code increases dramatically; that is, the code's "shelf-life" drops significantly.

In summary, the J2EE programming model promotes a model that anticipates growth, encourages component-oriented code reusability, and leverages the strengths of inter-tier communication. It is the tier integration that lies at the heart of the J2EE programming model.

1.3.1   Multitier Application Scenario

Figure 1.3 illustrates an application scenario in which the Web container hosts Web components that are almost exclusively dedicated to handling a given application's presentation logic. JSP pages, supported by servlets, generate dynamic Web content for delivery to the client. The EJB container hosts application components that use EIS resources to service requests from Web-tier components. This architecture decouples data access from the application's user interface. The architecture is also implicitly scalable. Application back-office functionality is relatively isolated from the end-user look and feel.

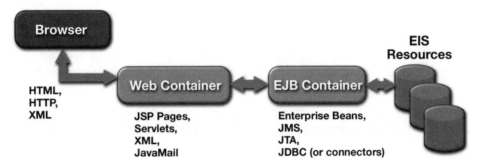

Figure 1.3 Multitier Application

It is worth noting that XML plays an integral role in this scenario. The ability to both produce and consume XML data messages in the Web container is an extremely flexible way to embrace a diverse set of client types. These platforms range from general purpose XML-enabled browsers to specialized XML rendering engines targeting vertical solutions. XML data messages typically use HTTP as their transport protocol. Java and XML are complementary technologies: The Java language offers portable code, XML provides portable data.

In the Web tier, the question of whether to use JSP pages or servlets comes up repeatedly. JSP technology is intended for application user interface components, while Java Servlets are preferred for request processing and application control logic. Servlets and JSP pages work together to provide dynamic content from the Web tier.

1.3.2   Stand-Alone Client Scenario

Figure 1.4 illustrates a stand-alone client scenario.

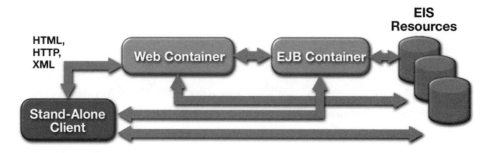

Figure 1.4   Stand-Alone Clients

The stand-alone client may be one of three types:

- EJB clients interacting directly with enterprise beans hosted in an EJB container within an EJB server, as shown in Figure 1.5. This scenario uses RMI-IIOP, and the EJB server accesses EIS resources using JDBC and the J2EE Connector architecture.

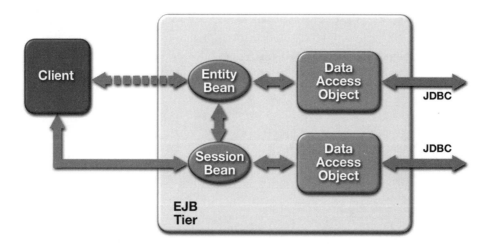

Figure 1.5   EJB-Centric Java Client

- Stand-alone clients, implemented in the Java language or another programming language, consuming dynamic Web content (usually XML data messages). In this scenario, the Web container essentially handles XML transformations and provides Web connectivity to clients. Presentation logic occurs in the client tier. The Web tier handles business logic and may directly access EIS resources. Ideally, business logic is implemented as enterprise beans to take advantage of the rich enterprise beans component model.

- Stand-alone Java application clients accessing enterprise information system resources directly using JDBC or Connectors. In this scenario, presentation and business logic are co-located on the client platform and may in fact be tightly integrated into a single application. This scenario is a classic two-tier client-server architecture, with its associated distribution, maintenance, and scalability issues.

1.3.3   Web-Centric Application Scenario

Figure 1.6 illustrates a three-tier Web-centric application scenario.

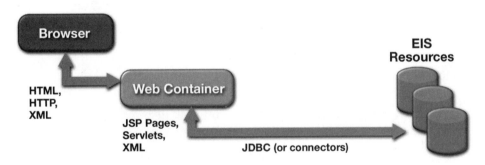

Figure 1.6   Web-Centric Application Scenario

There are a number of scenarios in which the use of enterprise beans in an application would be considered overkill: sort of like using a sledgehammer to crack a nut. The J2EE specification doesn't mandate a specific application configuration, nor could it realistically do so. The J2EE platform is flexible enough to support the application configuration most appropriate to a specific application design requirement.

As demonstrated in the book *J2EE Technology In Practice*, a three-tier Web-centric application scenario is widely used as the starting point for many J2EE applications. The Web container hosts both presentation and business logic, and it is assumed that JDBC and the J2EE Connector architecture are used to access EIS resources.

Figure 1.7 provides a closer look at the Web container in a Web application scenario.

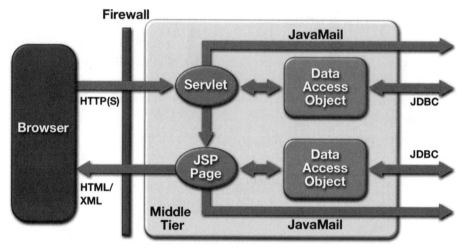

Figure 1.7   Web Container in a Three-Tier Scenario

Keep in mind that the term "Web container" has a precise meaning. It doesn't necessarily mean a distinct process running on a distinct piece of hardware. In many cases, J2EE platform providers may co-locate their Web and EJB containers, running them within the same Java Virtual Machine (JVM). J2EE applications deployed on such an implementation are still considered multitier applications, because of the division of responsibilities that the separate technologies imply.

1.3.4   Business-to-Business Scenario

Figure 1.8 illustrates a business-to-business scenario. This scenario focuses on peer-level interactions between both Web and EJB containers. The J2EE programming model promotes the use of XML data messaging over HTTP as the primary means of establishing loosely coupled communications between Web containers. This is a natural fit for the development and deployment of Web-based commerce solutions.

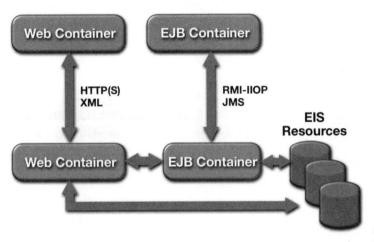

Figure 1.8   Business-to-Business Scenario

The peer-level communications between EJB containers is currently a more tightly coupled solution most suitable for intranet environments. With support for JMS and message-driven beans, the J2EE 1.3 platform makes developing loosely-coupled intranet solutions increasingly practical.

Future releases of the J2EE platform will provide additional functionality in the form of Java APIs for XML, which enable more complete support for loosely coupled applications through XML-based Web services.

1.4   How This Book Is Organized

The remainder of this book is divided into the following chapters:

- **Chapter 2, "J2EE Platform Technologies,"** provides an overview of the component, service, and communication technologies supported by the J2EE platform.

- **Chapter 3, "The Client Tier,"** presents implementation options for J2EE clients and provides guidelines for choosing among these options.

- **Chapter 4, "The Web Tier,"** describes technologies available for supporting development in the Web tier. It includes guidelines and techniques for using J2EE Web components and describes several Web application architectures.

- **Chapter 5, "The Enterprise JavaBeans Tier,"** describes the capabilities of the EJB tier of the J2EE platform and discusses design choices for implementing business logic.

- **Chapter 6, "Integrating with the Enterprise Information System Tier,"** describes recommended approaches for accessing enterprise information systems and how J2EE components must be configured to access them.

- **Chapter 7, "Packaging and Deployment,"** describes the capabilities provided by the J2EE platform for packaging and deploying J2EE applications, and provides heuristics and practical tips on how to use these capabilities.

- **Chapter 8, "Transaction Management,"** describes the transaction services provided by the J2EE platform and provides recommendations on how best to use those services.

- **Chapter 9, "Security,"** describes the mapping of the J2EE security model to enterprise computing environments and infrastructures.

- **Chapter 10, "J2EE Internationalization and Localization,"** new in this edition, explains how to expand an application's reach across the globe by customizing its interfaces and logic for multiple languages, countries, and cultures.

- **Chapter 11, "Architecture of the Sample Application,"** pulls all of the topics in the preceding chapters into a coherent programming model for interactive applications in the J2EE platform, and provides specific architectural guidelines.

- "Glossary," is a list of words and phrases found in this book and their definitions.

Additional information is available on the Java BluePrints Web site, listed in Section 1.6 on page 23. The Web site includes additional content, available only online, that describes in detail the architecture of the Java Pet Store sample application.

1.5   Summary

The challenge to IT professionals today is to efficiently develop and deploy distributed applications for use on both corporate intranets and over the Internet. Companies that can do this effectively will gain strategic advantage in the information economy.

The Java 2 Platform, Enterprise Edition is a standard set of Java technologies that streamline the development, deployment, and management of enterprise applications. The J2EE platform is functionally complete in the sense that it is possible to develop a large class of enterprise applications using only J2EE technologies. Applications written for the J2EE platform will run on any J2EE compatible server. The J2EE platform provides a number of benefits for organizations developing such applications, including a simplified development model; industrial-strength scalability; support for existing information systems; choices in servers, tools, and components; and a simple, flexible security model.

By providing the ability to deploy component-oriented enterprise applications across multiple computing tiers in a platform-neutral manner, the J2EE platform can give fast-moving enterprises a significant and measurable competitive edge.

1.6   References and Resources

- *J2EE Technology in Practice: Building Business Applications with the Java^{TM} 2 Platform, Enterprise Edition.* R. Cattell, J. Inscore, Enterprise Partners. Copyright 2001, Addison-Wesley.

- The Java BluePrints Web site <http://java.sun.com/blueprints>

- The Java Tutorial Web site <http://java.sun.com/docs/books/tutorial>

CHAPTER 2

J2EE Platform Technologies

by Vijay Ramachandran

THE J2EE platform specifies technologies to support multitier enterprise applications. These technologies fall into three categories: component, service, and communication.

The component technologies are those used by developers to create the essential parts of the enterprise application, namely the user interface and the business logic. The component technologies allow the development of modules that can be reused by multiple enterprise applications. The component technologies are supported by J2EE platform's system-level services. These system-level services simplify application programming and allow components to be customized to use resources available in the environment in which they are deployed.

Since most enterprise applications require access to existing enterprise information systems, the J2EE platform supports APIs that provide access to databases, enterprise information systems such as SAP and CICS, and services such as transaction, naming and directory, and asynchronous communication. Finally, the J2EE platform provides technologies that enable communication between clients and servers and between collaborating objects hosted by different servers.

This chapter will provide an overview of the J2EE platform technologies.

2.1 Component Technologies

A *component* is an application-level software unit. In addition to JavaBeans™ components, which are part of the J2SE™ platform, the J2EE platform supports the following types of components: applets, application clients, Enterprise JavaBeans™ (EJB™)components, Web components, and resource adapter components.

Applets and application clients run on a client platform, while EJB, Web, and resource adapter components run on a server platform.

Except for resource adapters, application architects and developers typically design and develop the components of a J2EE application. EIS and tool vendors design, develop, and provide resource adapter components, which are then deployed on the server and used by other components of the platform to access data in an EIS.

All J2EE components depend on the runtime support of a system-level entity called a *container*. Containers provide components with services such as lifecycle management, security, deployment, and threading. Because containers manage these services, many component behaviors can be declaratively customized when the component is deployed in the container. For example, an application component provider can specify an abstract name for a database that an Enterprise Java-Beans component needs to access, and a deployer will link that name with the information (such as a user name and password) needed to access the database in a given environment.

The following sections provide overviews of the different types of J2EE components and containers.

2.1.1   Types of J2EE Clients

The J2EE platform allows different types of clients to interact with server-side components.

- *Applets* are Java-based client components that usually execute within a Web browser, and that have access to all features of the Java programming language. J2EE applications can use applets for a more powerful user interface. Browser-based applet clients communicate over HTTP.

- An *application client* executes in its own client container. (The client container is a set of libraries and APIs that support the client code.) Application clients are user interface programs that can directly interact with the EJB tier of a J2EE platform-based application using RMI-IIOP. These clients have full access to J2EE platform services such as JNDI lookups, asynchronous messaging, and the JDBC™ API. An application client's container provides access to these J2EE services and handles RMI-IIOP communication.

- A *Java Web Start-enabled rich client* is a stand-alone client based on JFC/Swing APIs and enabled for the J2EE platform through the Java Web Start technology. A rich client has increased user interface features available to it, such as a better interactive environment and richer graphic capabilities, along with the J2EE platform features and services. Java Web Start technology enables application deployment through a single-step download-and-launch process performed by means of a Web browser. Rich clients communicate with the server using the J2SE environment to execute XML over HTTP(S). As Web service technologies gain ground in the future, these rich clients are well-positioned to efficiently use open communication standards such as JAX-RPC technology.

- A *wireless client* is based on Mobile Information Device Profile (MIDP) technology. MIDP is a set of Java APIs which, along with Connected Limited Device Configuration (CLDC), provides a complete J2ME environment for wireless devices.

2.1.2   Web Components

A *Web component* is a software entity that provides a response to a request. A Web component typically generates the user interface for a Web-based application. The J2EE platform specifies two types of Web components: servlets and JavaServer Pages™ (JSP™) pages. The following sections give an overview of Web components, which are discussed in detail in Chapter 4.

2.1.2.1   Servlets

A *servlet* is a component that extends the functionality of a Web server in a portable and efficient manner. A Web server hosts Java servlet classes that execute within a servlet container. The Web server maps a set of URLs to a servlet so that HTTP requests to these URLs invoke the mapped servlet. When a servlet receives a request from a client, it generates a response, possibly by invoking business logic in enterprise beans or by querying a database directly. It then sends the response—as an HTML or XML document—to the requestor.

A servlet developer uses the servlet API to:

- Initialize and finalize a servlet

- Access a servlet's environment

- Receive/forward requests and send responses

- Maintain session information on behalf of a client

- Interact with other servlets and other components

- Use a filter mechanism for pre- and post-processing of requests and responses

- Implement and enforce security at the Web tier

2.1.2.2   JavaServer Pages Technology

The JavaServer Pages (JSP) technology provides an extensible way to generate dynamic content for a Web client. A JSP page is a text-based document that describes how to process a request to create a response. A JSP page contains:

- Template data to format the Web document. Typically the template data uses HTML or XML elements. Document designers can edit and work with these elements on the JSP page without affecting the dynamic content. This approach simplifies development because it separates presentation from dynamic content generation.

- JSP elements and scriptlets to generate the dynamic content in the Web document. Most JSP pages use JavaBeans and/or Enterprise JavaBeans components to perform the more complex processing required of the application. Standard JSP actions can access and instantiate beans, set or retrieve bean attributes, and download applets. JSP technology is extensible through the development of custom actions, or tags, which are encapsulated in tag libraries.

2.1.2.3   Web Component Containers

Web components are hosted by servlet containers, JSP containers, and Web containers. In addition to standard container services, a *servlet container* provides the network services by which requests and responses are sent. It also decodes requests and formats responses. All servlet containers must support HTTP as a protocol for requests and responses; they may also support other request-response protocols such as HTTPS. A *JSP container* provides the same services as a servlet container. Servlet and JSP containers are collectively referred to as *Web containers*.

2.1.3   Enterprise JavaBeans Components

The Enterprise JavaBeans architecture is a server-side technology for developing and deploying components containing the business logic of an enterprise application. Enterprise JavaBeans components, also referred to as *enterprise beans*, are scalable, transactional, and multi-user secure. There are three types of enterprise beans: session beans, entity beans, and message-driven beans. Session and entity beans have two types of interfaces: a component interface and a home interface. The home interface defines methods to create, find, remove, and access metadata for the bean. The component interfaces define the bean's business logic methods. Message-driven beans do not have component and home interfaces.

An enterprise bean's component and home interfaces are required to be either local or remote. Remote interfaces are RMI interfaces provided to allow the clients of a bean to be location independent. Regardless of whether the client of a bean that implements a remote interface is located on the same VM or a different VM, the client uses the same API to access the bean's methods. Arguments and return results are passed by value between a client and a remote enterprise bean, and thus there is a serialization overhead.

A client of an enterprise bean that implements a local interface must be located in the same VM as the bean. Because object arguments and return results are passed by reference between a client and a local enterprise bean, there is no serialization overhead.

The following sections give an overview of enterprise beans. Enterprise beans are discussed in detail in Chapter 5.

2.1.3.1   Session Beans

A *session bean* is created to provide some service on behalf of a client and usually exists only for the duration of a single client-server session. A session bean performs operations such as calculations or accessing a database for the client. While a session bean may be transactional, it is not recoverable should its container crash.

Session beans can be stateless or can maintain conversational state across methods and transactions. If they do maintain state, the EJB container manages this state if the object must be removed from memory. However, the session bean object itself must manage its own persistent data.

2.1.3.2   Entity Beans

An *entity bean* is a persistent object that represents data maintained in a data store; its focus is data-centric. An entity bean is identified by a primary key. An entity bean can manage its own persistence or it can delegate this function to its container.

An entity bean can live as long as the data it represents. Persistence is handled in one of two ways:

- **Bean-managed persistence**—The developer handles persistence as part of the entity bean's source code.

- **Container-managed persistence**—The developer specifies the bean fields that need to be persistent and lets the EJB container manage persistence.

Beans with container-managed persistence are more portable across databases. In addition, entity beans with container-managed persistence can maintain relationships among themselves. This feature enables queries that join multiple database tables. With bean-managed persistence, a change in the underlying database may require the developer to change the entity bean's source code to conform to the SQL implemented by the new database.

2.1.3.3   Message-Driven Beans

A message-driven bean enables asynchronous clients to access the business logic in the EJB tier. Message-driven beans are activated only by asynchronous messages received from a JMS queue to which they listen. A client does not directly access a message-driven bean; instead, a client asynchronously sends a message to a JMS queue or topic. Because message-driven beans have no need to expose their methods to clients, they do not implement component or home interfaces. They also do not maintain state on behalf of a client.

2.1.3.4   EJB Component Containers

Enterprise beans are hosted by an *EJB container.* In addition to standard container services, an EJB container provides a range of transaction and persistence services and access to the J2EE service and communication APIs.

2.1.4   Components, Containers, and Services

The J2EE component types and their containers are illustrated in Figure 2.1.

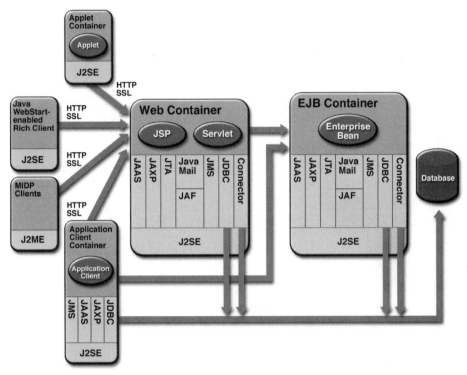

Figure 2.1   J2EE Components and Containers

Containers provide all application components with the J2SE platform APIs, which include the Java IDL and JDBC 2.0 core enterprise APIs. Table 2.1 lists the Standard Extension APIs that are available in each type of container. The J2EE platform APIs are described in Section 2.4 on page 42 and Section 2.5 on page 45.

Table 2.1   J2EE Required Standard Extension APIs

API	Applet	Application Client	Web	EJB
JDBC 2.0 Extension	N	Y	Y	Y
JTA 1.0	N	N	Y	Y

Table 2.1   J2EE Required Standard Extension APIs (continued)

API	Applet	Application Client	Web	EJB
JNDI 1.2	N	Y	Y	Y
Servlet 2.3	N	N	Y	N
JSP 1.2	N	N	Y	N
EJB 2.0	N	Y[a]	Y[b]	Y
RMI-IIOP 1.0	N	Y	Y	Y
JMS 1.0	N	Y	Y	Y
JavaMail 1.2	N	N	Y	Y
JAF 1.0	N	N	Y	Y
JAXP 1.1	N	Y	Y	Y
JAAS 1.0	N	Y	Y	Y
Connector 1.0	N	N	Y	Y

[a]   Application clients can only make use of the enterprise bean client APIs.

[b]   Servlets and JSP pages can only make use of the enterprise bean client APIs.

2.2   Platform Roles

The J2EE platform defines several distinct roles in the application development and deployment life cycle: J2EE product provider, application component provider, application assembler, deployer, system administrator, and tool provider. In general, the roles are defined to aid in identifying the tasks performed by various parties during the development, deployment, and running of a J2EE application. However, while some of these roles, such as system administrator and tool provider, perform tasks that are common to non-J2EE platforms, other roles have a meaning specific to the J2EE platform, because the tasks those roles perform are specific to J2EE technology. In particular, application component providers, application assemblers, and deployers must configure J2EE components and applications to use J2EE platform services (described in Section 2.3 on page 35).

The roles can be fulfilled by whatever personnel match an organization's actual application development and deployment workflow. Thus, each J2EE role may be performed by a different party or a single party may perform several roles. For example, a programmer may perform the roles of application component provider and application assembler.

The following sections define the J2EE platform roles. Subsets of some of these roles are defined in the EJB specification, including enterprise bean provider, EJB container provider, and EJB server provider. The JavaServer Pages specification defines the JSP container provider role, and the Java Servlet specification defines the roles of application developer, servlet container provider, Web container provider, and Web server provider.

2.2.1 J2EE Product Provider

A J2EE product provider, typically an operating system vendor, database system vendor, application server vendor, or a Web server vendor, implements a J2EE product providing the component containers, J2EE platform APIs, and other features defined in the J2EE specification. A J2EE product is free to implement interfaces not specified by the J2EE specification in an implementation-specific way.

A J2EE product provider provides application deployment and management tools. Deployment tools enable a deployer to deploy components on the J2EE product. The deployer role is described in Section 2.2.4 on page 34. Management tools allow a system administrator to manage the J2EE product and the applications deployed on the J2EE product. The form of these tools is not prescribed by the J2EE specification. The system administrator role is described in Section 2.2.5 on page 34.

2.2.2 Application Component Provider

Application component providers produce the building blocks of a J2EE application. They typically have expertise in developing reusable components as well as sufficient business domain knowledge. Application component providers need not know anything about the operational environment in which their components will be used. There are multiple roles for application component providers, including HTML page authors, document programmers, enterprise bean developers, and so on. These roles use tools provided by a tool provider to produce J2EE components and applications. The tool provider role is described in Section 2.2.6 on page 34.

2.2.3   Application Assembler

An application assembler takes a set of components developed by application component providers and assembles them into a complete J2EE application. Their expertise lies in providing solutions for a specific problem domain, for example, the financial industry. Application assemblers may not be familiar with the source code of the components that they use, but they use declarative descriptors for the components in order to know how to build applications from them. Like application component providers, they need not know anything about the operational environment in which their applications will be used. An application assembler will generally use GUI tools provided by either an application component provider or tool provider. An application assembler is responsible for providing assembly instructions describing external dependencies of the application that the deployer must resolve in the deployment process.

2.2.4   Deployer

A deployer, an expert in a specific operational environment, is responsible for deploying J2EE components and applications into that environment. A deployer uses tools supplied by the J2EE product provider to perform deployment tasks. A deployer installs components and applications into a J2EE server and configures components and applications to resolve all the external dependencies declared by the application component provider and application assembler.

2.2.5   System Administrator

A system administrator is responsible for configuring and administering an enterprise's computing and networking infrastructure. A system administrator is also responsible for overseeing the runtime well-being of the deployed J2EE applications. The system administrator typically uses runtime monitoring and management tools provided by the J2EE product provider to accomplish these tasks.

2.2.6   Tool Provider

A tool provider provides tools used for the development and packaging of application components. A variety of tools for use with the J2EE platform are possible, corresponding to the many component types supported by the J2EE platform as well as the various roles defined for the J2EE development and deployment process. Platform-independent tools can be used for all phases of development up to the deployment of an application. Platform-dependent tools are used for deployment, management, and monitoring of applications. Future versions of the J2EE specification may define more interfaces that allow such tools to be platform independent. For example, JSR 77 defines a tool API for application development, and JSR 88 defines an API for application management. These APIs are likely to be supported in the next version of the J2EE specification.

2.3   Platform Services

J2EE platform services simplify application programming and allow components and applications to be customized at deployment time to use resources available in the deployment environment. This section gives a brief overview of the J2EE platform naming, deployment, transaction, and security services.

2.3.1   Naming Services

J2EE naming services provide application clients, enterprise beans, and Web components with access to a JNDI naming environment (described in Section 2.4.3 on page 43). A *naming environment* allows a component to be customized without the need to access or change the component's source code. A container implements the component's environment and provides it to the component as a JNDI *naming context*.

A J2EE component locates its environment naming context using JNDI interfaces. A component creates a `javax.naming.InitialContext` object and looks up the environment naming context in `InitialContext` under the name `java:comp/env`. A component's naming environment is stored directly in the environment naming context or in any of its direct or indirect *subcontexts*.

A J2EE component can access named system-provided and user-defined objects. The names of system-provided objects, such as JTA `UserTransaction` objects, are stored in the environment naming context, `java:comp/env`. The J2EE platform allows a component to name user-defined objects, such as enterprise beans, environment entries, JDBC `DataSource` objects, and message connections. An object should be named within a subcontext of the naming environment according to the type of the object. For example, enterprise beans are named within the subcontext `java:comp/env/ejb` and JDBC `DataSource` references in the subcontext `java:comp/env/jdbc`.

2.3.2   Deployment Services

J2EE deployment services allow components and applications to be customized at the time they are packaged and deployed.

J2EE applications are deployed as a set of nested units. Each unit contains a *deployment descriptor,* an XML-based text file whose elements declaratively describe how to assemble and deploy the unit into a specific environment. Deployment descriptors contain many elements related to customizing J2EE platform services, such as transactions and security.

The following sections give an overview of J2EE platform deployment services. Deployment services are discussed in detail in Chapter 7.

2.3.2.1   Deployment Units

A *J2EE application* consists of one or more J2EE modules and one J2EE application deployment descriptor. An application deployment descriptor contains a list of the applications's modules and information on how to customize the application. A J2EE application consists of one or more Java Archive (JAR) files along with zero or more Resource Archive (RAR) files packaged into an Enterprise ARchive (EAR) file with an .ear extension.

A *J2EE module* consists of one or more J2EE components for the same container type and one component deployment descriptor of that type. A component deployment descriptor contains declarative data to customize the components in the module. A J2EE module without an application deployment descriptor can be deployed as a stand-alone J2EE module.

The three types of J2EE modules are:

- Enterprise JavaBeans modules contain class files for enterprise beans and an EJB deployment descriptor. EJB modules are packaged as JAR files with a .jar extension.

- Web modules contain JSP files, class files for servlets, GIF and HTML files, and a Web deployment descriptor. Web modules are packaged as JAR files with a .war (Web ARchive) extension.

- Resource adapter modules contain all Java interfaces, classes, native libraries, and other documentation, along with the resource adapter deployment descriptor. Together, these implement the Connector architecture for a particular EIS. Resource adapter modules are packages as JAR files with a .rar (Resource adapter ARchive) extension.

- Application client modules contain class files and an application client deployment descriptor. Application client modules are packaged as JAR files with a .jar extension.

2.3.2.2   Platform Roles in the Deployment Process

Each J2EE platform role performs specific activities related to deployment. An application component provider specifies component deployment descriptor elements and packages components into modules. An application assembler resolves references between modules and assembles modules into a single deployment unit. A deployer creates links between entities referred to by the application and entities in the deployment environment. A resource adapter provider specifies the deployment descriptor for the resource adapter elements and packages it along with the classes and libraries into separate modules.

2.3.3   Transaction Services

Transactions divide an application into a series of indivisible or "atomic" units of work. A system that supports transactions ensures that each unit fully completes without interference from other processes. If the unit can be completed in its entirety, it is committed. Otherwise, the system completely undoes (rolls back) whatever work the unit had performed. Transactions simplify application development because they free the application component provider from the complex issues of failure recovery and multi-user programming.

Transactions, as provided by the J2EE platform, have the following characteristics:

- J2EE transactions are flat. A flat transaction cannot have any child (nested) transactions.

- The J2EE platform implicitly handles many transaction details, such as propagating information specific to a particular transaction instance and coordinating among multiple transaction managers.

The following sections give an overview of J2EE platform transaction services. Transaction services are discussed in detail in Chapter 8.

2.3.3.1   Accessing Transactions

A *JTA transaction* is a transaction that can span multiple components and resource managers. A *resource manager local transaction* is a transaction that is specific to a particular enterprise information system connection.

JTA transactions are created and managed using the `javax.transaction.UserTransaction` interface. Different types of components access `UserTransaction` objects in different ways:

- Enterprise beans provide a mechanism for JTA transactions to be started automatically by their containers. Enterprise beans that use bean-managed transactions (described in Section 2.3.3.3 on page 39) use the method `EJBContext.getUserTransaction` to look up the `UserTransaction` object.

- Applets and application clients may or may not be able to directly access a `UserTransaction` object depending on the capabilities provided by the container. However, they can always invoke enterprise beans that use a `UserTransaction` object.

- Web components use JNDI to look up the `UserTransaction` object.

A resource manager local transaction is created and managed in a manner specific to a particular connection. For example, each SQL statement executed on a JDBC connection has its own transaction.

2.3.3.2   Web Component Transactions

Web components (JSP pages and servlets) are not designed to be transactional. Because of this, application component providers should only perform transactional work directly in Web components on a very limited basis. Preferably, an application component provider should delegate transactional work to the appropriate enterprise beans. When an enterprise bean is used to perform transactional work, the enterprise bean or container takes care of properly setting up the transaction.

Nevertheless, there are times when a Web component may need to directly demarcate transactions. It can do so using the `javax.transaction.UserTransaction` interface. You should, however, be aware of limitations in transaction propagation and state isolation, as described in the following discussions.

2.3.3.2.1 Transaction Propagation

Transactions are propagated from a Web component to an enterprise bean only when the Web component starts the transaction using the `UserTransaction` interface. Since Web components are server-side components, Web browsers and other clients don't have direct access to transactions, so a transaction initiated by a Web component *cannot* be propagated from the client of the component or between Web components and transactional resources such as JDBC connections.

2.3.3.2.2 State Isolation

A Web component can keep state for the lifetime of a client session or component. However, because Web components are not transactional components, their state cannot be isolated based on transactions. For example, separate servlets will see the same state of a client session even if they each start their own transaction.

2.3.3.3   Enterprise Bean Transactions

The J2EE platform provides two styles of transaction demarcation for enterprise beans: bean-managed and container-managed.

With *bean-managed transaction demarcation*, the enterprise bean is required to manage all aspects of a transaction. This entails operations such as:

- Creating the transaction object

- Explicitly starting the transaction

- Completing the transaction, either by committing the transaction when all updates are completed or rolling back the transaction if an error occurs

With *container-managed transaction demarcation*, the EJB container handles transaction management. The container performs the transaction demarcation based on the application assembler's deployment instructions; it handles starting and ending the transaction and maintaining the transaction context throughout the life of the transaction object. This greatly simplifies an application component provider's responsibilities and tasks, especially for transactions in distributed environments.

Both stateful and stateless session beans can use either container- or bean-managed transactions. However, a bean cannot use both types of transaction at the same time. The application component provider decides the type of transaction demarcation that a session bean will use and declares the transaction style via attributes in the enterprise bean's deployment descriptor. The attributes indicate whether the bean or container will manage the bean's transactions and, if the latter, how the container will manage the transactions. Entity beans can only use container-managed transaction demarcation.

2.3.4   Security Services

J2EE platform security services are designed to ensure that resources are accessed only by users authorized to use them. Access control involves two steps:

1. **Authentication**—An entity must establish its identity through *authentication*. It typically does so by providing *authentication data* (such as a name and password). An entity that can be authenticated is called a *principal*. A principal can be a user or another program. Users are typically authenticated by logging in.

2. **Authorization**—When an authenticated principal tries to access a resource, the system determines whether the principal is authorized to do so based on the security policies in force in the application's *security policy domain*.

The following sections give an overview of J2EE platform security services. Security services are discussed in detail in Chapter 9.

2.3.4.1   Security Methodologies

Containers provide two security methodologies: declarative and programmatic. *Declarative security* refers to the means of specifying an application's security structure in a form external to the application. An application component provider specifies declarative security in a component's deployment descriptor. *Programmatic security* refers to security mechanisms accessed within a program. An application component provider accesses programmatic security for EJB and Web components with J2EE platform security APIs.

2.3.4.2   Authentication

The J2EE platform allows an application component provider to choose how a principal is authenticated. A Web client can provide authentication data to a Web container using HTTP basic authentication, digest authentication, form-based authentication, or certificate authentication.

With *basic authentication,* the Web server authenticates a principal using the user name and password obtained from the Web client. Like basic authentication, *digest authentication* authenticates a user based on a user name and a password. However, the authentication is performed by transmitting the password in an encrypted form, which is much more secure than the simple base64 encoding used by basic authentication. With *form-based authentication,* the Web container can provide an application-specific form for logging in. With *certificate authentication,* the client uses a public key certificate to establish its identity and maintains its own security context.

There is no way to authenticate to an EJB container. However, authentication data is also often required when an enterprise bean accesses an external resource. An enterprise bean can provide authentication data to a resource directly, or it can request the container to perform this service for it. If the application component provider specifies that the container should propagate authentication data, the deployer specifies the authentication data for each resource factory reference declared by the enterprise bean. The container uses this authentication data when obtaining a connection to the resource.

2.3.4.3   Authorization

J2EE platform authorization is based on the concept of security roles. A *security role* is a logical grouping of users defined by an application component provider or application assembler. Each security role is mapped by a deployer to principals in the deployment environment. A security role can be used with declarative security or programmatic security.

An application component provider or application assembler can control access to an enterprise bean's methods by specifying the `method-permission` element in the bean's deployment descriptor. The `method-permission` element contains a list of methods that can be accessed by a given security role. If a principal is in a security role allowed access to a method, the principal may execute the method. Similarly, a principal is allowed access to a Web component only if the principal is in the appropriate security role. An application component provider controls access programmatically by using the `EJBContext.isCallerInRole` or `HttpServletRequest.isRemoteUserInRole` methods.

For example, suppose a payroll application specifies two security roles: `employee` and `administrator`. Salary update operations are executable only by a principal acting in the role of `administrator`, but salary read operations are executable by both `employee` and `administrator` roles. When the payroll application is deployed, the deployer provides a mapping between the set of administrator and employee principals (or groups) and their respective roles. When the salary update method is executed, the enterprise bean's container can check whether the principal or group propagated from the Web server is in a role that can execute that method. Alternatively, the method itself could use one of the security APIs to perform the check.

2.3.4.4   Java Authentication and Authorization Services

Java Authentication and Authorization Services (JAAS) enables an application to enforce access controls for authenticated users. It is based on the standard Pluggable Authentication Module (PAM) framework and supports user-based authorization. JAAS provides a framework and standard programming interface for authenticating users and for assigning privileges. Java applications using JAAS can provide both code-centric and user-centric access control. JAAS supports single sig-non and provides a flexible access control policy for user-based, group-based, and role-based authorization.

2.4   Service Technologies

The J2EE platform service technologies allow applications to access a wide range of services in a uniform manner. This section describes technologies that provide access to databases, transactions, XML processing, naming and directory services, and enterprise information systems.

2.4.1   JDBC API

The JDBC API provides database-independent connectivity between the J2EE platform and a wide range of tabular data sources. JDBC technology allows an application component provider to:

- Perform connection and authentication to a database server
- Manage transactions
- Move SQL statements to a database engine for preprocessing and execution
- Execute stored procedures
- Inspect and modify the results from Select statements

The J2EE platform requires both the JDBC 2.0 Core API (included in the J2SE platform), and the JDBC 2.0 Extension API, which provides row sets, connection naming via JNDI, connection pooling, and distributed transaction support. The connection pooling and distributed transaction features are intended for use by JDBC drivers to coordinate with a J2EE server. Access to databases and enterprise information systems is covered in detail in Chapter 6.

2.4.2   Java Transaction API and Service

The Java Transaction API (JTA) allows applications to access transactions in a manner that is independent of specific implementations. JTA specifies standard Java interfaces between a transaction manager and the parties involved in a distributed transaction system: the transactional application, the J2EE server, and the manager that controls access to the shared resources affected by the transactions.

The Java Transaction Service (JTS) specifies the implementation of a transaction manager that supports JTA and implements the Java mapping of the Object Management Group Object Transaction Service 1.1 specification. A JTS transaction manager provides the services and management functions required to support transaction demarcation, transactional resource management, synchronization, and propagation of information that is specific to a particular transaction instance.

2.4.3   Java Naming and Directory Interface

The Java Naming and Directory Interface™ (JNDI) API provides naming and directory functionality. It provides applications with methods for performing standard directory operations, such as associating attributes with objects and searching for objects using their attributes. Using JNDI, an application can store and retrieve any type of named Java object.

Because JNDI is independent of any specific implementations, applications can use JNDI to access multiple naming and directory services, including existing naming and directory services such as LDAP, NDS, DNS, and NIS. This allows applications to coexist with legacy applications and systems.

2.4.4   J2EE Connector Architecture

The J2EE Connector architecture is a standard API for connecting the J2EE platform to enterprise information systems, such as enterprise resource planning, mainframe transaction processing, and database systems. The architecture addresses the issues involved when integrating existing enterprise information systems (EIS), such as SAP, CICS, legacy applications, and nonrelational databases, with an EJB server and enterprise applications. The J2EE Connector architecture defines a set of scalable, secure, and transactional mechanisms for integrating an EIS with a J2EE platform. Adhering to the architecture simplifies this integration, enabling J2EE applications to use the strengths of the J2EE platform along with existing data in EISs.

The J2EE Connector architecture:

- Defines system contracts between J2EE-compliant application servers and resource adapters. Resource adapters, which are system libraries specific to an EIS, provide connectivity between J2EE application components and an EIS. Adapters are analogous to JDBC drivers for relational databases.

- Defines a common set of APIs so that Java applications and tools vendors can connect to and use an EIS through its resource adapters.

- Defines a standard packaging and deployment facility for resource adapters to facilitate their deployment in a J2EE environment.

To use the J2EE Connector architecture, an enterprise information system vendor provides a resource adapter for its EIS. The adapter is then either deployed as a separate module in the J2EE server or packaged and deployed along with the J2EE application. The EIS provider develops the resource adapter following the Connector architecture specification; it can be used on all J2EE platforms. Similarly, an application developed using the Connector API is deployable on all J2EE platforms that have the resource adapter for the EIS used by the application.

2.4.5   Java API for XML Processing Technology

The Java API for XML Processing (JAXP) technology supports the processing of XML documents using DOM, SAX, and XSLT. JAXP enables applications to parse and transform XML documents independent of a particular XML processing implementation. Depending on the needs of the application, developers have the flexibility to swap between XML processors, such as between high-performance or memory-conservative parsers, with no application code changes.

2.5   Communication Technologies

Communication technologies provide mechanisms for communication between clients and servers and between collaborating objects hosted by different servers. The J2EE specification requires support for the following types of communication technologies:

- Internet protocols

- Remote method invocation protocols

- Object Management Group protocols

- Messaging technologies

- Data formats

The following sections give an overview of J2EE platform communication technologies. Chapter 3 discusses how these communication technologies are used by clients.

2.5.1   Internet Protocols

Internet protocols define the standards by which the different pieces of the J2EE platform communicate with each other and with remote entities. The J2EE platform supports the following Internet protocols:

- **TCP/IP**—Transport Control Protocol over Internet Protocol. These two protocols provide for the reliable delivery of streams of data from one host to another. Internet Protocol (IP), the basic protocol of the Internet, enables the unreliable delivery of individual packets from one host to another. IP makes no guarantees as to whether the packet will be delivered, how long it will take, or if multiple packets will arrive in the order they were sent. The Transport Control Protocol (TCP) adds the notions of connection and reliability.

- **HTTP 1.0**—Hypertext Transfer Protocol. The Internet protocol used to fetch hypertext objects from remote hosts. HTTP messages consist of requests from client to server and responses from server to client.

- **SSL 3.0**—Secure Socket Layer. A security protocol that provides privacy over the Internet. The protocol allows client-server applications to communicate in a way that cannot be eavesdropped or tampered with. Servers are always authenticated and clients are optionally authenticated.

2.5.2   Remote Method Invocation Protocols

Remote Method Invocation (RMI) is a set of APIs that allow developers to build distributed applications in the Java programming language. RMI uses Java language interfaces to define remote objects and a combination of Java serialization technology and the Java Remote Method Protocol (JRMP) to turn local method invocations into remote method invocations. The J2EE platform supports the JRMP protocol, the transport mechanism for communication between objects in the Java language in different address spaces.

2.5.3   Object Management Group Protocols

Object Management Group (OMG) protocols allow objects hosted by the J2EE platform to access remote objects developed using the OMG's Common Object Request Broker Architecture (CORBA) technologies and vice versa. CORBA objects are defined using the Interface Definition Language (IDL). An application component provider defines the interface of a remote object in IDL and then uses an IDL compiler to generate client and server stubs that connect object implementations to an Object Request Broker (ORB), a library that enables CORBA objects to locate and communicate with one another. ORBs communicate with each other using the Internet Inter-ORB Protocol (IIOP). The OMG technologies required by the J2EE platform are Java IDL and RMI-IIOP.

2.5.3.1   Java IDL

Java IDL allows Java clients to invoke operations on CORBA objects that have been defined using IDL and implemented in any language with a CORBA mapping. Java IDL is part of the J2SE platform. It consists of a CORBA API and ORB. An application component provider uses the `idlj` IDL compiler to generate a Java client stub for a CORBA object defined in IDL. The Java client is linked with the stub and uses the CORBA API to access the CORBA object.

2.5.3.2   RMI-IIOP

RMI-IIOP is an implementation of the RMI API over IIOP. RMI-IIOP allows application component providers to write remote interfaces in the Java programming language. The remote interface can be converted to IDL and implemented in any other language that is supported by an OMG mapping and an ORB for that language. Clients and servers can be written in any language using IDL derived from the RMI interfaces. When remote interfaces are defined as Java RMI interfaces, RMI over IIOP provides interoperability with CORBA objects implemented in any language. RMI-IIOP contains:

- The `rmic` compiler, which generates:
  - Client and server stubs that work with any ORB.
  - An IDL file compatible with the RMI interface. To create a C++ server object, an application component provider would use an IDL compiler to produce the server stub and skeleton for the server object.
- A CORBA API and ORB.

Application clients must use RMI-IIOP to communicate with enterprise beans.

2.5.4   Messaging Technologies

Messaging technologies provide a way to asynchronously send and receive messages. The Java Message Service API provides an interface for handling asynchronous requests, reports, or events that are consumed by enterprise applications. JMS messages are used to coordinate these applications. The JavaMail™ API provides an interface for sending and receiving messages intended for users. Although either API can be used for asynchronous notification, JMS is preferred when speed and reliability are a primary requirement.

2.5.4.1   Java Message Service API

The Java Message Service (JMS) API allows J2EE applications to access enterprise messaging systems such as IBM MQ Series and TIBCO Rendezvous. JMS messages contain well-defined information that describe specific business actions. Through the exchange of these messages, applications track the progress of enterprise activities. The JMS API supports both point-to-point and publish-subscribe styles of messaging.

In *point-to-point messaging*, a client sends a message to the message queue of another client. Often a client will have all its messages delivered to a single queue.

Most queues are created administratively and are treated as static resources by their clients.

In *publish-subscribe messaging*, clients publish messages to and subscribe to messages from well-known nodes in a content-based hierarchy called *topics*. A topic can be thought of as a message broker that gathers and distributes messages addressed to it. By relying on the topic as an intermediary, message publishers are independent of subscribers and vice-versa. The topic automatically adapts as both publishers and subscribers come and go. Publishers and subscribers are *active* when the objects that represent them exist. JMS also supports the optional *durability* of subscribers that "remember" the existence of the subscribers while they are inactive.

The JMS API definitions must be included in a J2EE product, but a product is not required to include an implementation of the JMS `ConnectionFactory` and `Destination` objects. These are the objects used by an application to access a JMS service provider. A future version of the J2EE platform will require that a J2EE product provide support for both JMS point-to-point and publish-subscribe messaging, and thus must make those facilities available using the `ConnectionFactory` and `Destination` APIs.

2.5.4.2   JavaMail API

The JavaMail API provides a set of abstract classes and interfaces that comprise an electronic mail system. The abstract classes and interfaces support many different implementations of message stores, formats, and transports. Many simple applications will only need to interact with the messaging system through these base classes and interfaces.

The abstract classes in the JavaMail API can be subclassed to provide new protocols and add functionality when necessary. In addition, JavaMail API includes concrete subclasses that implement widely used Internet mail protocols and conform to specifications RFC822 and RFC2045. They are ready to be used in application development. Developers can subclass JavaMail classes to provide the implementations of particular messaging systems, such as IMAP4, POP3, and SMTP.

2.5.4.2.1 JavaBeans Activation Framework API

The JavaBeans Activation Framework (JAF) API integrates support for MIME data types into the Java platform. JavaBeans components can be specified for operating on MIME data, such as viewing or editing the data. The JAF API also provides a mechanism to map filename extensions to MIME types.

The JAF API is used by the JavaMail API to handle the data included in e-mail messages; typical applications will not need to use the JAF API directly, although applications making sophisticated use of e-mail may need it.

2.5.5   Data Formats

Data formats define the types of data that can be exchanged between components. The J2EE platform requires support for the following data formats:

- **HTML 3.2**—The markup language used to define hypertext documents accessible over the Internet. HTML enables the embedding of images, sounds, video streams, form fields, references to other HTML documents, and basic text formatting. HTML documents have a globally unique location and can link to one another.

- **Image files**—The J2EE platform supports two formats for image files: GIF (Graphics Interchange Format), a protocol for the online transmission and interchange of raster graphic data, and JPEG (Joint Photographic Experts Group), a standard for compressing gray-scale or color still images.

- **JAR file**—A platform-independent file format that permits many files to be aggregated into one file.

- **Class file**—The format of a compiled Java file as specified in the Java Virtual Machine specification. Each class file contains one Java language type—either a class or an interface—and consists of a stream of 8-bit bytes.

- **XML**—A text-based markup language that allows you to define the markup needed to identify the data and text in structured documents. As with HTML, you identify data using tags. But unlike HTML, XML tags describe the data, rather than the format for displaying it. In the same way that you define the field names for a data structure, you are free to use any XML tags that make sense for a given application. When multiple applications share XML data, they have to agree on the tag names they intend to use.

2.6   Summary

The primary focus of the Java 2 Platform, Enterprise Edition is a set of component technologies (Enterprise JavaBeans technology, JavaServer Pages technology, and Java servlets technology) that simplify the process of developing enterprise applications. The J2EE platform provides a number of system-level services that simplify application programming and allow components to be customized to use resources available in the environment in which they are deployed. In conjunction with the component technologies, the J2EE platform provides APIs that enable components to access a variety of remote services, and mechanisms for communication between clients and servers and between collaborating objects hosted by different servers.

2.7   References and Resources

- Java Web Start Web site `<http://java.sun.com/products/javawebstart>`

- Java Authentication and Authorization Service Web site
  `<http://java.sun.com/products/jaas>`

- *J2EE 1.3 Platform Specification* `<http://java.sun.com/j2ee>`

CHAPTER 3

The Client Tier

by Ray Ortigas

$\mathbf{F}$ROM a developer's point of view, a J2EE application can support many types of clients. J2EE clients can run on laptops, desktops, palmtops, and cell phones. They can connect from within an enterprise's intranet or across the World Wide Web, through a wired network or a wireless network or a combination of both. They can range from something thin, browser-based and largely server-dependent to something rich, programmable, and largely self-sufficient.

From a user's point of view, the client *is* the application. It must be useful, usable, and responsive. Because the user places high expectations on the client, you must choose your client strategy carefully, making sure to consider both technical forces (such as the network) and non-technical forces (such as the nature of the application). This chapter presents guidelines for designing and implementing J2EE clients amidst these competing forces.

This chapter cites examples from the Java Pet Store sample application, an online outlet for selling pets, and the Java Smart Ticket sample application, an e-commerce movie ticket service. The code for these sample applications is available on the Java BluePrints Web site. See "References and Resources" on page 73 for more information.

3.1   Client Considerations

Every application has requirements and expectations that its clients must meet, constrained by the environment in which the client needs to operate.

Your users and their usage patterns largely determine what type of client or interface you need to provide. For example, desktop Web browser clients are popular for e-mail and e-shopping because they provide a familiar interface. For another example, wireless handheld clients are useful for sales force automation because they provide a convenient way to access enterprise resources from the field in real time. Once you have decided what type of interface you need, you should design your client configuration with network, security, and platform considerations in mind.

3.1.1   Network Considerations

J2EE clients may connect to the enterprise over a wide array of networks. The quality of service on these networks can vary tremendously, from excellent on a company intranet, to modest over a dialup Internet connection, to poor on a wireless network. The connectivity can also vary; intranet clients are always connected, while mobile clients experience intermittent connectivity (and are usually online for short periods of time anyway).

Regardless of the quality of service available, you should always keep in mind that the client *depends* on the network, and the network is imperfect. Although the client *appears* to be a stand-alone entity, it cannot be programmed as such because it is part of a distributed application. Three aspects of the network deserve particular mention:

- Latency is non-zero.

- Bandwidth is finite.

- The network is not always reliable.

A well-designed enterprise application must address these issues, starting with the client. The ideal client connects to the server only when it has to, transmits only as much data as it needs to, and works reasonably well when it cannot reach the server. Later, this chapter elaborates on strategies for achieving those goals.

3.1.2   Security Considerations

Different networks have different security requirements, which constrain how clients connect to an enterprise. For example, when clients connect over the Internet, they usually communicate with servers through a firewall. The presence of a firewall that is not under your control limits the choices of protocols the client can use. Most firewalls are configured to allow Hypertext Transfer Protocol (HTTP) to pass across, but not Internet Inter-Orb Protocol (IIOP). This aspect of firewalls makes Web-based services, which use HTTP, particularly attractive compared to RMI- or CORBA-based services, which use IIOP.

Security requirements also affect user authentication. When the client and server are in the same security domain, as might be the case on a company intranet, authenticating a user may be as simple as having the user log in only once to obtain access to the entire enterprise, a scheme known as *single sign on*. When the client and server are in different security domains, as would be the case over the Internet, a more elaborate scheme is required for single sign on, such as that proposed by the Liberty Alliance, an industry collaboration spearheaded by Sun Microsystems.

The authentication process itself needs to be confidential and, usually, so does the client-server communication after a user has been authenticated. Both the J2EE platform and the client types discussed in this chapter have well-defined mechanisms for ensuring confidentiality. These mechanisms are discussed in Chapter 9.

3.1.3 Platform Considerations

Every client platform's capabilities influence an application's design. For example, a browser client cannot generate graphs depicting financial projections; it would need a server to render the graphs as images, which it could download from the server. A programmable client, on the other hand, could download financial data from a server and render graphs in its own interface.

Another aspect of the platform to consider is form factor. Desktop computers offer a large screen, a keyboard, and a pointing device such as a mouse or trackball. With such clients, users are willing to view and manipulate large amounts of data. In contrast, cell phones have tiny screens and rely on button-based interactions (usually thumb-operated!). With such clients, users can't (and don't want to) view or manipulate large amounts of data.

Applications serving multiple client platforms pose additional challenges. Developing a client for each platform requires not only more resources for implementation, testing, and maintenance but also specialized knowledge of each platform. It may be easier to develop one client for all platforms (using a browser- or a Java technology-based solution, for example), but designing a truly portable client requires developers to consider the lowest common denominator. Consequently, such a client implementation cannot take advantage of the various capabilities unique to each platform.

3.2   General Design Issues and Guidelines

While the J2EE platform encourages thin-client architectures, J2EE clients are not dumb. A J2EE client may handle many responsibilities, including:

- **Presenting the user interface**—Although a client presents the views to a user, the logic for the views may be programmed on the client or downloaded from a server.

- **Validating user inputs**—Although the EIS and EJB tier must enforce constraints on model data (since they contain the data), a client may also enforce data constraints by validating user inputs.

- **Communicating with the server**—When a user requests functionality that resides on a server, the user's client must present that request to the server using a protocol they both understand.

- **Managing conversational state**—Applications need to track information as a user goes through a workflow or process (effectively conversing with the application). The client may track none, some, or all of this information, known as conversational state.

How you handle these responsibilities on your client can significantly impact your development efforts, your application's performance, and your users' experience. Generally, the more responsibilities you place on the client, the more responsive it will be.

The next two sections consider browser clients and Java clients separately. You do not have to pick one or the other; a J2EE application can accommodate both browser and Java clients. The Java Pet Store sample application, for example, has a Web browser interface for shoppers and a Java application for administrators. Section 4.4.2.2 on page 107 explains how to design the Web tier to support multiple types of clients.

3.3   Design Issues and Guidelines for Browser Clients

Browsers are the thinnest of clients; they display data to their users and rely on servers for application functionality.

From a deployment perspective, browser clients are attractive for a couple of reasons. First, they require minimal updating. When an application changes, server-side code has to change, but browsers are almost always unaffected. Second, they are ubiquitous. Almost every computer has a Web browser and many mobile devices have a microbrowser.

This section documents the issues behind designing and implementing browser clients.

3.3.1   Presenting the User Interface

Browser clients download documents from a server. These documents contain data as well as instructions for presenting that data. The documents are usually dynamically generated by JSP pages (and less often by Java servlets) and written in a presentational markup language such as Hypertext Markup Language (HTML). A presentational markup language allows a single document to have a reasonable presentation regardless of the browser that presents it. These screenshots in Figure 3.1 show the Java Pet Store sample application running in two different browsers.

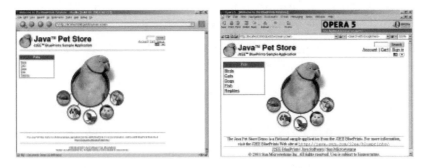

Figure 3.1   Java Pet Store Sample Application Shopping Client Rendered by Two Different Browsers

There are other alternatives to HTML, particularly for mobile devices, whose presentation capabilities tend to differ from those of a traditional desktop computer. Examples include Wireless Markup Language (WML), Compact HTML (CHTML), Extensible HTML (XHTML) Basic, and Voice Markup Language (VoiceML).

Browsers have a couple of strengths that make them viable enterprise application clients. First, they offer a familiar environment. Browsers are widely deployed and used, and the interactions they offer are fairly standard. This makes browsers popular, particularly with novice users. Second, browser clients can be easy to implement. The markup languages that browsers use provide high-level abstractions for how data is presented, leaving the mechanics of presentation and event-handling to the browser.

The trade-off of using a simple markup language, however, is that markup languages allow only limited interactivity. For example, HTML's tags permit presentations and interactions that make sense only for hyperlinked documents. You can enhance HTML documents slightly using technologies such as JavaScript in combination with other standards, such as Cascading Style Sheets (CSS) and the Document Object Model (DOM). However, support for these documents, also known as Dynamic HTML (DHTML) documents, is inconsistent across browsers, so creating a portable DHTML-based client is difficult.

Another, more significant cost of using browser clients is potentially low responsiveness. The client depends on the server for presentation logic, so it must connect to the server whenever its interface changes. Consequently, browser clients make many connections to the server, which is a problem when latency is high. Furthermore, because the responses to a browser intermingle presentation logic with data, they can be large, consuming substantial bandwidth.

3.3.2   Validating User Inputs

Consider an HTML form for completing an order, which includes fields for credit card information. A browser cannot single-handedly validate this information, but it can certainly apply some simple heuristics to determine whether the information is invalid. For example, it can check that the cardholder name is not null, or that the credit card number has the right number of digits. When the browser solves these obvious problems, it can pass the information to the server. The server can deal with more esoteric tasks, such as checking that the credit card number really belongs to the given cardholder or that the cardholder has enough credit.

When using an HTML browser client, you can use the JavaScript scripting language, whose syntax is close to that of the Java programming language. Be aware that JavaScript implementations vary slightly from browser to browser; to accommodate multiple types of browsers, use a subset of JavaScript that you know will work across these browsers. (For more information, see the *ECMA-Script Language Specification*.) It may help to use JSP custom tags that autogenerate simple JavaScript that is known to be portable.

Code Example 3.1 shows how to validate a Web form using Java-Script's DOM hooks to access the form's elements. For example, suppose you have a form for creating an account. When the user submits the form, it can call a JavaScript function to validate the form.

```
<form name="account_form" method="POST"
action="http://acme.sun.com/create_account"
onSubmit="return
checkFamilyName();">
<p>Family name: <input type="text" name="family_name"></p>
<!- ... -->
<p><input type="submit" value="Send it!" /></p>
</form>
```

Code Example 3.1   HTML Form Calling a JavaScriptValidation Function

Code Example 3.2 shows how the JavaScript validation function might be implemented.

```
<script language="JavaScript">
<!--
function checkFamilyName() {
    var familyName =
        window.document.account_form.family_name.value;
    if (familyName == "") {
        alert("You didn't enter a family name.");
        return false;
    }
    else {
        return true;
    }
}
-->
</script>
```

Code Example 3.2   JavaScript Validation Function Using DOM Hooks

Validating user inputs with a browser does not necessarily improve the responsiveness of the interface. Although the validation code allows the client to instantly report any errors it detects, the client consumes more bandwidth because it must download the code in addition to an HTML form. For a non-trivial form, the amount of validation code downloaded can be significant. To reduce download time, you can place commonly-used validation functions in a separate source file and use the `SCRIPT` element's `SRC` attribute to reference this file. When a browser sees the `SRC` attribute, it will cache the source file, so that the next time it encounters another page using the same source file, it will not have to download it again.

Also note that implementing browser validation logic will duplicate some server-side validation logic. The EJB and EIS tiers should validate data regardless of what the client does. Client-side validation is an optimization; it improves user experience and decreases load, but you should never rely on the client exclusively to enforce data consistency.

3.3.3   Communicating with the Server

Browser clients connect to a J2EE application over the Web, and hence they use HTTP as the transport protocol.

When using browser interfaces, users generally interact with an application by clicking hyperlinked text or images, and completing and submitting forms. Browser clients translate these gestures into HTTP requests for a Web server, since the server provides most, if not all, of an application's functionality.

User requests to retrieve data from the server normally map to HTTP GET requests. The URLs of the requests sometimes include parameters in a query string that qualify what data should be retrieved. For example, a URL for listing all dogs might be written as follows:

```
http://javapetstore.sun.com/product.screen?category_id=DOGS
```

User requests to update data on the server normally map to HTTP POST requests. Each of these requests includes a MIME envelope of type `application/x-www-form-urlencoded`, containing parameters for the update. For example, a POST request to complete an order might use the URL:

```
http://javapetstore.sun.com/cart.do
```

The body of the request might include the following line:

```
action=add&itemId=EST-27
```

The servlet API provides a simple interface for handling incoming GET and POST requests and for extracting any parameters sent along with the requests.

Section 4.4.2 on page 98 describes strategies for handling requests and translating these requests into events on your application model.

After a server handles a client request, it must send back an HTTP response; the response usually contains an HTML document. A J2EE application should use JSP pages to generate HTML documents; for more information on using JSP pages effectively, see Section 4.2.6.4 on page 86.

Security is another important aspect of client-server communication. Section 9.2.2 on page 284 covers authentication mechanisms and Section 9.4.2 on page 305 covers confidentiality mechanisms.

3.3.4 Managing Conversational State

Because HTTP is a request-response protocol, individual requests are treated independently. Consequently, Web-based enterprise applications need a mechanism for identifying a particular client and the state of any conversation it is having with that client.

The *HTTP State Management Mechanism* specification introduces the notion of a *session* and *session state*. A session is a short-lived sequence of service requests by a single user using a single client to access a server. Session state is the information maintained in the session across requests. For example, a shopping cart uses session state to track selections as a user chooses items from a catalog. Browsers have two mechanisms for caching session state: cookies and URL rewriting.

- A *cookie* is a small chunk of data the server sends for storage on the client. Each time the client sends information to a server, it includes in its request the headers for all the cookies it has received from that server. Unfortunately, cookie support is inconsistent enough to be annoying: some users disable cookies, some firewalls and gateways filter them, and some browsers do not support them. Furthermore, you can store only small amounts of data in a cookie; to be portable across all browsers, you should use four kilobytes at most.

- *URL rewriting* involves encoding session state within a URL, so that when the user makes a request on the URL, the session state is sent back to the server. This technique works almost everywhere, and can be a useful fallback when you cannot use cookies. Unfortunately, pages containing rewritten URLs consume much bandwidth. For each request the server receives, it must rewrite every URL in its response (the HTML page), thereby increasing the size of the response sent back to the client.

Both cookies and pages containing rewritten URLs are vulnerable to unauthorized access. Browsers usually retain cookies and pages in the local file system, so any sensitive information (passwords, contact information, credit card numbers, etc.) they contain is vulnerable to abuse by anyone else who can access this data. Encrypting the data stored on the client might solve this problem, as long as the data is not intended for display.

Because of the limitations of caching session state on browser clients, these clients should not maintain session state. Rather, servers should manage session state for browsers. Under this arrangement, a server sends a browser client a key that identifies session data (using cookies or URL rewriting), and the browser sends the key back to the server whenever it wants to use the session data. If the browser caches any information beyond a session key, it should be restricted to items like the user's login and preferences for using the site; such items do not need to be manipulated, and they can be easily stored on the client.

3.4   Design Issues and Guidelines for Java Clients

Java clients can be divided into three categories: *applications*, *applets*, and *MIDlets*. They all leverage the Java programming language and a small common set of Java libraries, but they are deployed differently.

3.4.0.0.1 Application Clients

Application clients execute in the Java 2 Runtime Environment, Standard Edition (JRE). They are very similar to the stand-alone applications that run on traditional desktop computers. As such, they typically depend much less on servers than do browsers.

Application clients are packaged inside JAR files and may be installed explicitly on a client's machine or provisioned on demand using Java Web Start technology. Preparing an application client for Java Web Start deployment involves distributing its JAR with a Java Network Launching Protocol (JNLP) file. When a user running Java Web Start requests the JNLP file (normally by clicking a link in a Web browser), Java Web Start automatically downloads all necessary files. It then caches the files so the user can relaunch the application without having to download them again (unless they have changed, in which case Java Web Start technology takes care of downloading the appropriate files).

For more information on Java Web Start and JNLP, see the Java Web Start home page listed in "References and Resources" on page 73.

3.4.0.0.2 Applet Clients

Applet clients are user interface components that typically execute in a Web browser, although they can execute in other applications or devices that support the applet programming model. They are typically more dependent on a server than are application clients, but are less dependent than browser clients.

Like application clients, applet clients are packaged inside JAR files. However, applets are typically executed using Java Plug-in technology. This technology allows applets to be run using Sun's implementation of the Java 2 Runtime Environment, Standard Edition (instead of, say, a browser's default JRE).

For more information on packaging applets, consult the *Java Tutorial*. For more information on serving applets from JSP pages using Java Plug-in technology, consult the *J2EE Tutorial*.

3.4.0.0.3 MIDlet Clients

MIDlet clients are small applications programmed to the Mobile Information Device Profile (MIDP), a set of Java APIs which, together with the Connected Limited Device Configuration (CLDC), provides a complete Java 2 Micro Edition (J2ME) runtime environment for cellular phones, two-way pagers, and palmtops.

A MIDP application is packaged inside a JAR file, which contains the application's class and resource files. This JAR file may be pre-installed on a mobile device or downloaded onto the device (usually over the air). Accompanying the JAR file is a Java Application Descriptor (JAD) file, which describes the application and any configurable application properties.

For a complete specification of a JAD file's contents, as well as deploying MIDP applications in general, see the *J2ME Wireless Toolkit User's Guide*.

3.4.1   Presenting the User Interface

Although a Java client contains an application's user interface, the presentation logic behind this interface may come from a server, as it would for a browser, or it may be programmed from the ground up on the client. In this section, we discuss the latter case.

Java applet and application clients may use the Java Foundation Classes (JFC)/Swing API, a comprehensive set of GUI components for desktop clients. Java MIDlets, meanwhile, may use the MIDP User Interface API, a GUI toolkit that is geared towards the limited input capabilities of today's mobile information devices. For example, Figure 3.2 shows the Java Smart Ticket sample application using the MIDP UI API and running on a Palm IIIc emulator.

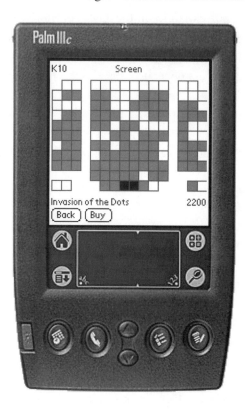

Figure 3.2   Java Smart Ticket Sample Application Client Running on a Palm OS Device

Implementing the user interface for a Java client usually requires more effort to implement than a browser interface, but the benefits are substantial. First, Java client interfaces offer a richer user experience; with programmable GUI components, you can create more natural interfaces for the task at hand. Second, and perhaps more importantly, full programmability makes Java clients much more responsive than browser interfaces.

When a Java client and a browser client request the same data, the Java client consumes less bandwidth. For example, when a browser requests a list of orders and a Java client requests the same list, the response is larger for the browser because it includes presentation logic. The Java client, on the other hand, gets the data and nothing more.

Furthermore, Java clients can be programmed to make fewer connections than a browser to a server. For example, in the Java Pet Store sample application, an administrator may view orders in a table and sort them by date, order identifier, and so on. He or she may also see order data presented in a pie chart or a bar chart, as shown in Figure 3.3.

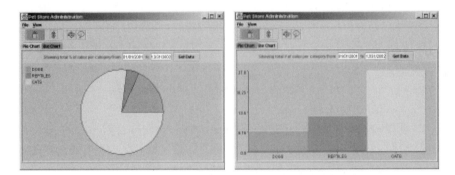

Figure 3.3   Java Pet Store Sample Application Administrator Client Displaying Order Data in Pie and Bar Charts Using the JFC/Swing API

Because the administrator client uses the JFC/Swing API, it can provide all of these views from the same data set; once it retrieves the data, it does not have to reconnect to the server (unless it wants to refresh its data). In contrast, an administrator client implemented using a browser must connect to the server each time the view changes. Even though the data does not change, the browser has to download a new view because the data and the view are intertwined.

For more information on programming JFC/Swing user interfaces, refer to the *JFC Swing Tutorial*. For more information on programming MIDP user interfaces, read *Programming Wireless Devices with the Java 2 Plaform, Micro Edition*.

3.4.2   Validating User Inputs

Like presentation logic, input validation logic may also be programmed on Java clients, which have more to gain than browser clients from client-side input validation. Recall that browser clients have to trade off the benefit of fewer connections (from detecting bad inputs before they get to the server) for the cost of using more bandwidth (from downloading validation code from the server). In contrast, Java clients realize a more responsive interface because they do not have to download validation logic from the server.

With Java clients, it is straightforward to write input validation logic. You use the Java programming language, as shown in Code Example 3.3 from the Java Smart Ticket sample application:

```
public void validateAll() throws ApplicationException {
    if (username.size() < 4) {
        /* Complain about username being too short... */
    }
    if (password.size() < 6) {
        /* Complain about password being too short... */
    }
    if (zipCode.size() != 5) {
        /* Complain about ZIP code not having 5 characters... */
    }
    if (creditCard.size() != 12) {
        /* Complain about credit card number not having
        12 digits... */
    }
}
```

Code Example 3.3   Java Smart Ticket Sample Application Code for Validating Inputs in a User Account Form

For more sophisticated input validation on JFC/Swing clients, consider using the InputVerifier class provided by the JFC/Swing framework. For more information, see "References and Resources" on page 73.

Of course, the best way to reduce client-side validation requirements is to make it impossible to enter bad data in the first place (especially if you are expecting a value of an enumerated type). For example, using a text field to enter a date is error-prone because a text field can receive many types of input. Providing a set of drop-downs that contain valid months, days, and years might be an improvement, but a user can still enter invalid input (such as Feb. 30). The best solution is to provide a calendar widget that intelligently constrains what date is chosen, and the only way to implement such a custom component is with a programmable client.

3.4.3 Communicating with the Server

Java clients may connect to a J2EE application as *Web clients* (connecting to the Web tier), *EJB clients* (connecting to the EJB tier), or *EIS clients* (connecting to the EIS tier).

3.4.3.0.1 Web Clients

Like browser clients, Java Web clients connect over HTTP to the Web tier of a J2EE application. This aspect of Web clients is particularly important on the Internet, where HTTP communication is typically the only way a client can reach a server. Many servers are separated from their clients by firewalls, and HTTP is one of the few protocols most firewalls allow through.

Whereas browsers have built-in mechanisms that translate user gestures into HTTP requests and interpret HTTP responses to update the view, Java clients must be programmed to perform these actions. A key consideration when implementing such actions is the format of the messages between client and server.

Unlike browser clients, Java clients may send and receive messages in any format. For example, in the Java Smart Ticket sample application, a user may look at a list of movies. If the user had a browser client, the list would have to be formatted in HTML before downloading it to the client. However, the Java client in this demo downloads a plain binary string representing the list.

A Java client could use another format, such as comma-separated values:

```
1,Big and Badder,2,The Dot,4,Invasion of the Dots
```

Or, the client could use key-value pairs:

```
id=1,title="Big and Badder"
id=2,title="The Dot"
id=4,title="Invasion of the Dots"
```

Or, the client could use XML:

```
<movies>
    <movie>
        <id>1</id>
        <title>Big and Badder</title>
    </movie>
    <movie>
        <id>2</id>
        <title>The Dot</title>
    </movie>
    <movie>
        <id>4</id>
        <title>Invasion of the Dots</title>
    </movie>
</movies>
```

Although the possibilities are endless, you can think of message formats as falling into a spectrum, with binary strings on one end and XML documents on the other. To understand the tradeoffs of message formats in general, it helps to consider these two extremes.

Binary messages consume little bandwidth. This aspect of binary messages is especially attractive in low-bandwidth environments (such as wireless and dial-up networks), where every byte counts. Code Example 3.4 illustrates how a Java client might construct a binary request to log into an application.

```
static final int LOGIN_USER = 1;
// ...

HttpConnection c;
DataOutputStream out;
String username, password;
/* Construct the body of the HTTP POST request using out... */

out.write(LOGIN_USER);
out.writeUTF(username);
```

```
out.writeUTF(password);
/* Send the HTTP request... */
```

Code Example 3.4   Java Client Code for Sending a Binary Request

Code Example 3.5 illustrates how a Java servlet might listen for requests from the Java client:

```
public void doPost(HttpServletRequest req,
    HttpServletResponse resp) throws IOException, ServletException {

    /* Interpret the request. */
    DataInputStream in =
        new DataInputStream(req.getInputStream());
    int command = in.readInt();

    resp.setContentType("application/binary");
    DataOutputStream out =
        new DataOutputStream(resp.getOutputStream());
    byte command = in.read();
    switch (command) {
    case LOGIN_USER:
        String username = in.readUTF();
        String password = in.readUTF();
        /* Check username and password against user database... */
    }
}
```

Code Example 3.5   Java Servlet Code for Interpreting a Binary Request

These examples also illustrate a substantial cost of HTTP-based messaging in general; you have to write code for parsing and interpreting messages. Unfortunately, writing such code, especially for multiple programmable clients, can be time-consuming and error-prone.

Java technologies for XML alleviate some of the burdens experienced with binary messaging. These technologies, which include the Java API for XML Processing (JAXP), automate the parsing and aid the construction of XML messages.

Messaging toolkits based on Java technology help interpret messages once they are parsed; these toolkits implement open standards such as the Simple Object Access Protocol (SOAP). The ability to parse and interpret messages automatically reduces development time and helps maintenance and testing.

A side benefit of using XML messages is that alternate clients are easier to support, as XML is a widely-accepted open standard. For example, StarOffice Calc and Macromedia Flash clients could both read order data formatted in XML from the same JSP page and present the data in their respective interfaces. Also, you can use XML to encode messages from a variety of clients. A C++ client, for example, could use a SOAP toolkit to make remote procedure calls (RPC) to a J2EE application.

The most common models for XML processing are DOM and the Simple API for XML (SAX). Unlike DOM, which provides an in-memory, tree-based data structure for random access, SAX offers event-based serial access, which makes processing messages faster. For more information on using XML effectively, see "References and Resources" on page 73.

Like browser clients, Java Web clients carry out secure communication over HTTPS. See Section 9.2.2 on page 284 for more information on Web authentication mechanisms and Section 9.4.2 on page 305 for more information on Web confidentiality mechanisms.

3.4.3.0.2 EJB Clients

When using Web clients, you must write code for translating user gestures into HTTP requests, HTTP requests into application events, event responses into HTTP responses, and HTTP responses into view updates. On the other hand, when using EJB clients, you do not need to write such code because the clients connect directly to the EJB tier using Java Remote Method Invocation (RMI) calls.

Unfortunately, connecting as an EJB client is not always possible. First, only applet and application clients may connect as EJB clients. (At this time, MIDlets cannot connect to the EJB tier because RMI is not a native component of MIDP.) Second, RMI calls are implemented using IIOP, and most firewalls usually block communication using that protocol. So, when a firewall separates a server and its clients, as would be the case over the Internet, using an EJB client is not an option. However, you could use an EJB client within a company intranet, where firewalls generally do not intervene between servers and clients.

When deploying an applet or application EJB client, you should distribute it with a client-side container and install the container on the client machine. This container (usually a class library) allows the client to access middle-tier services (such as the JMS, JDBC, and JTA APIs) and is provided by the application server vendor. However, the exact behavior for installing EJB clients is not completely specified for the J2EE platform, so the client-side container and deployment mechanisms for EJB clients vary slightly from application server to application server.

Clients should be authenticated to access the EJB tier, and the client container is responsible for providing the appropriate authentication mechanisms. For more information on EJB client authentication, see Section 9.2.2.2 on page 287.

3.4.3.0.3 EIS Clients

Generally, Java clients should not connect directly to a J2EE application's EIS tier. EIS clients require a powerful interface, such as the JDBC API, to manipulate data on a remote resource. When this interface is misused (by a buggy client you have implemented or by a malicious client someone else has hacked or built from scratch), your data can be compromised. Furthermore, non-trivial EIS clients must implement business logic. Because the logic is attached to the client, it is harder to share among multiple types of clients.

In some circumstances, it may be acceptable for clients to access the EIS tier directly, such as for administration or management tasks, where the user interface is small or nonexistent and the task is simple and well understood. For example, a simple Java program could perform maintenance on database tables and be invoked every night through an external mechanism.

3.4.4   Managing Conversational State

Whereas browser clients require a robust server-side mechanism for maintaining session state, Java clients can manage session state on their own, because they can cache and manipulate substantial amounts of state in memory. Consequently, Java clients have the ability to work while disconnected, which is beneficial when latency is high or when each connection consumes significant bandwidth.

To support a disconnected operation, a Java client must retrieve enough usable data for the user before going offline. The initial cost of downloading such data can be high, but you can reduce this cost by constraining what gets downloaded, by filtering on user preferences, or requiring users to enter search queries at the beginning of each session. Many applications for mobile devices already use such strategies; they also apply well to Java clients in general.

For example, you could extend the Java Smart Ticket sample application to allow users to download movie listings onto their phones. To reduce the size of the listings, you could allow users to filter on simple criteria such as genre (some users may not be in the mood for drama) or ZIP code (some users may only want to go to movie theaters within 10 miles of where they live). Users could then browse the personalized lists on their phones without needing to connect to the server until they want to buy a ticket.

Also note that the movie listings are candidates for persistence on the client, since they are updated infrequently, perhaps once every week. The Java Smart Ticket sample application client uses the MIDP Record Management Store (RMS) API to store data locally. Application clients, meanwhile, can use either local files (assuming they have permission) or the Java Native Launching Protocol and API (JNLP) persistence service. (Applets have very limited local storage because they normally use a browser's cookie store, although they can request permission to use local files as well.)

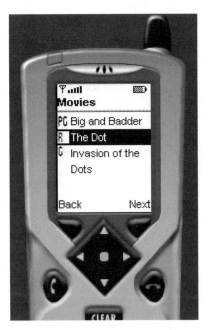

Figure 3.4   Java Smart Ticket Sample Application Listing Movie Information
Downloaded onto the Phone

The example of downloading movie listings illustrates a read-only interaction. The client retrieves data from the server, caches it, and does not modify the cached data. There may be times, however, when a Java client needs to update data it receives from the server and report its changes to the server. To stay disconnected, the client must queue updates locally on the client and only send the batch when the user connects to the server.

In the Java Smart Ticket sample application, the client allows users to pinpoint the exact seats they want to buy. When the user decides what show he or she wants to see, the client downloads the data for the show's seating plan and displays the plan to the user. The plan indicates which seats are available and which have already been taken, as shown in Figure 3.5.

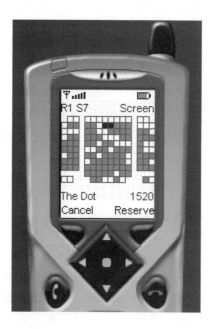

Figure 3.5   Java Smart Ticket Sample Application Displaying an Editable Seating Plan for a Particular Movie Showing

This example highlights two important issues. First, when Java clients manipulate enterprise data, they need to know about the model and some or all of the business rules surrounding the data model. For example, the client must understand the concept of booked and unbooked seats, and model that concept just like the server does. For another example, the client must also prevent users from trying to select booked seats, enforcing a business rule also implemented on the server. Generally, clients manipulating enterprise data must duplicate logic on the server, because the server must enforce all business rules regardless of what its clients do.

Second, when Java clients manipulate enterprise data, applications need to implement data synchronization schemes. For example, between the time when the user downloads the seating plan and the time when the user decides what seats he or she wants to buy, another user may buy some or all of those seats. The application needs rules and mechanisms for resolving such a conflict. In this case, the server's data trumps the client's data because whoever buys the tickets first—and hence updates the server first—gets the tickets. The application could continue by asking the second user if he or she wants the seats that the first user did not buy. Or, it could refresh the second user's display with an updated seating plan and have the user pick seats all over again.

3.5   Summary

The J2EE platform supports a range of client devices and client programming models. Supported devices include desktop systems, laptops, palmtops, cell phones, and various emerging non-traditional devices. The supported programming models include browser clients using HTML and JavaScript, browser plug-in clients such as Flash, office suite clients such as StarOffice, and programmable clients based on Java technologies.

Application developers should make an effort to provide users with the highest possible level of service and functionality supported by each client device. The primary consideration throughout the design of the client should be the network, since the client participates in a networked application. At the same time, there may be other important considerations, such as development and support capabilities, time to market, and other factors that affect the ultimate client solution chosen for a particular application.

3.6   References and Resources

- *The J2EE Tutorial.* S. Bodoff, D. Green, K. Haase, E. Jendrock, M. Pawlan. Copyright 2001, Sun Microsystems, Inc.
`<http://java.sun.com/j2ee/tutorial/index.html>`

- *The JFC/Swing Tutorial.* M. Campione, K. Walrath. Copyright 2000, Addison-Wesley. Also available as
`<http://java.sun.com/docs/books/tutorial/uiswing/index.html>`

- *The Java Tutorial, Third Edition: A Short Course on the Basics.* M. Campione, K. Walrath, A. Huml. Copyright 2000, Addison-Wesley. Also available as
`<http://java.sun.com/docs/books/tutorial/index.html>`

- *The Eight Fallacies of Distributed Computing.* P. Deutsch. Copyright 2001, Sun Microsystems, Inc.
`<http://java.sun.com/people/jag/Fallacies.html>`

- *Programming Wireless Devices with the Java 2 Plaform, Micro Edition.* R. Riggs, A. Taivalsaari, M. VandenBrink. Copyright 2001, Addison-Wesley.

- *eMobile End-to-End Application Using the Java 2 Platform, Enterprise Edition.* T. Violleau. Copyright 2000, Sun Microsystems, Inc.
`<http://developer.java.sun.com/developer/technicalArti-cles/javaone00/eMobileApplet.pdf>`

- *Java Technology and XML.* T. Violleau. Copyright 2001, Sun Microsystems, Inc. `<http://developer.java.sun.com/developer/technicalArti-cles/xml/JavaTechandXML/>`

- *A Note on Distributed Computing.* J. Waldo, G. Wyant, A. Wollrath, S. Kendall. Copyright November 1994, Sun Microsystems, Inc.
`<http://research.sun.com/research/techrep/1994/smli_tr-94-29.pdf>`

- *Cascading Style Sheets Level 2 Specification.* World Wide Web Consortium, May 1998. `<http://www.w3.org/TR/REC-CSS2/>`

- *Document Object Model (DOM) Level 2 Core Specification.* World Wide Web Consortium, November 2000. `<http://www.w3.org/TR/2000/REC-DOM-Level-2-Core-20001113/>`

- *ECMAScript Language Specification.* European Computer Manufacturers Association, December 1999. `<ftp://ftp.ecma.ch/ecma-st/Ecma-262.pdf>`

- *HTML 4.01 Specification.* World Wide Web Consortium, December 1999.
  `<http://www.w3.org/TR/html4/>`

- *Hypertext Transfer Protocol — HTTP/1.1.* The Internet Society, 1999.
  `<http://www.ietf.org/rfc/rfc2616.txt>`

- *HTTP State Management Mechanism.* The Internet Society, February 1997.
  `<http://www.ietf.org/rfc/rfc2109.txt>`

- Java Web Start Web site `<http://java.sun.com/products/javaweb-start/developers.html>`

- *Input Verification.* Sun Microsystems, 2001.
  `<http://java.sun.com/j2se/1.3/docs/guide/swing/InputChanges.html>`

- *Webmonkey.* Lycos, 2001. `<http://webmonkey.com/>`

CHAPTER 4

The Web Tier

by Greg Murray and Mark Johnson

A J2EE application's Web tier makes the application's business logic available on the World Wide Web. The Web tier handles all of a J2EE application's communication with Web clients, invoking business logic and transmitting data in response to incoming requests.

This chapter describes several ways of using Web-tier technology effectively in a J2EE application design, including examples from the sample application. The chapter is specifically *not* about Web page design.

4.1 The Purpose of the Web Tier

A server in the Web tier processes HTTP requests. In a J2EE application, the Web tier usually manages the interaction between Web clients and the application's business logic. The Web tier typically produces HTML or XML content, though the Web tier can generate and serve any content type. While business logic is often implemented as enterprise beans, it may also be implemented entirely within the Web tier.

The Web tier typically performs the following functions in a J2EE application:

- **Web-enables business logic**—The Web tier manages interaction between Web clients and application business logic.

- **Generates dynamic content**—Web-tier components generate content dynamically, in entirely arbitrary data formats, including HTML, images, sound, and video.

- **Presents data and collects input**—Web-tier components translate HTTP PUT and GET actions into a form that the business logic understands and present results as Web content.

- **Controls screen flow**—The logic that determines which "screen" (that is, which page) to display next usually resides in the Web tier, because screen flow tends to be specific to client capabilities.

- **Maintains state**—The Web tier has a simple, flexible mechanism for accumulating data for transactions and for interaction context over the lifetime of a user session.

- **Supports multiple and future client types**—Extensible MIME types describe Web content, so a Web client can support any current and future type of downloadable content.

- **May implement business logic**—While many enterprise applications implement business logic in enterprise beans, Web-only, low- to medium-volume applications with simple transactional behavior can implement business logic entirely within the Web tier.

4.2   Web-Tier Technologies

This section presents a quick review of Web technologies in the J2EE platform, first describing legacy technologies, and then the Web-tier component types that supersede them. Feel free to skip this section if you are already familiar with these technologies. If you need to refresh your understanding beyond what this section offers, see the J2EE Tutorial (a reference to the J2EE Tutorial is listed in "References and Resources" on page 127).

4.2.1   Traditional Web-Tier Technologies

Understanding the history of dynamic Web content generation provides a context for understanding the benefits of Web technology in the J2EE platform. The earliest versions of the World Wide Web relied on basic HTTP servers to serve static HTML pages to HTML browsers. However, it quickly became clear that dynamic content, generated on demand, would make the Web a platform for delivering applications as well as content.

Several mechanisms were developed to allow Web servers to generate content on demand, all of which can be thought of as Web server functional extensions. In this context, a Web application is simply a complex Web server extension.

Web-tier technologies in the J2EE platform provide a superset of the functionality offered by the older technologies described here. Easy migration from or seamless integration with legacy Web applications is one of the strengths of Web-tier technologies in the J2EE platform.

The earliest standard server extension mechanism was the Common Gateway Interface (CGI), which defines a type of stand-alone executable program used by a server to produce dynamic content. While CGI remains a popular option for Web applications, it has some important limitations. CGI has performance limitations, because each HTTP request to a CGI program usually results in the creation of a heavyweight process in the host operating system. CGI is also a simple interface that offers no portable support for high-level system services, such as load balancing, scalability, high availability, security, state maintenance, and resource management, making scalable CGI solutions difficult to develop and maintain. CGI's simplicity is a double-edged sword: It is easy to understand, but it does not offer many portable system services to the developer.

Some of CGI's limitation can be overcome with a server extension API, which allows developers to create libraries that generate dynamic content. Examples of such APIs include NSAPI (for Netscape servers), Apache extension modules (for Apache), and ISAPI (for Microsoft Internet Information Server). While extension libraries alleviate the overhead of CGI process creation, server extension APIs are nonportable between server vendors, locking applications into a particular vendor's API and product line. Worse, server extension libraries can compromise system stability, because an extension library crash can take down the entire server.

An improvement to server extension APIs is server-side scripting, in which a script running inside the server produces dynamic content. Fast CGI is a server-side scripting interface that replaces an operating system CGI program with a server-side CGI script. Server-side scripts that fail usually do not crash the server, because the script interpreter can easily intercede to recover from script failures. Although server-side scripts may be somewhat more portable than extension APIs, they are non-portable to the extent that they use server-specific features. Server-side scripts also do not provide uniform, portable access to high-level system services.

4.2.2   Web-Tier Technologies in the J2EE Platform

Web-tier technologies in the J2EE platform provide the benefits of server-side scripting, using compiled Java classes in a standardized, secure, and vendor-neutral environment. This section briefly describes and provides best practices for Web-tier technologies in the J2EE platform.

A Web application is a collection of Web-tier components, content, and configuration information, which operates as a single functional unit. The runtime support environment for a Web application is called a Web container. A Web application archive (.war) file contains all of the class files and resources for the Web application, along with an XML deployment descriptor file that configures the application. See Chapter 7 in particular for more on packaging and deploying Web applications.

The platform specification defines a contract between the Web container and each Web component, defining the component's lifecycle, the behavior the component must implement, and the services that the server must provide to the component.

The platform specification also defines two types of Web component technologies: Java Servlets ("servlets") and JavaServer Pages™ (JSP™ pages) technology.

A servlet is a Java class that extends a J2EE server, producing dynamic content in response to requests from the server. The server passes service requests to the servlet through the standard interface `javax.servlet`, which every servlet must implement.

A JSP page is an HTML page with special markup that provides customizable behavior for generating dynamic content at runtime. A JSP page is usually translated into a servlet when it is deployed. JSP technology provides a document-centric, rather than programmatic, way to specify dynamic content generation.

4.2.3   The Web Container

A J2EE Web application runs inside a J2EE server's Web container. The container manages each component's lifecycle, dispatches service requests to application components, and provides standard interfaces to context data such as session state and information about the current request.

The Web container provides a consistent interface to the components it hosts, so Web components are portable across application servers. And, because packaging and deployment of J2EE Web applications are standardized, a Web application can be deployed into any J2EE server without recompiling the code or rebuilding the application archive.

The next few sections describe Web-tier components in the J2EE platform and explain the benefits their features provide.

4.2.4 Java Servlets

A Java Servlet is a Java class that extends a J2EE-compatible Web server. Each servlet class produces dynamic content in response to service requests to one or more URLs.

Servlets offer some important benefits over earlier dynamic content generation technologies. Servlets are compiled Java classes, so they are generally faster than CGI programs or server-side scripts. Servlets are safer than extension libraries, because the Java Virtual Machine (JVM) can recover from a servlet that exits unexpectedly. Servlets are portable both at the source-code level (because of the Java Servlet specification) and at the binary level (because of the innate portability of Java bytecode). Servlets also provide a richer set of standard services than any other widely adopted server extension technology.

In addition to producing content, servlets have several features that support application structure. A developer can create classes that respond to events in a servlet's lifecycle by implementing listener interfaces. The sample application uses listener interfaces to initialize servlet data structures. A servlet can also be extended by one or more servlet filters, which are reusable classes that wrap calls to a servlet's `service` method, transforming the request or the response. Servlet filters can be organized into filter chains that perform successive transformations on servlet requests or responses.

Distributed servlets are more scalable than non-distributed servlets. The Web container can provide an application with load balancing and failover by migrating user sessions among cluster nodes. Distributed servlets are marked `distributable` in the Web application deployment descriptor. They must follow a set of restrictions beyond those required of non-distributed servlets. The additional restrictions ensure that servlet code operates properly across session migrations.

For an introduction to or review of servlets, see the section entitled "Java Servlet Technology" in *The J2EE Tutorial*.

4.2.5   JavaServer Pages (JSP) Technology

Most Web applications produce primarily dynamic HTML pages that, when served, change only in data values and not in basic structure. For example, all of the catalog pages in an online store may have identical structure and differ only in the items they display. JSP technology exists for producing such content.

A JSP page is a document containing fixed template text, plus special markup for including other text or executing embedded logic. The fixed template text is always served to the requester just as it appears in the page, like traditional HTML. The special markup can take one of three forms: directives, scripting elements, or custom tags (also known as "custom actions"). Directives are instructions that control the behavior of the JSP page compiler and therefore are evaluated at page compilation time. Scripting elements are blocks of Java code embedded in the JSP page between the delimiters <% and %>. Custom tags (discussed later in this section) are programmer-defined markup tags that generate dynamic content when the page is served. The JavaServer Pages specification defines a set of standard tags that are available in all platform implementations. Custom tags and scripting elements generate dynamic content that is included in a response when a page is being served.

JSP pages can specify dynamic content of any textual type, but they are primarily used for creating structured content such as HTML, XML, XHTML, and so on. JSP pages are easier to write than servlets, because they look like structured documents. JSP pages are a more natural development technology for page designers, who specialize in authoring structured documents. Although a JSP page looks to its author like a document, most J2EE implementations translate a JSP page into a servlet class when it is deployed. JSP pages are also compatible with a wide array of authoring tools that simplify page creation.

JSP pages differ from servlets in their programming model. A JSP page is primarily a document that specifies dynamic content, rather than a program that produces content. JSP page technology provides a "document-centric" alternative to "programmatic" servlets for creating dynamic, structured data.

4.2.5.1   XML JSP Page Syntax

The JSP specification defines an alternate XML syntax for JSP pages. Pages in standard JSP syntax cannot be well-formed XML because the markup does not conform to XML's requirements. Pages using the alternate JSP XML syntax can be validated against an XML Schema Definition Language (XSDL) schema to check for many potential errors that would otherwise appear only at runtime. XML syntax can also facilitate integration with development tools. For integrity, a single JSP file may not contain a mix of standard JSP syntax and XML syntax.

Writing JSP pages in XML syntax is different from using JSP pages to generate XML content. The XML JSP page syntax is a way to specify a JSP page using well-formed XML. JSP pages written in either standard or XML syntax are useful for generating dynamic XML content.

4.2.5.2   Custom Tags

JSP technology allows developers to define custom tags, which are markup tags that are replaced by dynamic content when the page is served. The dynamic content is created by a tag handler class, which a programmer creates and packages in a tag library archive file. A programmer defines the syntax for a tag and implements the tag's behavior in the handler class. Page authors can then import and use tags in tag libraries just as they use other markup tags.

Custom tags provide several benefits to a J2EE application design.

- Custom tags are reusable, as scripting elements generally are not.

- Libraries of custom tags provide high-level services for JSP pages that are portable across JSP containers.

- Custom tags ease maintenance, because they reduce repeated code. Changing a tag's handler class changes the tag's behavior everywhere it is used.

- Custom tags help developers focus on their core skills. Page authors can work exclusively with custom tags and standard markup, instead of with a jumble of tags and cryptic scripting elements. Meanwhile, programmers can focus on developing custom tag logic.

- Custom tags can provide non-programmers, such as page authors, with an intuitive syntax for invoking business logic.

- Custom tags can decouple business logic and data presentation. This separation eases maintenance, clarifies the intent of each component, and allows programmers and page authors to work relatively independently of one another.

4.2.5.3   Standard Tag Libraries

Standard tag libraries are sets of custom tags that provide a basic set of domain-neutral functionality for JSP pages. Standard tags typically perform such functions

as Web resource inclusion, request forwarding, conditional logic, collection itera-
tion, XSLT transformations, internationalization, state access, and HTML forms.
Some companies have produced tag libraries that are intimately integrated with their
tools and J2EE product lines. Other organizations have produced tag libraries for
general use in J2EE applications. Apache Taglibs, for example, is an open-source
project that contains dozens of custom tags.

The Java Standard Tag Library (JSTL) is now a part of the Java Community
Process (JSR-52, A Standard Tag Library for JavaServer Pages). Once standardized, JSTL will provide a rich layer of portable functionality to JSP pages. It will
be available in all compliant JSP containers. See the Apache Jakarta taglib page
listed in "References and Resources" on page 127 for more on JSTL.

Standard tag libraries often provide much of the basic functionality that JSP
pages need. Mature libraries have been tested and optimized by a community of
developers. Adopting a high-quality standard tag library can save application development time.

4.2.6   Web-Tier Technology Guidelines

This section provides guidelines for effective use of servlets and JSP pages.

4.2.6.1   Where to Use Servlets

Servlets are most effectively used for implementing logic and generating binary
content.

4.2.6.1.1 Use Servlets to Implement Services

Servlets are usually not visual components, except for some that generate binary
content. Instead, think of a servlet as an information service provided by an application. A servlet can perform whatever service it provides—templating, security, personalization, application control—and then select a presentation component (often a
JSP page) to which it forwards the request for display. The sample application
implements its templating services as a servlet (see Section 4.4.3.1 on page 110).
Just as a servlet can be thought of as a service, a servlet filter can be thought of as a
customization or an extension of the services that a servlet provides.

4.2.6.1.2 Use Servlets as Controllers

Servlets are the preferred technology for implementing a Web-tier controller, which
determines how to handle a request and chooses the next view to display. A control-

ler activates application operations and makes decisions, which are essentially procedural tasks that are best suited for program code in servlets.

JSP pages should not be used as controllers. Because JSP pages that are mostly logic are a mixture of markup tags and program code, they are difficult to read and maintain, especially for Web developers who are not programmers.

```
public class extends HttpServlet {
    protected void doPost(HttpServletRequest req,
                          HttpServletResponse res) throws... {

        String creditCard = req.getParameter("creditCard");
        String jspPage = "/process" + creditCard + ".jsp";
        ServletContext sc = getServletContext();
        RequestDispatcher rd = getRequestDispatcher(jspPage);
        rd.forward(req, res);
    }
}
```

Code Example 4.1   A Servlet Properly Used as a Controller

Code Example 4.1 is an example of a servlet used properly as a controller. The same controller is implemented improperly as a JSP page in Code Example 4.5 on page 91. Comparing the two, the pure servlet implementation is cleaner and easier to maintain.

See also Section 4.2.6.9 on page 91.

4.2.6.1.3 Use Servlets to Generate Binary Content

Binary content should be generated by servlets. Servlets that output binary content must set the Content-Type HTTP header to the MIME type of the content being generated. A servlet writes its binary data to an OutputStream acquired from the ServletRequest, as shown in Code Example 4.2.

```
public class JpgWriterServlet extends HttpServlet {
    public void service(HttpServletRequest req,
                        HttpServletResponse rsp) throws... {
        rsp.setHeader("Content-type", "image/jpg");
```

```
            OutputStream os = rsp.getOutputStream();
            // ... now write binary data to the OutputStream...
```

Code Example 4.2   A Servlet that Produces Binary Content

A servlet can write to either an `OutputStream` or a `PrintWriter`, but not both. JSP pages can't create binary content.

4.2.6.2   Avoid Writing Servlets That Print Mostly Static Text

Servlets composed mostly of `println` statements would be better implemented as JSP pages. JSP pages are for creating textual content that combines template data with dynamic data values. Servlets that print a great deal of text, and perform some logic between the print lines, are tedious to write and difficult to maintain. Every delimiter in the quoted strings written by the servlet must be properly escaped with a backslash, reducing readability. Updating the visual presentation of such a servlet requires modifying and recompiling a program, instead of updating a page of markup.

```
    public class PopulateServlet extends HttpServlet {
      public void doGet(HttpServletRequest  req,
                        HttpServletResponse res) throws ... {
      ...
      if (dbConnectionClosed) {
        PrintWriter out = response.getWriter();
        out.println("<html>");
        out.println("<body bgcolor=white>");
        out.println("<font size=\"+5\" color=\"red\">Can't con-
nect</font>");
        out.println("<br>Confirm your database is running");
        out.println("</body></html>");
      }
    }
```

Code Example 4.3   Bad Practice: a Servlet that Prints Static Content

In Code Example 4.3, a servlet is used inappropriately to generate static content. The code is difficult to read, requires careful delimiter escaping, and would probably need a programmer for nontrivial modifications.

A better design, shown in Code Example 4.4, demonstrates a servlet that detects an error and forwards the request to a JSP page, which reports the error. This maintains proper separation of function from presentation, allowing Web developers and programmers to focus on their core skills.

```
PopulateServlet.java:
public class PopulateServlet extends HttpServlet {
  protected void doGet(HttpServletRequest  req,
                       HttpServletResponse res) throws ... {
    ...
    if (dbConnectionClosed) {
      ServletContext ctx = getServletContext();
      ctx.getRequestDispatcher("/db_failed.jsp").forward(req, res);
    }
  }
}


db_failed.jsp:
<html>
 <body>
  <br><font color="red">Unable to Connect</font>
  <br>Confirm that your database is running
 </body>
<html>
```

Code Example 4.4   Servlet Logic that Delegates Display to a JSP Page

4.2.6.3   Use RequestDispatcher Methods forward and include Correctly

A servlet uses two RequestDispatcher methods, forward and include, to create a response using other components. However, the two methods are intended for fundamentally different operations. Use RequestDispatcher.forward to delegate processing of an entire request to another component, and use RequestDispatcher.include to build a response containing results from multiple Web resources.

When using the request dispatcher in a servlet, keep in mind that `RequestDispatcher.forward` requires that the body of the servlet response be empty. Writing something to the response and then calling `forward` either causes a runtime exception or discards any data previously written.

4.2.6.4   Where to Use JavaServer Pages

JSP pages are typically used for creating structured or free-form textual data. They are most appropriate where data values change between requests, but data structure either doesn't change, or changes very little.

4.2.6.4.1 Use JSP Pages for Data Presentation

JSP pages are most appropriately used for producing structured textual content. Enterprise application data view types typically include HTML, XHTML, and DHTML.

JSP pages are best used for content that is partially fixed, with some elements that are filled in dynamically at runtime. A JSP page contains fixed content called "template data" (not to be confused with the templating mechanism described in this chapter). Custom tags or scripting elements occur at various points in the template data, and are replaced at runtime with dynamic data, producing customized content.

JSP pages cannot create binary content. They are also usually not appropriate for creating content with highly variable structure or for controlling request routing. Servlets are better for those situations. (See Section 4.2.6.1 on page 82 for more on this topic.) JSP pages can reasonably activate business logic, if the implementation of that logic is in a custom tag instead of in a scriptlet; see Section 4.2.6.8 on page 89.

4.2.6.4.2 Use JSP Pages to Generate XML

JSP pages are an excellent technology for generating XML with fixed structure. They are particularly useful for generating XML messages in standard formats, where message tags are fixed and only attribute values or character data change each time the page is served. XML documents can also be created from templates, assembling several XML subdocuments into a composite whole.

4.2.6.4.3 Use JSP Pages to Generate Unstructured Textual Content

JSP pages are not limited to producing documents with structured markup. They can also create unstructured textual content such as ASCII text, fixed-width or delimited data, and even PostScript. For example, JSP pages would be an excellent choice for rendering personalized e-mail form letters to customers.

4.2.6.4.4 Use JSP Pages as Templates

JSP pages may also be appropriately used for assembling textual data from multiple sources, as described in Section 4.4.3.1 on page 110.

4.2.6.5 JSP Pages Character Encoding

JSP pages use class `javax.servlet.jsp.JSPWriter` to write content to the response stream. This class automatically ensures that any text output by the JSP page is properly encoded. But automatic encoding is also a limitation, because it means JSP pages cannot be used to produce binary content directly.

4.2.6.6 Avoid Heavy Use of Logic Tags

Standard tag libraries usually provide so-called "logic tags," which are custom tags that loop, perform iterations, evaluate expressions, and make decisions. Avoid using standard tag libraries to perform a great deal of logic in JSP pages. Using custom tags for logic provides little benefit, and violates separation of logic and presentation. JSP pages that are simply procedural programs written in XML syntax are at least as difficult to maintain as other types of programs.

Instead of creating "procedural" JSP pages, implement logic in a custom tag, servlet, or helper class. One powerful technique is to define custom tags for application logic, implementing the tag handlers using enterprise beans. A thin layer of code (the tag handler class) links the custom tag with enterprise bean lookup and method invocation. This approach provides the view (JSP page or servlet) with direct access to model data (in the enterprise beans), maintaining separation of presentation from function.

4.2.6.7 Use JSP Include Directives and Tags Appropriately

The JSP include directive and the JSP include tag have similar syntax but different purposes.

An include directive includes literal text "as is" in the JSP page and is not intended for use with content that changes at runtime. The include occurs only when the servlet implementing the JSP page is being built and compiled. For example, the following include directive includes a file at page compilation time:

```
<%@ include file="header.jsp" @%>
```

The JSP include tag includes either static or dynamic content in the JSP page when the page is being served. When used to include static content, the include tag works just the same as the include directive. But when an include tag includes dynamic content, the tag generates and includes the dynamic content in the context of the current request. The include occurs each time the JSP page is served. For example, the following JSP include tag includes dynamic content, which depends on the current request:

```
<jsp:include page="/servlets/currentUserInfoServlet"/>
```

In contrast, the JSP include directive is commonly used to modularize Web pages, to reuse content, and to keep Web page size manageable. For example, an include directive could include headers and footers on every page. Using a JSP include directive results in a larger servlet and, if abused, could lead to code bloat.

The JSP include tag is commonly used to insert dynamically generated content into a JSP page at the time it is served. An include tag is more flexible than an include directive, because it can select the content to include at runtime. But an include tag requires runtime processing, and is therefore slower than an include directive.

Each time a particular JSP page is requested, all of its included pages are evaluated and recompiled if necessary. A child page must redeclare the components it uses (for example, JavaBeans components and objects provided by the container). Pages share data by way of the HttpSession object.

The sample application uses primarily include tags, because most of its JSP pages produce dynamic content.

The include directive is problematic for internationalization, because the contentType:charset of the included page cannot be set independently of the including page. The include tag is the only choice for including content with page encoding in JSP version 1.1.

Implementation note: Some Web container implementations (including Tomcat) do not automatically track modifications to files included by an include directive. If you change a file that is included, you also need to force a recompile by "touching" (change the modification date of) the "parent" files that include the modified file.

4.2.6.8   Using Custom Tags to Avoid Scriptlets

Consider using custom tags instead of scriptlets in JSP pages for the following reasons:

- **Scriptlet code is not reusable**—Scriptlet code appears in exactly one place: the JSP page that defines it. If the same logic is needed elsewhere, it must be either included (decreasing readability) or copied and pasted into the new context.

  Custom tags can be reused by reference.

- **Scriptlets encourage copy/paste coding**—Because scriptlet code appears in only one place, it is often copied to a new context. When the scriptlet needs to be modified, usually all of the copies need updating. Finding all copies of the scriptlet and updating them is an error-prone maintenance headache. With time, the copies tend to diverge, making it difficult to determine which scriptlets are copies of others, further frustrating maintenance.

  Custom tags centralize code in one place. When a tag handler class changes, the tag's behavior changes everywhere it is used.

- **Scriptlets mix logic with presentation**—Scriptlets are islands of program code in a sea of presentation code. Changing either requires some understanding of what the other is doing to avoid breaking the relationship between the two. Scriptlets can easily confuse the intent of a JSP page by expressing program logic within the presentation.

  Custom tags encapsulate program logic so that JSP pages can focus on presentation.

- **Scriptlets break developer role separation**—Because scriptlets mingle programming and Web content, Web page designers need to know either how to program or which parts of their pages to avoid modifying. Poorly implemented scriptlets can have subtle dependencies on the surrounding template data. Consider, for example, the following line of code:

```
<% out.println("<a \"href=\"" + url + "\">" + text); %> </a>
```

It would be very easy to change this line in a way that breaks the page, especially for someone who does not understand what the line is doing.

Custom tags help the separation of developer roles, because programmers create the tags, and page authors use them.

- **Scriptlets make JSP pages difficult to read and to maintain**—JSP pages with scriptlets mix structured tags with JSP page delimiters and Java language code. The Java language code in scriptlets often uses "implicit" objects, which are not declared anywhere except in the JavaServer Pages specification. Also, even consistent indentation does not help readability much for nontrivial pages.

  JSP pages with custom tags are composed of tags and character data, which is much easier to read. JSP pages that use XML syntax can be validated as well.

- **Scriptlet compile errors can be difficult to interpret**—Many JSP page compilers do a poor job of translating line numbers between the source page and the generated servlet. Even those that emit error messages often depend on invisible context, such as implicit objects or surrounding template data. With poor error reporting, a missed semicolon can cost hours of development time.

  Erroneous code in custom tags will not compile either, but all of the context for determining the problem is present in the custom tag code, and the line numbers do not need translation.

- **Scriptlet code is difficult to test**—Unit testing of scriptlet code is virtually impossible. Because scriptlets are embedded in JSP pages, the only way to execute them is to execute the page and test the results.

  A custom tag can be unit tested, and errors can be isolated to either the tag or the page in which it is used.

Expressions sometimes also suffer from these problems, but they are somewhat less problematic than scriptlets because they tend to be small.

Custom tags maintain separation between developer roles. They encourage reuse of logic and state within a single source file. They also improve source code readability, and improve both testability and error reporting.

Some projects have Web page authors but few or no programmers. Page authors with limited programming skill can use scriptlets effectively if they use scriptlets for display logic only. Business logic should never be implemented in scriptlets.

4.2.6.9   Avoid Forwarding Requests from JSP Pages

When a JSP page calls `RequestDispatcher.forward`, either directly or with a custom tag, it is acting as a controller. Controllers are better implemented as servlets than as JSP pages, because controllers are logical components, not presentation components. Code Example 4.5 demonstrates a controller implemented as a JSP page.

```
<% String creditCard = request.getParameter("creditCard");
    if (creditCard.equals("Visa")) { %>
<jsp:forward page="/processVisa.jsp"/>
<% } else if (creditCard.equals("American Express")) { %>
<jsp:forward page="/processAmex.jsp"/>
<% } %>
```

Code Example 4.5   Bad Practice: JSP Page Acting as a Controller

In this example, the scriptlets and tags conditionally forward the request to another JSP page based on a request attribute. If each of the `forward` tags were replaced with a single line of Java code that performed the forward, the result would be a JSP page containing nothing but a scriptlet. This code would obviously be better implemented as a servlet. Code Example 4.1 on page 83 shows the code for a servlet implementation of this functionality.

4.3   Web-Tier Application Structure

The J2EE platform is a layered set of system services that are consistently available to J2EE applications across implementations. It is the top layer of a "stack" of services that support an application, shown in Figure 4.1. The J2EE platform runs on top of the J2SE platform, which itself runs on top of the host operating system. In the Web tier, a J2EE Web container provides services related to serving Web requests.

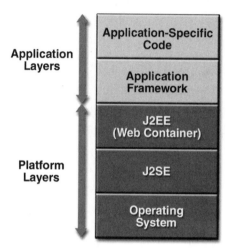

Figure 4.1   Platform and Application Layers

Just as the J2EE platform has layers, J2EE applications can benefit from architectural layering. The highest-level division between layers in an application's Web tier is between functions that are specific to a particular application and those that occur in all Web applications.

All Web-tier applications share a common set of basic requirements that are not provided by the J2EE platform itself. A software layer called an application framework can meet these requirements and can be shared between applications. As shown in Figure 4.1, application-specific code is written in terms of the application framework layer.

A Web-tier application framework sits on top of the J2EE platform, providing common application functionality such as dispatching requests, invoking model methods, and selecting and assembling views. Framework classes and interfaces are structural; they are like the load-bearing elements of a building, forming the application's underpinnings. Application developers extend, use, or implement framework classes and interfaces to perform application-specific functions. For example, a framework may offer an abstract class that a developer may extend to execute business logic in response to application events. A Web-tier application framework makes Web-tier technologies easier to use, helping application developers to concentrate on business logic.

The BluePrints recommended best practice is to choose an existing, proven Web-tier application framework for a J2EE application rather than designing and building a custom framework layer. A Web-tier application framework can provide the following benefits to your application:

- **Decouples presentation and logic into separate components**—Frameworks encourage separating presentation and logic because the separation is designed into the extension interfaces.

- **Separates developer roles**—Application frameworks generally provide different interfaces for different developers. Presentation component developers tend to focus on creating JSP pages using custom tags, while logic developers tend to write action classes, tag handlers, and model code. This separation allows both types of developers to work more independently.

- **Provides a central point of control**—Most frameworks provide a rich, customizable set of application-wide features, such as templating, localization, access control, and logging.

- **Facilitates unit testing and maintenance**—Because framework interfaces are consistent, automated testing harnesses are easy to build and execute.

- **Can be purchased instead of built**—Time not spent developing structural code is available for developing business logic.

- **Provides a rich set of features**—Adopting a framework can leverage the expertise of a group of Web-tier MVC design experts. The framework may include useful features that you do not have the experience to formulate or the time to develop.

- **Encourages the development and use of standardized components**—Over time, developers and organizations can accumulate and share a toolbox of preferred components. Most frameworks incorporate a set of custom tags for view construction.

- **Provides stability**—Frameworks are usually created and actively maintained by large organizations or groups, and are used and tested in a large installed base. Accordingly, framework code tends to be more stable than custom code.

- **Has community support**—Popular frameworks attract communities of enthusiastic users who report bugs, provide consulting and training services, publish tutorials, and produce useful add-ons. Open frameworks are particularly strong in this regard.

- **May reduce training costs and time**—Developers already trained and experienced in using a framework get up to speed more quickly and are more productive.

- **May simplify internationalization**—Most frameworks support a flexible internationalization strategy.

- **May support input validation**—Many frameworks have consistent ways to specify input validation. Validation is commonly available on the client side, on the server side, or both.

- **May be compatible with tools**—Good tools can improve productivity and reliability. Some frameworks are integrated with rapid application development tool sets.

All of these benefits come at a cost, of course. You always have less control over a design you have acquired rather than created yourself. Some frameworks must be purchased, although these are usually bundled with a tool set. Other people's code in your application means other people's *bugs* in your application. Still, most development projects find that a Web-tier framework improves design and implementation quality.

4.4   Web-Tier Application Framework Design

Model-View-Controller ("MVC") is the BluePrints recommended architectural design pattern for interactive applications. MVC, described in Chapter 11, organizes an interactive application into three separate modules: one for the application model with its data representation and business logic, the second for views that provide data presentation and user input, and the third for a controller to dispatch requests and control flow. Most Web-tier application frameworks use some variation of the MVC design pattern.

The MVC design pattern provides a host of design benefits. MVC separates design concerns (data persistence and behavior, presentation, and control), decreasing code duplication, centralizing control, and making the application more easily modifiable. MVC also helps developers with different skill sets to focus on their core skills and collaborate through clearly defined interfaces. For example, a J2EE application project may include developers of custom tags, views, application logic, database functionality, and networking. An MVC design can centralize control of such application facilities as security, logging, and screen flow. New data sources are easy to add to an MVC application by creating code that adapts the new data source to the view API. Similarly, new client types are easy to add by adapting the new client type to operate as an MVC view. MVC clearly defines the responsibilities of participating classes, making bugs easier to track down and eliminate.

This section describes how to use MVC to organize a J2EE Web application design using the sample application's Web Application Framework design as an example. Many of the key classes described (the controller, the templating service, the abstract action class, and so on) are usable for any application, not just for an online shopping application.

A J2EE application's Web tier serves HTTP requests. At the highest level, the Web tier does four basic things in a specific order: interprets client requests, dispatches those requests to business logic, selects the next view for display, and generates and delivers the next view. (See Figure 4.2.)

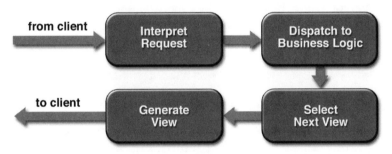

Figure 4.2   The Web-Tier Service Cycle

The Web-tier controller receives each incoming HTTP request and invokes the requested business logic operation in the application model. Based on the results of the operation and state of the model, the controller then selects the next view to display. Finally, the controller generates the selected view and transmits it to the client for presentation.

Figure 4.2 is deceptively simple. An enterprise application's Web tier commonly has the following requirements:

- An application design must have a strategy for serving current and future client types.

- A Web-tier controller must be maintainable and extensible. Its tasks include mapping requests to application model operations, selecting and assembling views, and managing screen flow. Good structure can minimize code complexity.

- Application model API design and technology selection have important implications for an application's complexity, scalability, and software quality.

- Choosing an appropriate technology for generating dynamic content improves development and maintenance efficiency.

The BluePrints best practice is to implement the Web tier of a J2EE enterprise application using an appropriate Web application framework. (See Section 4.4.5 on page 114.) The next several sections describe the general design of a J2EE application Web tier. If you choose to use a Web application framework, the following discussion will help you to understand what the framework does and how to use it. If you write your own Web-tier architectural code, the following design discussions will help you make educated decisions about how to use the technology.

4.4.1   Structuring the Web Tier

Overall structure is the most important consideration in a Web-tier design. Both the sample application and the various existing Web application frameworks implement some form of "Model 2" architecture, where a servlet manages client communication and business logic execution, and presentation resides mainly in JSP pages.

The literature on Web-tier technology in the J2EE platform frequently uses the terms "Model 1" and "Model 2" without explanation. This terminology stems from early drafts of the JSP specification, which described two basic usage patterns for JSP pages. While the terms have disappeared from the specification document, they remain in common use. Model 1 and Model 2 simply refer to the absence or presence (respectively) of a controller servlet that dispatches requests from the client tier and selects views.

A Model 1 architecture consists of a Web browser directly accessing Web-tier JSP pages. The JSP pages access Web-tier JavaBeans that represent the application model, and the next view to display (JSP page, servlet, HTML page, and so on) is determined either by hyperlinks selected in the source document or by request parameters. A Model 1 application control is decentralized, because the current page being displayed determines the next page to display. In addition, each JSP page or servlet processes its own inputs (parameters from GET or POST). In some Model 1 architectures, choosing the next page to display occurs in scriptlet code, but this usage is considered poor form. (See the design guideline Section 4.2.6.8 on page 89.)

A Model 2 architecture introduces a controller servlet between the browser and the JSP pages or servlet content being delivered. The controller centralizes the logic for dispatching requests to the next view based on the request URL, input parameters, and application state. The controller also handles view selection, which decouples JSP pages and servlets from one another. Model 2 applications are easier to maintain and extend, because views do not refer to each other directly. The Model 2 controller servlet provides a single point of control for security and logging, and often encapsulates incoming data into a form usable by the back-end MVC model. For these reasons, the Model 2 architecture is recommended for most interactive applications.

An MVC application framework can greatly simplify implementing a Model 2 application. Application frameworks such as Apache Struts and JavaServer Faces™ (see Section 4.4.5 on page 114) include a configurable front controller servlet, and provide abstract classes that can be extended to handle request dispatches. Some frameworks include macro languages or other tools that simplify application construction.

The Model 1 architecture can provide a more lightweight design for small, static applications. Model 1 architecture is suitable for applications that have very simple page flow, have little need for centralized security control or logging, and change little over time. Model 1 applications can often be refactored to Model 2 when application requirements change.

4.4.1.0.1 When to Switch from Model 1 to Model 2

JSP pages in a Model 1 application that use scripting elements, custom tags, or JavaScript to forward requests should be refactored to Model 2.

A Model 1 architecture is best when the page navigation is simple and fixed, and when a simple directory structure can represent the structure of the pages in the application. Such applications usually embed the page flow information in the links between the pages. The presence of forward in a JSP page implies that logic embedded in the page is making a decision about the next page to display.

Over time, as the application grows and changes, page flow logic accumulates. The application becomes difficult to maintain because the page flow logic is distributed across multiple pages. The best time to switch from Model 1 to Model 2 is before this maintenance problem arises. This is why it's usually best to choose Model 2 from the outset, basing the application on an existing Web controller framework that best meets application requirements. Model 1 remains a viable option for simple, static applications.

4.4.2   Web-Tier MVC Controller Design

The Model 2 architecture uses servlets for processing requests and selecting views. The Front Controller architectural design pattern centralizes an application's request processing and view selection in a single component. Each type of Web client sends requests to and receives responses from a single URL, simplifying client development. The Front Controller receives requests from the client and dispatches them to the application model. This single point of dispatch makes the Front Controller a logical place for such global facilities as security and logging. The Front Controller also selects and formats the next client view. The controller is also an application of the Mediator pattern, because it decouples view components from one another.

In the J2EE platform, a Front Controller is typically implemented as a servlet. The sample application's Front Controller servlet handles all HTTP requests. The user views, discussed in the next section, are mostly JSP pages chosen by the Front Controller.

4.4.2.1   Web-Tier Controller Design

A Web-tier MVC controller maps incoming requests to operations on the application model, and selects views based on model and session state. Web-tier controllers have a lot of duties, so they require careful design to manage complexity. Because most enterprise applications grow over time, extensibility is an important requirement. This section describes some strategies for the internal structure of a controller in the Web tier, illustrated by example code adapted from the Web Application Framework, part of the BluePrints sample application.

4.4.2.1.1 Identifying the Operation to Perform

When a controller receives an HTTP request, it needs to be able to distinguish what application operation is being requested. How can the client, for example, request

WEB-TIER APPLICATION FRAMEWORK DESIGN

that the server create a new user? There are several ways to indicate to the server which operation to perform. The more common methods include:

- Indicate the operation in a hidden form field, which a POST operation delivers to the controller; for example:

```
<FORM METHOD="POST" ACTION="http://myServer/myApp/myServlet">
    <INPUT TYPE="HIDDEN" NAME="OP" VALUE="createUser"/>
    <!-- other form contents... -->
</FORM>
```

- Indicate the operation in a HTTP GET query string parameter; for example:

```
http://myHost/myApp/servlets/myServlet?op=createUser
```

- Use a servlet mapping to map all URLs with a particular suffix or base URL to a specific servlet. A servlet mapping is a deployment descriptor definition that compares request paths to a pattern and dispatches matching requests to the corresponding servlet. For example, imagine that a Web application's deployment descriptor defines the following servlet mapping:

```
<servlet-mapping>
    <servlet-name>myServlet</servlet-name>
    <url-pattern>*.do</url-pattern>
</servlet-mapping>
```

Imagine also that the servlet's context path is `http://myServer/myApp/servlets`. The servlet container would direct a request with URL `http://myServer/myApp/createUser.do myServlet` to `myServlet`, because the request URL matches the pattern `*.do`. Servlet `myServlet` can extract the requested operation's name from the request URL. Chapter 11 of the Java Servlet 2.3 specification defines servlet mappings.

Of the three options discussed here, the BluePrints recommendation is to use servlet mappings when they are available. Servlet mappings provide the most flexible way to control where to route URLs based on patterns in the URLs. Most Web application frameworks (see Section 4.4.5 on page 114) use servlet mappings to direct requests to the appropriate front controller for an application.

The sample application uses a servlet mapping to handle request URLs. The servlet container maps all request URLs matching `*.do` to the main Web-tier controller servlet, `MainServlet.java`. Another servlet mapping routes all URLs matching `*.screen` to the templating service, which assembles composite views.

4.4.2.1.2 Invoking Model Methods

Once the controller has determined which operation to perform, it must invoke the corresponding application model method with parameters derived from the request. A naive controller design might use a large `if-then-else` statement, as shown in Code Example 4.6.

```
if (op.equals("createUser")) {
    model.createUser(request.getAttribute("user"),
                     request.getAttribute("pass"));
} else if (op.equals("changeUserInfo") {
    // ... and so on...
}
```

Code Example 4.6   A Poorly Designed Controller

The `if-then-else` approach leads to a very large `service` method, which is difficult to read and still more difficult to maintain. A better approach is to use the Command pattern. The sample application defines an abstract class `Action`, which represents a single application model operation. A controller can look up concrete `Action` subclasses by name and delegate requests to them. Sample code for the abstract class `Action` and a concrete class `CreateUserAction` appears in Code Example 4.7.

```
// Action.java:
public abstract class Action {
    protected Model model;
    public Action(Model model) { this.model = model; }
    public abstract String getName();
    public abstract Object perform(HttpServletRequest req);
};

// CreateUserAction.java:
public class CreateUserAction extends Action {
    public CreateUserAction(Model model) {
        super(model);
```

```
        }
    public String getName() { return "createUser"; }
    public Object perform(HttpServletRequest req) {
        return model.createUser(req.getAttribute("user"),
                                req.getAttribute("pass"));
    }
}
```

Code Example 4.7   An Abstract Action Class and a Concrete Subclass

Code Example 4.7 defines an abstract class `Action`, which has a name and a `perform` method that executes a model method corresponding to the name. For example, `Action`'s concrete subclass `CreateUserAction` has the name "createUser". Its `perform` method invokes the model method `createUser` using parameters extracted from the HTTP request.

```
public class ControllerServlet extends HttpServlet {
    private HashMap actions;
    public void init() throws ServletException {
        actions = new HashMap();
        CreateUserAction cua = new CreateUserAction(model);
        actions.put(cua.getName(), cua);
        //... create and add more actions
    }
    public void doPost(HttpServletRequest req,
                       HttpServletResponse resp)
        throws IOException, ServletException {

        // First identify operation "op" from URL.
        // method getOperation() is defined elsewhere.
        String op = getOperation(req.getRequestURL());
        // Then find and execute corresponding Action
        Action action = (Action)actions.get(op);
        Object result = null;
        try {
                result = action.perform(req);
        } catch (NullPointerException npx) {
                //... handle error condition: no such action
```

```
        }
        // ... Use result to determine next view (see next section)
    }
//... other methods...
}
```

Code Example 4.8   Using a Map to Identify and Execute Actions

Code Example 4.8 shows a controller servlet that maintains a hash map of
Action objects, each indexed by its name. When the servlet loads, the servlet container calls the method init, which fills the hash map with Action objects that
invoke model operations. The hash map key is the name of the operation. Each
time the servlet's service method receives a request, it identifies the name of the
operation to perform, looks up the corresponding Action in the hash map, and
executes it by invoking the Action's perform method. The Action returns a result
object that the servlet uses, along with other data, to decide which view to display
next. When this controller receives a request containing the name createUser, it
finds an instance of CreateUserAction in the hash map. It then invokes the
Action's perform method, which uses the model to create a user (as shown in
Code Example 4.7).

The code samples shown in this section are greatly simplified for clarity. The
Web Application Framework used by the sample application provides a full,
working example of this sort of controller called MainServlet. The servlet container dispatches requests with a servlet mapping: it forwards all URLs matching
*.do to the MainServlet. Code Example 4.8 demonstrates how to provide an
extensible framework for dispatching client requests.

The sample application improves the extensibility of the servlet code in Code
Example 4.8 even further by externalizing the map of requests to actions. The
controller in the sample application initializes the actions hash map from an
external XML file, which contains pairs of operation names and corresponding
Action class names. The controller servlet initializes the action map with the
request names and action classes referred to in the XML file. The XML file is
deployed as a resource in the Web application archive. Adding a new Action is as
simple as adding a concrete Action subclass to the application archive and defining a configuration file mapping that associates the request URL with the action
class. An example of such a mapping appears in Code Example 4.9. With no code

modification, the sample application controller servlet can dispatch requests using actions that did not even exist when the controller was written.

Dispatching service requests to the application model is only half of the Web-tier controller's job. It is also responsible for determining the next view to display.

4.4.2.1.3 Controlling Dynamic Screen Flow

The succession of views that a Web application user sees is called screen flow. A Web-tier controller controls screen flow by selecting the next view a user sees. In static Web sites, screens (usually Web pages) are statically linked to one another. By contrast, a controller dynamically chooses the "next" screen in response to both user actions and model operation results.

In this section, the term "view" means a Web resource with a URL from which Web content is available. A view might be a JSP page, a servlet, static content, or some combination of the three, assembled into a page. Typically, the "next" view to display depends on one or more of:

- The current view

- The results of any operation on the application model, returned by model method invocations

- Possibly other server-side state, kept in `PageContext`, `ServletRequest`, `HttpSession`, and `ServletContext`.

For example, the next view to display after a sign on view very likely depends on:

- The current view

- The user id and password contained in the request

- The success or failure of the sign on operation, and

- Possibly other server-side state. Examples of such state might include a maximum number of allowed users (application scope), or the URL the user was trying to access (request scope). See Section 4.4.7 on page 116 for a description of state and its scope.

The controller uses this data to determine which view to display next. A Web controller "displays a view" by forwarding the request to a JSP page, servlet, or other component that renders the view in a format compatible with the client; for example, returning HTML to a browser.

The controller in the sample application uses two components to select and generate views: a screen flow manager, which selects the next view to display; and a templating service, which actually generates the view content. The controller uses the screen flow manager to select a view, and forwards the request to the templating service, which assembles and delivers a view to the client. Both the screen flow manager and the templating servlet are generic components that are usable in any Web application. The component-based design reduces component coupling, promoting code reuse and simplifying the controller design.

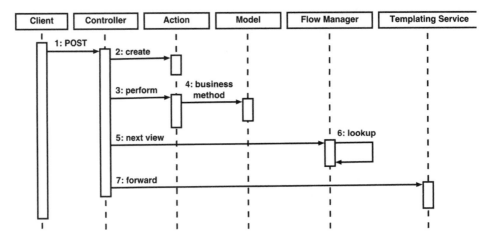

Figure 4.3   Web-Tier Controller OID

Figure 4.3 is an object interaction diagram that shows the Web-tier controller interacting with other Web-tier classes. The diagram shows the following sequence of calls:

1. The controller receives a POST from the client.

2. The controller creates an `Action` corresponding to the requested operation (as described in the previous section).

3. The controller calls the `Action`'s `perform` method.

4. `perform` calls a model business method.

5. The controller calls the screen flow manager to select the next view to display.

6. The screen flow manager determines the next view and returns its name to the controller.

7. The controller forwards the request to the templating service, which assembles and delivers the selected view to the client.

Most request URLs map to a specific view URL. For example, the screen flow map can define that the view `signoff.screen` always follows request URL `/signoff.do`. Sometimes the next screen to display depends on model operation results, server-side state, or user activity. For example, the next view following the request URL `/signin.do`, which signs a user into the system, depends on whether the sign in operation succeeded.

In the sample application, an application assembler configures the screen flow manager with an XML-based file called a screen flow map. The screen flow map defines a next view name for each request URL. For dynamic view selection, a screen flow map can also map a request URL to a flow handler, which is a Java class that selects the next view programmatically. Flow handlers are typically written by component providers or application assemblers.

4.4.2.1.4 Example

The Web Application Framework screen flow map `mappings.xml` configures the screen flow manager. Sample application Code Example 4.9 shows a URL action mapping that uses a flow handler to determine the next view in code.

```
<url-mapping url="signoff.do" screen="signoff.screen">
<action-class>
    com.sun.j2ee.blueprints.petstore.controller.web.actions.SignOffHT-
MLAction
    </action-class>
</url-mapping>
```

Code Example 4.9   Excerpt from the Sample Application Screen Flow Map

In Code Example 4.9, the `url-mapping` element defines a mapping for request URL `/signoff.do`. The `action` element declares an action of class `Signoff-HTMLAction`, which performs the business logic for this URL (signing off a user). An application assembler or a component provider wrote the action class `SignoffHTMLAction` to sign a user off of the application. The `screen` attribute tells the screen flow manager to display screen `signoff.screen` after the action completes.

Figure 4.4 shows the result of an HTTP POST to the URL `/signoff.do`.

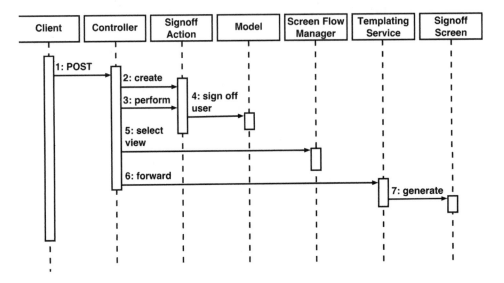

Figure 4.4   OID of POST to Flow Handler Defined in Code Example 4.9

The servlet container deployment descriptor has a servlet mapping from pattern `*.do` to the controller, so when a client POSTs a request to `/verifysignin.do`, the following actions occur:

1. The servlet container routes the request to the controller.

2. The controller creates an instance class `SignoffHTMLAction` and passes the request to it.

3. The controller calls the `SignoffHTMLAction's` `perform` method.

4. The `SignoffHTMLAction` object calls the model method that signs the user out of the application.

5. The controller asks the screen flow manager for the next view.

6. The controller forwards the request to the URL `signoff.screen`.

7. The templating servlet generates and delivers the requested view (a templated JSP page) to the client, so the user receives a view indicating that signoff succeeded.

The last piece of the puzzle not yet explained is how to map a view name in the design just described to an actual Web component (JSP page, servlet, and so on). Views and templating are discussed in Section 4.4.3 on page 110.

4.4.2.2   Serving Multiple Client Types

Web applications may support only one type of client with a single protocol, or multiple clients with different protocols, security policies, presentation logic, and workflows. Web clients may include several versions of a few different browsers, MIDP clients, so-called "rich" clients with stand-alone APIs, and Web service interfaces. Long-lived applications may need to be able to handle new types of Web clients.

Each type of client needs its own controller, which specializes in the protocols for that client type. A particular type of client may also need different presentation components for form factor or other reasons.

Following are some options for how to service requests from clients that use different application-level protocols. (Web-tier clients use HTTP for transport.) Each of the following alternatives expands upon Figure 4.2 by adding flexibility and increasing complexity.

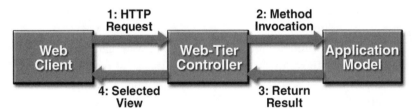

Figure 4.5   Using a Front Controller to Handle Browser Interaction

Applications with a single client type can implement a single front controller. For example, a browser-only application is shown in Figure 4.5. Its single Front Controller servlet receives HTTP requests from the browser, translates the contents of these requests into operations on the application model, and serves views of result data as HTML (or XML). Additional controllers can support new client types, as shown in Figure 4.6.

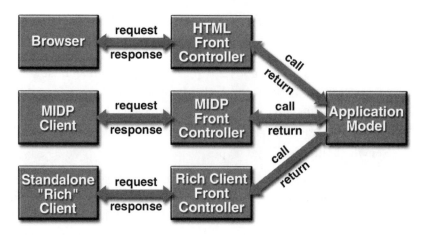

Figure 4.6   Supporting Multiple Client Types with Multiple Controllers

The multiple-controller approach in Figure 4.6 provides extensibility for any future Web client types, including those that do not yet exist. In fact, because servlets aren't limited to HTTP, this architecture can support even non-Web clients. Each controller can implement the workflow, presentation logic, and security constraints unique to its client type. Notice also that the code implementing the application model is shared by all of the controllers. This separation of model and controller ensures identical application behavior across client types and eases maintenance and testing.

Some application functionality, particularly security, can be easier to manage from a single point. Introducing a protocol router, as shown in Figure 4.7, can provide a single point of control for all Web clients, each of which still retain their own controllers.

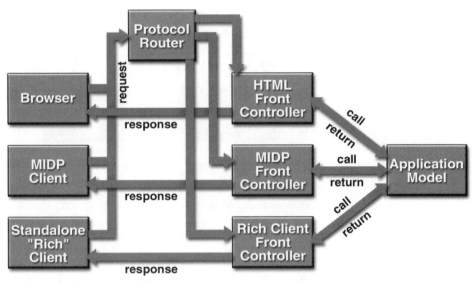

Figure 4.7 Using a Protocol Router for Centralized Control

The protocol router in Figure 4.7 is either a servlet or servlet filter that determines the client type and dispatches the request to the appropriate controller. The router typically uses the HTTP header User-agent to determine what sort of client is requesting service. The protocol router can implement application-wide functionality such as security or logging. The client-specific controllers can implement behavior specific to each client's particular protocol.

The Front Controllers in Figure 4.7 may or may not be servlets. If the Front Controllers are servlets, the protocol router dispatches requests to them using RequestDispatcher.forward. If the protocol router is a servlet, the Front Controllers can be a layer of simple objects to which the router delegates request processing.

Note that the controller alternatives shown in the last few figures can be implemented incrementally. Each of the approaches can be built on the preceding one. The BluePrints recommendation is to adopt and adapt the alternative that most closely matches current application requirements, and add new functionality as necessary.

Templating is an application of the Composite View design pattern, discussed in Chapter 11, which builds a page from a number of independent view components.

4.4.3   Web-Tier MVC View Design

MVC views display data produced by the MVC model. View components (also known as "presentation components") in the Web tier are usually JSP pages and servlets, along with such static resources as HTML pages, PDF files, graphics, and so on. JSP pages are best used for generating text-based content, often HTML or XML. Servlets are most appropriate for generating binary content or content with variable structure. (For an in-depth explanation of appropriate technology usage, see Section 4.2.6.1 on page 82 and Section 4.2.6.4 on page 86.)

HTML browsers are very lightweight clients, so the Web tier generates and often styles dynamic content for browsers. Heavyweight clients can implement relatively more view functionality in the Client tier, and less in the Web tier. Such clients include stand-alone rich clients, application clients, and clients that use special content formats such as MacroMedia Flash or Adobe Portable Document Format (PDF).

Web-tier components are not limited to serving HTML-over-HTTP Web browsers. The Web tier may also serve MIDP clients using proprietary protocols, rich clients using XML, or Web service peers requesting services with Electronic Business XML (ebXML) or Simple Object Access Protocol (SOAP) messages. Each of these examples uses a different application-level protocol, while using HTTP for transport. A properly designed Web tier unifies access to application functionality for any client type. The Web tier also provides virtual session management for some client types.

See Chapter 3 for more on J2EE client technologies.

4.4.3.1   Templating

One typical application requirement is that application views have a common layout. A template is a presentation component that composes separate subviews into a page with a specific layout. Each subview, such as a banner, a navigation bar, or document body content, is a separate component. Views that share a template have the same layout, because the template controls the layout.

For example, Figure 4.8 shows the layout of a single page created by a template. Across the top of the page is a banner, on the left is a navigation menu, a footer appears at the bottom, and the body content occupies the remaining space.

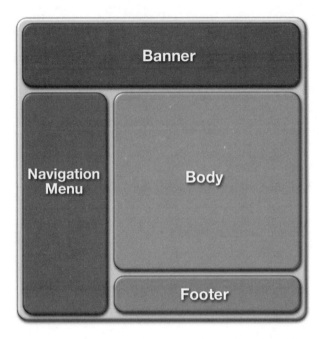

Figure 4.8   A Template Composes Other Views into a Consistent Layout

Using templates in an application design centralizes control of the overall layout of pages in the application, easing maintenance. Changing the layout in the template file changes the page layout for the entire application. More importantly, the individual subviews (like the "Navigation Menu" in Figure 4.8) are used by reference in the template instead of by copy-and-paste. Therefore, changing a subview means changing a single source file instead of changing all the files in which that subview occurs.

Template implementation is most easily explained by example. In the sample application, a JSP page called a template file specifies the page layout. The template file is a standard JSP page that uses custom tags to include subviews into each area of the page. The template references the individual subviews by name.

Code Example 4.10 is an example from the sample application that produces the layout shown in Figure 4.8. This file, called `template.jsp`, is a JSP page that produces HTML. The file specifies the page layout as standard HTML tags, and includes the content of other JSP pages using the custom tag insert, shown underlined in the code example.

```
<%@ taglib uri="/WEB-INF/tlds/taglib.tld" prefix="template" %>
<html>
<head>
    <title><template:insert parameter="title" /></title>
</head>

<body bgcolor="#FFFFFF">
<table width="100%" border="0" cellpadding="5" cellspacing="0">
  <tr>
    <td colspan="2">
      <template:insert parameter="banner" />
    </td>
  </tr>
  <tr>
    <td width="20%" valign="top">
      <template:insert parameter="sidebar" />
    </td>
    <!--- ... and so on ... -->
```

Code Example 4.10   The Template JSP Page for the Layout Shown in Figure 4.8

The JSP page includes the page named by the insert tag's parameter attribute at the point where the tag occurs. A separate screen definitions file for the application provides values for these parameters for each screen name.

The templating service is a single servlet that processes all screens. A servlet mapping routes all requests with URLs matching *.screen to a TemplateServlet, which assembles and serves the requested screen. Code Example 4.11 shows the definition of the screen called main.screen. The screen definitions file defines template.jsp as its template file and defines a series of screens. Each screen has a name and a list of values for the parameters in the template file. The templating service replaces each insert tag in the template file with the contents of the subview named by the tag's parameter attribute. For example, the templating service replaces all instances of <template:insert parameter="banner"/> with the contents of "/banner.jsp". The result is a fully-rendered screen.

```
<screen-definitions>
  <template>/template.jsp</template>
  <screen>
    <screen-name>main</screen-name>
    <parameter key="title">Welcome to the BluePrints Petstore</pa-
rameter>
    <parameter key="banner" value="/banner.jsp"/>
    <parameter key="sidebar" value="/sidebar.jsp"/>
    <parameter key="body" value="/main.jsp"/>
    <parameter key="mylist" value="/mylist.jsp"/>
    <parameter key="advicebanner" value="/advice_banner.jsp"/>
    <parameter key="footer" value="/footer.jsp"/>
  </screen>
  <!-- ... more screen definitions... -->
</screen-definitions>
```

Code Example 4.11   Screen Definition of Sample Application's "Main" View

The templating service described here is part of the sample application's Web Application Framework. The templating service is reusable as a component in other applications. Its design is based on the Composite View design pattern, which assembles a view from reusable subviews. For more information on the Composite View design pattern, please see Chapter 11.

4.4.4   Web-Tier MVC Model Design

An MVC application model both represents business data and implements business logic. Many J2EE applications implement their application models as enterprise beans, which offer scalability, concurrency, load balancing, automatic resource management, and other benefits. Simpler J2EE applications may implement the model as a collection of Web-tier JavaBeans components used directly by JSP pages or servlets. JavaBeans components provide quick access to data, while enterprise beans provide access to shared business logic and data.

Notice that the "application model" in Figure 4.5 on page 107 is generic: It implies no particular technology or tier. The application model is simply the programmatic interface to the application's business logic. Model API design and model technology selection are both important design considerations.

Section 11.4.1.2 on page 369 describes MVC model design considerations and patterns.

4.4.5   Web Application Frameworks

As the Model 2 architecture has become more popular, quite a number of Web-tier application frameworks have appeared. Some are vendor-specific frameworks integrated with specific servers and tools; others are freely available, open-source projects. Benefits of Web-tier application frameworks appear on page 93. Three frameworks of particular interest are:

- **J2EE BluePrints Web Application Framework ("WAF")**—The Web Application Framework forms the infrastructure of the sample application. This framework offers a Front Controller servlet, an abstract action class for Web-tier actions, a templating service, several generic custom tags, and internationalization support. WAF demonstrates both the mechanisms and effective use of a Web-tier framework layer in an application design. It is suitable for small, non-critical applications, and for learning the principles of Web-tier application framework design and usage.

- **Apache Struts**—Struts is a free, open-source, Web-tier application framework under development at the Apache Software Foundation. Struts is highly configurable, and has a large (and growing) feature list, including a Front Controller, action classes and mappings, utility classes for XML, automatic population of server-side JavaBeans, Web forms with validation, and some internationalization support. It also includes a set of custom tags for accessing server-side state, creating HTML, performing presentation logic, and templating. Some vendors have begun to adopt and evangelize Struts. Struts has a great deal of mindshare, and can be considered an industrial-strength framework suitable for large applications. But Struts is not yet a "standard" for which J2EE product providers can interoperably and reliably create tools.

- **JavaServer Faces**—A Java Community Process effort (JSR-127) is currently defining a standardized Web application framework called JavaServer Faces. Current standard Web-tier technologies offer only the means for creating general content for consumption by the client. There is currently no standard server-side GUI component or dispatching model. JavaServer Faces will be an architecture and a set of APIs for dispatching requests to Web-tier model JavaBeans; for maintaining stateful, server-side representations of reusable

HTML GUI components; and for supporting internationalization, validation, multiple client types, and accessibility. Standardization of the architecture and API will allow tool interoperation and the development of portable, reusable Web-tier GUI component libraries.

4.4.6 Separating Business Logic from Presentation

Placing business logic and presentation code in separate software layers is good design practice. The business layer provides only application functionality, with no reference to presentation. The presentation layer presents the data and input prompts to the user (or to another system), delegating application functionality to the business layer.

Separating business logic from presentation has several important benefits:

- **Minimizes impact of change**—Business rules can be changed in their own layer, with little or no modification to the presentation layer. Application presentation or workflow can change without affecting code in the business layer.

- **Increases maintainability**—Most business logic occurs in more than one use case of a particular application. Business logic copied and pasted between components expresses the same business rule in two places in the application. Future changes to the rule require two edits instead of one. Business logic expressed in a separate component and accessed referentially can be modified in one place in the source code, producing behavior changes everywhere the component is used. Similar benefits are achieved by reusing presentation logic with server-side includes, custom tags, and stylesheets.

- **Provides client independence and code reuse**—Intermingling data presentation and business logic ties the business logic to a particular type of client. For example, business logic implemented in a scriptlet is not usable by a servlet or an application client; the code must be reimplemented for the other client types. Business logic that is available referentially as simple method calls on business objects can be used by multiple client types.

- **Separates developer roles**—Code that deals with data presentation, request processing, and business rules all at once is difficult to read, especially for a developer who may specialize in only one of these areas. Separating business logic and presentation allows developers to concentrate on their area of expertise.

4.4.7   Web-Tier State

Data that a Web-tier component uses to create a response is called state. Examples of such data include the inventory data needed by a JSP page that lists items for sale, the contents of an online shopping cart maintained by a servlet, and the timestamp placed on an incoming request by a servlet filter.

State maintenance decisions have an enormous impact on application performance, availability, and scalability. Such decisions include choosing the tier to manage state, selecting the appropriate scope for each item of state, and effectively tracking conversational state in a distributed environment.

Note that the J2EE platform specification does not require that session state be recoverable after a crash or restart of a component container. Some J2EE implementations provide, as an extension, containers that can recover session state after a restart. Choosing such an implementation can simplify application design, but makes an application less portable, because it relies on a non-standard extension.

4.4.7.1   State Scope

Each item of Web-tier state has scope, which determines the accessibility and lifetime of the item. Web-tier state is accessible to servlets, servlet filters, and JSP pages. Briefly, Web-tier state can be maintained in four scopes:

Application scope is "global memory" for a Web application. Application-scope state is stored in the Web container's `ServletContext` object. (See the caveat on using context attributes in distributable servlets on page 126.) All servlets in an application share objects in application scope. The servlet developer is responsible for thread safety when accessing objects in application scope. An inventory object in application scope, for example, is accessible to all servlets, servlet filters, and JSP pages in the application. State in application scope exists for the lifetime of the application, unless it is explicitly removed.

Session scope contains data specific to a user session. HTTP is a "stateless" protocol, meaning that it has no way of distinguishing users from one another or for maintaining data on users' behalf. Session attributes are named object references that are associated with a user session. The servlet API allows a developer to create a session attribute and access or update it in subsequent requests. Session-scope state for an `HttpServlet` is stored in the Web container's `HttpSession` object (available from the `HttpServletRequest` argument to the `service` method). State in session scope is accessible to all Web components in the application and across multiple servlet invocations. However, it is accessible only within an individual user session. An online shopping cart is an example of data in session scope, because the contents of the cart are specific to a single client session and available across multiple server requests. A session ends when it is explicitly closed, when it times out after a period of inactivity, or when its container is shut down or crashes. Unless removed explicitly, state in session scope lasts until the session ends.

Request scope contains data specific to an individual server request, and is discarded when the `service` method returns. A Web component can read or modify data in request scope and then "forward" the request to another component. The component to which the request is forwarded then has access to the state. State in request scope is stored in a `ServletRequest` object, so it is accessible to any component receiving the request. Note that the values of query string parameters and form variables are also in request scope. For example, when a servlet places a timestamp in a `ServletRequest` and then forwards the request to another servlet, the timestamp is in request scope.

Page scope, applicable only to JSP pages, contains data that are only valid in the context of a single page. Page scope state is stored in a JSP page's `PageContext` object. When one JSP page forwards to or includes another, each page defines its own scope. Page scope state is discarded when the program flow of control exits the page.

4.4.7.2 Performance Implications of State Scope

Selecting the appropriate scope for an item of state depends largely on the purpose of that item in the application. It would not make sense, for example, to place a shopping cart class in application scope, because then all shoppers would have to share the same cart. Shopping carts, because they are specific to a user session, are most appropriately kept in session scope. But shopping cart contents maintained in Client-tier cookies would be in request scope, because they would be transmitted to the Web tier with each request. Maintaining session state in cookies is discouraged, even though this approach may be more easily scalable than using session attributes. See "Avoid Using Cookies Directly," starting on page 122 for more details.

Each state scope has implications for scalability, performance, and reliability. State in page or request scope is less likely to cause trouble, since such data are usually not large or long-lived enough to cause resource problems. State in application scope is usually manageable if it is read-only. Entity enterprise beans are the recommended technology for maintaining writable application-scope state. Entity beans are designed for scalable, concurrent access to shared data and logic. See Section 5.4 on page 142 for more information.

State in session scope has the greatest impact on Web application scalability and performance. Separate session-scope state accumulates for each connected user, unlike application-scope state, which is shared between all users and servlets. Also, session-scope state exists across requests, unlike request-scope state, which is discarded when a response is served.

4.4.7.2.1 How the Web Container Manages Session State

Application servers typically track user sessions with some combination of cookies and/or URL rewriting to store a session ID on the client. The session ID identifies the session, and the server is responsible for associating each `HttpServletRequest` with its corresponding `HttpSession` object. The J2EE server handles the details of using cookies and URL rewriting. The section "Maintaining Client State" in *The J2EE Tutorial* explains in detail how to manage Web-tier session state.

4.4.7.3   Web-Tier State Recommendations

When using enterprise beans, it's best to maintain session state with stateful session beans in the EJB tier. For Web-only applications, maintain the state in the Web tier as session attributes (using `HttpSession`). The following sections discuss the rationale for these recommendations.

4.4.7.3.1 Maintain Session State with Stateful Session Beans

Maintaining session state in stateful session beans is a BluePrints best practice. Web-tier components can access the session state through the stateful session bean's component interface and store just the reference as a session attribute. You can maximize the runtime performance of this approach by choosing a J2EE server product that permits use of local EJB interfaces from co-located Web components.

Reasons to prefer stateful session beans over other approaches to maintaining session state include:

- **Thread safety**—Enterprise beans are thread-safe. By contrast, sophisticated thread-safe servlets are difficult to write.

- **Lifecycle management**—The EJB container manages the lifecycle of enterprise beans components, automatically creating new instances, and activating and passivating instances as necessary to optimize performance.

- **Client type neutrality**—Enterprise beans can be accessed, either directly or through some sort of adapter, from multiple client types. This contrasts with HTTP session attributes, which are available only to HTTP clients.

For example, the sample application stores session state in stateful session beans `ShoppingClientControllerEJB` and `EJBClientControllerEJB`. For more on stateful session beans, see Chapter 5.

4.4.7.3.2 Maintain Web-Tier Session State in Session Attributes

Applications that don't use enterprise beans should maintain session state in session attributes, using `HttpSession`'s methods `getAttribute` and `setAttribute`. These methods allow the Web container to maintain the state in a way that is most effective for that particular application and server. Session attributes free the developer from the details of session state management, and ensure portability and scalability of Web components.

The alternative to using session attributes is to create your own solution. The Web container (via `HttpSession`) provides services such as cookie management, session IDs, and so on. Writing custom Web-tier state management code is usually redundant. Don't make work for yourself!

For more guidelines, see Section 4.4.7 on page 116, and also the section "Maintaining Client State" in *The J2EE Tutorial*.

Advantages of using session attributes include:

- **Easy implementation**—Because the application server handles the implementation of `HttpSession`, the developer is freed from bothering with the details of designing, implementing, and testing code for managing session state.

- **Optimization**—An application server's `HttpSession` implementation is optimized and tested for that server, and therefore will probably be more efficient and reliable than a custom solution.

- **Potentially richer feature set**—An application server's implementation of session state management may include such features as failover, cluster support, and so on, that go beyond the base-level requirements of the J2EE platform specifications. The system architect can select a server platform with the differentiating features that best suit application requirements, while maintaining J2EE technology compatibility and portability.

- **Portability**—The HttpSession interface is standardized, so it must pass the J2EE Compatibility Test Suite (CTS) across all J2EE-branded application servers. For more on the role of the CTS and J2EE branding, see the compatibility reference listed in "References and Resources" on page 127.

- **Scalability**—HttpSession can most effectively manage storage of Web-tier session state in caches and/or server clusters.

- **Evolvability**—Application server vendors are constantly improving their offerings. Servers will maintain existing interfaces for backward compatibility, even as they add features that improve performance and reliability. An HttpSession implementation that works properly today will work better tomorrow as improved server versions become available, with little or no change to the source code.

But session attributes have these important disadvantages:

- **Limited to Web clients**—The Web tier is by definition limited to servicing Web clients, so HttpSession interface is limited to HTTP communications. Other client types will require reimplementation of session state management.

- **Session state not guaranteed to survive Web container crashes**—Some application servers maintain persistent session state or provide failover, so sessions can span container crashes or restarts. But not all servers support that functionality, because the specification doesn't require it. As a result, restarting a container can invalidate all sessions in progress, losing all of their state. If this is a problem for your application, either consider selecting a server that provides persistent sessions or session failover (which compromises portability), or consider storing session state in the EIS tier.

4.4.7.3.3 Share Data among Servlets and JSP Pages with JavaBeans Components

The standard JSP tag useBean accesses an attribute in application, session, request, or page scope as a JavaBean component. Standard actions setProperty and getProperty get and set the attributes' properties using JavaBeans property accessors. Servlets have access to these attributes as well, so data shared between JSP pages and servlets is best maintained in JavaBeans classes. Code Example 4.12 shows a servlet setting a session-scope attribute of type UserDataBean, naming it UserData.

```
public void service(HttpServletRequest req,
                    HttpServletResponse res) throws... {
  HttpSession session = req.getSession();
  UserDataBean userData = new userData;
  userData.setName("Moliere");
  session.setAttribute("userData", userData);
  ...
```

Code Example 4.12 Setting a Session Attribute's Value to a JavaBean Instance

When servlets are called, or the same servlet is called again, it can access the UserDataBean using the method HttpSession.getAttribute, as shown in Code Example 4.13.

```
HttpSession session = req.getSession();
UserDataBean userData = (UserDataBean)session.getAttribute("userDa-
ta");
String userName = userData.getUsername();
```

Code Example 4.13 Accessing a Session Attribute JavaBean Instance from a Servlet

A JSP page can access the UserDataBean using the standard tag useBean, as shown in Code Example 4.14. This creates the named JavaBean instance if it does not already exist. The remainder of Code Example 4.14 shows how to get or set the properties of the userData attribute by using getProperty and setProperty.

```
<!-- Declare that the page uses session attribute UserData -->
<jsp:useBean id="userData" type="UserDataBean" scope="session"/>

<!-- get the userData property userData-->
<jsp:getProperty name="userData" property="username"/>

<!-- set all userData properties to values of corresponding
     request parameter names -->
<jsp:setProperty name="userData" property="*"/>

<!-- set userData property "username" to value of request
     parameter "username" -->
```

```
<jsp:setProperty name="userData" property="username"/>

<!-- set userData property "username" to value of request
     parameter "new_user_name" -->
<jsp:setProperty name="userData" property="username"
     param="new_user_name"/>

<!-- set userData property "username" to string "Unknown User" -->
<jsp:setProperty name="userData" property="username"
     value="Unknown User"/>
```

Code Example 4.14 Using JavaBean Properties in a JSP Page

These examples show how to share information between components in session scope. These techniques work similarly for application, page, and request scopes.

4.4.7.3.4 Avoid Using Cookies Directly

Avoid using cookies directly for storing session state in most applications. Implementation details of session state storage are best left to the application server. Using either a stateful session bean or a Web container's HttpSession implementation can provide reliable access to session state through a portable interface. Using the standard interface saves the development time of implementing and maintaining a custom solution.

Disadvantages to using cookies for session state include:

- Cookies are controlled by a low-level API, which is more difficult to use than the other approaches.

- All data for a session are kept on the client. Corruption, expiration, or purging of cookie files can result in incomplete, inconsistent, or missing information.

- Size limitations on cookies differ by browser type and version, but the least-common-denominator approach limits the maximum cookie size to 4,096 bytes. This limitation can be eliminated by storing just references to data (session ids, user ids, and so on) in cookies, and retrieving the data as necessary from another tier (at the cost of increased server complexity and resource usage).

- Servlets and JSP pages that rely exclusively on cookies for client-side session state will not operate properly for all clients. Cookies may not be available for many reasons: The user may have disabled them, the browser version may not support them, the browser may be behind a firewall that filters cookies, and so on.

- Because Web clients transmit to a server only those cookies that it created by that server, servers with different domain names can't share cookie data. For example, JavaPetStore.com may want to allow users to shop from their own shopping sites, as well as from JavaPetFood.com. But because JavaPet-Food.com can't access JavaPetStore.com's cookies, there's no easy way to unify the shopping sessions between the two servers.

- Historically, cookie implementations in both browsers and servers have tended to be buggy, or vary in their conformance to standards. While you may have control of your servers, many people still use buggy or nonconformant versions of browsers.

- Browser instances share cookies, so users cannot have multiple simultaneous sessions.

- Cookies work only for HTTP clients, because they are a feature of the HTTP protocol. Notice that while package `javax.servlet.http` supports session management (via class `HttpSession`), package `javax.servlet` has no such support.

Exceptions to this guideline exist. For example, a browser cookie could contain a user's login name and locale to facilitate sign on. Because of the drawbacks described here, cookies should be used to maintain session state only when there is a clear reason to do so.

4.4.8 Distributable Web Applications

The J2EE platform provides optional support for distributed Web applications. A distributed Web application runs simultaneously in multiple Web containers. When a Web application is marked `distributable` in its deployment descriptor, the container may (but is not required to) create multiple instances of the servlet, in multiple JVM instances, and potentially on multiple machines. Distributing a servlet improves scalability, because it allows Web request load to be spread across multiple servers. It can also improve availability by providing transparent failover between servlet instances.

4.4.8.1   Distributed Servlet Instances

By default, only one servlet instance per servlet definition is allowed for servlets that are neither in an application marked `distributable`, nor implement `SingleThreadModel`. Servlets in applications marked `distributable` have exactly one servlet instance per servlet definition for each Java virtual machine (JVM). The container may create and pool multiple instances of a servlet that implements `SingleThreadModel`, but using `SingleThreadModel` is discouraged.

At any particular time, session attributes for a given session are local to a particular JVM. The distributed runtime environment therefore acts to ensure that all requests associated with a given session are handled by exactly one JVM at a time. A servlet's session state may migrate to, or be failed-over to, some other JVM between requests.

4.4.8.2   Distributed Conversational State

Distributing multiple instances of a servlet across multiple JVM instances raises the issue of how to support conversational state. If each request a user makes can be routed to a different server, how can the system track that user's session state?

J2EE product providers solve this problem in different ways. One approach, called sticky server affinity, associates a particular client with a particular servlet instance for the duration of the session. This solves the session state problem, because each session is "owned" by a particular servlet. But this approach can compromise availability, because when a servlet, JVM instance, or server crashes, all of the associated sessions can be lost. Sticky server affinity can also make load balancing more difficult, because sessions are "stuck" on the servers where they started.

Another approach to solving the distributed conversational state problem is state migration. State migration serializes and moves or copies session state between servlet instances. This solution maintains the availability benefits of servlet distribution and facilitates load balancing, because sessions can be moved from more- to less-loaded servers. But state migration can increase network traffic between clustered servers. Each time a client updates session state, all redundant copies of that state must be updated. If session state is stored in a database (as is often the case), the database can become a performance bottleneck. The containers must also cooperate to resolve simultaneous update collisions, where two clients accessing the same session (one browser window opened from another, for example) update different copies of the same session state.

The J2EE platform specification gives the J2EE product provider the opportunity to add value by solving the issue of distributed conversational state in the implementation while maintaining the consistent J2EE interface. A good solution to this problem can be a selling point for a J2EE vendor. Designers considering a Web-tier-only architecture for high-performance applications should be sure to understand how prospective J2EE product providers address this issue.

Stateful session beans are designed specifically for handling distributed conversational state, but do so in the EJB tier, rather than in the Web tier. See Section 4.4.7.3.1 for more details.

4.4.8.3 Distributable Servlet Restrictions

Servlets used in a distributable application require some additional constraints. Most are necessary conditions for session state migration. These restrictions also apply for code in JSP pages and custom tags.

- **Session attributes must be either serializable or supported in distributed sessions by the Web container**—The Web container must accept instances of serializable classes as session attributes. A container must also accept a few other J2EE object types as session attributes: enterprise bean home and remote references, transaction contexts (`javax.transaction.UserTransaction`), and the JNDI context object for `java:comp/env` (`javax.naming.Context`). For any other types, the container may throw an `IllegalArgumentException` to indicate that the object cannot be moved between JVMs.

  Implementing `Serializable` in a session attribute does not guarantee that the container will use native Java serialization. The container is also not required to use any defined custom serialization methods, such as `readObject` or `writeObject`, that the class may define. It does ensure that session attribute values are preserved if the session is migrated. See Section 7.2.2 of the Java Servlet specification 2.3, and Section J2EE.6.5 of the J2EE platform specification 1.3 for more details.

- **Don't store application state in static or instance variables**—Web containers are not required to maintain static or instance variable values when a session migrates. Code that depends on state stored in such variables will likely not operate properly after session migration. Such state should be stored either as a session attribute, in an enterprise bean, or in a database.

- **Don't use context attributes to share state between servlets**—Context attributes are stored in `ServletContext` and are shared by all servlets in a Web application. But context attributes are specific to the JVM instance in which they were created. Servlets that communicate by sharing context attributes may not operate properly if distributed, because context attributes do not replicate between Web containers in different JVM instances. To share data between distributed servlets, place the data in a session object, store it in the EIS tier in a database or distributed cache, or use an enterprise bean.

  One exception to this guideline is to use context attributes as a shared data cache between the servlets in each Web container. Cache hits and misses affect only an application's performance, not its behavior.

- **Don't depend on servlet context events or HTTP session events**—The Web container is not required to propagate such events between containers in a distributed environment.

4.5   Summary

The Web tier of the J2EE platform makes J2EE applications available on the World Wide Web. JSP pages and servlets are Web components that supersede legacy technologies by providing portable high-level system services. These services include transactions, data access, state maintenance, security, and distribution. Using custom tags and standard tag libraries in JSP pages improves code quality and eases maintenance.

The Model-View-Controller (MVC) architectural design pattern is recommended for most interactive Web applications. MVC makes application functionality more reusable, and simplifies adding and modifying client types, data views, and workflow.

A Model 1 application is a set of JSP pages that are statically linked to one another. A Model 2 application has a centralized controller that dynamically performs request dispatching and view selection. Model 2 is the preferred architecture for Web applications, because it provides more flexibility and is more maintainable than a Model 1 design.

A Web-tier application framework is a domain-neutral layer of services, usually based on MVC, that simplifies constructing an interactive Web application. Such a framework can reduce an application's time-to-market, improve code quality, and ease maintenance. It's usually preferable to choose an existing framework rather than to build one.

The simplest framework design has a single controller that receives requests from browsers, dispatches calls to an application model, and displays results. Multiple controllers can support multiple types of Web-tier clients by communicating with them in their native protocols. A protocol router provides a single point of control for application-wide services such as security and logging.

A Web-tier templating mechanism can improve page layout consistency. The templating mechanism uses a template file to assemble individual views into a single composite view. A template file specifies layout for a set of composite views. Templating makes an application more flexible and makes content more reusable.

Servlets are useful for implementing application services, generating binary content, and controlling applications. JSP pages are best for creating textual content with embedded references to external data. Servlet filters can extend the functionality of an existing servlet, JSP page, or servlet filter.

Web application state resides in either application scope, session scope, request scope, or page scope. State in session scope has the greatest impact on scalability, because its size is proportional to the number of users. Using a stateful session bean is the recommended way to maintain session-scope state. Web-only applications should store session-scope state in HTTP session attributes.

Some J2EE products allow a Web application to be distributed for improved scalability and availability. How a platform implementation manages load in a distributed application is vendor-specific. JSP pages, custom tags, and servlets in a distributed Web application must follow additional programming restrictions.

4.6   References and Resources

For tutorials on using APIs described in this chapter, see the *Web Technology* section of:

- *The J2EE Tutorial*. S. Bodoff, D. Green, K. Haase, E. Jendrock, M. Pawlan, B. Stearns. Copyright 2002, Addison-Wesley. Also available online at `<http://java.sun.com/j2ee/tutorial>`

- *Core J2EE Patterns: Best Practices and Design Strategies*. D. Alur, J. Crupi, D. Malks. Copyright 2001, Prentice-Hall PTR.

- The Java™ Servlet 2.3 and JavaServer Pages™ 1.2 specifications (JSR-53) are available for download in PDF format at `<http://www.jcp.org/aboutJava/communityprocess/final/jsr053/>`

- For information on compatibility and the CTS, see `<http://java.sun.com/j2ee/compatibility.html>`

- The Apache Struts project can be found at `<http://jakarta.apache.org/struts/index.html>`

- The Apache Jakarta taglibs are available at `<http://jakarta.apache.org/taglibs/index.html>`

The Enterprise JavaBeans Tier

by Inderjeet Singh, Linda DeMichiel, and Beth Stearns

IN a multitier J2EE application, the Enterprise JavaBeans (EJB) tier hosts application-specific business logic and provides system-level services such as transaction management, concurrency control, and security. Enterprise JavaBeans technology provides a distributed component model that enables developers to focus on solving business problems while relying on the J2EE platform to handle complex system-level issues. This separation of concerns allows rapid development of scalable, accessible, robust, and highly secure applications. In the J2EE programming model, EJB components are a fundamental link between presentation components hosted by the Web tier and business-critical data and systems maintained in the enterprise information system tier.

This chapter describes the concepts central to the Enterprise JavaBeans architecture and provides guidelines and recommendations to best use EJB components. The chapter:

- Examines the nature of business logic and describes the problems a developer needs to resolve when implementing business logic

- Describes the component model that Enterprise JavaBeans architecture provides to address these problems

- Describes remote and local client views

- Provides details on the three types of enterprise beans: entity beans, session beans, and message-driven beans

- Recommends design guidelines for developing EJB components and applications

- Presents recommendations and practices to best utilize the EJB tier services provided by the J2EE platform

- Provides guidelines to facilitate application portability

5.1 Business Logic and Business Objects

Business logic, in a very broad sense, is the set of procedures or methods used to manage a specific business function. Taking the object-oriented approach enables the developer to decompose a business function into a set of components or elements called *business objects*. Like other objects, business objects have both state (or data) and behavior. For example, an employee object has data such as a name, address, social security number, and so on. It has methods for assigning it to a new department or for changing its salary by a certain percentage. To manage a business problem you must be able to represent how such business objects function and interact to provide the desired functionality. The set of business-specific rules that help identify the structure and behavior of the business objects, along with the pre- and post-conditions that must be met when an object exposes its behavior to other objects in the system, is known as *business logic*.

The following discussion demonstrates how to define the structure and behavior of a business object from the requirements imposed by the business problem it addresses. For example, the sample application uses a group of business objects:

- A catalog object to show available pets

- A shopping cart object to temporarily hold a client's selection of pets

- An account object to keep information about a client

- Order objects to keep track of placed orders

Using the account object as an example, its requirements include:

1. Each client must have a unique account.

2. Each account should have contact information for a client such as name, street address, and e-mail address.

3. Clients must be able to create new accounts and close (or remove) accounts.

4. Clients must be able to update contact information for their accounts.

5. Clients must be able to retrieve information for their accounts.

6. Clients can retrieve and update only their own account information.

7. The account information must be maintained in persistent storage.

8. Multiple clients must be able to access their account information at the same time.

9. Multiple clients cannot update the same account concurrently.

The first two requirements specify the structural attributes of the account object. Following these rules, the account object should have a field to hold account identification and several other fields to hold address, phone, and other contact information.

The behavior of the account object is described in requirements three, four, and five. For example, accounts should have methods to create a new account, to update contact information, and to get the account information.

The last four requirements specify general conditions that must be met so that the account object can properly carry out its functionality. For example, when a client updates an account, the client should be authorized to access that particular account and updated account information should be written to persistent storage. No other client should be able to access the particular account concurrently.

Similar analysis and requirement definitions could be performed for other objects. For example, an order object has a set of general conditions on its behavior that have a significant correlation to the behavior of an account object. That is, a client needs to be authorized before updating or reading the status of an order, order details need to be written to a persistent storage, and so on.

If you examine business objects in similar applications you will see that even though the actual structure and behavior of the object is tied closely to the business problem it is going to solve, many services that these business objects provide follow specific patterns that are quite generic in nature.

5.1.1   Common Requirements of Business Objects

This section describes common requirements of business objects.

5.1.1.1   Maintain State

A business object often needs to maintain state between method invocations. This state can be either conversational or persistent. Conversational state is state maintained in an object during the conversation between a client and the application. Persistent state is state that is stored in a database or other persistent store, outliving the conversation between a client and the application.

Consider a shopping cart object. The state of the shopping cart object represents the items and quantities of the items purchased by the client. The cart is initially empty and gains meaningful state when a user adds an item to the cart. When a user adds a second item to the cart, the cart should have both items in it. Similarly, when a user deletes an item from the cart, the cart should reflect the change in its state. When a user exits the application, the cart object is reclaimed and the conversational state no longer exists. When the object gains, maintains, and loses its state as a result of repeated interactions with the same client, we say the object maintains conversational state.

To understand persistent state, consider an account object. When a user creates an account, the account information needs to be stored permanently so that when the user exits the application and re-enters the application, the account information can be presented to the user again. The state of an account object needs to be maintained in persistent storage, such as a database that will survive system crashes.

5.1.1.2   Operate on Shared Data

Another common characteristic of business objects is that they often operate on shared data. In this case, measures must be taken to provide concurrency control and appropriate levels of isolation for access to the shared data. An example of such a scenario would be multiple users updating the same account information. If two users try to update the same account at the same time, a mechanism must be used to keep the data in a consistent state.

5.1.1.3   Participate in Transactions

A transaction can be described as a set of tasks that need to be completed as a unit. If one of the tasks fails, all the tasks in the unit will be rolled back. If all of them succeed, the transaction is said to be committed.

Business objects often need to participate in transactions. For example, order placement needs to be transactional because of the set of tasks required to complete an order—decrementing the quantity of the purchased item in inventory, storing the order details, and sending an order confirmation to the user. For the transaction to be completed, all of these tasks must succeed. If any one of these tasks fails, work done by other tasks needs to be undone.

In many business operations, transactions may span more than one remote data source. Such transactions—called distributed transactions—require special protocols to ensure data integrity. Chapter 8 discusses the issues involved in transaction management.

5.1.1.4   Service a Large Number of Clients

A business object should be able to provide its services to a large number of clients at the same time. This translates into a requirement for instance management algorithms that give each client an impression that a dedicated business object is available to service its request. Without such a management mechanism, the system will eventually run out of resources and will not be able to service any more clients.

5.1.1.5   Remain Available to Clients

A business object should remain available to clients even when systems crash, a service referred to as high availability. The EJB container in which a business object resides provides this service by utilizing strategies to mask various server errors from the clients.

5.1.1.6   Provide Remote Access to Data

A client should be able to remotely access services offered by a business object. This means that the business object should have some type of infrastructure to support servicing clients over the network. This in turn implies that a business object should be part of a distributed computing environment that takes care of fundamental issues in distributed systems, such as location and failure transparency.

5.1.1.7   Control Access

The services offered by business objects often require some type of client authentication and authorization mechanism to allow only a certain set of clients to access protected services. For example, it should be verified that a client is authorized to update account information in an account business object before allowing it to do so. In many enterprise scenarios, different levels of access control are needed. For example, employees should only be allowed to view their own salary objects, while a payroll administrator can view as well as modify all salary objects.

5.1.1.8   Reusable

A common requirement of business objects is that they be reusable by different components of the same application and/or by different applications. For example, an application used by the payroll department to keep track of employees' salary may have two business objects: employee and salary. A salary business object may use the services of an employee business object to get the grade level of an employee. An application that tracks the employee vacation allowances may want to use this employee object to get the name of the employee through the employee number. Business objects are able to be used by inter- and intra-application components when they are developed in a standard way and run in an environment that abides by these standards. If these standards are widely adopted by the vendor community, an application can be assembled from off-the-shelf components from different vendors. In addition to enabling rapid application development, this approach helps developers avoid vendor lock-in.

5.2   Enterprise Beans as J2EE Business Objects

As discussed in the previous section, business objects need to provide some generic services to clients, such as support for transactions, security, and remote access. These common services are complex in nature and are outside the domain of the business logic required to implement an application. To simplify development, enterprise applications need a standard server-side infrastructure that can provide such services.

The EJB tier of the J2EE platform provides a standard server-side distributed component model that greatly simplifies the task of writing business logic. In the EJB architecture, system experts provide the framework for delivering system-level services, and application domain experts provide the components that hold business-specific knowledge. The J2EE platform enables enterprise developers to concentrate on solving the problems of the enterprise instead of expending their efforts on system-level issues.

The Enterprise JavaBeans architecture defines components—called *enterprise beans*—that allow the developer to write business objects that use the services provided by the J2EE platform. There are three kinds of enterprise beans: session beans, entity beans, and message-driven beans.

- Session beans are intended to be private resources used only by the client that creates them. For this reason, session beans, from the client's perspective, appear anonymous.

- Entity beans are components that represent an object-oriented view of some entities that are stored in persistent storage, such as a database. In contrast to session beans, every entity bean has a unique identity that is exposed as a primary key.

- Message-driven beans are new to the EJB 2.0 architecture supported in the J2EE 1.3 platform. Message-driven beans are components that process asynchronous messages delivered via the Java Message Service (JMS) API. Message-driven beans, by implementing a JMS message listener interface, can asynchronously consume messages sent to a JMS queue or topic.

Later sections of this chapter discuss each type of enterprise bean in detail.

Enterprise beans live inside EJB containers, which provide life cycle management, transactions, security, persistence, and a variety of other services for them. An EJB container is part of an EJB server, which provides naming and directory services, e-mail services, and so on. When a client invokes an operation on an enterprise bean, the call is intercepted by its container. By interposing between clients and components at the method call level, containers can inject services that propagate across calls and components, and even across containers running on different servers and different machines. Because the container adds these services "behind the scenes," this mechanism simplifies development of both components and clients. Figure 5.1 illustrates this.

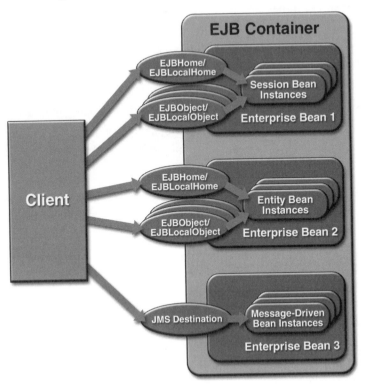

Figure 5.1   Client View of Enterprise Beans

5.2.1   Enterprise Beans and EJB Containers

The EJB architecture endows enterprise beans and EJB containers with a number of unique features that enable portability, reusability, and ease of use:

* Enterprise bean instances are created and managed at runtime by a container. If an enterprise bean uses only the services defined by the EJB specification, the enterprise bean can be deployed in any compliant EJB container. Specialized containers can provide additional services beyond those defined by the EJB specification. An enterprise bean that depends on such a service can be deployed only in a container that supports that service.

- The behavior of an enterprise bean is not wholly contained in its implementation. Service information, including transaction information (described in Chapter 8) and security information (described in Chapter 9), is separate from the enterprise bean implementation. (For transactions, this separation is particularly true when the bean opts to delegate transaction management to the container. However, beans that choose to do their own transaction management include calls to the appropriate methods of the `javax.transaction.UserTransaction` interface in their implementation class.) When service information is kept separate from the bean implementation, the service information can be customized during application assembly and deployment (described in Chapter 7). This makes it possible to include an enterprise bean in an assembled application without requiring source code changes or recompilation, even when it is redeployed in a different environment. Specifying service-level details in the deployment descriptor also greatly reduces the amount of code that a developer needs to write.

- The bean provider defines the client view of an enterprise bean. The client view of an enterprise bean can be either a remote view or a local view. A provider can define both types of views for a bean, but usually only one or the other is provided. The client view of an enterprise bean—either remote or local—is provided through two interfaces: a component interface and a home interface. Although the client view is unaffected by the container and server in which the bean is deployed, the client of a bean's local client view must be co-located in the same container as the bean. Because the client view is the same regardless of the container or server in which the bean is deployed, it ensures that both the beans and their clients can be deployed in multiple execution environments without changes or recompilation. The client view interfaces are implemented by classes generated by the container when a bean is deployed. It is by implementing these interfaces that the container can interpose on the client operations on a bean and inject its services. See Section 5.3 on page 140.

The following sections describe the home and component interfaces and the enterprise bean class. Note that only session and entity beans have client view interfaces. Message-driven beans are not directly accessible by clients. Access to message-driven beans is discussed in Section 5.6 on page 154.

5.2.1.1   Home Interface

The home interface provides methods for creating and removing enterprise beans. In addition, the home interface of an entity bean also contains methods to find instances of the bean based on certain search criteria, and it may contain home business methods.

The home interface for an enterprise bean with a remote client view must extend `javax.ejb.EJBHome`. The home interface for an enterprise bean with a local client view extends `javax.ejb.EJBLocalHome`.

Generally, the enterprise bean's remote home interface allows a client to do the following:

- Create new enterprise bean instances

- Remove enterprise bean instances

- Get the metadata for the enterprise bean through the `javax.ejb.EJBMetaData` interface. The `javax.ejb.EJBMetaData` interface is provided to allow application assembly tools to discover the metadata information about the bean.

- Obtain a handle to the home interface. The home handle can be serialized and written to stable storage. Later, possibly in a different Java virtual machine, the handle can be deserialized from stable storage and used to obtain a reference to the home interface.

- Find an existing entity bean instance. The home interface of an entity bean provides one or more methods for finding existing entity bean instances within the home. Every entity bean home contains a `findByPrimaryKey` method. A client that knows the primary key of an entity object can obtain a reference to the entity object by invoking the `findByPrimaryKey` method on the entity bean's home interface. The bean provider may define other finder methods in the entity bean's home interface as well.

- Provide business logic across all bean instances. The home interface of an entity bean may also define methods to provide business logic that is not specific to an individual bean instance.

An enterprise bean's local home interface is similar to the remote home interface. It allows clients to create and remove enterprise bean instances, but it does not provide methods for getting metadata or for obtaining a handle.

5.2.1.2   Component Interface

The component interface defines the set of business methods available to clients. An enterprise bean may have a remote and/or a local client view. The bean developer must define a component interface for each such client view that the bean provides. Usually, a bean provides either a local or remote view, but not both.

The remote component interface must extend `javax.ejb.EJBObject`, while the local component interface extends `javax.ejb.EJBLocalObject`. Implementations of these interfaces (which are generated by the container) delegate invocation of a business method to an instance of the enterprise bean class.

The `javax.ejb.EJBObject` and the `javax.ejb.EJBLocalObject` interfaces define the methods that allow clients to perform the following operations on a reference to an enterprise bean object:

- Obtain the home interface

- Remove the enterprise bean object

- Test whether a given enterprise bean object is identical to another

- Obtain an entity bean object's primary key

The `javax.ejb.EJBObject` interface for a bean with a remote client view defines a method that allows its clients to obtain a handle to the enterprise bean object. This method is not available to clients of a bean with a local client view.

5.2.1.3   Enterprise Bean Class

The enterprise bean *class* provides the actual implementation of the business methods of the bean. A business method defined on the enterprise bean class is called by the container when the client calls the corresponding method listed in the component interface. In the case of a message-driven bean, the container invokes the `onMessage` method defined on the message-driven bean class when a message arrives for the bean to service. Depending on whether the bean is an entity bean, a session bean, or a message-driven bean, the enterprise bean class must implement the `javax.ejb.EntityBean`, the `javax.ejb.SessionBean`, or the `javax.ejb.MessageDrivenBean` interface.

In addition to business methods, the home interface and the enterprise bean class also share responsibility for create methods and for finder methods and home methods (in the case of entity beans).

The create methods provide ways to customize a bean at the time it is created. For each `create...` method listed in the home interface, the bean class implements a corresponding `ejbCreate...` method. A message-driven bean class must also implement an `ejbCreate` method, even though it has no home interface.

Finder methods provide ways to locate a bean. For each finder method listed in the home interface of an entity bean with bean-managed persistence, the bean class implements the corresponding `ejbFind...` method. In the case of an entity bean with container-managed persistence, the `ejbFind...` methods are defined as query methods in the deployment descriptors, and their implementation is provided by the container.

Entity bean classes must also provide an implementation for each home method listed in the home interface. These home methods are implemented with corresponding `ejbHome...` methods.

An entity bean with container-managed persistence may also define select methods in its bean class. A select method is a query method for the internal use of the entity bean class and is not exposed in the home or component interface. The bean provider defines the semantics of a select method by specifying an Enterprise JavaBeans Query Language (EJB QL) query string in the deployment descriptor. The container provides the implementation of the select method. Select methods return values from the container-managed persistent and container-managed relationship fields of entity beans with container-managed persistence.

The following three sections contain in-depth discussions of the properties and uses of entity and session beans. Message-driven beans are covered in Section 5.6 on page 154.

5.3   Remote and Local Client Views

The EJB 2.0 specification introduces a local client view for session and entity beans, in addition to preserving the remote client view defined by the EJB 1.1 specification. As described in the previous sections, a session or entity bean can implement a local home interface and local component interface instead of (or in addition to) a remote home interface and remote component interface.

An enterprise bean defines a remote client view when it is designed for use in a distributed environment; that is, when its clients may potentially reside in a different JVM. Each method call on a bean's remote home or component interface results in a remote method invocation. Although necessary for distributed systems, remote method invocations have a certain amount of network overhead and can have performance limitations. In addition, the overhead of a remote invocation occurs even if the client and the bean are located on the same JVM. This can be particularly problematic in situations that require fine-grained access to objects. (See Section 5.7.3 on page 159 for a more complete discussion of how to handle fine-grained access.) While these limitations are unavoidable for distributed systems, proper design can reduce their impact.

Use of a local client view avoids the performance overhead of remote method invocation. To use a local client view, the enterprise bean and its client must be guaranteed to be located on the same JVM. By implementing a local home interface and local component interface, co-located enterprise beans can make direct, local method calls on the methods of other beans and avoid the remote invocation overhead. It is thus feasible to implement fine-grained access between beans using local interfaces.

5.3.1   Guidelines for Using Local or Remote Client Views

In certain situations it is preferable to use a local client view (local home and component interfaces) for an enterprise bean. In other situations, a remote client view (remote home and component interfaces) is more appropriate. Keep in mind that most of these considerations apply to session beans as well as entity beans, because both can implement local and remote client views.

- Use remote interfaces when the distribution of components (or their potential distribution) requires location independence in the deployment environment.

- Use remote interfaces when loose coupling between a bean and its client is desirable.

- Use remote interfaces to ensure that parameters are passed between a bean and a client using pass-by-value semantics rather than pass-by-reference semantics. Passing parameters by value prevents the bean from inadvertently modifying the client data, as the bean gets its own copy of the data separate from the client's copy. With local interfaces, which use pass-by-reference semantics, a reference to the same copy of the data is passed between the client and the bean. Both the client and the bean view and act on the same single copy of the data. Any actions the bean performs on the data affects the client's view of the data.

- Use remote interfaces for entity beans that require only coarse-grained access to the underlying data objects.

The use of local interfaces for enterprise beans may be better suited to some applications. Consider using local interfaces for session and entity beans under these circumstances:

- Use local interfaces for a session or entity bean if they are required to be located in the same container as their clients. For local interfaces to be used, the session or entity bean *must* be deployed in the same JVM as the client.

- Use local interfaces when tight coupling between a client and a bean is desirable.

- Use local interfaces when pass-by-reference semantics is preferable for parameter passing between a client and the bean. This is typically done to achieve higher performance by avoiding the overhead of object copying.

- Use local interfaces for entity beans that expose fine-grained access to the underlying data objects.

An entity bean that uses local interfaces is referred to as a lightweight entity bean because it avoids the performance costs of remote interfaces.

5.3.2   Entity Beans and Local Client Views

An entity bean is generally used with a local view. If the application is such that a remote view is necessary, the developer can use a session bean with a remote client view as a facade to entity beans with local views. See Section 5.7.2 on page 158 for more information.

Local interfaces offer other advantages for entity beans. Local interfaces enable entity beans with container-managed persistence to participate in container-managed relationships with other entity beans. With container-managed relationships, the EJB container manages the persistent relationships between entity beans, much like it manages the persistent state of entity beans. Container-managed relationships are described further in Section 5.4.2.2 on page 146.

5.4   Entity Beans

An entity bean represents an object view of business data stored in persistent storage or an existing application. The bean provides an object wrapper around the data to simplify the task of accessing and manipulating it. This object view of data lends itself to software reuse. For example, an entity bean representing customer account information can be used by order management, user personalization, and marketing in a uniform way.

An entity bean allows shared access from multiple clients and lives beyond the duration of the client's session with the server. If the state of an entity bean is being updated by a transaction at the time of a server crash, the entity bean's state is automatically reset to the state of the last committed transaction.

5.4.1   Guidelines for Using Entity Beans

A bean provider can use the following entity bean characteristics as guidelines when deciding whether to model a business object as an entity bean:

- Representing persistent data

  If the state of a business object needs to be stored in a persistent storage and its behavior primarily represents or is dependent upon the manipulation of such state, then it should be modeled as an entity bean.

- Representing objects with clearly-defined identity

  Instances of business objects typically have their own unique identity. A business object's identity distinguishes one object instance from another and makes it possible to locate a particular business object. For example, a business object representing a purchase order has a purchase order number that uniquely identifies that order. Entity beans provide a persistent identity for business objects. They should be used when accessing an object by its identity is important to the application.

- Providing concurrent access by multiple clients

  When multiple clients need to share the state and behavior of a business object, that object should be modeled as an entity bean. An entity bean maintains persistent state. However, this state is not specific to a particular client, but instead it is representative of the persistent state of a business object. By modeling business objects as entity beans, a bean provider can rely on an EJB server or container to ensure appropriate synchronization for entity beans when they are accessed concurrently from multiple transactions.

- Providing robust, long-lived persistent data management

  When a business object exists independently of user sessions and its state must survive container restarts, model it as an entity bean. Entity bean state survives container restarts and crashes and does not depend on a particular user session.

- Persisting data in a portable manner

  Use an entity bean to model persistent data that needs to be accessed in a portable way. Using entity beans with container-managed persistence guarantees that the bean's view of its own persistent state is always the same, regardless of how it is stored in the data storage system used in its deployment environment.

- Providing access through queries

  Unlike session beans and message-driven beans, entity beans with container-managed persistence provide a query capability and can be located by the container based on their identity or state. The bean provider can define queries that allow entities to be automatically found by the container on the basis of the values of their persistent data—such as customer location, order quantity, order identification number, and so on.

- Simplifying transaction handling

  Use an entity bean to have the container handle the transaction logic for the persistent data. By doing so, the developer does not have to include transaction handling code with the entity bean's business logic.

5.4.2   Entity Bean Persistence

The protocol for transferring the state of an entity between the enterprise bean instance and the underlying persistent store is referred to as object persistence. An entity bean can implement persistence in the following ways:

- Directly implementing persistence in the enterprise bean class or in one or more helper objects provided with the enterprise bean class (bean-managed persistence)

- Delegating the handling of its persistence to its container (container-managed persistence)

With bean-managed persistence, the bean provider writes database access calls. These calls can be coded directly into the enterprise bean class or encapsulated in a data access object that is part of the entity bean. If data access calls are coded directly in the enterprise bean class, it may be more difficult to adapt the entity component to work with a database that has a different schema or with a different type of database. Encapsulating these calls in a data access object makes it easier to adapt the enterprise bean's data access to different schemas or different database types, but requires regeneration of the data access objects used by the bean. The data access object approach should therefore only be used when use of container-managed persistence is not appropriate for the individual bean type. Data access objects are discussed in Section 5.7.5 on page 161.

With container-managed persistence, the bean provider relies on the container to manage the access to the persistent state of the bean. Unlike the case of bean-managed persistence, the bean provider does not have to write any database access calls.

The EJB 2.0 architecture significantly improves upon container-managed persistence. Rather than defining instance variables in the entity bean class for the bean state that is to be stored to the database, as with earlier EJB specifications, the bean provider defines public abstract accessor methods (get and set methods) for each container-managed persistent and container-managed relationship "field." The container provides the implementation of the get and set methods used at runtime. The "field" itself is invisible to the bean.

Container-managed persistence simplifies the task of writing entity beans, because the container takes the responsibility of generating the code to access the data source. Bean developers should take advantage of this feature and use container-managed persistence whenever possible to delegate to the container the task of maintaining the persistence state of an entity bean.

5.4.2.1   Example: A Customer Account Bean

The concept of a customer account is central to all clients in many e-commerce applications. Multiple clients need to share behavior such as creating an account, verifying an existing account, and updating account information. Updates to the state of an account object need to be written to persistent storage. The account object needs to live even when the client's session with the server is over. Therefore, in the sample application, an account object is modeled as an entity bean.

An Account bean conforming to the EJB 2.0 specification that uses container-managed persistence does not declare instance variables for its container-managed persistent fields. Instead, it uses accessor methods for the data fields, as shown in Code Example 5.1.

```
public abstract class AccountEJB implements EntityBean {
    // Container-managed persistent fields
    public abstract String getStatus();
    public abstract void setStatus(String status);
    ...
}
```

Code Example 5.1   Account Bean Implementation

5.4.2.2   Container-Managed Relationships

The EJB container provides automatic management of both the persistent state of entity beans and the persistent relationships among entity beans. Container-managed relationships may be unidirectional or bidirectional, and they may be of any cardinality. That is, a relationship may be a one-to-one relationship, a one-to-many relationship, or a many-to-many bidirectional relationship. Keep in mind that relationship integrity is maintained based on the direction of the relationship.

Relationships are implemented as container-managed relationships fields. Like persistent fields, container-managed relationships fields are abstract bean fields that are defined and accessed by public abstract get and set accessor methods in the enterprise bean class. The type of a container-managed relationship field is either an entity bean local component interface type or a collection of an entity bean local component interface type.

Entity bean relationships are manipulated by simply using the get and set accessor methods and the methods of the java.util.Collection API. Any change made to a container-managed relationship field is reflected in the relationship between the entity beans involved in the relationship and is automatically persisted by the container. The container also automatically enforces the integrity constraints of each relationship. For example, if the entity bean Supplier has a many-to-many bidirectional relationship with the entity bean Item, then if a supplier S stops supplying an item I, the container will automatically remove supplier S from the set of suppliers available to supply item I.

An entity bean must provide a local client view so that it can be used as the target of a container-managed relationship. It is important to note, however, that an entity bean is not required to have a local client view to make use of container-managed persistence.

The entity bean's deployment descriptor contains a description of the bean's abstract persistence schema. This schema is an abstract representation of an entity bean's persistent state and relationships, independent of the bean's implementation in a particular container or particular data store.

5.4.2.3   EJB QL, the EJB Query Language

A further advantage of using entity beans with container-managed persistence is that they support the use of EJB QL, the Enterprise JavaBeans Query Language. EJB QL is a query language similar to SQL that is new to EJB 2.0. By allowing the bean provider to specify queries defined on an entity bean's abstract persistence schema, EJB QL provides a datastore-independent, portable way to express how to find an entity object or collection of entity objects. EJB QL queries can also find container-managed persistent field values.

The container maps a query in EJB QL to operations on the underlying persistent data store. For example, in the case of a relational data store, the container maps an EJB QL query to an SQL query.

For each EJB QL finder or select method (except `findByPrimaryKey`), there must be a corresponding EJB QL query that defines its behavior. The container implements the finder or select method by translating the EJB QL statement into a query on the persistent store, such as a query on a relational database.

An EJB QL query always has a SELECT clause and a FROM clause, and may also have a WHERE clause that limits the query result set. The result of an EJB QL query may be either an entity bean or a persistent value, or collections of these.

For example, the Code Example 5.2 demonstrates how the sample application uses an EJB QL query for a finder method `findOrdersByStatus` to find orders that are in a particular status, such as `PENDING`.

```
SELECT DISTINCT OBJECT(o)
    FROM SupplierOrder o
    WHERE o.poStatus = ?1
```

Code Example 5.2   EJB QL Query Example

The query returns `SupplierOrder` objects, as indicated by the expression `OBJECT(o)`. The identifier o is analogous to an SQL correlation variable. The WHERE clause limits the orders to those whose status matches the value of the first parameter passed to the query (denoted by the expression `?1`).

Here are some guidelines for writing queries in EJB QL:

- Utilize parameters and write general queries that serve multiple purposes. For example, Code Example 5.2 uses the expression `?1` rather than `PENDING` to implement a general query that can be used to find orders in any status, not just `PENDING`.

- Use `distinct` to eliminate duplicates in a returned collection of objects. For example, Code Example 5.2 uses `distinct` to eliminate duplicate orders from the result of the query.

- Write select methods for complex queries that you do not want exposed to clients. For example, to avoid exposing an employee's salary to clients, an employee bean may use a select method to programmatically calculate an employee's bonus based on salary.

- Write complex select queries to select results on a tightly-coupled network of entity beans that can return data about the network, entity object, or container-managed persistent field data.

5.4.2.4   Benefits of EJB 2.0 Container-Managed Persistence

The EJB 2.0 approach to container-managed persistence offers a number of benefits:

- Provides a layer of data independence

  Container-managed persistence provides for data independence in two locations: between the client view and the entity bean and between the entity bean and the persistent store.

- Promotes an entity bean's portability

  With the EJB 2.0 container-managed persistence approach, it is easier to migrate an entity bean to different EJB containers and to different types of persistent stores. This migration can be done without recompiling the bean.

- Provides a datastore-independent query language

  EJB QL provides a way to specify queries for the finder and select methods of entity beans with container-managed persistence that is independent of their implementation in a particular database or other persistent store. It therefore allows such entity beans to be portable across particular storage systems.

- Provides for faster development

  Because the bean provider does not have to be concerned with the details of persistence management, development of the entity bean can be faster and simpler and the developer is further freed from systems-level concerns.

5.4.3 When to Use Bean-Managed Persistence

Despite the many advantages of container-managed persistence, there are situations in which it is more appropriate to develop entity beans using the bean-managed persistence approach. These include the following:

- Use bean-managed persistence when you need exact control over the database schema or need to customize code to match a specific legacy database schema.

- Use bean-managed persistence when it is important that the application be very finely tuned against the database that is in use.

- Use bean-managed persistence when portability is not an issue. Even in this case, however, it is recommended that data access objects (DAOs) be used. DAOs better enable the bean to be adapted to a different database schema or to evolve into an entity bean with container-managed persistence at a later date. See Section 5.7.5 on page 161.

- Use bean-managed persistence when the query needs of the application exceed the current capabilities of EJB QL. While EJB QL will continue to develop, it is not yet able to express a number of queries that are expressible in SQL.

- Use bean-managed persistence when your persistent store is not a database system or is a legacy database system that is not likely to be supported for container-managed persistence.

5.5   Session Beans

Session beans are used to implement business objects that hold client-specific business logic. The state of such a business object reflects its interaction with a particular client and is not intended for general access. Therefore, a session bean typically executes on behalf of a single client and cannot be shared among multiple clients. A session bean is a logical extension of the client program that runs on the server and contains information specific to the client. In contrast to entity beans, session beans do not directly represent shared data in the database, although they can access and update such data. The state of a session object is non-persistent and need not be written to the database.

A session bean is intended to be stateful. However, the Enterprise JavaBeans specification allows stateless session beans as a way to provide server-side behavior that doesn't maintain any specific state. The next sections discuss the properties and uses of both stateful and stateless session beans.

5.5.1   Stateful Session Beans

A stateful session bean contains conversational state on behalf of its client. The conversational state is defined as the session bean's field values plus all objects reachable from the session bean's fields. Stateful session beans do not directly represent data in a persistent data store, but they can access and update data on behalf of the client. As its name suggests, the lifetime of a stateful session bean is typically that of its client.

5.5.1.1   Uses of Stateful Session Beans

A bean provider can use the following session bean characteristics as guidelines when deciding whether to model a business object as a stateful session bean:

- Maintaining client-specific state

  Stateful session beans are designed to maintain a conversational state on behalf of a client; therefore, business objects representing client-centric business logic should be modeled as stateful session beans. Since stateful session bean instances are tied to a client, system resources held by stateful session beans usually cannot be shared among multiple clients.

- Representing non-persistent objects

    Stateful session bean state is not stored in persistent storage and cannot be rec-created after the client's session with the server ends. Therefore, business objects that are relatively short-lived and non-persistent—whose state must only be maintained for one entire session—should be modeled as stateful session beans. If a stateful session bean needs to save persistent state beyond its own lifetime, it should make use of one or more entity beans for this purpose.

5.5.1.2 Example: A Shopping Cart Bean

A shopping cart object represents the collection of products selected by a particular customer for purchase during a session. The contents of the shopping cart are specific to a particular customer session and need not be saved unless the customer is ready to place an order. The shopping cart object is short-lived. The data should not be shared, since it represents a particular interaction with a particular customer and is alive only for the customer's session with the server. The sample application models the concept of shopping cart as a local stateful session bean. As shown in Code Example 5.3, ShoppingCartLocal provides ability to add and delete items to the shopping cart.

```
public interface ShoppingCartLocal extends EJBLocalObject {
    public void addItem (String itemID);
    public Collection getItems (Locale locale);
    public void deleteItem (String itemID);
    public void updateItemQuantity (String itemID, int newQty);
    public void empty ();
}
```

Code Example 5.3   ShoppingCartLocal Interface

5.5.2 Stateless Session Beans

Stateless session beans are designed strictly to provide server-side behavior. The term stateless means that the session bean does not maintain any state information for a specific client. This means that all stateless session bean instances are equivalent when they are not involved in serving a client-invoked method. However, stateless session beans can have non-client specific state, for example, an open network or database connection.

5.5.2.1   Uses of Stateless Session Beans

A bean provider can use the following session bean characteristics as guidelines when deciding whether to model a business object as a stateless session bean:

- Modeling reusable service objects

    A business object that provides some generic service to all its clients can be modeled as stateless session beans. Such an object does not need to maintain any client specific state information across method invocations, so the same bean instance can be reused to service other clients. For example, in the sample application, the SignOn bean validates a customer id against a database as a stateless service.

- Providing high performance

    A stateless session bean can be very efficient as it requires fewer system resources by the virtue of being not tied to one client. Since stateless session beans minimize the resources needed to support a large number of clients, depending on the implementation of the EJB server, applications that use this approach may scale better than those using stateful session beans. However, this benefit may be offset by the increased complexity of the client application that uses the stateless session beans because the client may have to perform the state management functions.

- Providing procedural view of data

    In a procedural view of data, methods of the business object do not operate on instance variables. Instead, they behave like calls in a procedural language. If a business object exhibits such functionality then it should be modeled as a stateless session bean. For example, a stateless session bean can provide facade methods that hide the operations of multiple entity beans behind it.

5.5.2.2   Example: A Catalog Bean

The sample application uses a stateless session bean to model a catalog object. A catalog object represents different categories and products and provides browsing and searching services to its clients. Both of the primary functions of the catalog, browsing and searching, are generic services that are not tied to any particular client. Also, the catalog object operates on multiple rows in the database at the same time and provides a shared view of the data. Code Example 5.4 lists the services provided by the catalog object:

```
public interface CatalogLocal extends EJBLocalObject {
    public Page searchItems(String keywords, int start, int count,
Locale l);
    public Category getProduct(String productID, Locale l);
    public Page getProducts(String categoryID, int start, int count,
Locale l);
    ...
}
```

Code Example 5.4   Catalog Component Interface

5.6   Message-Driven Beans

A message-driven bean is a new type of enterprise bean introduced in EJB 2.0. A message-driven bean allows J2EE applications to receive JMS messages asynchronously. (Asynchronous messaging allows applications or components to communicate with other applications or components by exchanging messages in such a way that senders are independent of receivers. The sender sends its message and does not need to wait for the receiver to receive or process the message.)

Message-driven beans are components that receive inbound messages from a JMS provider. The primary responsibility of a message-driven bean is to process messages, because the bean's container automatically manages other aspects of the message-driven bean's environment. Message-driven beans contain business logic for handling received messages. A message-driven bean's business logic may key off the contents of the received message, or it may be driven by the mere fact of receiving the message. Its business logic may include such operations as:

- Doing some computation

- Initiating a step in a workflow

- Storing data

- Sending another message

Message-driven beans function as message listeners, consuming messages from a JMS destination (queue or a topic). While message-driven beans are currently limited to JMS messages, it is expected that their capabilities will be expanded in future EJB specifications to allow other messaging systems to be supported as well.

From a bean developer's standpoint, message-driven beans are much like stateless session beans, only simpler. They have the same life cycle as stateless session beans, but they do not have a component or home interface. The developer needs to be concerned with implementing only one business method for a message-driven bean, the onMessage method. The onMessage method contains the business logic that the message-driven bean executes upon receipt of a message. The bean typically examines the message and executes the actions necessary to process it. This may in turn involve the invocation of other components. Like session beans, message-driven beans may be used to drive workflow processes. In this case, however, it is the arrival of a particular message that causes the processing to be initiated.

A bean developer can choose to make the message-driven bean invocation part of a transaction. This can be done only when using container-managed transaction demarcation. When a message-driven bean is part of a transaction, then the message delivery is part of the subsequent transactional work. If the subsequent transaction fails, then the message delivery is rolled back along with the other transactional work. The message remains available in the JMS destination until picked up by another message-driven bean instance. Note that the message sender and message receiver, which is the message-driven bean, do not share the same transaction. Thus, the sender and receiver communicate in a loosely coupled but reliable manner.

Bean-managed transaction demarcation can also be used with a message-driven bean, but because the transaction is started within the onMessage method, the message delivery itself is not part of the transaction.

5.6.1   Uses of Message-Driven Beans

Consider using message-driven beans under the following circumstances:

- When you need to have asynchronous messaging in your application

- When you want to have messages automatically delivered. Automatic message delivery avoids polling for messages.

- When you want to integrate two applications in a loosely-coupled but reliable manner. Because JMS interfaces are available for most leading message-oriented middleware products, message-driven beans are widely used to integrate enterprise beans with packages and legacy applications. Chapter 6 discusses this approach further.

- When you want the message delivery to drive other events in the system. For example, workflow steps can be based on the mere fact of message delivery, or they can be based on the message content.

- When you want to create message selectors. A message selector is designed to take on only specific messages, thus making it possible to use message-driven beans as triggers.

5.6.2   Example: Invoice Message-Driven Bean

Code Example 5.5 shows a message-driven bean that updates purchase orders based on invoice information received in a JMS message. The message-driven bean listens for JMS messages containing invoice data. When it receives a message, its onMessage method extracts the invoice data from the message text. In this example, the data has been encoded in XML, which is parsed and then used to process an invoice.

```
public class InvoiceMDB implements
        MessageDrivenBean, MessageListener {
    public void onMessage(Message msg) {
        try {
            String msgTxt = ((TextMessage) msg).getText();
            Invoice invoice = Invoice.fromXML(msgText);
            // do further processing
        } catch (...) {
            // handle exceptions
        }
    }
}
```

Code Example 5.5   Message-Driven Bean Example

5.7   Design Guidelines

While you are free to write your application and enterprise bean code according to your own needs, we do recommend certain guidelines.

- Keep the code in enterprise beans as "client-neutral" as possible. Enterprise beans are meant to contain business logic that can be used by many client types. Methods in enterprise beans that serve only one client type make any logic within that method inaccessible to other client types. Code that is specific for a particular client type belongs with the software managing that client type. In particular, Web-tier and HTTP-related functions and data do not belong in an enterprise bean.

- Keep as much business logic as possible in the EJB tier. By doing so, you take advantage of the EJB container services and simplify your programming effort.

- Use stateful session beans to manage conversational state rather than managing conversational state in the client or Web tier. As with the previous point, this leverages the advantages of enterprise beans.

In addition to the guidelines discussed previously for choosing specific bean types, there are other design choices that you need to make when developing objects for the EJB tier. These choices include the types of objects that should be enterprise beans, and the role an enterprise bean may play in a group of collaborating components.

You may also need to consider the services provided by enterprise beans and the EJB container, and decide whether these services benefit your application. You should take into consideration these EJB services and advantages:

- The EJB architecture handles such system services as transaction management, security, scalability, persistent data access, distributed processing, and concurrency. An enterprise bean developer does not have to include code to handle these services. As a developer, you can focus on the application and business logic.

- Enterprise beans support multiple types of components.

- Enterprise beans support applications with a complex series of operations and accumulation of conversation state over time.

- Enterprise beans are portable across hardware platforms, operating systems, server implementations, and databases .

- Enterprise beans can be easily customized in the runtime environment.

- Enterprise beans are reusable software modules.

5.7.1 Remote versus Local Client Access for Entity Beans

As noted earlier, an entity bean must implement a local client view to be the target of a container-managed relationship. However, the requirements of the application might necessitate that the same entity bean implement a remote view as well. It is possible for an entity bean to use a local view and have the advantages of container-managed relationships, and to expose its functionality to remote clients. This can be done in the following two ways.

A bean provider can implement a session bean with a remote client view that serves as a facade to the local entity beans implementing the container-managed relationships. Clients use the methods of the remote session bean, which in turn provides a conduit to the functionality of the local entity bean or beans. Because the session bean implements a remote view, clients are not restricted to the same Java Virtual Machine as the session bean. The functionality of the local entity beans is available to remote clients through this session bean.

Alternatively, the bean provider can implement an entity bean with both a local and remote client view. This dual-purpose entity bean may have one or more entity beans with local interfaces behind it. The remote entity bean interface provides a coarse-grained view of the persistent data that is modeled by the network of entity beans related through their local interfaces. The remote entity bean may be accessed directly by clients of the EJB tier, or the bean provider may implement a remote session bean that serves as a facade to the entity bean with both the local and remote view. Note that if the same method is exposed through both local and remote interfaces, the method will be called with the pass-by-reference semantics in the local case, and with the pass-by-value semantics in the remote case. The bean provider needs to take care while writing and invoking the method to avoid any unintended side-effects.

5.7.2 Session Beans as a Facade to Entity Beans

A facade provides a unified interface to a set of interfaces. This section describes when and how to use a session bean as a facade to entity beans.

Entity beans represent an object-oriented view of data and provide business logic to manipulate this data. In an enterprise environment, entity beans often need to be shared among different applications representing different tasks. In such cases, use of application-specific stateful session beans to manage the inter-action of various entity beans provides a simpler interface to the client by giving the client a central point of entry. The client always interacts with this session bean and is unaware of the existence of other entity beans in the system. However, if the client interacts with only a few entity beans in a relatively simple way, the entity beans can be exposed directly.

Stateful session beans are logical extensions of the client programs. The decision to use one or many session bean facades depends on the types of clients the application supports. Since the sample application has only a single type of client, the shopping client, the sample application uses a single stateful session bean called ShoppingClientFacadeLocal. It's easy to imagine another client that would provide administration functionality such as inventory and order status monitoring. The work flow of such a client would be entirely different from a shopping client. Therefore, it is advisable to define another stateful session bean that encapsulates this administrative work flow. However, it is not recommended that a session bean be created as a facade for every entity bean in the system, as that approach would waste server resources.

5.7.3   Fine-Grained versus Coarse-Grained Object Access

Entity beans with local interfaces provide efficient access to fine-grained objects. Model these objects as local entity beans when you can assure that their clients are co-located on the same JVM, or implement the business objects with a local view and provide a remote enterprise bean facade to them.

As mentioned earlier, enterprise beans that are implemented as remote objects may consume significantly more system resources and network bandwidth to execute. Because of the overhead of remote access, remote entity beans should not be used for fine-grained access. Therefore, only model a business object as a remote entity bean if its clients are distributed. In such a case, keep the entity bean access coarse grained, and use a value object to pass data across the remote interface.

A *value object* is a serializable Java object that can be passed by value to the client. A value object can be used to aggregate state extracted from a remote entity bean for use by the client. By avoiding the use of fine-grained remote method calls to retrieve the persistent state of an entity bean, value objects help reduce the network overhead involved in remote access.

The sample application models the details of an order as a value object representing the state of a particular order in the database and providing getter methods to query the state of this account. An administration client makes just one remote call to execute `getOrdersByStatus` on the remote object account and gets back a collection of the serialized `OrderDetails` objects. The client can then query the state of these orders locally via the methods provided with the `OrderDetails` object.

5.7.3.1 Example: An Address Value Object

In the sample application, an address and credit card information are modeled as value objects. The definition of the `Address` class is shown in Code Example 5.6.

```java
public class Address implements java.io.Serializable {
    public Address (String streetName1, String streetName2,
        String city, String state, String zipCode, String country){
        this.streetName1 = streetName1;
        this.streetName2 = streetName2;
    ...
    }
    public String getStreetName1() {
        return streetName1;
    }
    ...
    private String streetName1;
    private String streetName2;
    ...
}
```

Code Example 5.6   `Address` value object

An `Address` does not exhibit complex behavior, but is merely a data structure that contains only data fields. An address is fine-grained, having only get and set methods. Moreover, it only has meaning if it is associated with an account.

When making the object pass-by-value it is important to make it immutable to reinforce the idea that the value object is not a remote object and changes to its state will not be reflected on the server; in other words, it is just a copy and not the remote reference. To make an `Address` object immutable, declare all its instance data private and supply only get methods. To change a pass-by-value object, the client must first remove it and then create a new object with the desired field values.

5.7.4   Master-Detail Modeling Using Enterprise Beans

In a master-detail relationship, one object serves as a pointer to another. Typically such a relationship is represented to the user as a list of items from which to select. This list is called a master record and its contents are provided by the master object. Selecting an item from this list leads to an expanded view of that item. The expanded view is provided by a detail object.

A master-detail relationship is a one-to-many type relationship among data sets. A set of purchase orders and a set of line items belonging to each purchase order is an example of a master-detail relationship. An application can use this master-detail relationship to enable users to navigate through the purchase order data and see the detail data for line items only when needed.

Entity beans with container-managed persistence are the preferred way to implement master-detail relationship modelling, since they support container-managed relationships. Further, container-managed relationships provide a cascade-delete facility that automatically enables the lifetime of the detail object to be dependent on the lifetime of the master, capturing an important aspect of this dependency.

5.7.5   Data Access Objects

In situations where the use of container-managed persistence is not suitable, *data access objects* can be used to encapsulate access to persistent data. A data access object (DAO) design pattern separates the interfaces to a system resource from the underlying strategy used to access that resource. Both entity beans with bean-managed persistence and session beans can use DAOs.

A DAO class provides an abstract API for manipulating a data source. This abstract API makes no reference to how the data source is implemented. The DAO simply has to know how to load itself from persistent store based on some identity information (a primary key or a file name, for example), how to store itself, and so on.

By encapsulating data access calls, data access objects allow adapting data access to different schemas or even to different database types. Data access objects for different schemas and databases can share a common interface enabling the application assembler to choose the appropriate object from among several at assembly time. Section 6.4.3 on page 188 extends this approach to show how access objects can be used to create an integration layer.

The DAO pattern is not limited to representing data in a database. It can also encapsulate XML data sources as DAO classes.

5.7.5.1 Clarifying Bean Implementations

When a session bean or an entity bean with bean-managed persistence needs to access a database within a method implementation, a corresponding method in the data access object implements the actual logic of fetching or updating data in the database. This removes the data access logic from the enterprise bean implementation. The bean's business logic is not cluttered with data access calls, such as JDBC calls, making it much cleaner and readable.

For example, consider the `Catalog` session bean. The business method `getProducts` needs to return all the products for a category. Whenever `getProducts` needs to operate on data residing in the database, it hands over control to a data access object. The data access object formulates the query, fetches the result set, and returns the data in the desired format to the bean's calling method.

In the sample application, the implementation of the `Catalog` session bean is provided by `CatalogEJB`. The code for `CatalogEJB.getProducts` appears in Code Example 5.7; the code for the corresponding data access object appears in Code Example 5.8.

```
public Page getProducts(String categoryId, int start, int count,
                        Locale l) {
    try {
        ... // initialize dao to an instance of CatalogDAOImpl
        return dao.getProducts(categoryId, start, count, l);
    } catch (.....) {
        // catch exceptions and throw an EJBException
    }
}
```

Code Example 5.7   `CatalogEJB.getProducts`

```
public Page getProducts(String categoryId, int start, int count, Lo-
cale l) {
    ... // initialize database connection and other variables
```

```
        String query = "select COUNT(*) from (product a join"
            + "product_details b on a.productid=b.productid) "
            + "where locale = ? and a.catid = ? ";
        PreparedStatement ps = con.prepareStatement(query,
            ResultSet.TYPE_SCROLL_INSENSITIVE,
            ResultSet.CONCUR_READ_ONLY);
        ps.setString(1, l.toString());
        ps.setString(2, categoryID);
        ResultSet rs = ps.executeQuery();
        ... // Create page from the result set and return it
    }
```

Code Example 5.8   `CatalogDAOImpl.getProducts`

5.7.5.2   Consequences of Using DAO Pattern

Potential consequences of using the data access object pattern include:

• Resource vendor independence

When a component uses a vendor-specific API, it is locked into that vendor's product line. The DAO pattern provides a layer of indirection that isolates vendor-specific code in a class or several classes, where it can easily be replaced if necessary or desirable.

• Resource implementation independence

- Similar types of resources are often available in various formats through various access methods. For example, persistent data can be implemented by a relational database, an object database, flat files in a file system, interaction with a remote persistence server, and so on. The DAO pattern separates the management of data access mechanism details from the behavior of application objects. Easier migration to container-managed persistence

  A data access object, by encapsulating persistence logic and separating it from business logic, facilitates migrating from bean-managed persistence to container-managed persistence.

- Enhanced extensibility

  It is easier to add new data source types using data access objects. Each such type requires only a new DAO class, plus integration of that class into the existing framework.

5.7.6 Implementing an Entity Bean without a Create Method

There are times when you do not want to provide create methods in an entity bean's home interface. Omit the create methods when you do not want the entity bean to create persistent data. Typically in these situations, some other system or process is responsible for creating the data underlying the entity bean's persistent representation. For example, database functions insert new data into a database, and clients use the entity bean to retrieve data.

5.7.7 Representing References to Entity Beans

References between enterprise beans are common in many applications. Entity beans reference other related beans, stateful session beans may keep references to entity beans in conversational state, and stateless session beans and message-driven beans may look up and pass references to other beans. Developers can represent references between entity beans in the following ways:

- Use a container-managed relationship

  With the EJB 2.0 architecture, model persistent references between entity beans using container-managed persistence as container-managed relationships. Container-managed relationships automatically maintain persistent references between entity beans and collections of entity beans.

- Store a reference to a home or component interface in a non-persistent field of an entity bean with bean-managed persistence or in an instance variable of a session or message-driven bean. Beans can retain references to other entity beans in instance fields.

- Use the referenced entity bean's primary key

  If a referenced entity bean's home interface is known, the referencing bean can use the `findByPrimaryKey` method in the referenced bean's home interface to find a bean's component interface.

- Do not pass `this` as a reference to an enterprise bean. Doing so circumvents the EJB container and causes errors.

5.8   Portability Guidelines

The best way to achieve application portability is to use only J2EE-compatible application servers and tools. These products pass the rigorous J2EE Compatibility Test Suite (CTS) that ensures "Write-Once-Run-Anywhere" portability for J2EE applications.

Another way to ensure portability is to use more than one application server in the development cycle. The J2EE Reference Implementation (J2EE RI) is a good choice for a second application server.

It is also helpful to use code generation wizards to write enterprise beans. Besides enhancing productivity, such wizards typically generate code that is consistent with the J2EE specifications, thereby eliminating inadvertent errors. For example, such wizards will typically ensure that your enterprise bean methods throw all required exceptions—`RemoteException`, `FinderException`, and so on. These tools are particularly useful for generating the deployment descriptor since the deployment descriptor content must follow a precise XML syntax. Writing them manually is prone to errors because it is easy to incorrectly order elements, duplicate element entries, or make simple typing mistakes.

Most application servers also ship with verification tools that validate the components and their deployment descriptors against the J2EE specifications. The

J2EE RI also ships with one such tool called the J2EE Verifier. Run these verification tools as part of your regular build process to enhance portability.

5.8.1 Typecast Remote References

A client program that needs to access a remote enterprise bean must use the `PortableRemoteObject.narrow` method for type narrowing. Type narrowing is needed when a client program looks up a home interface from JNDI, or a finder method returns a collection of references to remote enterprise beans. Code Example 5.9 shows how to do type narrowing when looking up a home object from JNDI.

```
try {
    Context ctxt = new InitialContext();
    Object objref = ctxt.lookup("java:comp/env/ejb/remote/admin");
    OrderProcessingCenterAdminFacadeHome adminHome =
        (OrderProcessingCenterAdminFacadeHome) PortableRemoteОb-
ject.narrow (objref, OrderProcessingCenterAdminFacadeHome.class);
    OrderProcessingCenterAdminFacade admin = adminHome.create();
} catch (....) {
```

Code Example 5.9   Using the `narrow` Method for Type Narrowing

Type narrowing is needed because many application servers use RMI-IIOP as the communication protocol to access remote beans. However, some application servers do not use RMI-IIOP and hence allow the use of Java language typecasts as well. For portability you cannot rely on an application server allowing Java language typecasts; you should always use the `PortableRemoteObject.narrow` method. The overhead on this method call is usually quite small. In addition, EJB containers that do not use RMI-IIOP typically optimize away all such overhead.

Note that the `narrow` method must not be used in the clients of local enterprise beans since they are in the same JVM. The local enterprise beans are always type-narrowed using the regular typecast of the Java programming language.

5.8.2 Mark Non-Serializable Fields Transient

To preserve a bean's state during passivation, the bean class must be serializable. This requires that all the non-transient fields of the bean class are serializable. Fields that are primitive types, such as `String` and `int`, are serializable. However, a reference field, which is a field whose value is a reference to a class instance, is serializable only if the referenced class implements java.io.Serializable. You must mark all fields of non-serializable types as transient. The JVM's serialization machinery ignores fields marked as transient.

For example, a database connection represented by java.sql.Connection is not serializable. It must be marked transient when declared inside an enterprise bean class.

5.8.3   Bean-Managed Persistence and Portability

Extra effort is required to achieve portability for an enterprise bean that uses bean-managed persistence, because the bean needs to ensure portability across all databases as well as JDBC drivers.

The foremost factor affecting portability relates to the SQL language. Many database vendors provide proprietary extensions to SQL to provide additional functionality and to achieve higher performance. Consider using only standard SQL constructs to achieve portability. If you do need to use proprietary extensions, consider using the Data Access Object design pattern to encapsulate vendor-specific code.

5.8.3.1   SQL and Database Connections

For maximum portability, it's important to close SQL statements before you close the database connection. Enterprise beans often need to open a database connection, execute a set of SQL statements, then close the connection. Some JDBC driver implementations throw an exception if a JDBC connection is closed while some of the driver database statements are open. To achieve portability across JDBC drivers, always close database statements before closing the database connection. The finally block in Code Example 5.10 illustrates how this can be done.

```
public Page searchItems(String searchQuery, ....) {
    Connection con = null;
    PreparedStatement ps = null;
    ResultSet rs = null;
    String query = "SELECT .....";
    try {
        con = dataSource.getConnection();
        ps = con.prepareStatement(query);
        rs = ps.executeQuery();
```

```
        // rest of the method body
    } catch (.... ) { // handle exceptions
    } finally {
        if (rs != null) rs.close();
        // Close PreparedStatement before Connection.
        if (ps != null) ps.close();
        if (c != null) c.close();
    }
    ...
}
```

Code Example 5.10 Closing Database Connections

5.8.3.2   Relying on Instance Fields

Bean providers should not rely on a bean's instance fields or container-managed persistence accessor methods within `ejbActivate`, `ejbLoad`, `ejbPassivate`, and `ejbStore` methods. This is because the container can choose several ways to manage the life cycle of its enterprise beans. For example, in the `ejbActivate` method the container is not required to load an entity bean's instance fields from its persistence store. Similarly, in the `ejbPassivate` method the container is not required to store the instance fields to its persistence store. In addition, the container is not required to allow accesses to resources from the `ejbActivate` or `ejbPassivate` methods.

5.8.3.3   Avoid Exposing Resource-Specific Details

Bean providers should be especially careful to avoid including backend resource-specific details in their components' interfaces, since doing so may limit where the components might be used. One easily overlooked form of resource dependence is the set of exceptions a method may throw. Because bean-managed persistence methods do not necessarily use a SQL database to manage their persistence, `SQLException` should not be thrown in the bean-managed persistence method signatures.

Instead of throwing `SQLException`, define system- and application-level exceptions for the class and throw those exceptions in response to error conditions. While using the Data Access Object (DAO) design pattern, catch the resource-specific exceptions, such as SQLException, in the DAO class and translate them to appropriate system-level or application-level exceptions.

Consider Code Example 5.11 from the sample application. In the method searchItems, an SQLException is translated to a CatalogDAOSysException, which extends java.lang.RuntimeException to indicate a system-level exception.

```
public class CatalogDAOImpl implements CatalogDAO {
    ....
    public Page searchItems(String searchQuery, int start,
                            int count, Locale l)
        throws CatalogDAOSysException {
    ....
    try {
        Connection con = getDBConnection();
        PreparedStatement ps = con.prepareStatement("SELECT ...");
        ...
        ps.executeQuery();
        ...
    } catch (SQLException se) {
        throw new CatalogDAOSysException("Malformed query.");
    }
    ...
}
```

Code Example 5.11   Throwing Exceptions

The code throws an application exception if the user input to searchQuery is incorrect. For errors such as an unavailable database connection, or general SQL exceptions, a system exception should be thrown.

5.9   Summary

Distributed enterprise applications require a number of common services. These include maintaining state, operating on shared data, participating in transactions, servicing a large number of clients, providing remote access to data, and controlling access to data. The middle tier of enterprise computing has evolved as the ideal place to provide these services. The J2EE platform promotes the Enterprise Java-

Beans architecture as a way to provide the system services that most enterprise applications need. The EJB architecture frees enterprise application developers from concerns about these services, enabling them to concentrate on providing robust, highly functional business logic.

The Enterprise JavaBeans architecture provides various types of enterprise beans to model business objects: entity beans, stateful and stateless session beans, and message-driven beans. Choose a particular enterprise bean type to model a business concept depending on the application's needs for robust data handling, efficient behavior, and maintaining client state during a user session.

An entity bean provides an object-oriented view of stored data, such as relational data stored in a database; a stateless session bean gives a procedural view of the data. An application component provider should use entity beans to model logical entities such as records in a database. When implementing behavior to visit multiple rows in a database and present a read-only view of data, stateless session beans are the best choice. They are designed to provide generic services to multiple clients.

Some business concepts actually require more than one view of data. An example would be a catalog that provides browsing and searching services as well as mechanisms to update the product information. In such cases, you can use a stateless session bean to operate on product information as a whole and an entity bean to provide access to a particular product.

Enterprise beans implemented as remote objects consume a significant amount of system resources and network bandwidth. Because of this overhead, they are not appropriate for modeling all business objects. Instead, an application component provider can implement certain enterprise beans as local objects, with a remote enterprise bean as a facade to the local beans. Or, you can use data access objects to encapsulate database access and value objects to model objects that are dependent on enterprise beans.

Also, it may not be appropriate to give clients direct access to all enterprise beans used by an application. Some enterprise beans may act as mediators for communication between clients and the EJB tier. Such beans can encapsulate work flow specific to an application or can serve as an entry point to a hierarchy of information.

5.10   References and Resources

For the complete Enterprise JavaBeans specification, see:

- *Enterprise JavaBeans Specification*, version 2.0. Copyright 2001, Sun Micro-systems, Inc. <http://java.sun.com/products/ejb>

For more information on EJB and its effective use, see:

- *Applying Enterprise JavaBeans: Component-Based Development for the J2EE Platform*. V. Matena, B. Stearns. Copyright 2001, Addison-Wesley.

- *Mastering Enterprise JavaBeans*, 2nd edition. E. Roman, S. Ambler, T. Jewell. Copyright 2002, Wiley.

- *Enterprise JavaBeans,* 3rd edition. R. Monson-Haefel. Copyright 2001, O'Reilly.

- *Core J2EE Patterns: Best Practices and Design Strategies*. D. Alur, J. Crupi, D. Malks. Copyright 2001, Prentice-Hall.

Integrating with the Enterprise Information System Tier

by Rahul Sharma and Beth Stearns

THIS chapter focuses on the integration of enterprise applications with existing enterprise information systems (EIS) and applications. Enterprise information systems provide the information infrastructure critical to the business processes of an enterprise. Examples of EISs include relational databases, enterprise resource planning (ERP) systems, mainframe transaction processing systems, and legacy database systems.

The EIS integration problem has assumed great importance because enterprises are striving to leverage their existing systems and resources while adopting and developing new technologies and architectures. Today, enterprise application development is more about integration rather than developing an enterprise application from scratch. Enterprises cannot afford to discard their existing investments in existing applications and EISs. The emergence of Web-based architectures and Web services has made it more imperative for enterprises to integrate their EISs and applications and expose them to the Web.

The EIS integration problem is one part of the broader scope of enterprise application integration (EAI). EAI entails integrating applications and enterprise data sources so that they can easily share business processes and data. This chapter focuses on the following aspects of EAI, and includes discussions of recommended guidelines:

- **Application integration**—Existing enterprise applications may be off-the-shelf bundled applications or they may be developed in-house. Two examples are supply chain management (SCM) and customer relationship management (CRM) applications. While such applications expose business level functionality used directly by end users or integrated with other enterprise applications, they usually do not expose the underlying data on which the business functionality is built.

- **Data integration**—An enterprise environment often contains more than one database system upon which its business processes run. These database systems may be relational, object-based, hierarchical, file based, or legacy stores. Data integration focuses on integrating existing data with enterprise applications. For example, an integration might entail integrating a Web-based order management system with an existing order and customer database.

- **Legacy integration**—Legacy integration involves integrating new enterprise applications with applications and EISs that have been in operation for some time, often referred to as an enterprise's "legacy" systems. An enterprise cannot afford any disruption in these legacy systems. This chapter focuses on how to connect enterprise applications to these legacy systems.

6.1   Integration Scenarios

A J2EE application may be configured in a number of different ways to access an enterprise information system. The following sections illustrate a few typical enterprise information system integration scenarios.

6.1.1   An Internet E-Store Application

The sample application illustrates an Internet E-Store application. Company A deploys the sample application to create an Internet E-Store. The application is composed of a set of enterprise beans, JSP pages, and servlets that collaborate to provide the overall functionality of the application. The database stores data related to product catalogs, shopping carts, customer registration and profiles, and order status.

The architecture of this application is illustrated in Figure 6.1.

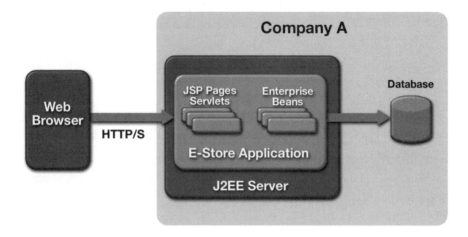

Figure 6.1   An Internet E-Store Application

A customer uses a Web browser to initiate an e-commerce transaction with the sample application. A customer

- Browses the catalog
- Makes a selection of products
- Puts the product selection into a shopping cart
- Enters a user name and password to initiate a secure transaction
- Fills in order-related information
- Places an order

Company A stores all persistent information about customers and their transactions in an existing database that already contains product and inventory information.

6.1.2   An Intranet Human Resources Application

Company B has developed and deployed an employee self-service application based on the J2EE platform. This application supports a Web interface to existing human resources applications supported by the enterprise resource planning system from Vendor X and provides additional business processes that are customized to the needs of Company B.

Figure 6.2 illustrates an architecture for this application. The middle tier is composed of enterprise beans and JSP pages that provide customization of business processes and support a company standardized Web interface. This application enables an employee (under the different roles of Manager, HR manager, and Employee) to perform various personnel management functions: personal information management, payroll management, compensation management, benefits administration, travel management, and cost planning.

The company's IT department deploys this application and enterprise resource planning system in a secure environment at a single physical location. Access to the application is permitted only to employees of the organization based on their roles and access privileges, and within the confines of the organization-wide intranet.

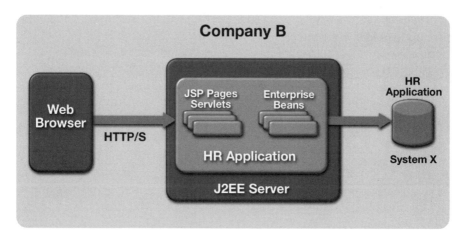

Figure 6.2   An Intranet Human Resources Application

6.1.3   A Distributed Purchasing Application

Company C has a distributed purchasing application whose Web-based interface an employee can use to perform multiple purchasing transactions. An employee can use the application to manage the procurement process, from creating a purchase requisition to getting invoice approval. This application also integrates with the existing financial applications in the enterprise for tracking financial aspects of the procurement business processes.

Figure 6.3 illustrates an architecture for this application. The application as developed and deployed on the J2EE platform is composed of JSP pages, enterprise beans, and existing information systems. The enterprise beans integrate a logistics application that provides integrated purchasing and inventory management functions from Vendor X and another that provides financial accounting functions from Vendor Y.

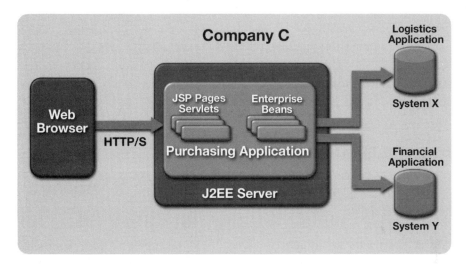

Figure 6.3   A Distributed Purchasing Application

Company C is a large decentralized enterprise with geographically distributed business units and departments. In this scenario, System X and System Y are managed by different IT departments and have been deployed at secured data centers in different geographic locations. The integrated purchasing application is deployed at a location different from either System X or System Y.

System X and System Y are in different security domains; they use different security technologies and have their own specific security policies and mechanisms. The distributed purchasing application is deployed in a security domain that is different from either that of System X or System Y.

6.1.4   An Order Fulfillment Application

This scenario is an extension of the Internet E-Store scenario described in Section 6.1.1 on page 172 and which the sample application demonstrates as well. Company A has an order fulfillment center that processes all orders placed on the Internet E-Store Web site. A separate department within Company A owns this center. This department maintains its own databases and has no access to the databases of the Internet E-Store Web site. To decouple the data models of the two departments, the order processing center requires that all orders sent to it are in XML format. Since an order might require significant processing, the order processing center receives orders asynchronously so that its clients can continue operation without waiting for an order to be fulfilled.

By using automated rules for small orders, the order processing center can process such orders without human intervention. All other orders require approval by an administrator. When an order is successfully completed, the center sends a confirmation e-mail to its customer. The administrator can also receive various kinds of sales data, such as daily sales volume, sales per category, and so forth.

6.2   J2EE Integration Technologies

To address the EIS integration problem, the J2EE platform provides the following EIS integration technologies:

- **J2EE Connector architecture**—The J2EE Connector architecture provides a standard architecture for integrating J2EE applications with existing EISs and applications. The Connector architecture enables adapters for external EISs to be plugged into the J2EE application server. Enterprise applications can then be developed using these adapters to support and manage secure, transactional, and scalable integration with EISs. The 1.0 version of the Connector architecture focuses on synchronous integration with EISs. The 2.0 version (under development as part of J2EE 1.4) extends the core functionality to add support for asynchronous integration with EISs. We expand on the synchronous and asynchronous integration later in this chapter.

- **Java Message Service (JMS)**—JMS is a standard Java API defined for enterprise messaging systems. It is meant to be a common messaging API that can be used across different types of messaging systems. A Java application uses the JMS API to connect to an enterprise messaging system. Once connected, the application uses the facilities of the underlying enterprise messaging system (through the API) to create messages and to communicate asynchronously with one or more peer applications.

- **JDBC™ API**—The JDBC API defines a standard Java API for integration with relational database systems. A Java application uses the JDBC API for obtaining a database connection, retrieving database records, executing database queries and stored procedures, and performing other database functions.

The following sections cover the Connector architecture, JMS, and the JDBC API in more detail. For other sources of information on these topics, please refer to "References and Resources" on page 200.

6.2.1 J2EE Connector Architecture

The J2EE Connector architecture is the standard architecture for integrating J2EE products and applications with heterogeneous enterprise information systems. The Connector architecture enables an EIS vendor to provide a standard resource adapter for its enterprise information system. Because a resource adapter conforms to the Connector architecture specification, it can be plugged into any J2EE-compliant application server to provide the underlying infrastructure for integrating with that vendor's EIS. The EIS vendor is assured that its adapter will work with any J2EE-compliant application server. The J2EE application server, because of its support for the Connector architecture, is assured that it can connect to multiple EISs.

The J2EE application server and EIS resource adapter collaborate to keep all system-level mechanisms—transactions, security, connection management—transparent to the application components. This enables an application component developer to focus on a component's business and presentation logic without getting involved in the system-level issues related to EIS integration.

Through its contracts, the J2EE Connector architecture establishes a set of programming design guidelines for EIS access. The J2EE Connector architecture defines two types of contracts: system and application level. The system-level contracts exist between a J2EE application server and a resource adapter. An application-level contract exists between an application component and a resource adapter. See Figure 6.4.

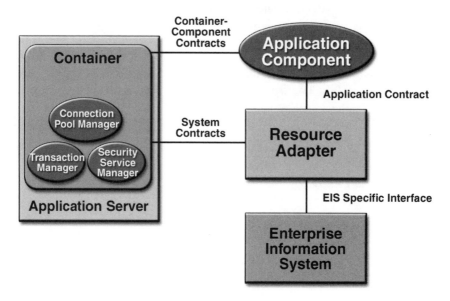

Figure 6.4   Connector Architecture System and Application Contracts

The application-level contract defines the client API that an application component uses for EIS access. The Connector architecture does not require that an application component use a specific client API. The client API may be the Common Client Interface (CCI), which is an API for accessing multiple heterogeneous EISs, or it may be an API specific to the particular type of resource adapter and its underlying EIS. There are advantages to using CCI, principally that tool vendors can build their tools on top of this API. Although the CCI is targeted primarily towards application development tools and EAI vendors, it is not intended to discourage vendors from using JDBC APIs. An EAI vendor will typically combine JDBC with CCI by using the JDBC API to access relational databases and using CCI to access other EISs.

The system-level contracts define a "pluggability" standard between application servers and EISs. By developing components that adhere to these contracts, an application server and an EIS know that connecting is a straight-forward operation of plugging in the resource adapter. The EIS vendor or resource adapter provider implements its side of the system-level contracts in a resource adapter, which is a system library specific to the EIS. The resource adapter is the component that plugs into an application server. Examples of resource adapters include an adapter that connects to an ERP system and one that connects to a mainframe transaction processing system.

There is also an interface between a resource adapter and its particular EIS. This interface is specific to the EIS, and it may be a native interface or some other type of interface. The Connector architecture does not define this interface.

The Connector architecture defines the services that the J2EE-compliant application server must provide. These services—transaction management, security, and connection pooling—are delineated in the three Connector system-level contracts. The application server may implement these services in its own specific way. The three system contracts, which together form a Service Provider Interface (SPI), are as follows:

- **Connection management contract**—This contract enables an application server to pool connections to an underlying EIS, while at the same time it enables application components to connect to an EIS. Pooling connections is important to create a scalable application environment, particularly when large numbers of clients require access to the underlying EIS.

- **Transaction management contract**—This contract is between the application server's transaction manager and an EIS that supports transactions. It gives the transaction manager the ability to manage transactions across multiple EIS resource managers. (A resource manager provides access to a set of shared resources.) The contract also supports local transactions, which are transactions that an EIS resource manager handles internally.

- **Security contract**—The security contract enables secure access to an EIS and protects the EIS-managed resources.

Future versions of the Connector architecture will add support for a thread management contract, enabling an application server to manage threads for its resource adapters.

6.2.2   Java Message Service API

The Java Message Service (JMS) API is a standard Java API defined for enterprise messaging systems. It is a common messaging API that can be used across different types of messaging systems. A Java application uses the JMS API to connect to an enterprise messaging system. Once connected, the application uses the facilities of the underlying enterprise messaging system (through the API) to create messages and to communicate asynchronously with one or more peer applications.

A JMS provider implements the JMS API for an enterprise messaging system and provides access to the services provided by the underlying message system. Application server vendors include a JMS provider with the application server. Currently, vendors plug a JMS provider into an application server in their own vendor-specific manner. The Connector architecture 2.0 version defines a standard for plugging a JMS provider into an application server, allowing a JMS provider to be treated similarly to a resource adapter. However, a JMS provider will have a JMS API as a client API for its underlying enterprise messaging system.

A client application, called a JMS client, uses the JMS API to access the asynchronous messaging facilities provided by the enterprise messaging system. The EJB tier is the best place to implement JMS clients in J2EE applications. Since JMS supports peer-to-peer messaging, both source (or producer) and destination (or consumer) applications act as clients to the JMS provider.

A JMS domain identifies the type of asynchronous message-based communication supported by a JMS provider and an enterprise messaging system. There are two domain types: queue-based point-to-point domains and publish-subscribe domains. A Java application using JMS has a different application programming model depending on the JMS domain. For example, a Java application uses the JMS-defined queue-based interfaces `QueueConnectionFactory` and `MessageQueue`, among other queue-based interfaces, to interact with a point-to-point domain.

6.2.3   JDBC and RDBMS Access

Relational database management systems (RDBMS) are the most prevalent form of enterprise data store. Many application component providers use the JDBC 2.0 or 3.0 API for accessing relational databases to manage persistent data for their applications.

The JDBC API has two parts: a client API for direct use by developers to access relational databases and a standard, system-level contract between J2EE servers and JDBC drivers for supporting connection pooling and transactions. Developers do not use the contract between J2EE servers and JDBC drivers directly. Rather, J2EE server vendors use this contract to provide pooling and transaction services to J2EE components automatically. Note that, according to the JDBC 3.0 specification, the JDBC system-level contracts can be the same as the Connector architecture system contracts. Conceptually, JDBC drivers are pluggable resource adapters.

An application component provider uses the JDBC client-level API for such operations as obtaining a database connection, retrieving database records, executing queries and stored procedures, and performing other database functions.

6.3   Application Integration Design Approaches

The EIS integration approaches may be classified as shown in Figure 6.5.

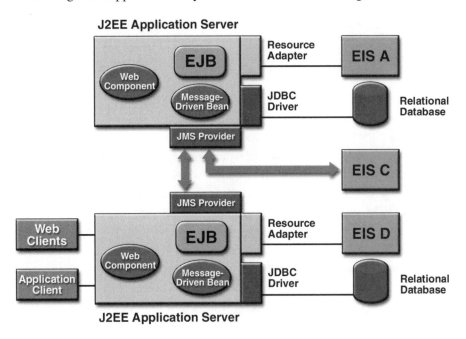

Figure 6.5   EIS Integration Design Approaches

- Data integration using the JDBC API (for relational databases) or Connector architecture (for non-relational databases)

- Asynchronous, message-based, loosely-coupled integration using the JMS and J2EE Connector architecture

- Synchronous, tightly-coupled integration using the Connector architecture

- Legacy connectivity using the Connector architecture

6.3.1   Synchronous Integration

This mode of integration involves synchronous communication between J2EE applications and the target EIS. Synchronous communication between a J2EE application and an EIS follows the request-response interaction model. An application initiates a request to the target EIS. The application then blocks its processing in the request invocation thread while it waits for a response from the EIS. The application continues its execution after it receives the response.

Most EISs utilize a synchronous request-reply interaction model. Typically, an EIS defines an API for remote function calls that applications use to issue synchronous requests to the EIS. For example, an EIS might define an API that includes a remote function to create an account receivable item in the EIS. An enterprise application invokes this remote function on the EIS to create an account receivable item and waits until it receives a reply containing the results of the function's execution on the EIS. This interaction is synchronous because the calling application's invocation thread waits synchronously while the function executes on the EIS and continues when the remote function returns.

The 1.0 version of the Connector architecture supports a synchronous request-response interaction mode where an application component initiates the synchronous request. The application server and resource adapter for the underlying EIS manage transaction and security through the system contracts provided in this synchronous request-response interaction mode. The resource adapter takes the responsibility to propagate the security and transaction context to its underlying EIS using an EIS-specific communication protocol.

Synchronous interaction leads to tight coupling between a J2EE application and an EIS. You should consider the implications of this when integrating applications with EISs. Consider a typical scenario where a J2EE application needs to access an EIS to process client-initiated requests. The application itself may be designed to handle multiple concurrent client requests. It may employ either a multithreaded implementation or multiple application instances may be running on multiple application server processes. When an application instance receives a client request, it synchronously invokes an EIS function. The invocation thread in the application process is then blocked from further processing until it receives a reply from the target EIS.

Suppose that the target EIS has a limited load capacity; that is, the EIS is capable of handling only a limited number of concurrent requests on a limited number of connections. As a result, the EIS is unable to process the same number of concurrent requests as the application. In a tightly-coupled synchronous integration, the application's response time and throughput for client requests may drop since it must wait for synchronous invocations on the EIS to complete.

Synchronous remote function calls typically expose underlying distribution and transaction management mechanisms, which may be vendor specific or based on a middleware standard. When these mechanisms are exposed, the application may become tightly coupled to the middleware mechanisms for transactions, distribution, and security. This causes problems if the application needs to integrate with other types of EISs, because its communication model must be redesigned to handle different middleware mechanisms.

The tight coupling that results from synchronous communication also raises issues about the relationship between an application and an EIS. The dependency between the two may cause the application's performance to be impeded by communication failures. For example, if the EIS is down or unavailable, an application request may return immediately with an error. The application logic needs to include code to initiate retries of such failed requests, or the EIS may successfully execute a request but be unable to reply because of a communications failure after the request was received. To handle this, the application logic must include timeouts or it will hang indefinitely waiting for a response.

6.3.2   Asynchronous Integration

Asynchronous integration involves message-based communication between a J2EE application and EIS. An application sends a request to an EIS. The request sender continues its own processing—that is, the application's thread does not block—while the EIS handles the request asynchronously. The request sender does not have to wait for the EIS processing to complete and for the reply to come back. Instead, the thread sends the message and continues processing client requests.

There are two forms of asynchronous message-based communication: queue-based communication and publish-subscribe messaging. Queue-based communication, or point-to-point messaging, involves a message queue that is independent of both sending and receiving applications. The message queue acts as a message buffer between the communicating applications. The sender application sends a message to this queue, while the receiver application receives its messages from the queue.

With a publish-subscribe messaging mechanism, an application publishes messages on a specific topic. Multiple applications, called subscribers, can subscribe to this topic and receive the published messages. The publish-subscribe facility manages delivery of published messages to applications subscribing to the topic.

Regardless of the messaging communication, a message represents structured data exchanged through asynchronous message-based communication. A message carries information used within a single enterprise's business processes or across the business processes of multiple enterprises. For example, a message can represent information required to invoke an EIS function. Another message can carry the returned value of this function invocation.

When using asynchronous communication, an application and an EIS are said to be loosely coupled. With loose coupling, an application thread can continue processing client requests without blocking on EIS performance or communication glitches. The application is not bound to the EIS or the communication delivery mechanism.

An enterprise messaging system may support both publish-subscribe and queue-based messaging, as well as the following services:

- **Message routing**—A messaging system processes and routes messages to one or more peer applications. The messaging system uses the routing information carried within a message.

- **Transaction management**—A messaging system can act as a transactional resource manager, allowing a client application to use a transaction model to interact with the messaging system. For example, a client application can produce a set of messages and use a transaction to group the messages together into a single atomic unit of work. When the transaction commits, the messaging system sends the set of messages as one unit. If the transaction rolls back, the messaging system discards the entire set of messages produced within the rolled back transaction.

- **Reliable message delivery**—A messaging system can provide different levels of message delivery semantics, from making an attempt to deliver the message (called at-most-once delivery) to guaranteeing that the message is delivered (called exactly-once delivery).

- **Message priority and ordering**—A messaging system can permit applications to assign priorities to messages and to indicate that messages should be delivered in serial order. The messaging system delivers messages assigned a higher priority ahead of those assigned a lower priority.

- **Message transformation**—Advanced messaging systems support message transformation and the use of rules engines. When a message flows through such a messaging system, it may be transformed based on the system's configured set of rules and defined message schemas. For example, the messaging system may transform the format of a particular message to one that is better understood by the intended consumer. The message system first transforms the message, then routes the message to the appropriate consumer application.

6.3.3 Comparing Approaches

When designing your application, you need to decide whether to use synchronous or asynchronous integration with its target EISes and existing applications. Both synchronous and asynchronous integration approaches are valid for application integration, and the choice should be based on the integration requirements and use cases. Base your decision on the following guidelines.

- **Quality of services required**—The use of a queue or a publish-subscribe system provides higher quality of services, such as message routing and reliable message delivery, than synchronous communications.

- **Application throughput**—Asynchronous messaging can lead to better throughput because a queue buffers messages, supports message routing, and guarantees message delivery.

- **Transactional integration**—A synchronous communication model is more suitable when an application needs to perform secure and transactional access to one or more EISes synchronously for client request processing. In such cases an application can afford the overhead of tighter coupling with an EIS to ensure higher quality request processing and error handling.

- **Programming model complexity**—An asynchronous communication programming model is more complex than the more common synchronous request-response model. While the asynchronous model provides more services, the cost is greater application complexity and more work on the part of developers.

6.3.4 Data Integration

A J2EE application developed using the J2EE component model may need to integrate with existing data. The existing data may be relational, object-based, hierarchical, or some legacy representation. The problem is magnified when the existing data is huge (such as millions of records) and the schema is complex. Often, it's not possible to change the database schema because other applications depend on it.

The JDBC API is recommended for integration with relational databases. This book does not provide a primer for JDBC since there are numerous other sources to learn about JDBC. (See "References and Resources" on page 200.) Instead, this chapter focuses on J2EE application design issues related to database access.

For non-relational and legacy databases, the J2EE Connector architecture defines a simple tool-focused Common Client Interface (CCI) API that resource adapters can implement. (Note that Connector architecture does not require CCI, but recommends it for toolability.) CCI provides a remote function call API that can be used to develop or generate higher-level abstractions to simplify access to the underlying EISs.

Data integration can be handled on two levels:

- Model a J2EE application using the EJB programming model. Use entity beans and stateful and stateless session beans to partition a J2EE application. Develop the EJB components and then map them to the existing schema. Whenever possible, use EJB container-managed persistence. See Chapter 5.

- Develop or generate abstractions (called access objects) that represent the underlying existing data and stored procedures. These abstractions bridge the gap between the EJB components and the existing data. See Section 6.4.3 on page 188.

6.4   Developing an Integration Layer

The J2EE application programming model for EIS integration defines a set of design choices, guidelines, and recommendations for application component providers. These guidelines enable an application component provider to develop an application based on its overall functional and system requirements. The application programming model focuses on the following aspects:

- Programming access to data and functions

- Using tools to simplify and reduce application development effort involved in accessing EISes

- Getting connections to an EIS and managing connections

- Supporting the security requirements of an application

The following sections describe each of these aspects from the perspective of relational database access using JDBC API, with the exception of transactions, which are discussed in Chapter 8. An important point to note is that the following sections are not meant to be a programmer's guide to using the JDBC API. While the following discussions refer to the JDBC API, the concepts are generic and apply to any client APIs (including the Common Client Interface) supported by resource adapters.

6.4.1   Programming Access to Data and Functions

When an application requires access to an enterprise information system, an application component provider is responsible for developing code to access resources managed by the enterprise information system, including tables, stored procedures, business objects, and transaction programs. The application component provider also has to write the business and application logic when developing functionality for applications that target enterprise information system.

In the J2EE programming model, a container assumes primary responsibility for managing connection pooling, transactions, and security. The level of service provided is based on the declarative specification of the application requirements by an application component provider or deployer. This leaves an application component provider to concentrate on developing code to access the data and functions managed by an enterprise information system.

6.4.2   Using Tools for EIS Integration

Application development tools can simplify EIS integration. By supporting end-to-end application development, tools also minimize the difficulties of working with vendor-specific client APIs. Different tools provide different functionality within the application development process. Generally, tools can be divided into these functional areas:

- Data and function mining tools, which enable application component providers to look at the scope and structure of data and functions in an existing information system

- Object-oriented analysis and design tools, which enable application component providers to design an application in terms of enterprise information system functionality

- Application code generation tools, which generate higher level abstractions for accessing data and functions. A mapping tool that bridges different programming models, such as an object to relational mapping, falls into this category.

- Application composition tools, which enable application component providers to compose application components from generated abstractions (such as those described in previous bullets). These tools typically use the JavaBeans component model to enhance ease of programming and composition.

- Deployment tools, which are used by application component providers and deployers to set transaction, security, and other deployment time requirements

6.4.3   Developing EIS Access Objects

A component can access data and functions in an enterprise information system in several ways, either directly by using the appropriate client API or indirectly by abstracting the complexity and low-level details of an EIS access API into higher level *access objects*. Access objects can take different forms—they can be data access objects (as described in Chapter 5), command beans, or records. There are advantages to using access objects, as follows:

- An access object can adapt a low-level API for accessing EIS data and functions to an easy-to-use API that is consistent across multiple types of enterprise information systems. For example, an access object may follow a design pattern that maps EIS function parameters to setter methods and return values to getter methods. The application component provider uses an EIS function by first calling the appropriate setter methods to set up the parameters, then calling the method corresponding to the EIS function, and finally calling the getter methods to retrieve the results.

- An access object facilitates a component's ability to adapt to different EIS resources. For example, a component can use an access object to adapt its persistent state management to a different database schema or to a different type of database.

- A component can be composed from access objects that support the JavaBeans model or, by using application development tools, the component can be linked with generated access objects. This simplifies the application development effort.

Access objects primarily provide a programming technique to simplify application development. Because of this, we recommend that they be used whenever an application component provider needs to access data or functions in an EIS. In some cases, tools may be available to generate such access objects. In other cases, the application component provider may need to hand-code an access object.

6.4.3.1   Types of Access Objects

There are different types of access objects, and these different access objects are used for different purposes. This section highlights the different access objects and their purposes.

6.4.3.1.1 Command Beans

An access object can encapsulate one or more EIS functions, such as business functions or stored procedures. This type of access object is referred to as a command bean. An application component uses a command bean to interact with a resource adapter and execute an EIS function. The command bean is associated with a remote EIS function, hiding the low-level programming aspects of accessing the function. The application component, rather than having to program through the CCI or EIS client-side API, instead accesses the EIS function by programming to the command bean's interface.

Code Example 6.1 implements a command bean that drives a purchase requisition business process in an enterprise resource planning system by mapping purchasing functions to method calls on a `PurchaseFunction` object.

```
PurchaseFunction pf = // instantiate access object for
                      // PurchaseFunction
// set fields for this purchase order
pf.setCustomer ("Wombat Inc");
pf.setMaterial (...);
pf.setSalesOrganization (...);
pf.execute ();
// now get the result of purchase requisition using getter methods
```

Code Example 6.1   Command Bean Code

6.4.3.1.2 Data Access Objects

When an access object encapsulates access to persistent data, such as that stored in a database management system, it is called a data access object (DAO). Often, tools generate data access objects based on the database schema. Data access objects can provide a consistent API across different types of database management systems. The sample application uses data access objects that correspond to order objects stored in different types of databases.

The principal advantage of data access objects is that they decouple the user of the object from the programming mechanism that accesses the underlying data. The DAO exposes the same interface to its clients regardless of the API it uses to access the EIS data. Even changes to the schema or function specification of the EIS may not impact the DAO's user interface. This means that the user's programming model does not have to change when EIS access mechanisms change or there are modifications to the EIS schema.

Code Example 6.2 shows a data access object that provides access to products in a product catalog. This product catalog is stored in a non-relational database. CatalogDAO is an object that provides a simple interface for getting products in the product catalog. CatalogDAO extends a DAO base class that may be specific to a tool or an EAI framework.

```
public class CatalogDAO extends com.example.tool.DAO {
    private RecordFactory rf;
    public CatalogDAO(Connection cx, RecordFactory rf) {
        super(cx);
        this.rf = rf;
    }
    public Collection getAllProducts() throws DAOException {
        try {
            MappedRecord input =
                rf.createMappedRecord("PRODUCT_INPUT_RECORD");
            input.put("ORDER-ID", "*");
            IndexedRecord output =
                rf.createIndexedRecord("PRODUCT_INFO_RECORD");
            InteractionSpecImpl ixSpec = new InteractionSpecImpl();
            ixSpec.setFunctionName("GET_PRODUCTS");
            ixSpec.setInteractionVerb
                (InteractionSpec.SYNC_SEND_RECEIVE);
            Interaction ix = cx.createInteraction();
            ix.execute(ixSpec, input, output);
```

```
            java.util.Iterator iterator = output.iterator();
            while (iterator.hasNext()) {
                // Get a record element and extract value
                // Add element to the collection
            }
            // Return Collection
        } catch (ResourceException re) {
            // ... Handle exception
        }
    }
    // other DAO class methods ....
}
```

Code Example 6.2   Example of a Data Access Object

Code Example 6.3 shows how an application component might use the
CatalogDAO data access object. The application component first instantiates the
CatalogDAO object and then uses a get method to retrieve products in the product
catalog.

```
public Product getProduct(String productID, Locale locale) {
    try {
        CatalogDAO dao =ProductCatalogDAOFactory.getDAO ();
        return dao.getProduct (productID, locale);
    } catch (...) {
        //... Handle exceptions
    }
}
```

Code Example 6.3   Using a Data Access Object

An access object can aggregate access to other access objects, thus providing
a higher level of abstraction and functionality. For example, a PurchaseOrder
aggregate access object can access a purchase order business function using a
command bean and can also use a data access object to maintain persistent
attributes of the purchase order. An aggregate access object can also encapsulate

logic to process multiple access objects in a specific order. Such aggregate access objects are generated by tools.

6.4.3.1.3 Record Objects

Another type of access object, called a record object, is used to represent a data structure. It can be used to hold input or output data for an EIS function. A record object can be a custom implementation, in which case a tool generates the object from the meta information in a repository, or it can be a generic implementation, in which case it extracts meta information from a metadata repository at runtime. Such meta information includes type mapping and data representation.

6.4.3.2   Using Access Objects

A component can use access objects in different ways depending on the functionality they offer. Some common ways to use access objects are:

- Define a one-to-one association between components and access objects. That is, each access object encapsulates the EIS functionality required by a particular component. This approach enables components to have Web access to the EIS resources encapsulated by an access object.

- Define components to aggregate the behavior of multiple access objects. This approach is often used when a component accesses multiple EIS resources or adds additional business logic to the functionality defined by multiple EIS resources.

6.4.3.3   Guidelines for Access Objects

There are some general guidelines to follow in developing access objects:

- An access object should not make assumptions about the environment in which it will be deployed and used.

- An access object should be designed to be usable by different types of components. For example, if an access object follows the set-execute-get design pattern described previously, then its programming model should be consistent across both enterprise beans and JSP pages.

- An access object should not define declarative transaction or security requirements of its own. It should follow the transaction and security management model of the component that uses it.

- All programming restrictions that apply to a component apply to the set of access objects associated with it. For example, an enterprise bean isn't allowed to start new threads, to terminate a running thread, or to use any thread synchronization primitives. Access objects should conform to the same restrictions.

6.4.4 Guidelines for Connection Management

It is important that application servers and components manage connections efficiently. Connections are expensive to create and remove. If an application server creates a new connection for each component's request, and then destroys the connection when the component completes its work, it is virtually impossible to support large numbers of users. To avoid this problem, J2EE application servers support connection pooling. While each application server can implement its own connection pooling mechanism, adhering to the Connector architecture ensures that pooling is efficient, scalable, and extensible.

An application server, by providing connection pooling, enables connections to be shared among client sessions so that a larger number of concurrent sessions can access an EIS. If each component acquires an EIS connection and holds it until its removal, it is difficult to scale up an application to support thousands of users. Since holding on to an EIS connection across long-lived instances or transactions is expensive, and since there is often a physical limitation to the number of connections to an EIS, components must manage connections efficiently. Application component providers need to follow sound connection management practices.

Connection management is especially important when applications migrate from two-tier to multitier component-based architecture. For example, a two-tier JDBC application may share a single connection across an entire application. However, after migrating to component-based partitioning, the same application must deal with shared connections across multiple component instances.

Application developers should follow the standard J2EE programming model for connection management; that is, application code should use the JNDI namespace to look up a connection factory instance. The same programming model is used for the creation of JDBC, CCI, or JMS connections.

In the standard programming model, the component provider specifies connection factory requirements for an application component in the deployment descriptor. For example, a bean provider specifies four elements in the deployment descriptor for a connection factory reference. (Refer to the EJB 2.0 specification for details on deployment descriptor elements for EJB components.)

- `res-ref-name`: `jdbc/CatalogDB`

- `res-type`: `javax.sql.DataSource`

- `res-auth`: `Application` or `Container`

- `res-sharing-scope`: `Shareable` or `Unshareable`

The `res-auth` element should be set to `Container` so that the container manages the EIS sign on while creating connections. See Section 6.4.5 on page 196.

The application component looks up a connection factory instance in the component's environment using the JNDI API.

```
// obtain the initial JNDI Naming context
Context ctxt = new InitialContext();
// perform JNDI lookup to obtain resource manager connection factory
javax.sql.DataSource ds = (javax.sql.DataSource)
    ctxt.lookup("java:comp/env/jdbc/CatalogDB");
```

The JNDI name passed in the method `NamingContext.lookup` is the same as that specified in the `res-ref-name` element.

Next, the application component invokes the `getConnection` method on the connection factory to get an EIS connection. The returned connection instance represents an application-level handle to an underlying physical connection.

```
// Invoke factory to obtain a connection
java.sql.Connection con = ds.getConnection();
```

Once it has acquired the connection, the application component uses it to interact with the EIS. When the application component completes its work, it should invoke the `Connection.close` method on the acquired connection instance. Closing the connection enables the application server to manage the connection pool more effectively.

The bean provider can control the extent that connections are shared. By default, other enterprise beans in the application that use the same resource in the same transaction context can share the connection. The bean provider can set the `res-sharing-scope` deployment descriptor element to `Unshareable` to indicate that a connection not be shared. Keep in mind, though, that sharing connections to a resource manager allows the container to optimize connection and local transaction use. It is recommended that connections be marked `Shareable`.

6.4.4.1   Connection Management by Component Type

A J2EE application is typically composed of components of different types: JSP pages, servlets, and enterprise beans. These component types vary in terms of their support for container-managed activation and passivation, execution of an instance for multiple clients, sharing of an instance across multiple clients, and other factors. Since connection management can vary by component type, an application component provider must account for such differences when deciding on a connection management model for an application. Here are a few examples that illustrate these differences.

A JSP page or servlet acquires and holds on to a connection to an EIS, whether that connection is initiated through the CCI or JDBC, in relation to the life cycle of its HTTP session. The JSP page or servlet can handle multiple HTTP requests across a single HTTP session, provided that those requests come from Web clients using the same EIS connection.

A stateful session bean can share an open connection and its client-specific query results across multiple methods. However, keep in mind that stateless session beans are designed to retain no state specific to a client. As a result, while stateless session beans can share a connection across methods, they maintain no client-specific state associated with the connection.

For entity beans, the EJB specification identifies methods that are allowed to perform EIS access through a connection. These include `ejbCreate`, `ejbPostCreate`, `ejbRemove`, `ejbFind`, `ejbActivate`, `ejbLoad`, `ejbStore`, and any business methods from the remote interface. An entity bean cannot access an EIS from within the `setEntityContext` and `unsetEntityContext` methods because a container does not have a meaningful transaction or security context when these two methods are called.

6.4.5   Security Guidelines

An application component provider follows the security model defined for the particular J2EE component—enterprise bean, JSP page, or servlet. Here are some guidelines for handling security in all types of components:

- An application component provider should declaratively specify security requirements for an application in the deployment descriptor. The security requirements include security roles, method permissions, and the authentication approach for EIS sign on.

- Security can be managed at the application level by an application component that is security aware. The component provider should include a simple programmatic interface through which the component manages security. This programmatic interface allows the application component provider to make access control decisions based on the security context—the principal and role—associated with the caller of a method and to do programmatic sign on to an EIS. (See Section 6.4.5.1.2 on page 198.)

- Other development roles, such as the J2EE server provider, deployer, and system administrator, should satisfy an application's security requirements in the operational environment. These security requirements are specified in the deployment descriptor.

6.4.5.1   EIS Sign On

From a security perspective, the mechanism for getting a connection to a resource is referred to as *EIS sign on*. A user requests a connection to be established under its security context. This security context includes various attributes, such as role, access privileges, and authorization level for the user. All application-level invocations to the database using this connection are then provided through the security context associated with the connection.

    If the EIS sign on mechanism involves authentication of the user, then an application component provider can authenticate the user in one of two ways.

- The component provider allows the deployer to set up the EIS sign on information and the container manages sign on. For example, the deployer sets the user name and password for establishing the database connection. The container then takes the responsibility of managing the database sign on. This is sometimes referred to as container-managed EIS sign on.

- The component provider implements sign on to the database from the component code. The component provides explicit security information for the user requesting the connection. This is referred to as application-managed EIS sign on.

We recommend that a component let the container manage EIS sign on. This removes the burden of managing security information for the sign on from the application component provider. It also enables J2EE servers to provide additional useful security services, such as single sign on across multiple EISs and principal mapping across security domains.

Container-managed EIS sign on has other advantages. It enables the application component provider to avoid hard-coding security details in the component code. A component with hard-coded security logic is less portable because its code must be changed if deployed on containers with different security policies and mechanisms.

6.4.5.1.1 Container-Managed Sign On

This section illustrates how the application component provider delegates the responsibility of setting up and managing EIS sign on to the container. The deployer sets up the EIS sign on so that the user account for connecting to the database is always eStoreUser. The deployer also configures the user identification and authentication information—user name and password—that is needed to authenticate eStoreUser to the database.

Here is how to use the JDBC API for container-managed EIS sign on. Code Example 6.4 shows the component code for invoking the connection request method on the javax.sql.DataSource with no security parameters. As in the previous example, the component instance relies on the container to do the sign on to the database using the security information configured by the deployer. Code Example 6.5 contains the corresponding connection factory reference deployment descriptor entry, where the res-auth element specifies that sign on is performed by the container.

```
// Obtain the initial JNDI context
Context ctxt = new InitialContext();
// Perform JNDI lookup to obtain connection factory
javax.sql.DataSource ds = (javax.sql.DataSource) ctxt.lookup
```

```
           ("java:comp/env/jdbc/CatalogDB");

    // Invoke factory to obtain a connection.
    // The security information is not given; thus it will be
    // configured by the deployer.
    java.sql.Connection conn = ds.getConnection ();
```

Code Example 6.4   Container-Managed Sign On with JDBC

```
    <resource-ref>
        <description>description</description>
        <res-ref-name>jdbc/CatalogDB</res-ref-name>
        <res-type>javax.sql.DataSource</res-type>
        <res-auth>Container</res-auth>
    </resource-ref>
```

Code Example 6.5   Connection Factory Reference Element

6.4.5.1.2 Application-Managed Sign On

With application-managed sign on, the application component provider performs a programmatic sign on to the database. The component passes explicit security information (user name, password) to the connection request method. Application-managed sign on can be accomplished using the JDBC API. The component passes the security information—the user's name and the password—to the connection request method of the javax.sql.DataSource. See Code Example 6.6.

```
    // Obtain the initial JNDI context
    Context ctxt = new InitialContext();
    // Perform JNDI lookup to obtain factory
    javax.sql.DataSource ds = (javax.sql.DataSource) ctxt.lookup
            ("java:comp/env/jdbc/CatalogDB");
    // Get connection passing in the security information
    java.sql.Connection conn = ds.getConnection
            ("eStoreUser", "password");
```

Code Example 6.6   Application-Managed Sign On with the JDBC API

6.4.5.2   Handling EIS Access Authorization

An application component provider relies on both the container and the EIS for authorizing access to EIS data and functions. The application component provider specifies security requirements for application components declaratively in a deployment descriptor. A set of security roles and method permissions can be used to authorize access to methods on a component. For example, an application component provider declaratively specifies the `PurchaseManager` role as the only security role that is granted permission to call the `purchase` method on a `PurchaseOrder` enterprise bean. The `purchase` method in turn drives its execution through an ERP logistics application by issuing a purchase requisition. In effect, this application has authorized only end-users with the `PurchaseManager` role to do a purchase requisition. This is the recommended authorization model.

An application component provider can also programmatically control access to enterprise information system data and functions based on the principal or role associated with the client who initiated the operation. For example, the EJB specification allows component code to invoke `getCallerPrincipal` and `isCallerInRole` to get the caller's security context. An application component provider can use these two methods to perform security checks that cannot be expressed declaratively in the deployment descriptor.

An application can also rely on an enterprise information system to do access control based on the security context under which a connection to the enterprise information system has been established. For example, if all users of an application connect to the database as `dbUser`, then a database administrator can set explicit permissions for `dbUser` in the database security domain. The database administrator can deny `dbUser` permission to execute certain stored procedures or to access certain tables.

6.5   Summary

This chapter has described designs and guidelines for integrating enterprise information systems into enterprise applications. These guidelines enable an application component provider to develop an enterprise application based on its overall functional and system requirements for EIS integration. The chapter focuses on accessing EIS resources from a component, using tools to simplify and reduce application development effort involved in accessing EISes, obtaining and managing connections to EISes, and supporting the security requirements of an application.

The current version of the J2EE platform includes the Connector architecture version 1.0, which provides full support for integrating all types of enterprise information systems, including database and legacy systems, with the J2EE platform. The JDBC API is also available for accessing relational databases. Asynchronous messaging is available through the JMS API.

6.6   References and Resources

We recommend the following publications for more information on enterprise application integration. For more details on the J2EE Connector architecture:

- *The J2EE Connector Architecture.* R. Sharma, B. Stearns, T. Ng. Copyright 2001, Sun Microsystems, Inc.

- The J2EE Connector Specification, versions 1.0 and 2.0. Sun Microsystems, Inc. <http://java.sun.com/products/j2ee>

For complete information on JDBC, see:

- *JDBC API Tutorial and Reference, Second Edition.* S. White, M. Fisher, R. Cattell, G. Hamilton, M. Hapner. Copyright 2001, Sun Microsystems, Inc.

- *JDBC 2.0 API*, (JDBC specification). Copyright 1998, 1999, Sun Microsystems, Inc. Available at <http://java.sun.com/products/jdbc>

- *JDBC 3.0 API*, (JDBC specification). Copyright 2000, Sun Microsystems, Inc. Available at <http://java.sun.com/products/jdbc>

- *JDBC 2.0 Standard Extension API* (JDBC extension specification). Copyright 1998, 1999, Sun Microsystems, Inc. Available at <http://java.sun.com/products/jdbc>

For more information on JMS, see:

- *Java Message Service, Version 1.0.2* (JMS Specification). Copyright 1998, Sun Microsystems, Inc. Available at <http://java.sun.com/products/jms>

- *Java Message Service API and Tutorial.* M. Hapner, R. Sharma, K. Haase. Copyright 2002, Sun Microsystems, Inc.

Packaging and Deployment

by Inderjeet Singh and Vijay Ramachandran

THE Java 2 Platform, Enterprise Edition, enables developers to assemble applications from components. The process of assembling components into modules, and modules into enterprise applications, is called *packaging*. Well-designed, reusable components can be customized to their operational environment. The process of installing and customizing an application in an operational environment is called *deployment*. To be customizable, components need to be configurable. However, application developers should not have to repeatedly reinvent a configuration mechanism. They need a standard mechanism that provides flexibility for configuration and supports using tools to help the process.

The J2EE platform provides facilities to make the packaging and deployment process simple. It uses Java Archive (JAR) files as the standard package for modules and applications, and XML-based description and customization of components and applications. This chapter begins with an overview of the packaging and deployment process for the J2EE platform. It describes how to perform each stage in the process and provides guidelines for each stage. It concludes by discussing requirements for tools that support the deployment process.

7.1 Packaging Components

A J2EE component (such as a servlet or an enterprise bean) is an independent functional software unit that conforms to interfaces defined by a component specification, and has only explicit dependencies on its environment. A component may be a single class, but more often is a collection of classes, interfaces, and resources. The

J2EE platform offers five types of components: enterprise beans, servlets and JSP pages, applets, application clients, and connectors.

The J2EE platform specification provides a way to bundle one or more components into a *module*, which is the smallest unit of independent deployment for any component type. A module may be deployed directly into a J2EE container, or one or more modules may be combined to form a *J2EE application*. For example, several enterprise bean components may be packaged into an EJB module that provides all or part of an application model, and that EJB module may be further combined with other modules to create a J2EE application.

Modules and applications for the J2EE platform are packaged and deployed as *deployment units*, which are compressed archive files similar to JAR files, but with a specified internal structure and file extension. There are four types of J2EE platform modules:

- EJB modules contain enterprise beans and related classes.

- Web modules contain web-tier components and resources.

- Application client modules contain application client classes.

- Resource adapter modules contain Java connectors, resource adapters, and support libraries and resources.

The deployment unit for each type of module has a structure defined by the corresponding component technology specification. For example, a Web module deployment unit is called a "Web archive," which has (among other things) a WEB-INF directory containing support files for the module. One or more J2EE platform modules can be composed into a J2EE application, which has its own type of deployment unit.

In addition to components and resources, each deployment unit contains a *deployment descriptor*, which is an XML file that specifies the explicit dependencies between each component and its environment. Deployment descriptors specify two kinds of information:

- **Structural information**—Meta-data that describes the components contained in the deployment unit, their relationships to each other, and their external dependencies. Structural information corresponds to hard-coded features that are not configurable at deployment time. Such information includes the names of enterprise bean home and remote interfaces and implementation classes, entity bean primary key classes, the persistence mechanisms used, and so on. Environment entry declarations and resource requirements are also part of structural information. A component container uses structural information to manage component instances at runtime.

Changing structural information in a deployment descriptor can cause a component to operate incorrectly or not at all, because it must be consistent with inherent hard-coded features. For example, an entity bean is an entity bean because it implements the EntityBean interface, and a deployment descriptor that says otherwise is simply wrong.

- **Assembly information**—This optional information describes how the contents of a deployment unit are composed with other deployment units to produce a new component. Assembly information includes enterprise bean relationship names, descriptive entries, security roles, method permissions, and the values of environment entries.

  Assembly information in a deployment descriptor can be changed without breaking the corresponding component, although doing so may alter the behavior of the assembled application.

See Code Example 7.1 and the text following it for an example of structural and assembly information.

Each J2EE developer role has specific packaging and deployment responsibilities.

7.2   Roles and Tasks

Three development roles play a part in the J2EE packaging and deployment process: application component providers, application assemblers, and deployers. The packaging and deployment tasks that each role performs are summarized in Figure 7.1.

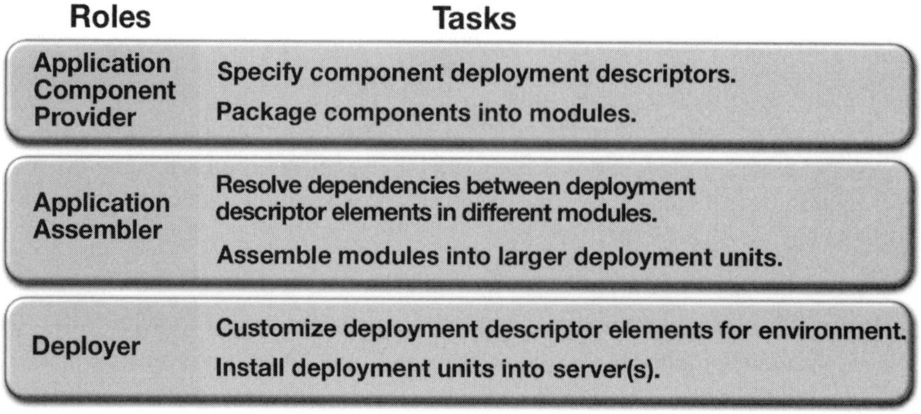

Figure 7.1   J2EE Packaging and Deployment Tasks

Developers in each of these roles create deployment units and perform specific tasks with the deployment descriptors of the deployment units they create.

7.2.1   Application Component Provider Tasks

Application component providers develop enterprise beans, HTML and JSP pages, servlets, applets, application clients, and associated helper classes. They also create the deployment descriptor for each component. Code Example 7.1 contains an excerpt from the sample application's enterprise bean deployment descriptor:

```
<session>
    <description>This is the Catalog ejb</description>
    <display-name>The Catalog</display-name>
    <ejb-name>TheCatalog</ejb-name>
    <local-home>
        com.sun.j2ee.blueprints.catalog.ejb.CatalogLocalHome
    </local-home>
    <local>com.sun.j2ee.blueprints.catalog.ejb.CatalogLocal</local>
    <ejb-class>
        com.sun.j2ee.blueprints.catalog.ejb.CatalogEJB
    </ejb-class>
    <session-type>Stateless</session-type>
    <transaction-type>Container</transaction-type>
```

```
<env-entry>
    <env-entry-name>
        ejb/catalog/CatalogDAOClass
    </env-entry-name>
    <env-entry-type>java.lang.String</env-entry-type>
    <env-entry-value>
        com.sun.j2ee.blueprints.catalog.dao.CatalogDAOImpl
    </env-entry-value>
</env-entry>
<resource-ref>
    <res-ref-name>jdbc/CatalogDataSource</res-ref-name>
    <res-type>javax.sql.DataSource</res-type>
    <res-auth>Container</res-auth>
</resource-ref>
</session>
```

Code Example 7.1   Descriptor Elements for an Entity Bean

Code Example 7.1 shows the deployment descriptor declaration of the sample application's catalog session bean. For this example, assembly information is shown in *italics* and structural information is in regular code font. Notice that structural information defines the public interface of the bean and the resources the bean uses. Structural information corresponds to hard-coded features of the bean, such as the classes it uses and the environment entries and resources it accesses. Assembly information, such as the bean's name, its description, and the values of environment entries, can be changed without causing inconsistencies with the code. Notice also that additional whitespace and newlines are significant within deployment descriptor text elements, and so should usually be avoided, except when it is truly desired. For example, text content to be used as a label may include whitespace, but resource reference names must not.

An application component provider typically creates the structural information in a deployment descriptor and may assign default values for some assembly informations. Application assemblers and deployers change or define the assembly information to configure the component for its role in an application, but usually leave structural information unchanged.

7.2.2   Application Assembler Tasks

Application assemblers combine existing components into applications and provide application assembly information for the application as a whole. Code Example 7.2 is an excerpt from the sample application's Web deployment descriptor:

```
<web-app>
    ...
    <servlet>
        <servlet-name>MainServlet</servlet-name>
        <display-name>HTML Client Front Controller</display-name>
        <description>no description</description>
        <servlet-class>
            com.sun.j2ee.blueprints.waf.controller.web.MainServlet
        </servlet-class>
    </servlet>

    <servlet-mapping>
        <servlet-name>webTierEntryPoint</servlet-name>
        <url-pattern>*.do</url-pattern>
    </servlet-mapping>
    ...
</web-app>
```

Code Example 7.2   Web Application Assembly Information

In the sample application, the application assembler uses the deployment descriptor to configure servlet class `MainServlet` to serve all URLs ending in suffix `.do`. The application assembler also defines the error pages that the application uses, its security constraints and roles, and so on. The only structural information shown in Code Example 7.2 is the servlet class. Everything else is assembly information created by the application assembler.

7.2.3   Deployer Tasks

Deployers deploy J2EE components and applications into an operational environment. They use tools created by the J2EE product provider to install J2EE modules and applications and configure them to their runtime environment. The J2EE platform and its related specifications for releases prior to the J2EE 1.4 release define some requirements for deployment tools, but do not define the interface between the deployment tools and containers; therefore, deployment tools for these releases are vendor-specific. Thus, prior to the J2EE 1.4 release, the deployment process is not standardized and portable across products. However, the J2EE 1.4 release will standardize the deployment process so that work a deployer performs will be portable across products.

Although the details differ from product to product, deployment typically involves two high-level tasks:

1. **Installation**—The deployer moves the media to the server, generates the additional container-specific classes and interfaces that enable the container to manage the components at runtime, and installs the components and additional classes and interfaces into the J2EE server.

2. **Configuration**—The deployer resolves all the external dependencies declared by the application component provider and follows the application assembly instructions defined by the application assembler. For example, the deployer configures the data sources that the application uses to persist data and maps the security roles defined by the application assembler to the operational environment's user groups and accounts. In some cases, a qualified deployer may customize the application components' business logic at deployment time, using tools provided with a J2EE product. For example, a deployer may write application code that wraps an enterprise bean's business methods or may add a company's logo to a login JSP page.

7.3   Packaging J2EE Applications

A J2EE application is packaged as a portable deployment unit called an enterprise archive (EAR) file. An EAR file is standard JAR file with a .ear extension. An EAR file contains:

- One or more J2EE modules

- A J2EE application deployment descriptor

Creation of a J2EE application is a two-step process. First, application component providers create EJB, Web, and application client modules. Second, the application assembler packages these modules together to create a J2EE application module that is ready for deployment. This section discusses issues involved in both of these steps.

All J2EE modules are independently deployable units. This enables component providers to create independent units of functionality without having to implement full-scale applications.

Figure 7.2 illustrates the various types of J2EE modules (EJB, Web, application client, and application) and how they can be deployed. Although the figure shows only an independently deployed EJB module (at the bottom of the figure), all four types of J2EE modules can be deployed independently.

To assemble an application, an application assembler resolves dependencies between components by creating links in the corresponding modules' deployment descriptors. Each component may have dependencies on other components within the same archive, on components in different archives, or both. All such dependencies must be resolved before deployment. For example, in the sample application, the Web components in the WAR file need to refer to `ShoppingClientController`, `Catalog`, `Account`, `Order`, and `ShoppingCart` enterprise beans in the EJB JAR file. The application assembler ensures that the description of the enterprise beans in the WAR file matches their descriptions in the EJB JAR file.

The J2EE specifications place a number of requirements on components and deployment units, most of which are essential for proper component operation. Yet component containers are not required to enforce many of these rules at runtime. Application assemblers should run verifier tools (such as the one included with the J2EE SDK) on assembled EAR files to verify that their contents are internally consistent. A verifier performs a number of static checks to ensure that the deployment descriptor and the archive file contents are referentially valid and conform to the EJB, servlet, and J2EE specifications. Common errors that a verifier can identify include mandatory naming convention violations, missing exception declarations, missing deployment descriptor entries, unresolved external component and resource references, name collisions, structural information that conflicts with code, and inaccessible support classes and interfaces. In addition, a vendor-supplied verifier can check the consistency of product-specific deployment information. An intelligent verifier can guide a deployer through the process of resolving these inconsistencies, provide contextual help, and even present suggested solutions. While verification does not guarantee correct runtime behavior, it can catch a wide class of errors before deployment.

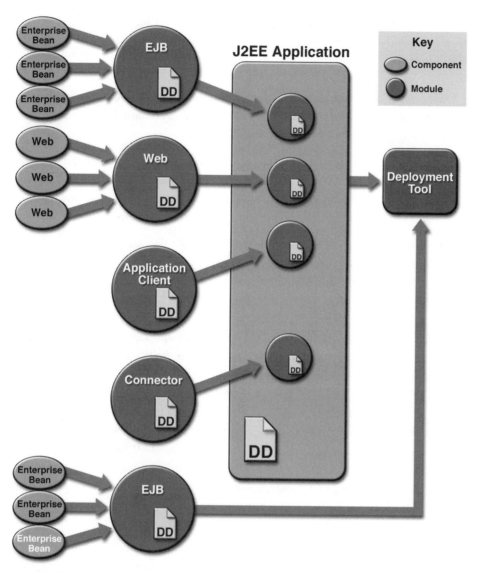

Figure 7.2   J2EE Packages

The following sections discuss the different types of J2EE modules and give some heuristic rules and practical tips on how best to package different component types.

7.3.1   EJB Modules

An EJB module is packaged and deployed as an EJB JAR file, a JAR file with a `.jar` extension. It is the smallest deployable and usable unit of enterprise beans. An EJB module contains:

- Java class files for the enterprise beans and their remote and home interfaces. Each entity bean requires that the EJB module also contain the bean's primary key class.

- Java class files for any classes and interfaces that the enterprise bean code depends on that are not included with the J2EE platform. This may include superclasses and superinterfaces, and the transitive closure of classes and interfaces used as method parameters, results, and exceptions.

- An EJB deployment descriptor that provides both the structural and application assembly information for the enterprise beans in the EJB module. The application assembly information is optional and is typically included only with assembled applications.

An EAR file differs from a standard JAR file in one key aspect: It includes a deployment descriptor (called `META-INF/ejb-jar.xml`) that contains meta-information about one or more enterprise beans.

In addition to the EJB JAR file for server-side use, an EJB JAR file producer should create a client JAR file containing all class files that a client program needs to access the enterprise beans contained in the EJB JAR file. Server-side component implementation classes are not included in a client JAR file.

A class may be included in an EJB JAR file or client JAR file either by direct inclusion of a class file, or by external reference to some other JAR file in the same J2EE application.

7.3.2   EJB Module Packaging Guidelines

These guidelines cover how to group EJB components into useful modules and provide pointers on packaging EJB modules.

7.3.2.1   Packaging Components into EJB Modules

A typical enterprise application contains many enterprise beans. Some of these enterprise beans may be off-the-shelf components, while others may use third-party libraries. The application assembler, therefore, must choose from the following packaging options:

1. Package each enterprise bean for an application in its own EJB module. In this approach, each enterprise bean has its own deployment descriptor and is packaged in one EJB module along with its dependent classes. One advantage of this approach is that it maximizes reusability of each enterprise bean by leaving the application assembler free to pick and choose among these EJB modules to compose additional J2EE applications. This option is recommended if your enterprise beans are each highly reusable. In such a case, the application assemblers will be able to reuse precisely those enterprise beans that they wish to reuse, and no more.

2. Package all enterprise beans for an application in one EJB module. In this approach, all enterprise beans and their dependent classes are packaged together in one EJB module. This approach is the simplest to implement. The application assembler does not have to specify references to the enterprise beans present in this EJB module as unresolved. This makes the job of application assemblers easier. Application assemblers who only wish to use a subset of the enterprise beans in the EJB module will still be able to do so, but may end up with a bloated application. The deployer in this case may have to deploy superfluous enterprise beans.

3. Package all related (closely-coupled) enterprise beans for an application in one EJB module. In this approach, all off-the-shelf components are used as is (that is, in their own EJB modules). All in-house enterprise beans are grouped based on their functional nature and put in one EJB module. For example, all enterprise beans related to account management can be put in one EJB module.

The third option is more modular and thus is recommended for most J2EE applications. It strikes the right balance between maximum reusability (option 1) and maximum simplicity (option 2). It promotes the black-box use of third-party components, which is especially important in the case where those components are digitally signed (although this is not a requirement of the J2EE platform). Another value of the third option arises when a J2EE server deploys each EJB module on a separate Java virtual machine for load balancing. In such cases, the third option is most efficient since it groups closely-coupled enterprise beans together, allowing many remote calls to be optimized to local calls. Another advantage of option 3 is that it promotes reusability at the functional level rather than at the enterprise bean level. For example, making a single Account enterprise bean reusable is more difficult than providing a reusable set of classes that provide account management functionality collectively. Logical grouping also makes sense from a tool point of view. A deployment or assembly tool may show the EJB module as a group under a single icon. The following discussions provide guidelines on various ways to group enterprise beans.

7.3.2.1.1 Grouping by Related Functionality

A group of enterprise beans that is packaged into the same EJB module may not easily be separated without knowing significant implementation details of each enterprise bean. To reuse one bean from an EJB module, you must generally deploy the entire module, including beans that you don't use. It thus makes good sense to package together a group of enterprise beans only if they will be commonly deployed and used together.

All utility classes used by a bean may be packaged into the EJB module of that bean. But redundant copies of utility classes increase the virtual machine size of most J2EE implementations and may cause potential conflicts during upgrades. Packaging related beans together reduces the number of copies of utility classes in memory. For these reasons, it is recommended that utility classes used by only one bean be packaged within the same EJB JAR file as that bean. Utility classes that are shared between modules should be packaged into utility JAR files and accessed referentially by their clients.

Grouping related beans in functional packages makes components easier to use with development tools. J2EE application assembly tools commonly display EJB modules in a palette of reusable components. Tools also typically visually group together enterprise beans from the same EJB module. For example, when server-side components related to accounting are grouped in a single code library or EJB module, they show up as accounting components in the development user interface.

7.3.2.1.2 Grouping Interrelated Beans

Enterprise beans can call one another at runtime, and one enterprise bean can delegate some of its functionality to another. Though some J2EE servers will support highly efficient cross-application dependencies, enterprise beans that depend on one another should be grouped together in the same JAR file for both organizational and performance reasons. In particular, all local beans that refer to one another should be packaged in the same JAR file.

Where beans call one another, an EJB module may be delivered preassembled, with all the enterprise bean cross-references resolved within the same unit. This makes the tasks of both the assembler and the deployer much easier. Locating an appropriate accounting bean for use by a teller bean across a number of servers may prove tedious, despite the best efforts and user interface wizardry of the authors of a J2EE deployment tool. Where one bean delegates to another, many servers will partition deployed EJB modules across different process and even machine boundaries. A bean that makes frequent calls to another bean in a separate address space can cause performance problems.

7.3.2.1.3 Grouping for Circular References

When two enterprise beans refer to each other, the result is a circular dependency. Neither bean can function without the other, and so neither is reusable without the other. In some cases redesign may eliminate these dependencies. When circular references are necessary, you should also package the components together in the same EJB module to ensure reusability.

7.3.2.1.4 Grouping with Common Security Profiles

While each EJB module allows a number of abstract security roles to be specified, enterprise beans are often written with a discrete set of users in mind. Enterprise beans that have the same security profile should be grouped together to keep security role names consistent.

7.3.2.2   Local Interfaces in the JNDI Namespace

Many EJB implementations expose enterprise bean home interfaces at defined, vendor-specific places in the Java Naming and Directory Interface (JNDI) namespace. A vendor-specific auxiliary deployment descriptor then usually binds the component's `ejb-name` (a component's application-global symbolic name) to its JNDI name (the name of the actual component).

But because there is no need for remote access to local interfaces, local home interfaces need not be exposed in the global JNDI namespace. While the component may look up local home interfaces using JNDI, and receive valid results, the container is not required to expose local beans anywhere in the JNDI namespace. Instead, the container implements all JNDI lookups of local interfaces, returning an appropriate object on request.

7.3.2.3   EJB Module Deployment Recommendations

This section provides a few minor defensive deployment recommendations for EJB modules.

Enterprise bean classes may have public methods that aren't declared in the bean's home and component interfaces. Deployment descriptors should not indicate transaction or security attributes for such methods. An EJB container cannot provide transactional behavior or enforce security constraints on such methods, because it can interpose only on public component or home interface method invocations.

Occasionally the primary key class for an entity bean using container-managed persistence will be either undefined or unknown to the component provider. In such cases, set the `prim-key-class` deployment descriptor element for the entity bean to `java.lang.Object`.

Some entity beans simply wrap a layer of functionality around existing enterprise data, managing and updating that data with container-managed persistence. Deployers should be certain that undeploying such beans does not cause the table representing the beans to be dropped, unless that behavior is what is desired. Likewise, the same component may be used in multiple places in an application; for example, `ContactInfo` for both `Customer` and `Supplier` components. When such beans use container-managed persistence, the deployer should consider whether all instances of the component should be stored in one table or multiple tables and configure the persistence behavior accordingly. A deployer can typically control these features by using vendor-specific deployment information (see Section 7.5.2.1 on page 245).

7.3.3   Web Modules

A Web module is packaged and deployed as a Web archive (WAR) file, a JAR file with a `.war` extension. It is the smallest deployable and usable unit of Web resources. A Web module contains:

- Java class files for the servlets and the classes that they depend on, optionally packaged as a library JAR file

- JSP pages and their helper Java classes

- Static documents (for example, HTML, images, sound files, and so on)

- Applets and their class files

- A Web deployment descriptor

Unlike other deployment unit types, a WAR file usually cannot be loaded by a classloader, because its internal directory structure differs from that of a loadable JAR file (see Section 7.3.4.2 on page 216). Like other module types, a WAR file may be deployed independently as a Web application or packaged in an EAR file and deployed as a J2EE application.

7.3.4   Packaging Components into Web Modules

The Web module is the smallest indivisible unit of Web resources that an application component provider supplies to the application assembler. This section contains guidelines for how to package Web-tier components into Web modules.

7.3.4.1   Request Path Elements

Understanding how Web application components map into a server address space requires an understanding of the structure of a request Uniform Resource Identifier (URI). The URI representing a request to a Web component is called a *request path*. After the protocol and hostname, a request URI has the following components:

- The *context path* locates the Web application in the Web server's namespace at deployment time. It can be thought of as the path to the "root directory" of a Web application (called the *context root*), relative to the root of the Web server namespace. A context path is always either empty (meaning that the root of the Web application is the root of the Web server namespace) or it both begins with a slash and does not end with one.

- The *servlet path* is the part of the URI that matched the servlet mapping for the request. It appears directly after the context path and never begins with a slash.

- The *path info* is any part of the request URI that is not part of the context path or the servlet path that follows the server path but precedes the query string. The HTTP GET query string, for example, typically appears as path info. Path info may be empty.

For example, consider the following request URI:

```
http://localhost/webapps/sample_app/jsp/Login.jsp/foo?uid=123
```

If the servlet mapping pattern that matched this request is jsp/*.jsp, then the context path is /webapps/sample_app, the servlet path is jsp/Login.jsp, and the path info is foo. Except for URL encoding details, a valid request URI is always a context path, followed by a servlet path, followed by path info.

The deployer maps the context root of a Web application into a Web server's namespace using vendor-specific tools. The servlet specification does not define a mechanism for this mapping.

7.3.4.2   Web Application Directory Structure

The Java Servlet specification defines a mandatory directory structure for a Web application deployment unit. This structure is defined in Section 9.4 of the Java Servlet specification, version 2.3. The Web application directory structure applies to the internal structure of a WAR file. The Java Servlet specification recommends, but does not require, that this same structure also be used as a runtime representation. Figure 7.3 shows this structure graphically.

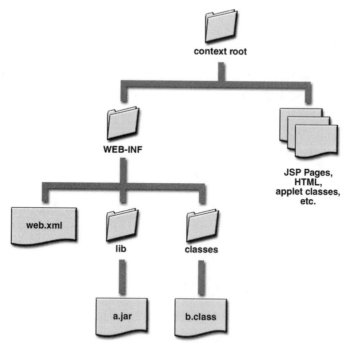

Figure 7.3   Web Application Directory Structure

The root directory of the Web application is the context root, which is mapped to the context path at deployment time. The context root contains the application's JSP pages, content, graphics, applet classes, and other files that the application serves to clients. These files are shown on the right in Figure 7.3.

Also under the context root is the WEB-INF directory, which contains files that are not intended to be served to clients. The WEB-INF directory has a specific structure, and has the following contents:

- The *deployment descriptor* file, called web.xml

- A directory called *lib*, which contains JAR files that will automatically be added to application components' classpath at runtime. Third-party libraries often reside in this directory.

- A directory called *classes*, which contains any classes needed by the application that are not in a JAR file. Such classes must be organized in directories by package, as usual.

Both the context root and WEB-INF may contain other files and directories in addition to those that are required. Files and directories in WEB-INF are accessible to Web components such as servlets and JSP pages, but can never be accessed directly by clients. Sensitive files, such as configuration files and security descriptors, should reside in the WEB-INF directory to protect them from unauthorized access by clients. Web-tier components may access these files using the methods ServletContext.getResource or ServletContext.getResourceAsStream.

Because servlet classes, servlet filter classes, tag libraries, and server-side utility classes are never served to clients, they should always reside either in JAR files in WEB-INF/lib or as class files in WEB-INF/classes. The BluePrints best practice for such classes is to package them into JAR files in WEB-INF/lib for ease of management.

7.3.4.3   Hyperlinks within a Web Module

Hyperlinks in a Web application should reference pages or components within the same module using relative, rather than absolute, paths. Using absolute URLs in paths assumes a fixed context path. If the context path changes for some reason, every absolute URL in the application will also need to be changed. For example, a component or static page that references another page in the same module using path ../help/purchasing.html will work correctly regardless of the value of the context path. By contrast, a link that used path /myapp/help/purchasing.html in a link would require changes if the context path were ever changed from /myapp to some other value.

Legacy content may include absolute URLs. URLs for legacy content often can be mapped into a Web application's namespace using a Web server's proprietary aliasing features.

7.3.4.4   Decoupling Application Components

Web components may directly invoke one another via HTTP, creating dependencies between components and applications. To avoid these dependencies, components that call one another should be packaged in the same Web module and deployed together.

Sometimes calling components between applications is unavoidable. Unfortunately, hard-coding a path to a component in another application makes the referencing application dependent on the context path of the referenced application. For example, if a servlet mapped to /apps/myStore/servlets/orderServlet invokes a servlet at /apps/warehouseApp/servlets/checkInventory, then application myStore requires that application warehouseApp be available at context path /apps/warehouseApp. If that context path changes, application myStore will require a code modification to operate properly.

Dependencies of a component on its environment should always be explicit. The BluePrints best practice for accessing components between applications is to externalize the dependency by using environment entries in the deployment descriptor instead of hard-coding paths to external components. In the example above, an application component provider could define an environment entry in the Web application's deployment descriptor, as shown in Code Example 7.3.

```
<env-entry>
    <description>
        Path to the warehouse checkInventory service
    </description>
    <env-entry-name>warehouseCheckInventory</env-entry-name>
    <env-entry-value>
        /apps/warehouseApp/servlets/checkInventory
    </env-entry-value>
    <env-entry-type>java.lang.String</env-entry-type>
</env-entry>
```

Code Example 7.3   Externalizing a Dependency between Applications

Any component of the myStore application could then access the inventory service indirectly by looking up its path in the environment entry.

```
InitialContext ctx = new InitialContext();
String invPath = (String)ctx.lookup("java:comp/env/warehouseCheck-
Inventory");
// ... invoke servlet using invPath...
```

Code Example 7.4   Accessing Another Application Indirectly

When the `myStore` application is deployed, a deployer ensures that the `env-entry-value` for the environment entry corresponds to a valid path. The application `myStore` accesses application `inventoryApp` indirectly through deployment information, so the dependency can be managed without changes to application code.

7.3.4.5   Cross-Linked Static Content

Cross-linked Web pages must be packaged in a single Web module to avoid broken links. Moreover, cross-linked HTML Web pages are typically reusable as a bundle, so it makes sense to package them together. As recommended in Section 7.3.4.3, the best practice is to use relative paths where possible for static content.

One way to make absolute URLs independent of context path is to use JSP pages with a custom action for linking. At runtime, the custom action can generate an HTML a tag with an `href` attribute that includes the context path.

```
<%@ taglib uri="http://java.sun.com/j2ee/blueprints/sampletags"
prefix="newtag" %>

This hyperlink is portable: <newtag:alink href="/a/b/c.html">Link
Here</newtag:alink>
```

Code Example 7.5   Using A Custom Action for Context Path Independence

Code Example 7.5 is an example of a JSP page that uses a custom tag called `alink`, which outputs an HTML a tag with the context path prepended to its `href` attribute value.

```
public int doStartTag() {
    HttpServletRequest req =
        (HttpServletRequest)pageContext.getRequest();
    String contextPath = req.getContextPath();
    try {
        pageContext.getOut().println(
            "<a href=\"" + contextPath + href + "\">");
    } catch (Exception e) { ... }
        return EVAL_BODY_INCLUDE;
    }
```

```
    public int doEndTag() {
        JspWriter out = pageContext.getOut();
        try { pageContext.getOut().println("</a>");
        } catch (Exception e) { ... }
        return EVAL_PAGE;
    }
}
```

Code Example 7.6   Tag Handler for Context Path-Independent Hyperlinks

Method `doStartTag` in Code Example 7.6 builds a URL from the context path from the `pageContext` and the value of the `alink` tag's `href` attribute. It outputs an HTML a tag with `href` set to the constructed URL. Method `doEndTag` simply closes the a tag. Code Example 7.7 shows the result of serving the JSP page.

```
This hyperlink is portable: <a href="/the/context/path/a/b/c.html">
Link Here</a>
```

Code Example 7.7   Result of JSP Page

The string `/the/context/path` in Code Example 7.7 is the context path inserted by the custom action's tag handler class `ALink`. Small to medium amounts of Web content that do not change often can easily be converted to JSP pages that manage the context path portably.

7.3.4.6   Logical Grouping of Functionality

A Web module that has a clearly defined purpose is easier to reuse in different scenarios than one with less well-defined overall behavior. For example, a well-designed Web module concerned purely with inventory management can be reused in many e-commerce applications that need inventory management capability. Such a module would be ideal for adding a Web-based interface for inventory management to the sample application.

7.3.4.7   Utility Libraries

In general, it is good practice to group utility classes into libraries, include those libraries in an application EAR file, and access them by reference from Web-tier components. This technique avoids unnecessary code duplication in the deployed application. All such libraries in a Web component deployment unit must be in the directory WEB-INF/lib. The J2EE 1.3 Specification section J2EE.8.2 explains how to access classes from JAR files in a J2EE application.

7.3.4.8   Accessing EJB Components from Web Components

When a Web component uses enterprise beans, package the EJB component's client EJB jar in the Web archive's WEB-INF/lib directory. Putting the client EJB jar in this directory places the files in that JAR in the Web container's classpath. Avoid mixing Web components and EJB components in the same JAR file, because doing so makes reuse impossible. Instead, package each Web application that provides a specific service in an individual WAR file, then create J2EE application EAR files by combining Web modules (WAR files) with EJB client JAR files.

When packaging, keep in mind that Web components that use local interfaces must reside within the same J2EE application EAR file as the enterprise beans that implement those interfaces.

7.3.5   Application Client Modules

Application client modules are packaged in JAR files with a .jar extension. Application client modules contain:

- Java classes that implement the client
- An application client deployment descriptor

An application client uses a client JAR file created by the EJB JAR file producer. The client JAR file consists of all the class files that a client program needs to access the enterprise beans in an EJB module.

7.3.6 Resource Adapter Modules

A Java Connector is packaged and deployed as a resource adapter archive (RAR) file, a JAR file with a `.rar` extension. It is the smallest deployable and usable unit of a Java Connector. A resource adapter module contains:

- Java class files for the classes and interfaces that implement both the Connector architecture contracts and the resource adapter itself, packaged as one or more JAR files

- Resource adapter utility classes

- Platform-dependent, native support libraries for the resource adapter

- Help files and documentation

- A resource adapter deployment descriptor

A resource adapter module requires a native support library compatible with each platform it supports to implement the platform-specific parts of the resource adapter. Note also that the support classes and interfaces for a resource adapter must be packaged as a JAR file within the RAR file. See the J2EE Connector Architecture Specification for details.

7.4 Deployment Descriptors

Deployment descriptors describe the contents of deployment units and configure components and applications to their environment. They also externalize the relationships between components, so those relationships can be managed without writing or changing program code. Deployment tools usually automatically generate deployment descriptors, so you do not have to edit and manage them directly.

There are five types of deployment descriptors, each of which corresponds to a type of deployment unit:

- EJB deployment descriptors are defined in the Enterprise JavaBeans specification.

- Web deployment descriptors are defined in the Java Servlet specification.

- Application and application client deployment descriptors are both defined in the J2EE platform specification.

- Resource adapter deployment descriptors for Java Connectors are defined by the J2EE Connector architecture specification.

Each deployment descriptor type is defined in its corresponding specification as an XML Document Type Definition (DTD).

Deployment descriptors contain information used by a component's container and also contain information that the component can access directly by way of the JNDI. The JNDI is a standard interface to an enterprise object name service.

7.4.1   J2EE Naming Environment

J2EE containers provide their components with a *naming environment*, which the component uses to look up client components, resources, and configuration information by name.

A component's deployment descriptor both specifies and resolves the explicit dependencies between the component and its environment. A component provider must declare any names a component uses in the component's deployment descriptor. An application assembler and/or deployer resolves each name by setting its value in a deployment descriptor. At runtime, a component instance looks up the resource or configuration information using a JNDI naming context provided by the container.

The JNDI naming context is the component's API for accessing the naming environment. To avoid collision with names of other enterprise resources in JNDI, and to avoid portability problems, all names in a J2EE application should begin with the string java:comp/env. Because all instances of a particular application component share naming environment entries, components may not change values in the naming context.

The naming context serves two general purposes: It provides parameters for component behavior and it decouples components from resources and from each other.

7.4.1.0.1 Parameterized Component Behavior

When a component is written in terms of parameters in the naming environment, its behavior can be changed externally instead of by changing code. A component provider can write component code whose behavior depends on the value of an *environment entry*, which is a named value defined by the component provider in the component's deployment descriptor. The assembler and/or deployer customizes the component's behavior by setting the environment entry's value.

An example of a component customized by an environment entry appears in Section 7.4.2.1.1.

Using environment entries to create configurable components is a BluePrints best practice. Parameterized components are more flexible than those that require code changes to modify behavior.

7.4.1.0.2 Decoupling Components and Resources

The naming environment's second purpose is to provide components with access to other components and resources by name, instead of directly. Decoupling components from one another provides two major benefits. First, a component's implementation can change with no impact on components referring to it, as long as the referenced component's public interface does not change. Second, because component instances are always accessed through a home interface rather than created by direct construction, the container can interpose on method calls and manage the component instance life cycle.

Users in different roles each use the naming environment in a different way. The component provider writes code that looks up components and resources by name in the naming environment, and declares usage of that name in the referencing component's deployment descriptor. The assembler and/or deployer configures the name to correspond to an object in the target environment, binding the name to a component or resource.

For examples of decoupling component code from other components, see Section 7.4.2.1.2. An example of decoupling component code from resources appears in Section 7.4.2.1.3.

The J2EE platform specification requires that components access one another and all external resources by way of the naming environment instead of loading component and connection factory classes directly. Decoupling components from resources and from each other lets the container make efficient decisions about how components access one another. Decoupling components from their resources provides deployment flexibility because each resource's implementation can be changed with no changes to component code.

7.4.2   Specifying Deployment Descriptor Elements

This section describes how to define specific deployment descriptor elements. It begins by describing elements common to all component types, and then covers elements specific to enterprise beans and Web components.

7.4.2.1   Common Elements

There are deployment descriptor elements common across the different J2EE component types. These include environment entries, references to enterprise beans, references to connection factories, references to resources in the environment, and security-related elements.

7.4.2.1.1 Declaring Environment Entries

Environment entries allow customization of a component during deployment or assembly without the need to access or change the component's source code.

Customization requires cooperation between developer roles. A component provider writes component code whose behavior depends on the value of an environment entry, then defines the environment entry name and type in the component's deployment descriptor. An application assembler or deployer sets the environment entry's value to configure component behavior without changing the source code. An application assembler may set some environment entries to configure components for an application. A deployer may change values previously assigned by component providers and/or application assemblers to configure the application to its environment. The deployer must ensure that the values of all the environment entries declared by a component are set to meaningful values. The application component provider or application assembler may include a <description> element in each environment entry to help the deployer with this task. Description elements also commonly appear as help text in deployment tools.

Environment entries are declared with the env-entry element. Code Example 7.8 uses an environment entry to determine whether to send confirmation e-mail when an order is processed. Code Example 7.9 shows how to set the value of the environment entry.

```
public static boolean getSendConfirmationMail() {
    boolean boolVal = false;
    try {
        InitialContext ic = new InitialContext();
        Boolean bool = (Boolean)
            ic.lookup(
                "java:comp/env/ejb/CRMmail/SendConfirmationMail");
        if (bool != null) {
            boolVal = bool.booleanValue();
        }
    } catch (NamingException ne) {
```

```
        ...
    }
    return boolVal;
}
```

Code Example 7.8   Looking up a Naming Environment Entry

```
<env-entry>
    <description>
        If true, customer receives confirmation e-mail
        when an order is received
    </description>
    <env-entry-name>CRMmail/sendConfirmationMail</env-entry-name>
    <env-entry-type>java.lang.Boolean</env-entry-type>
    <env-entry-value>false</env-entry-value>
</env-entry>
```

Code Example 7.9   Environment Entry Element

7.4.2.1.2 Declaring and Resolving References to Enterprise Beans

J2EE components look up enterprise bean home interface references by name using JNDI. The deployment descriptors of both the referencing and referenced beans link the two beans together.

A component (an enterprise bean or Web-tier component) looks up an enterprise bean with JNDI using a *logical name*, which is the referencing component's local name for the reference. The application component provider indicates the lookup dependency by declaring all logical names used by a component in that component's deployment descriptor. Each enterprise bean in the application has an ejb-name, which is a global identifying name assigned by the application assembler. The application assembler resolves lookup dependencies by mapping logical names to ejb-names in the referencing component's deployment descriptor.

Code Example 7.10 through Code Example 7.12, taken from the sample application, illustrate how deployment descriptors link together a reference from a component to the referenced bean's home interface. Figure 7.4 graphically demonstrates the relationships between these code samples.

In Code Example 7.10, ShoppingClientControllerEJB performs a JNDI lookup of logical name java:comp/env/ejb/cart. (In other words, it looks up cart in the ejb subcontext of the environment naming context java:comp/env.)

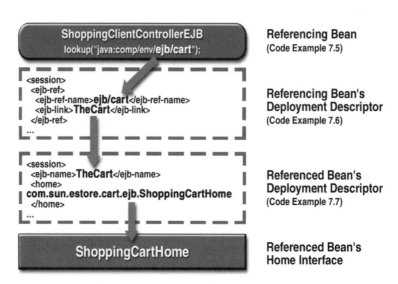

Figure 7.4   An Enterprise Bean Reference Resolves to a Home Interface

Code Example 7.11 shows part of the deployment descriptor for the referencing bean (ShoppingClientControllerEJB) that resolves the lookup of ejb/cart. The component provider declares and names an enterprise bean reference, using an ejb-ref-name element within an ejb-ref element. The reference's logical name is ejb/cart (relative to java:comp/env). The application assembler resolves the lookup dependency by adding an ejb-link element to the ejb-ref element, binding that lookup to the ejb-name TheCart.

Code Example 7.12 is an excerpt from the ShoppingCart bean's deployment descriptor. A session element declares the enterprise bean, and an ejb-name element within the session element defines the bean's ejb-name (TheCart). Among other things, the session element declares the bean's home interface class.

Figure 7.4 shows a direct mapping from a home interface name to the actual home interface; in J2EE implementations, the map from an ejb-name to the actual component is vendor-specific. For example, the J2EE reference implementation maps the ejb-name to the JNDI name of the bean's actual home interface in a separate XML file containing vendor-specific deployment information. See Section 7.5.2.1 on page 245 for an example and additional explanation.

An application assembler is usually the role that chooses ejb-names and binds them to logical names (with ejb-link), because the application assembler usually handles tying components together into applications. The deployer must ensure that all enterprise bean ejb-ref references are resolved (using ejb-link) to valid ejb-name elements in the referenced bean's deployment descriptor. Deployment verification tools can check that all such references are consistent.

```java
public class ShoppingClientControllerEJB implements SessionBean {
    public ShoppingCart getShoppingCart() {
        if (cart == null) {
            try {
                ShoppingCartHome cartHome =
                    EJBUtil.getShoppingCartHome();
                cart = cartHome.create();
            } catch (CreateException ce) {
                ...
            }
        }
        return cart;
    }
}


public static ShoppingCartHome getShoppingCartHome() {
    try {
        InitialContext initial = new InitialContext();
        Object objref = initial.lookup("java:comp/env/ejb/cart");
        return (ShoppingCartHome) PortableRemoteObject.
            narrow(objref, ShoppingCartHome.class);
    } catch (NamingException ne) {
        throw new GeneralFailureException(ne);
    }
}
```

Code Example 7.10 Looking Up a Home Interface by a Logical Name

```
<session>
    <ejb-name>TheShoppingClientController</ejb-name>
    <home>com.sun.estore.control.ejb.
        ShoppingClientControllerHome</home>
    ...
    <ejb-ref>
        <ejb-ref-name>ejb/cart</ejb-ref-name>
        <ejb-link>TheCart</ejb-link>
        <ejb-ref-type>Session</ejb-ref-type>
        <home>com.sun.blueprints.cart.ejb.ShoppingCartHome</home>
        <remote>com.sun.blueprints.cart.ejb.ShoppingCart</remote>
    </ejb-ref>
    ...
</session>
```

Code Example 7.11   Declaring and Resolving an Enterprise Bean Reference

```
<session>
    <display-name>TheCart</display-name>
    <ejb-name>TheCart</ejb-name>
    <home>com.sun.blueprints.cart.ejb.ShoppingCartHome</home>
    <remote>com.sun.blueprints.cart.ejb.ShoppingCart</remote>
    <ejb-class>com.sun.blueprints.cart.ejb.ShoppingCartEJB</ejb-
class>
    <session-type>Stateful</session-type>
    <transaction-type>Container</transaction-type>
</session>
```

Code Example 7.12   Defining the Referenced Bean's `ejb-name`

While this mechanism may at first seem complicated, it provides the required late binding between application components. The referencing bean's deployment descriptor both declares an explicitly named dependency of the bean on its environment and resolves that dependency by providing the `ejb-name` of the referenced bean. The referenced bean's deployment descriptor defines the global `ejb-name` that serves as the reference target.

An enterprise bean that is a target of `ejb-link` can be in the same EJB module or in another EJB module within the same J2EE application. The target enterprise bean must be type-compatible with the declared enterprise bean reference. This means that the target enterprise bean must be of the type indicated in the `ejb-ref-type` element and that the `home` and `remote` elements of the target enterprise bean must be type-compatible with the `home` and `remote` elements declared in the enterprise bean reference.

Always define all external resource references in a component's deployment descriptor. Even if your platform implementation indicates the JNDI name for a resource, the container is required by the specification to provide access only if the resource reference is declared in the deployment descriptor. Accessing JNDI objects without declaring them as external references may work for some implementations, but such behavior is not portable, and is not guaranteed to work properly. This advice also applies to environment resource references and EJB references (see the next section), and to all J2EE module types.

7.4.2.1.3 Declaring References to Connection Factories

A connection factory is an object that creates connections to a resource manager. For example, an object that implements the `javax.sql.DataSource` interface is a connection factory for `java.sql.Connection` objects, which are connections to database management systems.

Declaration and resolution of connection factory references is similar to declaration and resolution of enterprise beans. A component provider declares a lookup of a connection factory using a `resource-ref` element in the referencing component's deployment descriptor and gives the reference a logical name (that is, the name by which the component looks up the connection factory) using a `res-ref-name` element. This allows the component module consumer (that is, application assembler or deployer) to discover all the connection factory references used by the component. The component provider also indicates the type of the connection factory, not the type of connection the factory produces. For example, a JDBC connection factory's type is `DataSource`, not `Connection`.

The deployer must bind the connection factory references to the actual resource factories configured in the target environment. The details of how to accomplish this binding are specific to the implementation. For example, in the J2EE reference implementation, a deployer uses the JNDI `LinkRef` mechanism to create a symbolic link to the actual JNDI name of the connection factory, which is defined by the container. The deployer must also provide any additional configuration information that the resource manager needs to open and manage the resource.

Code Example 7.13 illustrates the mail connection factory reference in the entry for the `Mailer` enterprise bean.

```
<session>
    <display-name>TheMailer</display-name>
    <ejb-name>TheMailer</ejb-name>
    <home>com.sun.blueprints.mail.ejb.MailerHome</home>
    <remote>com.sun.blueprints.mail.ejb.Mailer</remote>
    ...
    <resource-ref>
        <res-ref-name>mail/MailSession</res-ref-name>
        <res-type>javax.mail.Session</res-type>
        <res-auth>Container</res-auth>
    </resource-ref>
</session>
```

Code Example 7.13 Connection Factory Reference Element

Note that the connection factory type must be compatible with the type declared in the `res-type` element. The `res-auth` subelement of the `resource-ref` element specifies whether resource sign on is managed by an application component or by its container. See Section 6.4.5.1 on page 196 for more information on resource sign on.

The `Mailer` enterprise bean calls `MailHelper` to open a mail session. Code Example 7.14 contains the code from the `MailHelper` class that requests a mail session object declared as java:comp/env/mail/MailSession in the JNDI context.

```
public void createAndSendMail(String to, String subject,
                             String htmlContents) {
    try {
        InitialContext ic = new InitialContext();
        Session session = (Session) ic.
            lookup("java:comp/env/mail/MailSession");
        ...
```

```
    }
  }
```

Code Example 7.14 Looking Up a Connection Factory

By default, enterprise beans in the same transaction context may share connections. Where possible, it is good practice to allow the application server to optimize efficiency by sharing connections. In some cases, sharing can cause incorrect component behavior; for example, a connection may be session-based, requiring sign on or maintaining state that might be interfered with by other components. In these cases, turn off connection sharing by setting the connection factory's `res-sharing-scope` deployment descriptor element to `Unshareable`.

7.4.2.1.4 Declaring Resource Environment References

Resource environment references are like connection factory references, except that the logical name resolves to the actual resource instead of resolving to a factory that creates connections to the resource. An application component provider declares references to resources in the environment using a `resource-env-ref` element in the referencing component's deployment descriptor. The application component provider defines the reference's logical name (using `resource-ref-env-name`) and type (using `resource-ref-env-type`).

The deployer binds the resource environment reference to the actual resource in the container. As for connection factories, the mechanism for associating resource environment references with actual resources is vendor-specific.

For example, the sample application includes a Web service that sends purchase orders to suppliers based on incoming orders. Code Example 7.15, derived from the sample application, shows code of a message-driven enterprise bean looking up a message queue to which the component sends purchase orders. Notice that the queue's logical name is in JNDI subcontext `java:comp/env/jms`, because the resource is a JMS Queue. Code Example 7.16 shows the part of the message-driven bean's deployment descriptor that declares and names the resource environment reference. The actual runtime resolution of the resource reference is performed by the container in an implementation-specific way.

```
String spqName = "ja-
va:comp/env/jms/SUPPLIER_PURCHASE_ORDER_QUEUE";
InitialContext ic = new InitialContext();
Queue supplierPoQueue = (Queue)ic.lookup(spqName);
```

Code Example 7.15   Looking Up a Resource Environment Reference

```
<message-driven>
    <ejb-name>ORDER_APPROVAL_MDB_QUEUE</ejb-name>
    ...
    <resource-env-ref>
        <resource-env-ref-name>
            jms/SUPPLIER_PURCHASE_ORDER_QUEUE
        </resource-env-ref-name>
        <resource-env-ref-type>
            javax.jms.Queue
        </resource-env-ref-type>
    </resource-env-ref>
</message-driven>
```

Code Example 7.16   Declaring a Resource Environment Reference

7.4.2.1.5 Security Elements

An application component provider uses the `security-role` element to define logical security roles that can be assumed by an authenticated principal. Code Example 7.17 illustrates how the sample application defines the `gold_customer` security role.

```
<security-role>
    <role-name>gold_customer</role-name>
</security-role>
```

Code Example 7.17   Security Role Element

The `security-role-ref` element is used to link a role name used by the method `isCallerInRole` with a security role. In the sample application, this method is used by the `Order` entity bean to enforce business rules based on whether the user is a preferred customer.

Code Example 7.18 and Code Example 7.19 illustrate how the `security-role-ref` element establishes a link between the string `GOLD_CUSTOMER` used by method `isCallerInRole` to the security role named `gold_customer`.

```
private int getBonusMiles() {
    int miles = (totalPrice >= 100) ? 1000 : 500;
    if (context.isCallerInRole("GOLD_CUSTOMER"))
        miles += 1000;
    return miles;
}
```

Code Example 7.18   Referencing a Security Role Name

```
<security-role-ref>
    <role-name>GOLD_CUSTOMER</role-name>
    <role-link>gold_customer</role-link>
</security-role-ref>
```

Code Example 7.19   Linking a Security Role Name and Security Role

An application component provider declaratively controls access to an enterprise bean's methods by specifying the `method-permission` element in the enterprise bean's deployment descriptor. The component provider defines this element to list the set of methods that can be accessed by each security role. The authorization scenario described in Section 9.3.8 on page 302 illustrates how `method-permission` elements affect the execution of enterprise bean methods.

7.4.2.2   Enterprise Bean Elements

Enterprise beans have component-specific deployment descriptor elements for persistence and transaction control.

7.4.2.2.1 Transaction Elements

Transaction elements are deployment descriptor elements that control an enterprise bean's transactional behavior. An enterprise bean requires a transaction element that indicates whether the bean uses container- or bean-managed transaction demarcation. If transaction demarcation is container-managed, the bean's methods also have transaction attributes.

An application assembler must ensure that transaction attributes are defined for all methods of the deployed enterprise beans that use container-managed transaction demarcation. If the transaction attributes have not been assigned by the application component provider, they must be assigned by the application assembler. Code Example 7.20 illustrates how transaction attributes are declared for an Account entity bean. The container-transaction element for Account specifies that when method changeContactInformation is invoked, it must be within the scope of a transaction. See Section 8.6.3 on page 264 for detailed information about the values that a transaction attribute can take.

```
<container-transaction>
    <method>
        <ejb-name>TheAccount</ejb-name>
        <method-intf>Remote</method-intf>
        <method-name>changeContactInformation</method-name>
        <method-params>
            <method-param>
                com.sun.blueprints.util.ContactInformation
            </method-param>
        </method-params>
    </method>
    <trans-attribute>Required</trans-attribute>
</container-transaction>
```

Code Example 7.20   Transaction Elements

7.4.2.2.2 Persistence Elements

The application component provider must specify whether a bean manages its own persistence or uses container-managed persistence. When a bean uses container-managed persistence, the application component provider must specify the fields of the bean. Code Example 7.21 illustrates how the Account entity bean uses the persistence-type element to declare that it will manage its own persistence.

```
<entity>
    <description>Account of a shopper</description>
```

```
    <display-name>TheAccount</display-name>
    ...
    <persistence-type>Bean</persistence-type>
</entity>
```

Code Example 7.21 Persistence Element

7.4.2.3   Web Component Elements

Some of the more commonly used Web component deployment descriptor elements are discussed in this section.

7.4.2.3.1 Servlet

The one deployment descriptor element that *must* be specified for a Web component is the `servlet` element, shown in Code Example 7.22. This element associates a logical identifier (`servlet-name`) with the name of the servlet class or the JSP file associated with the component.

```
<servlet>
    <servlet-name>webTierEntryPoint</servlet-name>
    <display-name>HTML Client Front Controller Servlet
        </display-name>
    <description>no description</description>
<servlet-class>
    com.sun.j2ee.blueprints.waf.controller.web.MainServlet
    </servlet-class>
</servlet>
```

Code Example 7.22 `Servlet` Element

7.4.2.3.2 Servlet Mapping

The `servlet-mapping` element specifies the URLs that the Web component is aliased to handle. While the element is called `servlet-mapping`, it is used to map URLs to both servlets and JSP pages. Code Example 7.23 aliases `Main` servlet to handle all requests to the URL namespace `*.do`.

```
<servlet-mapping>
    <servlet-name>webTierEntryPoint</servlet-name>
    <url-pattern>/control/*</url-pattern>
</servlet-mapping>
```

Code Example 7.23 Servlet Mapping Element

7.4.2.3.3 Error Pages

The `error-page` element can be used to invoke an error page automatically when the Web application throws a Java language exception. Code Example 7.24 shows how to enable the J2EE server to send `errorpage.jsp` to the browser client if the Web application ever throws any exception of the type `java.lang.Exception` or its subclass.

```
<error-page>
    <exception-type>java.lang.Exception</exception-type>
    <location>/errorpage.jsp</location>
</error-page>
```

Code Example 7.24 Error Page Element

7.4.2.3.4 Form-Based Authentication Configuration

Form-based authentication is the preferred mechanism for authenticating application users in the J2EE platform. Code Example 7.25 illustrates how to configure a Web application to activate form-based authentication when the Web server receives a request for the URL /control/placeorder. The `security-constraint` element specifies that the URL /control/placeorder is a protected resource. The `login-config` element specifies that the URL formbasedloginscreen will be displayed when an unauthenticated user tries to access /control/placeorder. This page contains an HTML form that prompts for a user name and password.

```
<security-constraint>
    <web-resource-collection>
        <web-resource-name>MySecureBit0</web-resource-name>
        <description>no description</description>
        <url-pattern>/control/placeorder</url-pattern>
        <http-method>POST</http-method>
```

```
            <http-method>GET</http-method>
        </web-resource-collection>
        <auth-constraint>
            <description>no description</description>
            <role-name>gold_customer</role-name>
            <role-name>customer</role-name>
        </auth-constraint>
        <user-data-constraint>
            <description>no description</description>
            <transport-guarantee>NONE</transport-guarantee>
        </user-data-constraint>
    </security-constraint>
    <login-config>
        <auth-method>FORM</auth-method>
        <realm-name>default</realm-name>
        <form-login-config>
            <form-login-page>formbasedloginscreen</form-login-page>
            <form-error-page>formbasedloginerrorscreen
                </form-error-page>
        </form-login-config>
    </login-config>
```

Code Example 7.25 Form-Based Authentication Configuration

7.4.3 Naming Convention Recommendations

Logical names are the names a component uses to refer to external objects. For example, Code Example 7.10 (on page 230) looks up a home interface using a logical name, java:comp/env/ejb/cart, and Code Example 7.11, using ejb-link, binds that logical name to the ejb-name TheCart. Code Example 7.12 declares the shopping cart object and gives it the physical name TheCart.

Each component has its own scope for the logical names it uses, so components can use the same logical name to refer to different objects, and the references will not collide. For example, although a Customer bean and a Supplier bean might both look up an associated enterprise bean by the logical name ejb/Address, each would access a different bean if each reference were bound (with ejb-link) to a different element. Each time a component performs a lookup using the same name, the same object (or an equivalent one) is returned from the naming context.

There are few requirements or restrictions on the internal structure of logical names. Conventions for logical names help to organize references of different types and make it more clear to an application assembler or deployer just what sort of object she is dealing with.

7.4.3.0.1 Naming Environment Entries

The name of an environment entry should use the subcontext of the component it configures. Code Example 7.26 from the sample application shows that the environment entry `CatalogDAOClass` appears in JNDI subcontext `java:comp/env/ejb/catalog`, because this environment entry is specific to the `Catalog` enterprise bean. Environment entries that configure an application globally, or configure more than one component, may be placed in the `java:comp/env` subcontext.

```
<env-entry>
    <env-entry-name>ejb/catalog/CatalogDAOClass</env-entry-name>
    <env-entry-type>java.lang.String</env-entry-type>
    <env-entry-value>...</env-entry-value>
</env-entry>
```

Code Example 7.26   Environment Entry Declared for Enterprise Bean

7.4.3.0.2 Naming Enterprise Bean References

JNDI subcontext `java:comp/env/ejb` should be used for the logical names of all EJB references. An additional subcontext level that groups tightly-coupled beans may also be useful. Code Example 7.27 illustrates how the sample application uses the JNDI subcontext `java:comp/env/ejb/controller` to group the shopping client controller and the shopping facade beans, since these two beans are intimately related. Grouping related classes into subcontexts can clarify for the application assembler or deployer which enterprise beans work with or depend on each other.

```
<ejb-local-ref>
    <ejb-ref-name>
        ejb/controller/ShoppingClientController
    </ejb-ref-name>
```

```
        <ejb-ref-type>Session</ejb-ref-type>
        <local-home>...</local-home>
        ...
        <ejb-link>TheShoppingClientController</ejb-link>
    </ejb-local-ref>

    <ejb-local-ref>
        <ejb-ref-name>ejb/controller/ClientFacade</ejb-ref-name>
        <ejb-ref-type>Session</ejb-ref-type>
        <local-home>...</local-home>
        ...
        <ejb-link>TheShoppingClientFacade</ejb-link>
    </ejb-local-ref>
```

Code Example 7.27   Declaring and Naming EJB References

7.4.3.0.3 Naming Connection Factory References

The J2EE platform specification version 1.3 provides several guidelines for logical names for connection factory resource references. Consistent logical naming groups resources by resource manager type, making it clear to the application assembler or deployer what sort of resource needs to be configured for each reference. Table 7.1 shows recommended JNDI subcontexts for common J2EE resource connection factory types.

7.4.3.0.4 Naming Environment Resource References

Logical names for environment resource references should follow the same conventions as for connection factories. For example, JMS message destinations should be placed in the `java:comp/env/jms` subcontext.

Table 7.1 Recommended JNDI Subcontexts for Connection Factories

Resource Manager Type	Connection Factory Type(s)	JNDI Subcontext
JDBC	`javax.sql.DataSource`	`java:comp/env/jdbc`
JMS	`javax.jms.TopicConnectionFactory` `javax.jms.QueueConnectionFactory`	`java:comp/env/jms`
JavaMail	`javax.mail.Session`	`java:comp/env/mail`
URL	`java.net.URL`	`java:comp/env/url`
Connector	`javax.resource.cci.ConnectionFactory`	`java:comp/env/eis`

7.5 Deployment Tools

Although deployment can be configured directly by editing XML text files, the process is handled best by specialized tools such as the DeployTool provided with the J2EE SDK. This section describes the actions that a deployment tool performs and outlines requirements on packaging and development tools. The recommendations in the remainder of this chapter are intended primarily for J2EE product providers who distribute packaging and deployment tools with their products. Developers can better understand what to expect from such tools by understanding the recommendations.

7.5.1 Deployment Tool Actions

This section discusses what happens behind the scenes when a J2EE application is deployed on a J2EE server. Since many J2EE applications may be deployed on an individual J2EE server, J2EE servers typically register each application under a different identifier. The deployment of a J2EE application involves three different types of components: enterprise beans, Web components, and application clients.

For each enterprise bean, the J2EE server must perform the following tasks:

1. Generate and compile the stubs and skeletons for the enterprise bean.

2. Set up the security environment to host the enterprise bean according to its de-

ployment descriptor, enforcing the application's security policy on access to the enterprise bean's methods.

3. Set up the transaction environment for the enterprise bean according to its deployment descriptor. This is needed so that the calls to the methods of the enterprise bean happen in the correct transaction context.

4. Register the enterprise bean, its environment properties, resources references, and so on, in the JNDI namespace.

5. Create database tables for enterprise beans that use container-managed persistence.

For each Web component, the J2EE server must perform the following tasks:

1. Transfer the contents of the Web component underneath the context root of the server. Since there may be more than one J2EE application installed, the server may install each in a specific directory. For example, the J2EE SDK installs each application under a context root specified at deployment time. The sample application is installed in the `petstore` directory.

2. Initialize the security environment of the application. This involves configuring the form-based login mechanism, role-to-principal mappings, and so on.

3. Register environment properties, resource references, and EJB references in the JNDI namespace.

4. Set up the environment for the Web application. For example, it performs the alias mappings and configures the servlet context parameters.

5. Precompile JSP pages as specified in the deployment descriptor.

The tool used to deploy an application client, and the mechanism used to install the application client, are not specified by the J2EE specification. Very sophisticated J2EE products may allow the application client to be deployed on a J2EE server and automatically made available to some set of (usually intranet) clients. Other J2EE products may require the J2EE application bundle containing the application client to be manually deployed and installed on each client machine. Another approach would be for the deployment tool on the J2EE server to produce an installation package that could be taken to each client to install the application client. Java Web Start technology is recommended to manage installation and automatic upgrading of application client programs.

7.5.2   Deployment Tool Requirements

Deployment tools have different requirements during development and during production deployment. A developer's deployment needs are different than the needs of a deployer installing a production application on a mission-critical system.

When an application is being developed, it must be deployed before it can be tested. Developers want fast response times and the ability to undeploy, redeploy, and partially deploy applications easily and quickly. They will often make minor changes to Java classes, and hence will not want to go through a lengthy deployment process over and over again. They also need extensive debugging facilities. Many Java development environments will contain a J2EE server optimized for these purposes.

When deploying a production application on a mission-critical server, the priorities are robustness, performance, and stability. Often, to avoid downtime and unforeseen problems, the application is first brought up on parallel systems. The foremost consideration of the deployer is to be able to connect all legacy systems to the newly developed application. A deployer may also want detailed logging of the deployment process.

The following sections explore packaging and deployment issues from a tools perspective and point out differences, if any, in light of the two different deployment times.

7.5.2.1   Vendor-Specific Deployment Information

The J2EE platform specification defines deployment unit requirements for each of the four J2EE module types and for a J2EE application itself. Each specification defines how the archive file must be structured to operate correctly with a J2EE deployment tool. In addition to application code and a deployment descriptor, an application requires a certain amount of additional vendor- or environment-specific binding information. For example, when the J2EE reference implementation receives an application EAR file from a deployer, it also needs the following information:

- A JNDI name for each enterprise bean's home interface

- A mapping of the application's abstract security roles to user and group names

- JNDI lookup names and account information for all databases

- JavaMail session configuration information

Note that these issues arise only at deployment time—they in no way affect the ability to deploy an application on servers from different J2EE product providers.

Each vendor implements these vendor-specific bindings in a different way. For example, the J2EE reference implementation represents vendor-specific information as a separate XML document (called `sun-j2ee-ri.xml`) within the application archive. Code Example 7.28 is an excerpt derived from the sample application's vendor-specific deployment information.

```
<j2ee-ri-specific-information>
    <server-name>localhost</server-name>
    <enterprise-beans>
        <module-name>customerEjb.jar</module-name>
        <unique-id>0</unique-id>
        ...
        <ejb>
            <ejb-name>AccountEJB</ejb-name>
            <jndi-name>ejb/local/customer/account</jndi-name>
            <ejb-ref>
                <ejb-ref-name>ejb/local/creditcard</ejb-ref-name>
                <jndi-name>
                localejbs/BluePrints_Petstore/CreditCardEJB3
                </jndi-name>
            </ejb-ref>
            ...
</j2ee-ri-specific-information>
```

Code Example 7.28 Vendor-Specific Deployment Information

The J2EE platform specification does not specify how an `ejb-name` maps to a home interface. Instead, the specification leaves this detail to the platform implementer's discretion, which provides the implementer with more design flexibility in the platform implementation.

The J2EE reference implementation provides one example of how a J2EE platform implementation might map an `ejb-name` to a home interface. A deployer using the J2EE reference implementation provides vendor-specific deployment information that maps each `ejb-name` to a `jndi-name`, which is the name of the actual bean home interface in the naming environment, as configured in the EJB container. As shown in Code Example 7.28, the J2EE reference implementation's vendor-specific deployment information binds the `ejb-name` AccountEJB to a corresponding `jndi-name`, `localejbs/BluePrints_Petstore/CreditCardEJB3`. This separation of standard deployment information from vendor-specific information ensures the reusability of deployment descriptors across vendor platforms and implementation versions while enabling vendor-specific bindings and extensions.

Vendors may find it useful to use XML attribute IDs to link vendor-specific information to components and entities within a J2EE application. The J2EE reference implementation links standard and vendor-specific deployment descriptor information by component name.

The J2EE specifications define the internal structure of deployment units, and the content and structure of deployment descriptors. BluePrints recommends the following practices for deployment tools and descriptors:

- Deployment tools should follow the J2EE specifications closely, so that each deployment unit may be opened and used by the deployment tools of as many vendors as possible.

- Deployment descriptors written by deployment tools should always conform to the DTDs specified in the J2EE specifications.

- Vendor-specific deployment information should be kept outside of the deployment descriptor, but within the deployment unit itself, perhaps in an auxiliary XML such as the one the J2EE reference implementation uses.

- A deployment tool should preserve, not remove, any files that it does not recognize within a deployment unit, because such files might be deployment information from some other tool.

- Likewise, tools should always preserve optional deployment descriptor entries, instead of throwing away entries they don't use or recognize.

- Finally, vendor-specific deployment information should have reasonable fallback default values to make deployment as simple as possible.

7.5.2.2   Single Point of Entry for Deployment

A high-end mission-critical server often consists of multiple physical servers. Often the number of Web containers is greater than the number of EJB containers. In such cases, the deployer shouldn't have to install applications individually on each machine. The deployment process should have a single point of entry—either a stand-alone deployment tool or the deployment component of a J2EE server. For example, the J2EE SDK deployment tool provides a single point of entry to the J2EE server. This central component then takes care of distributing appropriate components on both the Web and the EJB containers.

This approach has the following benefits:

- It simplifies the deployment process, because the deployer has to interact with only one deployment tool. The deployer also clearly understands when deployment is complete. The tool also determines which components are required to be deployed on each machine.

- It provides a place for centralized logging and auditing.

- It provides better fault tolerance. Since the deployment tool has complete control over all application components on all servers, it can detect server failures and perform failovers. It can also detect when a server comes back up and redeploy the application to bring it in sync. An added advantage is that the deployer does not have to worry about load-balancing, because the runtime environment handles it automatically.

- It simplifies undeployment and upgrading.

7.5.2.3 Remotely Accessible Deployment

Deployers often need to deploy multiple applications on multiple J2EE servers. To handle such scenarios more easily, the deployment tool should be remotely accessible as either a Web-based or client-server application. The deployment tool bundled with the J2EE SDK takes a client-server approach, using RMI-IIOP to communicate with the administration back-end of the J2EE server. The tool can access and deploy applications on multiple J2EE servers.

7.5.2.4 Undeployment Capability

In development-time deployment, undeployment capability is critical to quickly update new application components. In a high-end implementation, it isn't acceptable to restart the server to add or remove new software applications. High-end servers will therefore likely support dynamic deployment and undeployment. Low-end J2EE servers may not need to support this capability.

Another useful development feature of high-end J2EE products is incremental deployment and undeployment. For many J2EE servers, deploying a J2EE application may be an atomic (and slow) process. Waiting for an entire application to deploy when an application component changes can slow the development process unacceptably. Servers that allow deployment and undeployment capability of only parts of an application, and that incorporate this feature into their tools, greatly accelerate the development cycle.

7.5.2.5   JNDI Namespace Management

Deployers need to bind external references in a J2EE application to entities in their environment. Examples of such references include databases and enterprise beans. Since binding happens through the JNDI namespace, container providers need to provide tools to create and manage the JNDI namespace. These tools also need to control access to the JNDI namespace according to the security policy of their environment.

7.5.2.6   Name Collision Management

Application assemblers may use third-party enterprise beans, without control over the names used for such enterprise beans. As a result, name collisions are bound to occur. Packaging tools should automatically detect and handle such name collisions by adjusting names through the `ejb-link` element of the bean's deployment descriptors.

7.5.2.7   Deployment Descriptor Versioning

The lifetime of many enterprise applications may be measured in years and even decades. An important goal of the J2EE platform is to provide compatibility even when systems and application components are upgraded. To maintain deployment descriptor portability both across platforms and across implementation versions, separate standard and vendor-specific deployment information. Packaging and deployment tools should follow the versioning conventions described in the J2EE, EJB, and servlet specifications.

7.6   Summary

The J2EE platform provides facilities to simplify the deployment process. It uses JAR files as the standard package for components and applications, and XML-based deployment descriptors for platform configuration and component customization.

Tools that read and write application deployment descriptors also simplify deployment, because they present users with an intuitive view of application structure and component capabilities.

The J2EE packaging and deployment process involves three J2EE roles: application component provider, application assembler, and deployer.

Application component providers create components, package them into modules, and write their deployment descriptors. They design components with business logic that is customizable via deployment descriptors, instead of by modifications to the source code. When packaging components into modules, application component providers need to balance between the competing goals of reusability and simplicity.

Application assemblers resolve dependencies between deployment descriptor elements in different modules and assemble modules into larger deployment units. Deployers customize deployment descriptor elements for the application's deployment environment and install deployment units. The deployer must ensure that the values of all environment entries declared by an enterprise bean are meaningful.

The packaging and deployment process is handled best by specialized tools. While both component providers and deployers need to deploy applications, their deployment needs are different. Component providers want fast response times, and the ability to undeploy, redeploy, and partially deploy applications easily and quickly. Deployers in a production environment require robustness, performance, and stability. Deployment tools need to address both sets of requirements while supporting such J2EE platform goals as portability and backwards compatibility.

7.7   References and Resources

The following references are for those readers interested in more information on packaging and deployment.

- *The Java™ 2 Platform, Enterprise Edition, Specification.* J2EE Enterprise Team. Copyright 2000, Sun Microsystems, Inc.

- *Enterprise JavaBeans™ Specification.* Copyright 2001, Sun Microsystems, Inc.

- *The J2EE Connector Architecture Specification.* Copyright 2001, Sun Microsystems, Inc.

- *The Java™ Servlet 2.3 Specification.* Copyright 2001, Sun Microsystems, Inc. `<http://jcp.org/aboutJava/communityprocess/first/jsr053/index.html>`

- Java™ Web Start Web site `<http://java.sun.com/products/javaweb-start/developers.html>`

Transaction Management

by Tony Ng

TRANSACTION management is a mechanism for simplifying the development of distributed multiuser enterprise applications. It is also one of the standard services offered by the J2EE platform. By enforcing strict rules on an application's ability to access and update data, transaction management ensures data integrity. A transactional system ensures that a unit of work either fully completes or has no effect at all. Transaction management frees an application programmer from dealing with the complex issues of data access, including synchronized updates, failure recovery, and multiuser programming.

This chapter begins with a general overview of transactional concepts and J2EE platform support for transaction management. Then it describes the Java™ Transaction API (JTA), the interface used by the J2EE platform to manage and coordinate transactions. Finally, the chapter describes the transactional models available to each type of J2EE component and to enterprise information systems.

8.1 Transactional Concepts

A *transaction* is a logical unit of work that either modifies some state, performs a set of operations, or both. An individual transaction may involve multiple data and logical operations, but these operations always occur as an indivisible atomic unit, or they do not occur at all. For example, enrolling a patient in a health care plan may involve first acquiring release forms from the patient, verifying the patient's employment, checking her health and insurance history against remote data sources, and so on. All of the activities described can be subtasks of a single transaction, because failure of any one of these subtasks should cause the entire transaction to fail.

This section provides a brief introduction to basic concepts in conventional and distributed transactional systems. See "References and Resources" on page 277 for references to in-depth treatment of these topics.

8.1.1   ACID Transaction Properties

Enterprise transactions share the properties of atomicity, consistency, isolation, and durability, denoted by the acronym ACID. These properties are necessary to ensure safe data sharing.

Atomicity means that a transaction is considered complete if and only if all of its operations were performed successfully. If any operation in a transaction fails, the transaction fails. In the health care example described above, a patient can be enrolled only if all required procedures complete successfully, so enrollment is atomic.

Consistency means that a transaction must transition data from one consistent state to another, preserving the data's semantic and referential integrity. For example, if every health care policy in a database requires both a patient covered by the policy and a plan describing the coverage, every transaction in the health insurance application must enforce this consistency rule. While applications should always preserve data consistency, many databases provide ways to specify integrity and value constraints so that transactions that attempt to violate consistency will automatically fail.

Isolation means that any changes made to data by a transaction are invisible to other concurrent transactions until the transaction commits. Isolation requires that several concurrent transactions must produce the same results in the data as those same transactions executed serially, in some (unspecified) order. In the health plan enrollment example, isolation ensures that updates made to a patient record will not be globally visible until those updates are committed.

Durability means that committed updates are permanent. Failures that occur after a commit cause no loss of data. Durability also implies that data for all committed transactions can be recovered after a system or media failure.

An ACID transaction ensures that persistent data always conform to their schema, that a series of operations can assume a stable set of inputs and working data, and that persistent data changes are recoverable after system failure.

8.1.2 Transaction Participants

An application that uses transactions is called a *transactional application*. In a J2EE application, a transactional application may consist of multiple servlets, JSP pages, and enterprise beans. A *resource manager* is an external system accessed by an application. A resource manager provides and enforces the ACID transaction properties for specific data and operations. Examples of resource managers include a relational database (which support persistent storage of relational data), an EIS system (managing transactional, external functionality and data), and the Java Message Service (JMS) provider (which manages transactional message delivery). A transactional application accesses a resource manager through a *transactional resource* object. For example, a JDBC `java.sql.Connection` object is used to access a relational database. A *resource adapter* is a system library that makes the API of a resource manager available to an application server. A *Connector* is a resource adapter that has an API conforming to the Java Connector architecture, the standard architecture for integrating J2EE applications with EISes.

8.1.3 Transaction Demarcation

Transactional programs must be able to start and end transactions, and be able to indicate whether data changes are to be made permanent or discarded. Indicating transaction boundaries for a program is called *transaction demarcation*.

A program starts a transaction by executing a *begin* operation. The program may then read or modify data within the scope of the new active transaction. When the program is ready to make its data changes permanent, it executes a *commit* operation, causing the transaction to persist any data modified or created during the active state. Successful completion of the commit operation results in a permanent change to the transactional resource. If a commit operation fails (for example, due to inadequate resources or data consistency violations), the resource manager executes a *rollback*, discarding any changes made since the transaction began. An application may also explicitly request a rollback during an active transaction.

8.1.4 Distributed Transactions

Distributed enterprise systems often need to access and update multiple transactional resources in order to accomplish some business goal. Consider, for example, a travel agency application. Creating a typical business travel itinerary with a confirmed and paid plane ticket requires successful completion of user authentication, credit card processing, and flight reservation, as well as local creation of the itinerary itself. Such a transaction, involving independent, cooperating transactional systems, is called a *distributed transaction*.

Distributed transactions are more complex than non-distributed transactions because of latency, potential failure of one or more resource managers, and interoperability concerns. On a network, a failed transaction can be difficult to distinguish from one that is merely slow. Resource managers that do not "know" about each other cannot coordinate transactions by themselves. A transactional application could itself handle rollbacks and commits for multiple distributed resources, but only at the cost of a great deal of complex, non-reusable logic.

The most common solution to the problem of coordinating distributed transactions is to introduce a third participant, called a *transaction manager*, into the design. The transaction manager acts as a mediator between applications and the multiple resources the applications use. Figure 8.1 shows the three participants in a distributed transaction: the transactional application, the resource manager, and the transaction manager, which coordinates the transactions of multiple resource managers, providing the application with ACID transactions across *multiple* resources. In many cases, the transaction manager uses the X/Open XA protocol to communicate with multiple resource managers. In the J2EE platform, the XA protocol is encapsulated by the JTA XAResource interface. Please refer to "References and Resources" on page 277 for more information on the X/Open XA protocol.

At any time during a distributed transaction, the transaction manager maintains an association between each transaction (which has a unique global ID), application threads, and connections to the resource managers. For example, a transaction manager may associate a single transaction ID with a thread of an application, an SQL connection that has updated a table, a JMS provider waiting to transmit a message, and a resource adapter or Connector executing an external business function. A *transaction context* is the association of a transaction with an application component or a resource manager. The transparent forwarding of a transaction context from one component to another component or from a component to a resource manager is called *transaction context propagation*.

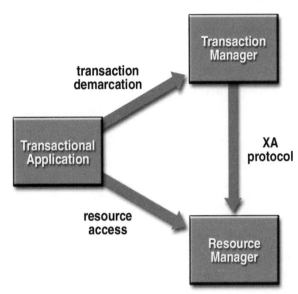

Figure 8.1   Distributed Transaction Participants

8.1.5   Two-Phase Commit Protocol

Resource managers that do not "know" about one another can't cooperate directly in distributed transactions; instead, the transaction manager controls the transaction, indicating to each resource manager whether and when to commit or roll back, based on the global state of the transaction. A transaction manager coordinates transactions between resource managers using a *two-phase commit* protocol. The two-phase commit protocol provides the ACID properties of transactions across multiple resources.

In the first phase of two-phase commit, the transaction manager tells each resource to "prepare" to commit; that is, to perform all operations for a commit and be ready either to make the changes permanent or to undo all changes. Each resource manager responds, indicating whether or not the prepare operation succeeded. In the second phase, if all prepare operations succeed, the transaction manager tells all resource managers to commit their changes; otherwise, it tells them all to roll back and indicates transaction failure to the application.

A particular resource manager may participate in multiple simultaneous distributed transactions. The ACID properties apply for all resource managers involved in a particular distributed transaction, as well as for all pending transactions within a particular resource manager.

8.2   J2EE Platform Transactions

Enterprise applications require safe, reliable, recoverable data access, so support for transactions is an essential element of the J2EE architecture. The J2EE platform supports a combination of servlets and JSP pages accessing multiple enterprise beans within a single transaction. Each component may acquire multiple connections to multiple resource managers.

The J2EE platform supports both programmatic and declarative transaction demarcation. The component provider can programmatically demarcate transaction boundaries in the component code with the Java Transaction API. Enterprise beans support declarative transaction demarcation, in which the enterprise bean container automatically starts and completes transactions based on configuration information in the components' deployment descriptor. In both cases, the J2EE platform assumes the burden of implementing transaction management.

J2EE transaction management is transparent to component and application code. A J2EE application server implements the necessary low-level transaction protocols, such as interactions between a transaction manager and resource managers, transaction context propagation, and distributed two-phase commit protocol. The J2EE platform requires only support for so-called "flat" transactions, which cannot have any child (nested) transactions.

An application can perform distributed transactions because a transaction manager propagates the transaction context across multiple resource managers. Transaction managers can also cooperate to propagate transaction context across J2EE server boundaries. Consider a large retail store chain. The transaction manager for a store's application server may also interoperate with the transaction managers for other stores within the same enterprise, permitting customers to pay for an item at one location and have it delivered from another. Such transactional capabilities pave the way for a high level of integration across the enterprise.

The next few sections provide examples of these transactional scenarios, which involve multiple distributed transaction participants.

8.2.1   Accessing Multiple Resources within a Transaction

As of version 1.3 of the J2EE platform, a J2EE product is required to support access within a single transaction to:

- A single JDBC database (multiple connections to the same database are allowed)

- A single Java Message Service (JMS) provider, and

- Multiple Enterprise Information Systems (EISs) through resource adapters (Connectors) specifying the XATransaction transaction level

Please refer to Section 8.8 on page 273 for more on these three types of resource managers.

Access to multiple JDBC databases within a single transaction is not required by J2EE version 1.3, and neither is support for multiple JMS providers within a transaction. Some product providers may add value to their product line by including these extra, non-standard transactional capabilities. For example, the J2EE reference implementation supports access to multiple JDBC databases in one transaction through XA-capable JDBC drivers.

8.2.1.0.1 Example: Transactions across Multiple Resource Managers

The following scenario illustrates a J2EE transaction that spans multiple resource managers. In Figure 8.2, a client invokes a method on enterprise bean X. Bean X accesses database A using a JDBC connection. Then enterprise bean X calls a method on another enterprise bean Y, which sends a JMS message to some other system using a JMS provider. Enterprise bean Y then invokes a method on enterprise bean Z, which updates and returns some data from an external EIS system using a resource adapter that implements the J2EE Connector architecture. The transaction manager in the J2EE server coordinates activities with the three resource managers. The server ensures that the database update by bean X, the message transmission by bean Y, and the EIS operation performed by bean Z are either all committed, or all rolled back.

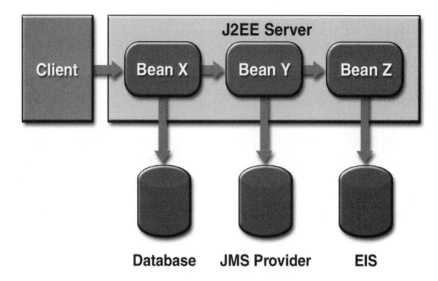

Figure 8.2   A Database, a JMS Provider, and an EIS within a Single Transaction

An application component provider does not have to write extra code to ensure consistent transactional behavior. Enterprise beans X, Y, and Z access their resources using the JDBC API, JMS, and the J2EE Connector architecture, respectively. Behind the scenes, the J2EE server's transaction manager enlists the connections to all three systems as part of the transaction. When the transaction commits, the J2EE server and the resource managers perform a two-phase commit to ensure atomic update of the two systems.

8.2.2   Transactions across Servers

J2EE products can distribute transactions across multiple application servers.

8.2.2.0.1 Example: Transactions across J2EE Servers

In Figure 8.3, a client invokes enterprise bean X, which updates data in enterprise information system A, and then calls another enterprise bean Y that is hosted by a different J2EE server. Enterprise bean Y performs read-write access to enterprise information system B.

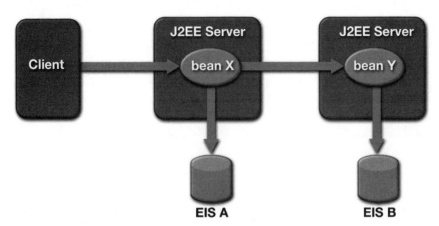

Figure 8.3 A Transaction Can Span Multiple J2EE Servers

When X invokes Y, the two J2EE servers cooperate to propagate the transaction context from X to Y. This transaction context propagation is transparent to the application code. At transaction commit time, the two J2EE servers use a distributed two-phase commit protocol to ensure that the two enterprise information systems are updated within a single transaction.

8.3 J2EE Transaction Technologies

The Java Transaction API and the J2EE platform specifications define the overall transactional behavior in the J2EE architecture. The JTA specification defines the contracts between applications, application servers, resource managers, and transaction manager. The J2EE platform specification defines the requirements for the J2EE transaction management and runtime environment.

8.3.0.0.1 Java Transaction API (JTA)

JTA specifies standard Java interfaces between a transaction manager and the distributed transaction participants it coordinates: applications, application servers, and resource managers. JTA defines interfaces that let applications, application servers, and resource managers participate in transactions regardless of their implementations.

A *JTA transaction* is a transaction managed and coordinated by the J2EE platform. A J2EE product is required to support JTA transactions as defined in the J2EE specification. A JTA transaction can span multiple components and enterprise information systems. A transaction is propagated automatically between components and to enterprise information systems accessed by components within the transaction. For example, a JTA transaction may comprise a servlet or JSP page accessing multiple enterprise beans, some of which access one or more resource managers.

JTA transactions begin either explicitly in code or implicitly by an EJB server. A component can explicitly begin a JTA transaction using interface `javax.transaction.UserTransaction`. An EJB container implicitly begins a JTA transaction when a client accesses an enterprise bean that uses container-managed transaction demarcation.

Most J2EE application component providers use only the JTA `UserTransaction` interface, and then only when choosing to use bean-managed transactions rather than container-managed transactions. An application component provider uses the JTA `UserTransaction` interface to demarcate JTA transaction boundaries in components. The JTA `TransactionManager` and `XAResource` interfaces are low-level APIs between a J2EE server and enterprise information system resource managers and are not intended to be used by applications.

The main benefit of using JTA transactions is the ability to combine multiple components and enterprise information system accesses into one single transaction with little programming effort. The J2EE platform propagates transactions between multiple components and enterprise information systems with no additional programming effort. Enterprise beans using container-managed transaction demarcation (See Section 8.6.2 on page 264) do not need to begin or commit transactions programmatically, because the EJB container automatically handles the demarcation.

JTA transactions are recommended when accessing EIS resources; see Section 8.7.3 on page 269.

8.4   Client Tier Transactions

The J2EE platform does not require transaction support in applets and application clients, though like distributed transactions, a J2EE product might choose to provide this capability for added value. So, whether applets and application clients can directly access a `UserTransaction` object depends on the capabilities provided by the container. To ensure portability, applets and application clients should delegate transactional work to enterprise beans, either directly or by way of the Web tier.

8.5   Web Tier Transaction Guidelines

Servlets and JSP pages in a two-tier application can access enterprise information systems within the scope of a JTA transaction. Servlets and JSP pages support only programmatic transaction demarcation. A servlet or JSP page can use JNDI to look up a UserTransaction object (using the standard defined name java:comp/UserTransaction), and then use the UserTransaction interface to demarcate transactions.

Code Example 8.1 illustrates the use of the JTA UserTransaction interface to demarcate transactions within a Servlet:

```
Context ic = new InitialContext();
UserTransaction ut =
    (UserTransaction) ic.lookup("java:comp/UserTransaction");
ut.begin();
// access resources transactionally here
ut.commit();
```

Code Example 8.1   Web Component Using a JTA Transaction

Calling UserTransaction.begin associates the calling thread with a new transaction context. Subsequent accesses of transactional resources such as JDBC connections or resource adapter connections implicitly enlist those resources into the transaction. The call to UserTransaction.commit commits the transaction, transparently engaging the two-phase commit protocol if necessary.

A servlet or JSP page may start a transaction only in its service method. A transaction that is started by a servlet or JSP page must be completed before the service method returns; in other words, transactions may not span Web requests. If the service method returns with a pending UserTransaction (that is, begin has been called, but not commit or rollback), the container aborts the transaction and rolls back all data updates. JTA transactions are not supported in servlet filters and Web application event listeners.

8.5.0.0.1 Web Tier Transaction Guidelines

In a multitier environment, data presentation and user interaction are the primary responsibilities of servlets and JSP pages. Data presentation and user interaction are usually not transactional operations. Because transactions tend to be associated with business logic, database access and other transactional work should be handled by transactional enterprise beans instead of by the JTA in the Web tier.

In designs that do not use enterprise beans, or where for some reason you choose to use Web tier transactions, the following guidelines apply. JTA transactions, threads, and transactional resources (for example, JDBC connections) have many complex and subtle interactions. Web components should follow the guidelines stated in the transaction management chapter of the J2EE specification (version 1.3, section J2EE.4.2):

- JTA transactions must be started and completed only from the thread in which the `service` method is called. If the Web component creates additional threads for any purpose, these threads must not attempt to start JTA transactions. These additional threads will not be associated with any JTA transaction.

- Transactional resources such as JDBC connections acquired and released by threads other than the `service` method thread should not be shared between threads.

- Transactional resource objects should not be stored in static fields.

- Web components that implement `SingleThreadModel` may store references to transactional resources in class instance fields. By definition, only one thread can ever access an instance of a Web component implementing `SingleThreadModel`; therefore, that instance can assume that fields referencing any transactional resources will not be shared with any other thread.

- Web components that do not implement `SingleThreadModel` should not store transactional resource objects in class instance fields. Transactional resource objects for such components should be acquired and released within the same invocation of the `service` method.

8.6   Enterprise JavaBeans Tier Transactions

Enterprise beans offer two types of transaction demarcation: bean-managed and container-managed. In container-managed transaction demarcation, six different transaction attributes—Required, RequiresNew, NotSupported, Supports, Mandatory, and Never—can be associated with an enterprise bean method. An application component provider or assembler specifies the type of transaction demarcation and transaction attributes for the methods of the enterprise beans in the deployment descriptor.

This section discusses the types of transactions and the attributes of container-managed transactions and presents guidelines for choosing among the available options.

8.6.1 Bean-Managed Transaction Demarcation

With bean-managed transaction demarcation, an enterprise bean uses the javax.transaction.UserTransaction interface to explicitly demarcate transaction boundaries. Session beans and message-driven beans can choose to use bean-managed demarcation; entity beans must always use container-managed transaction demarcation.

Code Example 8.2 illustrates the use of the JTA UserTransaction interface to demarcate transactions in an enterprise bean with bean-managed transaction demarcation.

```
UserTransaction ut = ejbContext.getUserTransaction();
ut.begin();
// perform transactional work here
ut.commit();
```

Code Example 8.2   Enterprise Bean Using a JTA Transaction

The UserTransaction interface is used the same way in the EJB tier as in the Web tier except that the reference to the interface is obtained by calling EJBContext.getUserTransaction instead of by way of a JNDI lookup. As noted in Section 8.5 on page 261, resource managers are implicitly enlisted into a transaction, if one is active, the first time they are accessed from the thread that started the transaction. It is not necessary for Web components to explicitly demarcate transactions of the resource managers.

8.6.2   Container-Managed Transaction Demarcation

The EJB container manages transaction boundaries for enterprise beans that use container-managed transaction demarcation. A transaction attribute for an enterprise bean method determines that method's transactional semantics, defining the behavior the EJB container must provide when the method is called. Transaction attributes are associated with enterprise bean methods in the bean's deployment descriptor. For example, if a method has a transaction attribute `RequiresNew`, the EJB container begins a new JTA transaction every time this method is called and attempts to commit the transaction before the method returns. The same transaction attribute can be specified for all the methods of an enterprise bean or different attributes can be specified for each method of a bean. Refer to Section 8.6.3 for more information on transaction attributes.

Even in container-managed demarcation, an enterprise bean has some control over the transaction. For example, an enterprise bean can choose to roll back a transaction started by the container using the method `setRollbackOnly` on the `SessionContext`, `EntityContext` and `MessageDrivenContext` object.

There are several benefits of using container-managed transaction demarcation:

- The transaction behavior of an enterprise bean is specified declaratively instead of programmatically. This frees the application component provider from writing transaction demarcation code in the component.

- It is less error-prone because the container handles transaction demarcation automatically.

- It is easier to compose multiple enterprise beans to perform a certain task with specific transaction behavior. An application assembler that understands the application can customize the transaction attributes in the deployment descriptor without code modification.

8.6.3   Transaction Attributes

A *transaction attribute* is a value associated with a method of an enterprise bean that uses container-managed transaction demarcation. A transaction attribute is defined for an enterprise bean method in the bean's deployment descriptor, usually by an application component provider or application assembler. The transaction attribute controls how the EJB container demarcates transactions of enterprise bean methods. In most cases, all methods of an enterprise bean will have the same transaction attribute. For optimization purposes, it is possible to have different attributes for different methods. For example, an enterprise bean may have methods that do not need to be transactional.

A transaction attribute must be specified for the methods in the component interface of a session bean and for the methods in the component and home interfaces of an entity bean.

8.6.3.0.1 Required

If the transaction attribute is `Required`, the container ensures that the enterprise bean's method will always be invoked with a JTA transaction. If the calling client is associated with a JTA transaction, the enterprise bean method will be invoked in the same transaction context. However, if a client is not associated with a transaction, the container will automatically begin a new transaction and try to commit the transaction when the method completes.

8.6.3.0.2 RequiresNew

If the transaction attribute is `RequiresNew`, the container always creates a new transaction before invoking the enterprise bean method and commits the transaction when the method returns. If the calling client is associated with a transaction context, the container suspends the association of the transaction context with the current thread before starting the new transaction. When the method and the transaction complete, the container resumes the suspended transaction.

8.6.3.0.3 NotSupported

If the transaction attribute is `NotSupported`, the transactional context of the calling client is not propagated to the enterprise bean. If a client calls with a transaction context, the container suspends the client's transaction association before invoking the enterprise bean's method. After the method completes, the container resumes the suspended transaction association.

8.6.3.0.4 Supports

It the transaction attribute is `Supports` and the client is associated with a transaction context, the context is propagated to the enterprise bean method, similar to the way the container treats the `Required` case. If the client call is not associated with any transaction context, the container behaves similarly to the `NotSupported` case. The transaction context is not propagated to the enterprise bean method.

8.6.3.0.5 Mandatory

The transaction attribute `Mandatory` requires the container to invoke a bean's method in a client's transaction context. If the client is not associated with a transaction context when calling this method, the container throws `javax.transaction.TransactionRequiredException` if the client is a remote client or `javax.ejb.TransactionRequiredLocalException` if the client is a local client. If the calling client has a transaction context, the case is treated as `Required` by the container.

8.6.3.0.6 Never

The transaction attribute `Never` requires that the enterprise bean method explicitly *not* be called within a transaction context. If the client calls with a transaction context, the container throws `java.rmi.RemoteException` if the client is a remote client or `javax.ejb.EJBException` if the client is a local client. If the client is not associated with any transaction context, the container invokes the method without initiating a transaction.

8.6.4   Enterprise JavaBeans Tier Transaction Guidelines

As mentioned previously, the recommended way to manage transactions is through container-managed demarcation. Declarative transaction management provides one of the major benefits of the J2EE platform by freeing the application component provider from the burden of managing transactions. Furthermore, the transaction characteristics of an application can be changed without code modification by switching the transaction attributes, making components useful in more contexts. Transaction demarcation should be selected with great care by someone who understands the application well. Bean-managed transaction demarcation is only for advanced users who want fine-grain control over the transactional behavior of the application.

8.6.4.1   Transaction Attributes Guidelines

Most enterprise beans perform transactional work (for example, accessing a JDBC database). The default choice for a transaction attribute should be `Required`. Using this attribute ensures that the methods of an enterprise bean are invoked within a JTA transaction. In addition, enterprise beans with the `Required` transaction attribute can be easily composed to perform work within the scope of a single JTA transaction.

Message-driven beans may use only the `Required` and `NotSupported` transaction attributes. Entity beans that use EJB 2.0 container-managed persistence should use only the `Required`, `RequiresNew`, or `Mandatory` transaction attributes for most component and home interface methods.

The `RequiresNew` transaction attribute is useful when the bean method needs to commit unconditionally, whether or not a transaction is already in progress. An example of this requirement is a bean method that performs logging. This bean method should be invoked with the `RequiresNew` transaction attribute so that logging records are created even if the calling client's transaction is rolled back.

The `NotSupported` transaction attribute can be used when the resource manager responsible for the transaction is not supported by the J2EE product. For example, if a bean method is invoking an operation on an enterprise resource planning system that is not integrated with the J2EE server, the server has no control over that system's transactions. In this case, the bean's transaction attribute should be set to `NotSupported` to clearly indicate that the enterprise resource planning system is not accessed within a JTA transaction.

Using the transaction attribute `Supports` is not recommended. An enterprise bean with this attribute would have transactional behavior that differed depending on whether the caller is associated with a transaction context, possibly leading to a violation of the ACID rules for transactions.

The transaction attributes `Mandatory` and `Never` can be used when it is necessary to verify the transaction association of the calling client. These attributes may make it more difficult to use the component inside an application because it restricts the calling client's transaction context.

8.6.4.2 Container-Managed Persistence Transaction Attributes Guidelines

As previously mentioned, entity beans that use EJB 2.0 container-managed persistence can only use `Required`, `RequiresNew`, or `Mandatory` transaction attributes for most business methods and methods on the home interface. Because accessing the container-managed persistence (CMP) and container-managed relationship (CMR) fields of an entity bean requires transactions, the `Mandatory` transaction attribute should be used for all get and set methods of an entity bean's CMP and CMR fields. Use of the `RequiresNew` transaction attribute for get and set methods of CMR fields is *not* recommended, because it is illegal to iterate through the same collection object corresponding to a CMR field in different transactions.

8.7   EIS Tier Transactions

Most enterprise information systems support some form of transactions. For example, a typical JDBC database allows multiple SQL updates to be grouped in an atomic transaction.

Components should always access an enterprise information system within the scope of a transaction to guarantee the integrity and consistency of the underlying data. Such systems can be accessed within a JTA transaction or a resource manager local transaction.

8.7.1   JTA Transactions

When an enterprise information system is accessed within the scope of a JTA transaction, any updates performed on the system will commit or roll back depending on the outcome of the JTA transaction. Multiple connections to information systems can be opened and all updates through the connections will be atomic if they are performed within the scope of a JTA transaction. The J2EE server is responsible for coordinating and propagating transactions between the server and the enterprise information system.

If the J2EE product supports multiple enterprise information systems in one transaction, a J2EE application can access and perform updates on multiple enterprise information systems atomically, without extra programming effort, by grouping all updates within a JTA transaction. Code Example 8.3 illustrates this use:

```
InitialContext ic = new InitialContext("java:comp/env");
DataSource db1 = (DataSource) ic.lookup("OrdersDB"); // JDBC
ConnectionFactory db2 =
    (ConnectionFactory) ic.lookup("InventoryEIS"); // Connector CCI
java.sql.Connection con1 = db1.getConnection();
javax.resource.cci.Connection con2 = db2.getConnection();

UserTransaction ut = ejbContext.getUserTransaction();
ut.begin();
// perform updates to OrdersDB using connection con1
// perform updates to InventoryEIS using connection con2
ut.commit();
```

Code Example 8.3   Accessing Multiple Transactional Resources

8.7.2   Resource Manager Local Transactions

A *resource manager local transaction* (or *local transaction*) is a transaction specific to a particular enterprise information system connection. A local transaction is managed by the underlying enterprise information system resource manager. The J2EE platform usually does not have control of or knowledge about any local transactions begun by components. Access to a transactional enterprise information system is usually within a local transaction if no JTA transaction has been initiated. For example, if a servlet accesses a JDBC database without starting a JTA transaction, the database access will be within the scope of a local transaction, specific to the database.

Local transactions may also be used when the enterprise information system is not integrated using the Connector architecture. For example, if no Connector resource adapter is available for an object-oriented database, a J2EE server cannot propagate any JTA transactions to the object-oriented database, and any access will be within local transactions. For this reason, applications should use the Connector architecture to integrate enterprise information systems that are not included as part of the J2EE platform.

8.7.3   EIS Tier Transaction Guidelines

Enterprise information systems such as databases should be accessed within the scope of a JTA transaction. Transactional access guarantees data consistency and integrity, and ensures that work performed by multiple components through multiple enterprise information system connections is grouped as an atomic unit. It also groups as an atomic unit work performed on one or more independent enterprise information systems.

Where JTA transaction control is not possible, such as with resource managers that do not support the JTA, consider using resource manager local transactions with compensating transactions (see the next section). Keep in mind that each local transaction requires an explicit commit or rollback. In addition, components using local transactions need extra logic to deal with individual enterprise information system rollbacks or failures.

8.7.4   Compensating Transactions

A *compensating transaction* is a transaction or a group of operations that undoes the effect of a previously committed transaction. A distributed transaction may include both JTA transactions and resource manager local transactions, but local transactions require explicit management. JTA-enabled resource managers handle rollback automatically by simply discarding any changes made since a transaction began. But each resource manager local transaction requires a compensating transaction that can undo the local transactions effects in case a rollback occurs.

Compensating transactions are useful if a component needs to access an enterprise information system that either does not support full JTA transactions or is not supported by a particular J2EE product. The J2EE platform supports JTA transactions for JDBC and JMS access. JTA transaction support for EIS access is determined by the transaction level of the resource adapter (see Section 8.8.3 on page 274). An XATransaction resource adapter automatically supports JTA transactions.

A LocalTransaction resource adapter (see Section 8.8.3 on page 274) accesses an EIS within the scope of a resource manager local transaction. Performing atomic operations on multiple EISs can be challenging when some of those systems do not participate in the JTA transaction. Compensating transactions meet this challenge by providing programmatic "rollback" of operations already committed by resource manager local transactions. Compensating transactions must be manually coded into application logic; the JTA provides no standard way to handle them.

For example, suppose an application needs to perform an atomic operation that involves updating two enterprise information systems: a database that supports JTA transactions and an enterprise resource planning system that does not. The application would need to define a compensating transaction for the update to the enterprise resource planning system. The approach is illustrated in Code Example 8.4.

```
updateERPSystem();
try {
    UserTransaction.begin();
    updateJDBCDatabase();
    UserTransaction.commit();
}
catch (RollbackException ex) {
    undoUpdateERPSystem();
}
```

Code Example 8.4   Compensating Transaction

The methods `updateERPSystem` and `updateJDBCDatabase` contain code to access and perform work on enterprise information systems. The `undoUpdateERPSystem` method contains code to undo the effect of `updateERPSystem` if the JTA transaction does not commit successfully.

Compensating transactions have a few pitfalls:

- **Committed transactions cannot always be undone**—Consider Code Example 8.4. If for some reason the method `undoUpdateERPSystem` fails, the data will be left in an inconsistent state.

- **Server crashes can compromise atomicity**—For example, if the system crashes immediately after the method `updateERPSystem`, the two database updates will not occur, resulting in a partial transaction

- **Resource manager local transaction commits can violate isolation**—When using compensating transactions with non-JTA resources, committed resource manager local transactions may subsequently be undone. In Code Example 8.4, a concurrent enterprise information system client may be using data from the committed update to the enterprise resource planning system, and this data may potentially be rolled back later. In other words, updates committed by a resource manager local transaction may be visible to other transactions, even before the distributed transaction commits.

8.7.4.1   Compensating Transaction Guidelines

Compensating transaction code should be encapsulated in a session enterprise bean with a bean-managed transaction. The session bean may implement all of the enterprise information system access logic itself, or delegate some or all of the access logic to other enterprise beans. If an enterprise bean's only responsibility is to access an enterprise information system that does not support JTA transactions, its transaction attribute should be set to `NotSupported` to indicate that a JTA transaction will not be used in the enterprise bean.

An application that depends on compensating transactions must have extra logic to deal with potential failures and inconsistencies. The extra work and pitfalls of compensating transactions mean applications should avoid using them when possible. Instead, use JTA transactions to simply and safely achieve ACID transaction properties across multiple components and enterprise information systems.

8.7.5   Isolation Level

An *isolation level* defines how concurrent transactions to an enterprise information system are isolated from one another. Enterprise information systems usually support the following isolation levels:

- `ReadCommitted`—This level prevents a transaction from reading uncommitted changes from other transactions.

- `RepeatableRead`—This level prevents a transaction from reading uncommitted changes from other transactions. In addition, it ensures that reading the same data multiple times will return the same value even if another transaction modifies the data.

- `Serializable`—This level prevents a transaction from reading uncommitted changes from other transactions and ensures that reading the same data multiple times will return the same value even if another transaction modifies the data. In addition, it ensures that if a query retrieves a result set based on a predicate condition and another transaction inserts data that satisfy the predicate condition, re-execution of the query will return the same result set.

Isolation level and concurrency are closely related. The isolation level indicates the degree of responsibility given to the EIS for managing concurrent data access. A lower isolation level typically allows greater concurrency, at the expense of more complicated logic to deal with potential data inconsistencies. A higher isolation level typically allows simpler logic, at the expense of system performance due to internal EIS data locking to enforce ACID transaction properties. A useful guideline is to use the highest isolation level provided by enterprise information systems that gives acceptable performance.

For consistency, all enterprise information systems accessed by a J2EE application should use the same isolation level. The J2EE specification version 1.3 does not define a standard way to set isolation levels when an enterprise information system is accessed within JTA transactions. If a J2EE product does not provide a way to configure the isolation level, the enterprise information system default isolation level will be used. For most relational databases, the default isolation level is `ReadCommitted`.

The isolation level should not change within a transaction, especially if some work has already been done. Some enterprise information systems will force a commit if you attempt to change the isolation level.

8.7.6   Performance with Multiple Resource Managers

The J2EE platform provides distributed transaction support across multiple resource managers, including JDBC databases, JMS providers, and EISes. The performance impact of using multiple resource managers in the same transaction is an important concern. Typically, a transaction that accesses more than one resource manager uses the two-phase distributed commit protocol, resulting in additional transaction processing overhead. Distributed transactions also cause additional administrative overhead; for example, partial failures of in-doubt transactions must always be resolved. Therefore, an application should minimize the use of multiple resource managers in the same transaction where possible (for example, by consolidating data into one EIS). However, JTA transactions should definitely be used when accessing multiple transactional resources. The benefits of data integrity and ease of programming that JTA transactions provide definitely outweigh the additional overhead incurred by two-phase commit.

8.8   J2EE Resource Manager Types

The J2EE architecture defines transactional behavior for three types of resource managers: JDBC-compliant databases, J2EE Connector-enabled information systems, and JMS providers. All three types of resource managers may be used within the scope of a single distributed transaction. Each type has somewhat different requirements and transactional semantics. This section describes these resource manager types and the requirements the J2EE platform specification places on them. It also explains their transactional semantics.

8.8.1   JDBC Databases

A J2EE product is required to provide transactional access to one JDBC resource per transaction. Transactional access to JDBC resources is available from servlets, JSP pages, and enterprise beans. Multiple components accessing the same JDBC resource within the scope of the same transaction are supported. For example, a servlet may start a transaction, modify a database, and invoke methods on an enterprise bean that modifies that same database, all within the scope of the same transaction.

Products that support access to multiple JDBC resources within a single transaction must do so with platform-specific APIs. Applications that use these features are not portable.

8.8.2   JMS Providers

A J2EE product is required to support at least one JMS provider per transaction. Transaction access to a JMS provider is available from servlets, JSP pages, and enterprise beans. Like JDBC connections, multiple components, potentially in different tiers, must be able to access the JMS provider within the same transaction scope. As with JDBC databases, accessing multiple JMS providers within a single transaction requires platform-specific APIs, sacrificing portability.

The transactional semantics of JMS message transmission refers to the transmission of the message itself, not necessarily any side-effect that transmission may cause. Each transaction groups a set of produced messages and a set of consumed messages into an atomic unit of work. Messages that are produced within a transaction are not immediately transmitted; instead, they are sent only once the transaction is committed. The messages are discarded if the transaction is rolled back. Similarly, messages are not consumed within a transaction until the transaction is committed. If the transaction is rolled back, messages will be redelivered and will remain available for consumption.

In JMS, transactions are *never* propagated between the sender and the recipient of a JMS message. In other words, the sender and the recipient of a JMS message can never be in the same transaction. The JMS transaction semantics provides atomicity on the sending and receiving of messages. For example, if an application sends two messages within a transaction T1, either both messages will be sent or they will both be discarded. On the recipient side, if both messages are delivered in a different transaction T2, the JMS provider will attempt to re-deliver the messages again if transaction T2 is rolled back. These are separate operations, and transaction T1 and T2 are independent of each other.

The transaction semantics of JMS presents one potential deadlock scenario for J2EE applications. Suppose an application A sends a JMS message to application B and suspends processing until it receives a message (for example, an acknowledgement message) from application B. If this work is done in a single transaction, application A will wait forever because the message from application A to B will not be sent until the transaction commits. To avoid this problem, the sending and receiving of messages in application A should be broken into two separate transactions.

8.8.3   J2EE Connector Architecture

The J2EE Connector architecture defines a standard architecture for integrating with heterogeneous EIS resources. It defines the contracts for a J2EE server as well as for resource adapters, which are system-level software drivers for specific EIS resources. These standard contracts provide pluggability between application servers and EISs.

A resource adapter can choose to support three different levels of transactions:

- **NoTransaction**—No transaction support is provided.

- **LocalTransaction**—Resource manager local transactions are supported.

- **XATransaction**—Resource adapter supports XA and the JTA XAResource interface. A resource adapter supporting XATransaction must also support LocalTransaction.

If a NoTransaction resource adapter is used as part of a JTA transaction, the action performed through the resource adapter will be independent of the transaction. In other words, the operations performed will not be rolled back even if the JTA transaction itself is rolled back.

If a LocalTransaction resource adapter is used in a JTA transaction, no other transactional resources (for example, JDBC or JMS access) can be used in the same transaction. This is because a LocalTransaction resource adapter does not support two-phase commit and thus cannot be mixed with other transactional resource managers in the same transaction.

The XATransaction resource adapter is the most flexible and can be mixed with other transactional resources in the same JTA transaction. For example, a J2EE application can update a JDBC database, send a JMS Message, and access an EIS resource in the same transaction provided the resource adapter used to access the EIS supports XATransaction. Note that this scenario is illegal if the resource adapter only supports LocalTransaction because a LocalTransaction resource adapter cannot be mixed with other transactional resources in the same transaction. This scenario is still valid if the resource adapter only supports the NoTransaction transaction level. However, the access to the EIS will not be part of the JTA transaction. Table 8.1 summarizes the behavior for resource adapters with different transactional levels.

Table 8.1 Transactional Behavior for Resource Adapters

Transaction Level	Work Performed as Part of JTA Transaction	Mixing with Other Transactional Resources
NoTransaction	No	Allowed
LocalTransaction	Yes	Not Allowed
XATransaction	Yes	Allowed

Applications should use an XATransaction resource adapter whenever possible for maximum flexibility and data integrity. If an XATransaction resource adapter is not available, a LocalTransaction resource adapter can provide similar transaction behavior as long as there is only one resource adapter in the transaction. An application may need to use a compensating transaction (see Section 8.7.4 on page 269) if it is necessary to access multiple resources within a single transaction. An application should use a NoTransaction resource adapter only if transactional access to a particular EIS is not important.

8.9   Summary

This chapter provides the guidelines for using transactions on the J2EE platform. It describes the J2EE transactional model available to each J2EE component type—application clients, JSP pages and servlets, and enterprise beans—and enterprise information systems.

The J2EE platform provides powerful support for writing transactional applications. It contains the Java Transaction API, which allows applications to access transactions in a manner that is independent of specific implementations and provides a means for declaratively specifying the transactional needs of an application. These capabilities shift the burden of transaction management from J2EE application component providers to J2EE product vendors. Application component providers can thus focus on specifying the desired transaction behavior and rely on a J2EE product to implement the behavior.

8.10   References and Resources

- *Transaction Processing: Concepts and Techniques*. J. Gray, A. Reuter. Copyright 1992, Morgan Kaufman Publishers.

- *Principles of Transaction Processing for the Systems Professional*. P. Bernstein, E. Newcomer. Copyright 1996, Morgan Kaufman Publishers.

- *Distributed TP: The XA Specification*. The Open Group. Copyright 1992.

- The Java Transaction Architecture specification
  `<http://java.sun.com/products/jta>`

- The Java Connector Architecture specification
  `<http://java.sun.com/j2ee/download.html>`

Security

by Ron Monzillo

IN an enterprise computing environment, failure, compromise, or lack of availability of computing resources can jeopardize the viability of the enterprise. An organization must take steps to identify threats to security. Once they are identified, steps should be taken to reduce these threats.

Although J2EE products, and hence J2EE applications, may not displace existing enterprise security infrastructures, they do offer significant value when integrated with these existing infrastructures. The J2EE application programming model attempts to leverage existing security services rather than require new services or mechanisms.

This discussion begins with a review of some security concepts and mechanisms. It describes the security concerns and characteristics of enterprise applications and explores the application of J2EE security mechanisms to the design, implementation, and deployment of secure enterprise applications.

9.1 Security Threats and Mechanisms

Threats to enterprise-critical assets fall into a few general categories:

- Disclosure of confidential information

- Modification or destruction of information

- Misappropriation of protected resources

- Compromise of accountability

- Misappropriation that compromises availability

Depending on the environment in which an enterprise application operates, these threats may manifest themselves in different forms. For example, in a traditional single system environment, a threat of disclosure might manifest itself in the vulnerability of information kept in files. In a distributed environment with multiple servers and clients, a threat of disclosure might also result from exposures occurring as the result of networking.

Although not all threats can or need be eliminated, there are many circumstances where exposure can be reduced to an acceptable level through the use of the following security mechanisms: authentication, authorization, signing, encryption, and auditing. The following sections describe J2EE platform security mechanisms and indicate how to use the mechanisms to secure J2EE applications.

9.2   Authentication

In distributed component computing, *authentication* is the mechanism by which callers and service providers prove to one another that they are acting on behalf of specific users or systems. When the proof is bidirectional, it is referred to as *mutual authentication.* Authentication establishes the call identities and proves that the participants are authentic instances of these identities. An entity that participates in a call without establishing or proving an identity (that is, *anonymously*) is called *unauthenticated.*

When a client *program* run by a user makes the calls, the caller identity is likely to be that of the *user.* When the caller is an *application component* acting as an intermediary in a call chain originating with some user, the identity may be associated with that of the user, in which case the component would be *impersonating* the user. Alternatively, one application component may call another with an identity of its own and unrelated to that of its caller.

Authentication is often achieved in two phases. First, an *authentication context* is established by performing a service-independent authentication requiring knowledge of some secret. The authentication context encapsulates the identity and is able to fabricate *authenticators* (proofs of identity*).* Then, the authentication context is used to authenticate with other (called or calling) entities. The basis of authentication entails controlling access to the authentication context and thus the ability to authenticate as the associated identity. Among the possible policies and mechanisms for controlling access to an authentication context are:

- Once the user performs an initial authentication, the processes the user starts inherit access to the authentication context.

- When a component is authenticated, access to the authentication context may be available to other related or trusted components, such as those that are part of the same application.

- When a component is expected to *impersonate* its caller, the caller may *delegate* its authentication context to the called component.

9.2.1   Protection Domains

Some entities may communicate without requiring authentication. A *protection domain* is a set of entities that are assumed or known to trust each other. Entities in such a domain need not be authenticated to one another.

Figure 9.1 illustrates that authentication is only required for interactions that cross the boundary of a protection domain. When one component interacts with others in the same protection domain, no constraint is placed on the identity that it can associate with its call. The caller may *propagate* the caller's identity, or *choose* an identity based on knowledge of authorization constraints imposed by the called component, since the caller's ability to *claim* an identity is based on trust, not authentication. If the concept of protection domains is employed to avoid the need for authentication, there must be a means to establish the boundaries of protection domains so that trust in unproven identities does not cross these boundaries. Entities that are universally trusting of all other entities should not be trusted as a member of any protection domain.

In the J2EE architecture, a container provides an authentication boundary between external callers and the components it hosts. The boundaries of protection domains don't always align with those of containers. Containers enforce the boundaries, and implementations are likely to support protection domains that span containers. Although a container is not required to host components from different protection domains, an implementation may choose to do so.

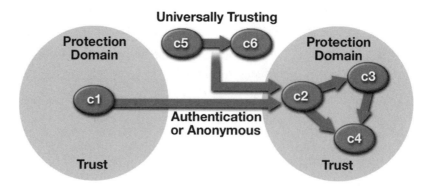

Figure 9.1   Protection Domain

For *inbound* calls, it is the container's responsibility to make an authentic representation of the caller identity available to the component in the form of a *credential*. An X.509 certificate and a Kerberos service ticket are examples of credentials used in computing environments. They are analogous to credentials such as a passport or a driver's license used in person-to-person interactions.

For *outbound* calls, the container is responsible for establishing the identity of the calling component. In general, it is the job of the container to provide bidirectional authentication functionality to enforce the protection domain boundaries of the deployed applications.

Without proof of component identity, the interacting containers must determine whether there is sufficient inter-container trust to accept the container-provided representations of component identity. In some environments, trust may simply be presumed; in others it may be evaluated more explicitly based on inter-container authentication and possibly the comparison of container identities to lists of trusted identities. If a required proof of identity is not provided, and when a sufficient inter-container trust relationship is absent, a container should reject or abandon a call.

Figure 9.2 illustrates these authentication concepts in two scenarios: an authenticated user scenario and an unauthenticated user scenario.

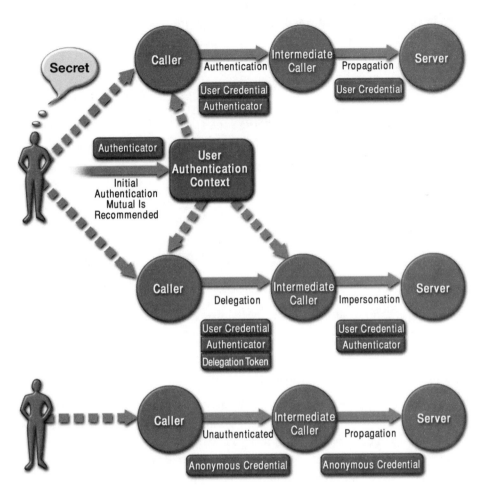

Figure 9.2 Authentication Scenarios

The authenticated user invokes a calling component that employs the user's authentication context to prove its identity to an intermediate component. When the called component makes a call, it propagates the identity of its caller. The propagated identity is unproven, so it will be accepted only if the targets trust the caller—that is, if they reside in the same protection domain.

The figure also differentiates identity propagation from delegation and subsequent impersonation. In propagation, the service providers bear the burden of determining whether they should accept propagated identities as authentic. In delegation, the user provides the called component with access to its authentication context, enabling the called component to impersonate the user in subsequent calls. Impersonation requires the user to trust the impersonator to act in its behalf.

The lower portion of the figure depicts the propagation of an unauthenticated user identity in the form of an anonymous credential. An anonymous credential is the one form of unproven identity that may be propagated independent of trust.

9.2.2   Authentication Mechanisms

In a typical J2EE application, a user would employ a client container to interact with enterprise resources in the Web or EJB tiers. Resources available to the user may be protected or unprotected. Protected resources are distinguished by the presence of *authorization rules* (see Section 9.3 on page 293) that restrict access to some subset of non-anonymous identities. To access a protected resource, a user must present a non-anonymous credential such that its identity can be evaluated against the resource authorization policy. In the absence of a trust relationship between the client and resource containers, the credential must be accompanied by an authenticator that demonstrates the user's right to claim the identity as its own. This section describes the various authentication mechanisms supported by the J2EE platform and how to configure them.

9.2.2.1   Web Tier Authentication

An application component provider can designate that a collection of Web resources (Web components, HTML documents, image files, compressed archives, and so on) is protected by specifying an authorization constraint (described in Section 9.3.7.1 on page 299) for the collection. When an unauthenticated user tries to access a protected Web resource, the Web container will prompt the user to authenticate with the Web container. The request will not be accepted by the Web container until the user identity has been proven to the Web container and shown to be one of the identities granted permission to access the resource. Caller authentication performed on the first access to a protected resource is called *lazy authentication.*

When a user tries to access a protected Web-tier resource, the Web container activates the authentication mechanism defined in the application's deployment descriptor. J2EE Web containers must support three authentication mechanisms: HTTP basic authentication, form-based authentication, and HTTPS mutual authentication. In addition, they are encouraged to support HTTP digest authentication.

In *basic authentication,* the Web server authenticates a principal using the user name and password obtained from the Web client. In *digest authentication* a Web client authenticates to a Web server by sending the server a message digest along with its HTTP request message. The digest is computed by employing a one-way hash algorithm to a concatenation of the HTTP request message and the client's password. The digest is typically much smaller than the HTTP request and doesn't contain the password.

Form-based authentication lets developers customize the authentication user interface presented by an HTTP browser. Like HTTP basic authentication, form-based authentication is a relatively vulnerable authentication mechanism, since the content of the user dialog is sent as plain text and the target server is not authenticated.

In single-sign on environments, discretion must be exercised in customizing an application's authentication interface. It may be preferable to provide a single enterprise-wide custom user authentication interface rather than implementing a set of application-specific interfaces.

With *mutual authentication,* the client and server use X.509 certificates to establish their identity. Mutual authentication occurs over a channel protected by SSL. Hybrid mechanisms featuring either HTTP basic authentication, form-based authentication, or HTTP digest authentication over an SSL protected channel are also supported. SSL is used to protect the authenticators during network communication and to authenticate the server to the client such that authenticators are not exchanged with the wrong entities.

9.2.2.1.1 Authentication Configuration

An authentication mechanism is configured using the `login-config` element of the Web component deployment descriptor. Code Example 9.1, Code Example 9.2, and Code Example 9.3 illustrate the declarations of the authentication mechanisms required of J2EE Web containers.

```
<web-app>
    <login-config>
        <auth-method>BASIC</auth-method>
        <realm-name>jpets</realm-name>
    </login-config>
</web-app>
```

Code Example 9.1   HTTP Basic Authentication Configuration

```
<web-app>
    <login-config>
        <auth-method>FORM</auth-method>
        <form-login-config>
            <form-login-page>login.jsp</form-login-page>
            <form-error-page>error.jsp</form-error-page>
        </form-login-config>
    </login-config>
</web-app>
```

Code Example 9.2   Form-Based Authentication Configuration

```
<web-app>
    <login-config>
        <auth-method>CLIENT-CERT</auth-method>
    </login-config>
</web-app>
```

Code Example 9.3   Client Certificate Authentication Configuration

9.2.2.1.2 Hybrid Authentication

In both HTTP basic and form-based authentication, passwords are not protected for confidentiality. This vulnerability can be overcome by running these authentication protocols over an SSL-protected session that ensures that all message content, including the client authenticators, are protected for confidentiality. Code Example 9.4 demonstrates how to configure HTTP basic authentication over SSL using the transport-guarantee element. Form-based authentication over SSL is configured in the same way.

```
<web-app>
    <security-constraint>
        ...
        <user-data-constraint>
            <transport-guarantee>CONFIDENTIAL</transport-guarantee>
        </user-data-constraint>
```

```
        </security-constraint>
    </web-app>
```

Code Example 9.4   SSL Hybrid Authentication Mechanism

9.2.2.1.3 Changing Authentication Identity

Sometimes users need to change authentication identities. This could happen when an authenticated user tries to visit a protected Web resource and is rebuffed for lack of access authority to the resource. Although the user can exit the browser and restart the authentication process, this is not always acceptable. Applications should give the user an opportunity to invalidate the authentication session and reauthenticate as a more appropriately privileged identity.

The `error-page` element may be used in the deployment descriptor of a Web application to configure a resource to be invoked by the Web container when the processing of an HTTP request produces a particular HTTP error code. This functionality may be employed to redirect an unauthorized request to a resource within the Web container that gives the user an opportunity to invalidate its authentication session. For example, the error-handling resource could return a form to the user containing the URI and parameters of the unauthorized request. The form would provide the user with an option to invalidate the current authentication session. Choosing to invalidate would cause the form containing the URI and parameters to be submitted to the Web container, where a session invalidation resource would be invoked. This resource would invalidate the current authentication session by calling `HttpSession.invalidate`. It then redirects the user, via the embedded URI and parameters, to the original unauthorized resource.

9.2.2.2   EJB Tier Authentication

Prior to J2EE 1.3 and EJB 2.0, the J2EE platform did not require that EJB containers implement specific authentication mechanisms. Moreover, in many environments, network firewall technology prevents direct interaction (via RMI) between client containers and enterprise beans. As a result, it is common for an EJB container to rely on the authentication mechanisms and network accessibility of a Web container to vouch for the identity of users accessing enterprise beans via protected Web components. As illustrated in Figure 9.3, such configurations use the Web container to enforce protection domain boundaries for Web components and the enterprise beans that they call.

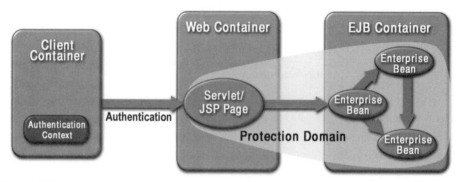

Figure 9.3   Typical J2EE Application Configuration

9.2.2.2.1 Common Secure Interoperability (CSIv2)

The J2EE 1.3 platform requires EJB containers and EJB client containers to support version 2 of the Common Secure Interoperability (CSIv2) protocol. CSIv2, a standard of the Object Management Group (OMG), defines a wire protocol for securing invocations made over RMI-IIOP. CSIv2 is designed to be used in environments where protecting the integrity or confidentiality of messages and authenticating servers to clients are enforced at the transport layer, perhaps by SSL or TLS. CSIv2 defines the Security Attribute Service (SAS) protocol that can be used above the transport to perform client authentication and impersonation where such functionality cannot be achieved using the underlying transport. The impersonation mechanism, called *identity assertion,* makes it possible for an intermediate to assert an identity other than its own, based on trust by the target in the intermediate. Identity assertion can be used by an intermediate J2EE container to propagate the identity of its callers in its calls. J2EE containers employ the CSIv2 identity assertion mechanism to establish the identities used by components to call other components as defined by application deployers. Figure 9.4 illustrates the CSIv2 architecture.

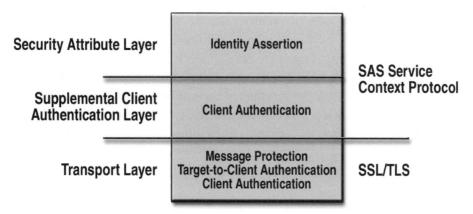

Figure 9.4   CSIv2 Protocol Architecture

CSIv2 defines an annotation language for application servers to use to communicate security requirements to clients. Application servers use this language in their *Interoperable Object References (IORs)* so that their security requirements are available to inform the actions of their clients. A target's security requirements are conveyed as a mechanism definition for each CSIv2 layer. Each of these defines the combination of supported and required security functionality that must be satisfied by clients of the target. When a J2EE application is deployed on an application server, the deployer must define the CSIv2 security policy to be communicated to clients and enforced by the application server. The most notable aspects of this policy are whether the target requires an integrity and/or confidentiality protected transport, whether the target requires client authentication, and the mechanism or mechanisms required for client authentication.

9.2.2.3   Client Identity Selection

The container of a J2EE server-side component establishes the invocation identity used when the component calls other J2EE components. The invocation identity established by the container depends on the identity selection policy defined by the deployer. A deployer may associate one of two identity selection policies with a component; `use-caller-identity` or `runas(role-name)`. The `use-caller-identity` policy causes the container to use the identity of a component's caller in all calls made by the component. The `runas(role-name)` policy causes the container to use a static identity selected by the deployer from the principal identities mapped to the named security role.

Component identity selection policies may be defined for J2EE Web and EJB resources. Application developers who wish to hold component callers account-able for actions the components perform on their behalf should associate a use-caller-identity policy with the components. Use of the runas(role-name) identity selection policy breaks the chain of traceability and may be used to afford the caller with the privileges of the component. Code Example 9.5 depicts the configuration of client identity selection policies in an EJB deployment descriptor.

```
<enterprise-beans>
    <entity>
        <security-identity>
            <use-caller-identity/>
        </security-identity>
        ...
    </entity>

    <session>
        <security-identity>
            <run-as>
                <role-name> guest </role-name>
            </run-as>
        </security-identity>
        ...
    </session>
    ...
</enterprise-beans>
```

Code Example 9.5   Configuring EJB Identity Selection Policies

Code Example 9.6 depicts the configuration of client identity selection policies in Web component deployment descriptors. In the absence of a run-as specification, the use-caller-identity policy is assumed.

```
<web-app>
    <servlet>
        <run-as>
```

```
                <role-name> guest </role-name>
            </run-as>
            ...
        </servlet>
        ...
    </web-app>
```

Code Example 9.6   Configuring Identity Selection Policies for Web Components

9.2.2.4   Enterprise Information System Tier Authentication

In integrating with enterprise information systems, J2EE components may use different security mechanisms and operate in different protection domains than the
resources they access. In these cases, the calling container can be configured to
manage the authentication to the resource for the calling component. This form of
authentication is called *container-managed resource manager sign on*. The J2EE
architecture also recognizes that some components require an ability to manage the
specification of caller identity and the production of a suitable authenticator directly.
For these applications, the J2EE architecture provides a means for an application
component to engage in what is called *application-managed resource manager sign
on*. Application-managed resource manager sign on is used when the ability to
manipulate the authentication details is a fundamental aspect of the component's
functionality.

The `resource-ref` elements of a component's deployment descriptor
(described in greater detail in Section 9.2.4 on page 293) declare the resources used
by the component. The value of the `res-auth` subelement declares whether sign
on to the resource is managed by the container or application. Components that
manage resource sign on can use the `EJBContext.getCallerPrincipal` or
`HttpServletRequest.getUserPrincipal` methods to obtain the identity of their
caller. A component can map the identity of its caller to a new identity and/or
authentication secret as required by the target enterprise information system. With
container-managed resource manager sign on, the container performs *principal
mapping* on behalf of the component.

Care should be taken to ensure that access to any component that encapsulates
or is provided by its container with a capability to sign on to another resource is
secured by appropriate authorization rules (see Section 9.3.6 on page 297).

The Connector architecture discussed in Section 6.2.1 on page 177 offers a
standard API for application-managed resource manager sign on. The Connector

provided API will ensure portability of components that authenticate with enterprise information systems.

9.2.3   Authentication Call Patterns

In a multitier, multicomponent application, certain call patterns should be avoided for usability reasons. For example, an application that calls protected EJB resources from unprotected Web resources can run into problems. This is because the Web tier's lazy authentication paradigm only provides users with an opportunity to authenticate when they attempt to access a protected resource. An unauthenticated user who attempts to visit an authentication-protected EJB resource from an unprotected Web resource will not be provided an opportunity to satisfy the authentication requirement of the EJB resource. One way to ensure that users of such applications can authenticate is to place protected Web resources in front of protected EJB components. Another approach is to include a link to a protected Web resource (perhaps appearing as an authenticate button) on Web resources that call protected EJB resources. This approach gives the user the option of authenticating by visiting a protected Web resource linked behind the button prior to accessing an EJB resource. This is especially useful where the user may have been denied access by the EJB container through an unprotected page.

Other call patterns should be avoided for security reasons. For example, when an application is deployed with a hybrid authentication mechanism, the deployer must ensure that the `transport-guarantee` element of each protected Web resource is set to `CONFIDENTIAL`. Otherwise, the client authenticator won't be fully protected. When form-based login is used over SSL, the `transport-guarantee` of the login page should be set to `CONFIDENTIAL`.

9.2.3.1   Self-Registration

Some Web-based applications must authenticate users whose identities cannot be known in advance of their first use of the application. In contrast to typical computer user authentication environments, where a user must wait for an administrator to set up the user's account, such applications require an automated means for users to register an authentication identity for themselves. To self-register, the user is required to provide his or her identity and may be required to provide a password to protect the account along with one or more additional forms of identification, agree to some contractual obligations, and/or provide credit card information for payment.

Once the registration dialog is complete, the user may authenticate as necessary to access the protected resources of the site.

The self-registration mechanisms provided by J2EE platforms are platform-specific. Applications that depend on these mechanisms should do so in a fashion that allows them to evolve, employing standard facilities and APIs as they are added to the platform. In the absence of portable self-registration mechanisms, application developers should resist the temptation to move user authentication and authorization into the application.

9.2.4   Exposing Authentication Boundaries with References

The application component provider is responsible for declaring references made by each component to other J2EE components and to external resources. These declarations are made in the deployment descriptor. In addition to their role in locating services, such declarations inform the deployer of all the places in the application where authentication may be necessary. Enterprise bean references are declared using `ejb-ref` elements. Enterprise information system references are declared with `resource-ref` elements. In both cases, the declarations are made in the scope of the calling component, and the collection of declared references serves to expose the application's inter-component/resource call tree.

J2EE platform deployment tools should present enterprise bean references to application deployers so that deployers know to secure interactions between the calling and called components. Deployers should use this knowledge to define CSIv2 security mechanism definitions that will appropriately secure the enterprise beans in all the ways that they are called. Deployers should use knowledge of the inter-container interactions that may occur as a result of the inter-component calls to configure appropriate inter-container security mechanisms and trust relationships.

9.3   Authorization

Authorization mechanisms limit interactions with resources to collections of users or systems for the purpose of enforcing integrity, confidentiality, or availability constraints. Such mechanisms allow only authentic caller identities to access components. Mechanisms provided by the J2EE platform can be used to control access to code based on identity properties, such as the location and signer of the calling code, and the identity of the user of the calling code. As mentioned in the section on authentication, caller identity can be established by selecting from the set of authentication contexts available to the calling code. Alternatively, the caller may propagate the identity of its caller, select an arbitrary identity, or make the call anonymously.

In all cases, a credential is made available to the called component. The credential contains information describing the caller through its identity attributes. In the case of anonymous callers, a special credential is used. These attributes uniquely identify the caller in the context of the authority that issued the credential. Depending on the type of credential, it may also contain other attributes that define shared authorization properties, such as group memberships, that distinguish collections of related credentials. The identity and shared authorization attributes in the credential are referred to as the caller's *security attributes.* In the J2SE platform, the identity attributes of the code used by the caller may also be included in the caller's security attributes. Access to the called component is determined by comparing the caller's security attributes with those required to access the called component.

In the J2EE architecture, a container serves as an authorization boundary between the components it hosts and their callers. The authorization boundary exists inside the container's authentication boundary so that authorization is considered in the context of successful authentication. For inbound calls, the container compares security attributes from the caller's credential with the access control rules for the target component. If the rules are satisfied, the call is allowed. Otherwise, the call is rejected.

There are two fundamental approaches to defining access control rules: *capabilities* and *permissions*. Capabilities focus on what a caller can do. Permissions focus on who can do something. The J2EE application programming model focuses on permissions. In the J2EE architecture, the job of the deployer is to map the permission model of the application to the capabilities of users in the operational environment.

9.3.1   Declarative Authorization

The deployer establishes the container-enforced access control rules associated with a J2EE application. The deployer uses a deployment tool to map an application permission model, which is typically supplied by the application assembler, to policy and mechanisms specific to the operational environment. The application permission model is defined in a deployment descriptor.

The deployment descriptor defines logical privileges called *security roles* and associates them with components to define privileges required to be granted permission to access components. The deployer assigns logical privileges to specific callers to establish the capabilities of users in the runtime environment. Callers are assigned logical privileges based on the values of their security attributes. For example, a deployer might map a security role to a security group in the operational environment. As a result, any caller whose security attributes indicate membership in the group is assigned the privilege represented by the role. As another example, a deployer might map a security role to a list containing one or more principal identities in the operational environment. Callers then authenticated by one of these identities are assigned the privilege represented by the role.

The EJB container grants permission to access a method only to callers that have at least one of the privileges associated with the method. Security roles also protect Web resource collections, that is, a URL pattern and an associated HTTP method, such as GET. The Web container enforces authorization requirements similar to those for an EJB container.

In both tiers, access control policy is defined at deployment time, rather than during application development. The deployer can modify the policy provided by the application assembler. The deployer refines the privileges required to access the components, and defines the correspondence between the security attributes presented by callers and the container privileges. In any container, the mapping from security attributes to privileges is scoped to the application so that the mapping applied to the components of one application may be different from that of another application.

9.3.2 Programmatic Authorization

A J2EE container makes access control decisions before dispatching method calls to a component. The logic or state of the component doesn't factor in these access decisions. However, a component can use two methods, `EJBContext.isCallerInRole` (for use by enterprise bean code) and `HttpServletRequest.isUserInRole` (for use by Web components), to perform finer-grained access control. A component uses these methods to determine whether a caller has been granted a privilege selected by the component based on the parameters of the call, the internal state of the component, or other factors such as the time of the call.

The application component provider of a component that calls one of these functions must declare the complete set of distinct `roleName` values to be used in all calls. These declarations appear in the deployment descriptor as `security-role-ref` elements. Each `security-role-ref` element links a privilege name embedded in the application as a `roleName` to a security role. Ultimately, the deployer establishes the link between the privilege names embedded in the application and the security roles defined in the deployment descriptor. The link between privilege names and security roles may differ for components in the same application.

In addition to testing for specific privileges, an application component can compare the identity of its caller, acquired using `EJBContext.getCallerPrincipal` or `HttpServletRequest.getUserPrincipal`, to the distinguished caller identities embedded in the state of the component when it was created. If the identity of the caller is equivalent to a distinguished caller, the component can allow the caller to proceed. If not, the component can prevent the caller from further interaction. The caller principal returned by a container depends on the authentication mechanism used by the caller. Also, containers from different vendors may return different principals for the same user authenticating by the same mechanism. To account for variability in principal forms, an application developer who chooses to apply distinguished caller state in component access decisions should allow multiple distinguished caller identities, representing the same user, to be associated with components. This is recommended especially where application flexibility or portability is a priority.

9.3.3   Declarative versus Programmatic Authorization

There is a trade-off between the external access control policy configured by the deployer and the internal policy embedded in the application by the component provider. The external policy is more flexible after the application has been written. The internal policy provides more flexible functionality while the application is being written. In addition, the external policy is transparent and completely comprehensible to the deployer, while internal policy is buried in the application and may only be completely understood by the application developer. These trade-offs should be considered in choosing the authorization model for particular components and methods.

9.3.4   Isolation

When designing the access control rules for protected resources, take care to ensure that the authorization policy is consistently enforced across all the paths by which the resource may be accessed. For example, when method-level access control rules are applied to a component, care must be taken that a less-protected method does not serve to undermine the policy enforced by a more rigorously protected method. Such considerations are most significant when component state is shared by disparately-protected methods or URL patterns. The simplifying rule of thumb is to apply the same access control rules to all the access paths of a component and to partition an application as necessary to enforce this guideline unless there is some specific need to architect an application otherwise.

As a point of information, the CSIv2 annotations defined in IORs pertain to all the methods of an enterprise bean. This means that one cannot differentiate the protection of methods of an enterprise bean with respect to authentication, integrity, or confidentiality.

9.3.5 Affects of Identity Selection

When setting an application's access control policy, the application component provider bases policy decisions on assumptions about the call identities selected by the application callers. When a call passes through intermediary components, the caller identity at the destination component may depend on the identity selection decisions made by the intermediaries. The destination component may assume that caller identities have been propagated along the call chain so that the caller identity is that of the caller who initiated the chain. In other cases, the called component must assume that one or more of the callers in its call path will employ an identity selection policy other than identity propagation. The application assembler is responsible for communicating component identity selection policies in the deployment descriptors. In the absence of a specific representation of identity selection policy from the assembler, the deployer should assume that a component will call other components using the identity of its caller.

9.3.6 Encapsulation for Access Control

An application's component model may impose authorization boundaries around what might otherwise be unprotected resources, using accessor components to implement the authorization barrier. If accessor components are used in this way, access control can either be done externally by the container, internally by the component, or both.

An accessor component may encapsulate the mapping to an authentication context suitable for interacting with an external resource. When using principal mapping to authenticate and gain access to enterprise information system resources, authorization mechanisms applied to the accessor component can control who is authorized to access a mapping. Depending on the form of the mapping, the authorization rules may be more or less complex. For example, if all access to a resource is performed via a single conceptually omnipotent enterprise information system tier identity, then the J2EE application can implement secure access to the resource by limiting who can use the accessor. If the mapping of authentication context is many-to-many, then the authorization configuration of the accessor may need to define which of a collection of mappings are accessible to a caller and which should be assumed by default if a caller does not assert the mapping it requires.

9.3.6.1   Shared Accessor Identity

An accessor component may be given access to an external resource either by container-managed sign on or bean-managed sign on. Permissions associated with the methods of the component ensure that access to the external resource is granted only to those J2EE principals that have access to the component.

9.3.6.2   Private Accessor Identity

An enterprise bean, such as a stateful session bean, can use bean-managed sign on to an external resource. The session bean relies on a protected entity bean to map the J2EE principal to the corresponding principal in the external resource's realm, and also to the corresponding authenticator if necessary. In this scenario, either one protected entity bean holds all the mappings, and that bean limits access to a particular mapping to specific principals (returned by `getCallerPrincipal`), or there is one entity bean per mapping. Section 9.3.2 on page 295 describes how application developers who place a priority on application flexibility and portability must account for variability in `getCallerPrincipal` return values.

9.3.7   Controlling Access to J2EE Resources

A client typically uses a J2EE application's container to interact with enterprise resources in the Web or EJB tiers. These resources may be protected or unprotected. Protected resources have authorization rules defined in deployment descriptors that restrict access to some subset of non-anonymous identities. To access protected resources, users must present non-anonymous credentials to enable their identities to be evaluated against the resource authorization policy.

9.3.7.1   Controlling Access to Web Resources

To control access to a Web resource, an application component provider or application assembler specifies a `security-constraint` element with an `auth-constraint` subelement in the Web deployment descriptor. Code Example 9.7 illustrates the definition of a protected resource in a Web component deployment descriptor. The descriptor specifies that the URL `/control/placeorder` can be accessed only by users acting in the role of `customer`.

```
<security-constraint>
    <web-resource-collection>
        <web-resource-name>placeorder</web-resource-name>
        <url-pattern>/control/placeorder</url-pattern>
        <http-method>POST</http-method>
        <http-method>GET</http-method>
    </web-resource-collection>
    <auth-constraint>
        <role-name>customer</role-name>
    </auth-constraint>
</security-constraint>
```

Code Example 9.7   Web Resource Authorization Configuration

9.3.7.2   Controlling Access to Enterprise Beans

An application component provider or application assembler that has defined security roles for an enterprise bean can also specify the methods of the bean's remote, home, local, and local home interfaces that each security role is allowed to invoke. This is done in the form of `method-permission` elements. Ultimately, the assignment of users to roles determines if a resource is protected. When the roles required to access the enterprise bean are assigned only to authenticated users, the bean is protected.

Code Example 9.8 contains two styles of method specifications. The first refers to all of the methods of all of the interfaces (that is, remote, home, local, and local home) of an enterprise bean. The second refers to a specific method that occurs on an interface of an enterprise bean. If there are multiple methods with the same overloaded name, this style refers to all overloaded methods. Method specifications can be further qualified to identify methods with overloaded names by parameter signature, or to refer to methods of a specific interface of the enterprise bean.

```
<method-permission>
    <role-name>admin</role-name>
        <method>
            <ejb-name>TheOrder</ejb-name>
            <method-name>*</method-name>
        </method>
</method-permission>

<method-permission>
    <role-name>customer</role-name>
    <method>
        <ejb-name>TheOrder</ejb-name>
        <method-name>getDetails</method-name>
    </method>
    <method>
    . . .
</method-permission>
```

Code Example 9.8   Enterprise Bean Authorization Configuration

In addition to the authorization policy defined in method-permission elements, method specifications may be added to the exclude-list to indicate that access to them is to be denied independent of caller identity and whether the methods are the subject of a method-permission element. Code Example 9.9 demonstrates the use of the exclude-list.

```
<exclude-list>
    <method>
        <ejb-name>SpecialOrder</ejb-name>
        <method-name>*</method-name>
    </method>
    <method>
    ...
</exclude-list>
```

Code Example 9.9   Enterprise Bean Excluded `method-permission`

9.3.7.3   Unprotected Resources

Many applications feature unprotected Web-tier content, available to any caller without authentication. Unprotected resources are characterized by the absence of a requirement that their caller be authenticated. In the Web tier, unrestricted access is provided simply by leaving out an authentication rule.

Some applications also feature unprotected enterprise beans. For example, the sample application allows anonymous, unauthenticated users to access certain EJB resources. In the EJB tier, the application assembler uses the `unchecked` element in the `method-permission` element to indicate that the methods covered by the specification are to be authorized by the container, independent of the identity of the caller. Code Example 9.10 demonstrates the use of the `unchecked` element.

```
<method-permission>
    <unchecked/>
    <method>
        <ejb-name>Catalogue</ejb-name>
        <method-name>browseSpecials</method-name>
    </method>
    <method>
    ...
</method-permission>
```

Code Example 9.10   Enterprise Bean Unchecked `method-permission`

9.3.8   Example

To understand how each application, and each component within an application, can apply its own authorization requirements, consider the following examples.

One application is assembled from two enterprise beans, EJB 1 and EJB 2, each with one method. Each method calls `isCallerInRole` with the role name `MANAGER`. The deployment descriptor includes a `security-role-ref` element for the call to `isCallerInRole` in each enterprise bean. The `security-role-ref` for EJB 1 links `MANAGER` to the role `good-managers` and the `security-role-ref` element for EJB 2 links `MANAGER` to the role `bad-managers`. The deployment descriptor defines two method-permission elements. One establishes that the role `employees` can access all methods of EJB 1 and the other does the same for EJB 2. The deployment descriptor has 3 `security-role` elements: `employees`, `good-managers`, and `bad-managers`. The deployer assigns User 1 to roles `employees` and `good-managers` and assigns User 2 to roles `employees` and `bad-managers`.

A second application, with one enterprise bean EJB 3, is also deployed in the container. EJB 3 also makes a call to `isCallerInRole` with the role name `MANAGER`. The deployment descriptor for this second application contains a `security-role-ref` element that links `MANAGER` to the role `good-managers`. Similarly, the deployment descriptor defines one `method-permission` element that establishes that the role `employees` can access all the methods of EJB 3. The deployment descriptor has 2 role elements, `employees` and `good-managers`. The deployer assigns User 2 to roles `employees` and `good-managers`.

Figure 9.5 illustrates the configuration of method permissions as a relationship between roles and methods. It also illustrates the mapping of caller security attributes to roles, and the link between privilege names embedded in the application and roles.

Table 9.1 lists the authorization decisions that occur when different users initiate method calls on these enterprise beans. For example, when User 1 initiates a method call on EJB 2's method, the container dispatches the call because the `method-permission` element specifies the security roles `employees` and `good-managers`, and the deployer has assigned User 1 to the `employees` security role. However, the `isCallerInRole("MANAGER")` method returns false, because the `security-role-ref` element for EJB 2 links `MANAGER` to the security role `bad-managers`, which is not satisfied for User 1. When User 1 invokes a method on EJB 3, the call isn't even dispatched, because User 1 isn't assigned to any security roles.

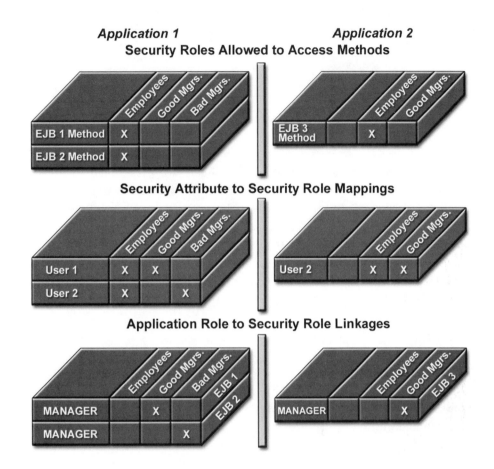

Figure 9.5   Authorization Scenario

Table 9.1   Authorization Decisions

Call	Call Dispatched?	isCallerInRole?
User 1 - EJB 1	yes	true
User 1 - EJB 2	yes	false
User 1 - EJB 3	no	never called
User 2 - EJB 1	yes	false

Table 9.1   Authorization Decisions (continued)

Call	Call Dispatched?	isCallerInRole?
User 2 - EJB 2	yes	true
User 2 - EJB 3	yes	true

9.4   Protecting Messages

In a distributed computing system, a significant amount of information is transmitted through networks in the form of messages. Message content is subject to three main types of attacks. Messages might be intercepted and modified for the purpose of changing the affects they have on their recipients. Messages might be captured and reused one or more times for the benefit of another party. Messages might be monitored by an eavesdropper in an effort to capture information that would not otherwise be available. Such attacks can be minimized by using integrity and confidentiality mechanisms.

9.4.1   Integrity Mechanisms

Integrity mechanisms ensure that communication between entities is not being tampered with by another party, especially one that can intercept and modify their communications. Integrity mechanisms can also be used to ensure that messages can only be used once.

Message integrity is ensured by attaching a *message signature* to a message. The message signature is calculated by using a one-way hash algorithm to convert the message contents into a typically smaller, fixed-length *message digest* that is then *signed* (that is, cryptographically enciphered, typically using a public key mechanism). A message signature ensures that modification of the message by anyone other than the caller will be detectable by the receiver.

In the J2EE architecture, a container serves as an authentication boundary between callers and the components it hosts. Information may flow in both directions on a call (that is, a call may have input, output, or input and output parameters). The deployer is responsible for configuring containers to safeguard interactions between components. A deployer should configure the containers involved in a call to implement integrity mechanisms either because the call will traverse open or unprotected networks or because the call will be made between components that do not trust each other.

The performance cost associated with applying integrity protection to all message communication is as much a property of the operational environment as it is a consequence of the cost of the protection. One way to safeguard the integrity of application messages without unnecessarily limiting the space of operational environments is to capture application-specific knowledge identifying which messages must be integrity protected. The place to capture this information is in the application's deployment descriptor.

9.4.2   Confidentiality Mechanisms

Confidentiality mechanisms ensure private communication between entities. Privacy is achieved by encrypting the message contents. Symmetric (or shared secret) encryption mechanisms generally require less computing resources than asymmetric (or public key) mechanisms. It is therefore quite common to use an asymmetric mechanism to secure the exchange of a symmetric encryption key that is then used to encrypt the message traffic.

The deployer is responsible for configuring containers to apply confidentiality mechanisms that ensure sensitive information is not disclosed to third parties. Despite the improved performance of shared secret mechanisms, message encryption costs are significant. They can have an adverse effect on performance when confidentiality mechanisms are applied where they are not needed. The application assembler should supply the deployer with information on those components that should be protected for confidentiality. The deployer then configures the corresponding containers to employ a confidentiality mechanism whenever interactions with these components occurs over open or unprotected networks. In addition to applying confidentiality mechanisms where appropriate, the deployer should configure containers to reject call requests or responses with message content that should be protected but isn't. Message integrity may be verified as a side effect of enforcing confidentiality.

The J2EE platform requires that containers support transport layer integrity and confidentiality mechanisms based on SSL/TLS so that security properties applied to communications are established as a side effect of creating a connection.

9.4.3   Identifying Sensitive Components

It is recommended that the application assembler identify the components with method calls whose parameters or return values should be protected for integrity or confidentiality. The deployment descriptor is used to convey this information. For

enterprise beans, this is done in a `description` subelement of the target EJB component. For servlets and JSP pages, this is done in the `transport-guarantee` subelement of the `user-data-constraint` subelement of a `security-constraint`. In
cases where a component's interactions with an external resource are known to carry
sensitive information, these sensitivities should be described in the `description`
subelement of the corresponding `resource-ref`.

9.4.4   Ensuring Confidentiality of Web Resources

In addition to understanding how to configure Web transport guarantees, it is important to understand the properties of HTTP methods and the effects these properties
have when following a link from one Web resource to another. When a resource
contains links to other resources, the nature of the links determines how the protection context of the current resource affects the protection of requests made to the
linked resources.

When a link is *absolute* (that is, the URL begins with `https://` or `http://`),
the HTTP client container will ignore the context of the current resource and
access the linked resource based on the nature of the absolute URL. If the URL of
the link begins with `https://`, a protected transport will be established with the
server before the request is sent. If the URL of the link begins with `http://`, the
request will be attempted over an insecure transport. When the link is *relative*, the
HTTP client container will protect an access to a linked resource based on
whether the resource in which the link occurs was protected.

The application developer should consider these link properties most carefully when a linked request must carry confidential data back to the server. There
are a few choices available to ensure security in such cases. For example, an application developer might choose to use secure absolute links to ensure the transport
protection of requests that carry confidential data. This solves the security
problem at the expense of constraining the application to a very specific naming
environment.

When an application opts for portability and uses relative links, another
option is for the deployer to configure the application so that wherever there is a
confidential interaction from one resource to another, both are deployed with a
confidential transport guarantee. This approach ensures that an HTTP client container does not send an unprotected request to a protected resource.

As a related point, the POST method is favored over the GET method for
delivering confidential request data, since data sent via GET appears in browser
location bars and in both client- and server-side logs.

9.5   Auditing

Auditing is the practice of capturing a record of security-related events to hold users or systems accountable for their actions. The value of auditing is not solely to determine whether security mechanisms are limiting access to a system. When security is breached, it is usually much more important to know who has been allowed access than who has been denied access. Knowing who has interacted with a system allows the determination of accountability for a breach of security. Moreover, to use auditing to evaluate the effective security of a system, there must be a clear understanding of what is audited and what is not.

The deployer is responsible for configuring the security mechanisms to be applied by the enterprise containers. Each configured mechanism may be thought of as a constraint that the containers will attempt to enforce on interactions between components. It should be possible for the deployer or system administrator to review the security constraints established for the platform and to associate an audit behavior with each constraint so that the container will audit one of the following:

- All evaluations where the constraint was satisfied

- All evaluations where it was not satisfied

- All evaluations independent of outcome

- No evaluations

It is also prudent to audit all changes (resulting from deployment or subsequent administration) to the audit configuration or the constraints being enforced by the platform. Audit records must be protected so that attackers cannot escape accountability for their actions by expunging incriminating records or changing their content.

The J2EE programming model shifts the burden of auditing from developers and integrators to those who are responsible for application deployment and management. Therefore, although not currently mandated by the J2EE specification, it is recommended that J2EE containers provide auditing functionality that facilitates the evaluation of container-enforced security policy.

9.6   Summary

A primary goal of the J2EE platform is to relieve the application developer from the details of security mechanisms and facilitate the secure deployment of an application in diverse environments. The J2EE platform addresses this goal by defining a clear separation of responsibility among those who develop application components, those who assemble components into applications, and those who configure applications for use in a specific environment. By allowing the component provider and application assembler to specify the parts of an application that require security, deployment descriptors provide a means outside of code for the developer to communicate these needs to the deployer. They also enable container-specific tools to give the deployer easier ways to engage the security constraints recommended by the developer.

An application component provider identifies all of the security dependencies embedded in a component including:

- The names of all the role names used by the component in calls to `isCallerInRole` or `isUserInRole`

- References to all of the external resources accessed by the component

- References to all the inter-component calls made by the component

An application component provider may also provide a method permission model, along with information that identifies the sensitivity with respect to privacy of the information exchanged in particular calls.

An application assembler combines one or more components into an application package and then rationalizes the external view of security provided by the individual components to produce a consistent security view for the application as a whole. The objective of the application assembler is to provide this information so that it can inform the actions of a deployer.

A deployer is responsible for taking the security view of the application provided by the application assembler and using it to secure the application in a specific operational environment. The deployer uses a platform-specific deployment tool to map the view provided by the assembler to the policies and mechanisms that are specific to the operational environment. The security mechanisms configured by the deployer are implemented by containers on behalf of the components hosted in the containers.

J2EE security mechanisms combine the concepts of container hosting, plus the declarative specification of application security requirements, with the availability of application-embedded mechanisms. This provides a powerful model for secure, interoperable, distributed component computing.

9.7   References and Resources

For additional information on security in the J2EE platform, consult the following:

- *The Java™ 2 Platform, Enterprise Edition, Specification*, v1.3. Copyright 2000, Sun Microsystems, Inc. <http://java.sun.com/j2ee>

- *Enterprise JavaBeans™ 2.0 Specification*. Copyright 2001, Sun Microsystems, Inc. <http://java.sun.com/products/ejb/docs.html>

- *The Java™ Servlet 2.3 Specification*. Copyright 2001, Sun Microsystems, Inc. <http://jcp.org/aboutJava/communityprocess/first/jsr053/>

- Document formal/01-12-30 (CORBA 2.6 - chapter 26 - *Secure Interoperability*). The Object Management Group. Copyright 1997-2002. <http://www.omg.org/cgi-bin/doc?formal/01-12-30>

- *The J2EE™ Tutorial*, S. Bodoff, D. Green, K. Haase, E. Jendrock, M. Pawlan, B. Stearns. Copyright 2002, Addison-Wesley. <http://java.sun.com/j2ee/tutorial>

- INTERNET-DRAFT, *The SSL Protocol Version 3.0*. A. Freier, P. Karlton, and P. Kocher, IETF Transport Layer Security Working Group, 1996. <http://www.netscape.com/eng/ssl3/draft302.txt>

- RFC-2617, *HTTP Authentication: Basic and Digest Access Authentication*. J. Franks, P. Hallam-Baker, J. Hostetler, S. Lawrence, P. Leach, A. Luotonen, and L. Stewart. Copyright 1999, The Internet Society. <http://www.ietf.org/rfc/rfc2617.txt>

- RFC-2818, HTTP Over TLS. E. Rescorla. Copyright 2000, The Internet Society. <http://www.ietf.org/rfc/rfc2818.txt>

- *Applied Cryptography*. B. Schneier. Copyright 1996, John Wiley & Sons, Inc.

J2EE Internationalization and Localization

by Greg Murray

Eₙₜₑᵣₚᵣᵢₛₑₛ are going global. Large organizations are expanding their reach across continents and cultures. Even small, family-owned companies are finding new customer bases and supply chain partners in parts of the world that they would not previously have considered. The Internet provides the communications backbone for increasing global interconnectedness.

To operate in a global arena, information systems must address a number of additional fundamental requirements, including:

- **Language requirements**—Users of a global application may speak any of dozens of languages. The relationship between geographic region and language spoken is complex; applications targeted at a single country often require multiple language interfaces. Representation of such quantities as numbers, dates, times, and currency vary by region.

- **Cultural concerns**—Some cultures use their traditional calendar instead of or in addition to the Gregorian calendar. A customer's interest level in a particular product may vary by culture. Products and services that are highly sought-after in one culture may be offensive in another.

- **Political differences**—Countries vary in customs law and information privacy requirements. Some governments place limitations on ideas, images, or speech.

- **Financial considerations**—Currencies are not necessarily freely convertible. Forms of payment may differ; for example, not all customers can be assumed to have a credit card or purchase order number. Governments have different requirements for customs restrictions, tariffs, and taxes.

- **Geographical factors**—Product pricing, available shipping modes, and delivery time may vary by both supply and product delivery location.

These are just a few of the scores of issues that arise when doing business in a global environment. This chapter presents techniques for creating flexible international J2EE applications and explains Java platform internationalization APIs.

10.1   Internationalization Concepts and Terminology

Internationalization terminology is commonly used inconsistently, even within the internationalization field. This section presents definitions of common internationalization terms as they are used in the rest of the chapter. For more detail and precision, see Unicode Technical Report 17 (UTR-17; see the reference listed in Section 10.9 on page 345).

10.1.1 Internationalization, Localization, and Locale

The set of political, cultural, and region-specific elements represented in an application is called a locale. Applications should customize data presentation to each user's locale. Internationalization, also known as "I18n," is the process of separating locale dependencies from an application's source code. Examples of locale dependencies include messages and user interface labels, character set, encoding, and currency and time formats. Localization (also called "L10n") is the process of adapting an internationalized application to a specific locale. An application must first be internationalized before it can be localized. Internationalization and localization make a J2EE application available to a global audience.

Class `java.util.Locale` represents a locale in the Java 2 Platform, Standard Edition (J2SE). A `Locale` object is an identifier in a program that determines such factors as how numbers, currency, and time should be displayed, and the human language used to present data in a user interface.

An internationalized J2EE application does not assume a single locale. Requests from clients arrive with an associated locale, which implies a locale for the response. A J2EE application often serves requests for many locales simultaneously. Determining the request locale and enforcing an appropriate response locale are important issues covered in Section 10.3.1 on page 321.

In many projects, application internationalization is an afterthought. But internationalizing an existing application usually requires a great deal of refactoring. Because internationalization affects all J2EE application tiers, it is fundamentally an architectural issue. Internationalization is much easier to achieve if it is integrated into the application design. A project's design phase should identify and separate locale dependencies if the application might ever need to support multiple locales.

10.1.1.1 Standard Locale Naming Convention

The J2SE standard class `java.util.ResourceBundle` (see Section 10.2.1 on page 316) defines a naming convention for locales, which should be used whenever organizing resources by locale. A locale name consists of international standard 2-character abbreviations for language (ISO 639) and country (ISO 3166), and an optional variant, which is a browser- and vendor-specific code for identifying platform differences. The Java platform does not define the possible values and semantics of variants. Any of the three parts of a locale may be empty and are separated by underscore characters ('_'). Examples of locale names might include `fr` (French), `de_CH` (Swiss German), and `en_US_POSIX` (United States English on a POSIX-compliant platform). For more on this naming convention, see the J2SE javadoc for class `java.util.ResourceBundle`.

10.1.2 Character Sets

A character set is a set of graphic, textual symbols, each of which is mapped to a set of nonnegative integers. For example, ASCII (ANSI X3.4-1968, ISO 646) defines a character set that is commonly used for representing American English. Japanese schools and official Japanese government documents use the Joyo Kanji, a fixed set of 1,945 characters. For the purposes of this chapter, "character set" means "coded character set," as defined in UTR-17.

A character set assigns a nonnegative integer, called a code point, to each character. For example, the ASCII code point for lowercase 'a' is 97 (hex 61).

10.1.2.2 ASCII

The most common character set used to represent American English is ASCII (American Standard Code for Information Interchange). Code points in 7-bit ASCII (called US-ASCII) range from 0 to 127. ASCII contains upper- and lower-case Roman alphabets, European numerals, punctuation, a set of control codes (non-graphic code points from decimal 0 to 31), and a few miscellaneous symbols.

Many early Internet protocols were based on 7-bit ASCII, greatly complicating Web application support of languages other than American English.

10.1.2.3 The 8859 Series

The ISO 8859 character set series was created to overcome some of the limitations of ASCII. Each ISO 8859 character set may have up to 256 characters. ISO 8859-1 ("Latin-1") comprises the ASCII character set, plus characters with diacritics (accents, diaereses, cedillas, circumflexes, and the like), and additional symbols. The ISO 8859 series defines thirteen character sets (ISO 8859-1 through -10 and ISO 8859-13 through -15) that can represent texts in dozens of languages.

10.1.2.4 Unicode

Unicode (ISO 10646) defines a standardized, universal character set with 21-bit code points. Unicode was designed to represent virtually all character sets currently in use around the world today and can be extended to accommodate additions. Unicode encompasses alphabetic scripts, ideographic writing systems, and phonetic syllabaries, and may be rendered in any direction.

The Java programming language internally represents characters and String objects as 16-bit encoded Unicode (version 3.0 for Java 1.4). Programs written in the Java programming language can therefore process data in multiple languages, natively performing localized operations such as string comparison, parsing, and collation.

Unicode characters in Java program source files may be represented as escape sequences, using the notation \u*XXXX*, where *XXXX* is the character's 16-bit code point in hexadecimal. Unicode-escaped strings are very useful when program source files are not encoded as Unicode. Unicode escape sequences also provide support for multiple scripts using a single file encoding.

10.1.3 Encodings

An encoding maps a character set's code points to units of a specific width, and defines byte serialization and ordering rules. The Unicode 3.0 encoding UTF-32BE encodes Unicode code points as 32-bit unsigned integers with big-endian byte ordering. For the purposes of this chapter, "encoding" means "character encoding form serialized by character encoding scheme," as defined by UTR-17.

Many character sets have more than one encoding. For example, Java programs can represent Japanese character sets using the EUC-JP or Shift-JIS encodings, among others. Each encoding has rules for representing and serializing a character set.

J2SE package `java.io` contains classes that support reading and writing character data streams in various encodings. These classes all have names that end in `Reader` (for example, `BufferedReader` and `InputStreamReader`) and `Writer` (`BufferedWriter`, `PrintWriter`).

JSP pages and servlets both use `PrintWriter` to produce responses, which automatically performs encoding. Servlets may output binary data with `OutputStream` classes, which perform no encoding. An application that uses a character set that cannot use the default encoding (ISO 8859-1) must explicitly set a different encoding. A reference to the encoding section of the J2SE documentation is listed in Section 10.9 on page 345.

10.1.3.5 UTF-8

UTF-8 (Unicode Transformation Format, 8 bit form) is a variable-width character encoding that encodes 16-bit Unicode characters as one to four 8-bit quantities. UTF-8 unifies US-ASCII with Unicode. A byte in UTF-8 is equivalent to 7-bit ASCII if its high-order bit is zero; otherwise, the character comprises a variable number of bytes. Another encoding, UCS-2, encodes each Unicode character in a fixed width of 16 bits. Documents encoded in UTF-8 tend to be smaller than documents encoded in UCS-2, because most characters are encoded in one byte instead of two.

Many new Web standards specify UTF-8 as their character encoding. UTF-8 is compatible with the majority of existing Web content and provides access to the Unicode character set. Current versions of browsers and email clients support UTF-8. UTF-8 is one of the two required encodings for XML documents (the other is UTF-16). Encoding internationalized content in UTF-8 is a BluePrints recommendation.

10.2   Using J2SE Internationalization APIs in J2EE Applications

J2SE internationalization APIs include utility classes and interfaces for externalizing application resources, formatting messages, formatting currency and decimals, representing dates and times, and collating. The next few sections explain how to use J2SE internationalization APIs in J2EE applications.

10.2.1 Resource Bundles

J2SE applications store locale-specific resources such as GUI item labels, menu items, and help text in classes called resource bundles. Resource bundles support internationalization by separating localized data from the code that uses it. Each resource bundle class contains localized resources for a particular locale. A resource bundle is a map of key/value pairs, where the keys are names that are shared across locales, and the values are resources localized to the resource bundle's locale. Application code references locale-specific resources by key rather than storing them directly.

Figure 10.1   Resource Bundles Map Key Strings to Localized Resources

For example, Figure 10.1 shows four separate resource bundles for English, French, German, and Japanese, which map the key YesLabel to localized strings for "Yes," "Oui," "Ja," and "Hai," respectively. Application source code would look up the localized string by name (YesLabel) from the resource bundle corresponding to the desired locale. The resource bundle class names are formed from the base name of the bundle for the default locale (MyBundle in this example), plus an optional underscore and locale, using the naming convention described in Section 10.1.1.1 on page 313.

Subclasses of abstract class `java.util.ListResourceBundle` keep named resources in an internal list, while subclasses of `java.util.PropertyResourceBundle` store them in external, textual property files. Application clients or rich clients can load resource bundle classes dynamically corresponding to the client's locale.

J2EE applications can also use resource bundles. Code Example 10.1 shows a very simple resource bundle for two messages in English.

```
public class WebMessages extends java.util.ListResourceBundle{
    public Object [][] getContents(){
        return contents;
    }
    static final Object[][] contents = {
        //Messages
        {"com.sun.blueprints.messages.welcome",
            "Welcome to the Java(TM) Pet Store"},
        {"com.sun.messages.come_back_soon",
            "Come Back Soon"}
    }
}
```

Code Example 10.1   An English Resource Bundle

Class `WebMessages` associates the localized English string `Welcome to Java(TM) Pet Store` with the name `com.sun.blueprints.messages.welcome` and associates the string `Come Back Soon` with the name `com.sun.messages.come_back_soon`. Application code retrieves localized strings by name from an instance of this class.

Adding support for new languages is as simple as creating another subclass of `ListResourceBundle`. Code Example 10.2 shows the source code for a resource bundle that provides localized Japanese text for one of the messages in Code Example 10.1.

```
public class WebMessages_ja extends java.util.ListResourceBundle{
    public Object [][] getContents(){
        return contents;
    }
```

```
static final Object[][] contents = {
    //Messages
    {"com.sun.blueprints.messages.welcome",
        "\uE382\u88E3\u8186\uE381\u9383\u819D"}
        // (Unicode for Japanese phrase)
}
}
```

Code Example 10.2   A Japanese Resource Bundle

Class `WebMessages_ja` defines a Japanese localized string for one of the keys used by class `WebMessages`. Note that the resource bundle's class file name ends with `_ja`, indicating that it is Japanese. Static method `ResourceBundle.getResource` determines the class name of the resource bundle to load for a locale by appending a suffix to the name of the bundle. The suffix follows the standard locale naming convention described in Section 10.1.1.1 on page 313.

Note that a locale-specific resource bundle class need not specify localized messages for all keys. Class `ResourceBundle` always uses the most specific localized string it can find, falling back to the class name with no suffix if a string cannot be found. Because Code Example 10.2 does not define a localized string for key `com.sunw.messages.come_back_soon`, a request for the string associated with that key will return `Come Back Soon`, the string defined in the default bundle defined in Code Example 10.3.

Code Example 10.3 shows code, possibly from a servlet or JSP page, that retrieves a resource bundle for a locale, and uses it to print a localized string.

```
// Get Japanese resource bundle
ResourceBundle messages = ResourceBundle.getResource("WebMessages",
Locale.JAPAN);
// Get localized string
String greeting =
messages.getString("com.sun.blueprints.messages.welcome");
// Output welcome message
out.println(greeting);
```

Code Example 10.3   Getting Messages from a Resource Bundle

Remember that an application should deliver content corresponding to the locale of the client, not the locale of the component container. As previously mentioned, UTF-8 encoding is recommended because it can display multiple languages on a single Web page and has wide browser support.

When a locale is not specified, resource bundles default to the container's default locale. The container's default locale should be set to a value appropriate for the majority of an application's users.

10.2.2 Message Formatting

Of course, localized content cannot be limited to static strings retrieved from resource bundles. The J2SE standard class `java.text.MessageFormat` provides a generic way to create concatenated message strings. A `MessageFormat` object contains a pattern string with embedded format specifiers. Method `MessageFormat.format` formats an array of objects using the format specifiers embedded in the pattern and returns the result as a `StringBuffer`.

```
String pattern = "Order number {0}, line item {1}: this item is out
    of stock.";
MessageFormat mf = new MessageFormat(pattern);
Object[] objs = new Object[] {
    new Integer(orderNumber),
    new Integer(lineNumber)
};
StringBuffer result = new StringBuffer();
String message = mf.format(objs, result, new FieldPosition());
//... use formatted message...
```

Code Example 10.4 Using `MessageFormat` to Format a Message

Code Example 10.4 illustrates how to use `MessageFormat` to format a message. The `MessageFormat` holds the pattern and uses it to format the result string, substituting formatted objects (`Integer` objects in this case) in place of format specifiers {0} and {1}. Code Example 10.4 is internationalized because it retrieves a format pattern from a resource bundle for the desired locale.

`MessageFormat` is recommended for formatting system-level messages such as error or logging strings. While `MessageFormat` is powerful, it is too programmatic for creating most internationalized dynamic Web content; instead, consider using

JSP pages for that purpose. `MessageFormat` can be used very effectively to internationalize JSP custom tags.

10.2.3 Date Formatting

Virtually all enterprise applications store, compare, and perform arithmetic on date values. Both calendars and textual representations of date and time values vary by locale. Calendars vary among regions, cultures, and organizations. For example, many cultures use lunar calendars, and some companies have their own corporate calendar. Even two locales that use the same calendar may represent times and dates differently.

The standard class `java.util.Date` represents date values. Its subclass, `java.sql.Date`, represents date values returned from JDBC data sources.

The standard J2SE platform abstract class `java.util.Calendar` represents abstract operations on date and time values, including assignment, comparison, and week day. Concrete subclasses of `Calendar` (`java.util.GregorianCalendar`, for example) implement abstract calendar operations in terms of a specific calendar system.

For textual representation of dates and times, the J2SE platform offers the standard abstract class `java.text.DateFormat` (and related classes). `DateFormat` provides a locale-sensitive API for parsing, formatting, and normalizing dates. Concrete subclass `java.text.SimpleDateFormat` implements date and time value formatting for all supported locales.

J2EE applications should represent date and time values using class `java.util.Date`, interpret them using class `Calendar`, and parse and format them using class `DateFormat`. See *The Java Tutorial* for examples of how to use these classes together.

10.2.4 Collation

Collation is the process of ordering text using language- or script-specific rules, rather than using binary comparison, and is therefore locale-specific. A character set may have multiple collating sequences, some of which may have to do with properties of the script. For example, alphabets (like Roman) with a concept of upper- and lowercase can have multiple collating sequences that treat letter case differently. Lists of numbers may be ordered numerically or lexically. International character sets may have diacritics, non-phonetic lexical symbols, ligatures, equivalent characters (Greek σ and ς for example), and other features that affect collation.

The J2SE standard abstract class `java.text.Collator` and related classes provide locale-aware collation. `Collator` is recommended for ordering lists of items in internationalized J2EE applications. For example, a component that produces ordered lists of catalog entries could use `Collator` to place the entries in an order appropriate to the client's locale.

Dependence on database collation services is discouraged. Collating in database queries or stored procedures requires complex bean-managed persistence code. Most databases only support one sort order at a time. Database collation services have other limitations and, in any case, are nonportable.

`Collator` is recommended because its behavior is independent of the source of the data being ordered. In an enterprise application, the same locale-aware collation code could be used for data retrieved from enterprise beans using container-managed persistance (CMP), data received from a Web client or Web service, data retrieved using JDBC, or data accessed by a Connector. `Collator` gives the developer more control over the results of the collation. It is also portable, and its data source independence ensures that collation is consistent throughout the application.

10.3   Web Tier Internationalization

This section presents some design considerations for internationalizing Web-tier components.

10.3.1 Tracking Locales and Encodings

An internationalized Web application must be able to determine the encoding of an incoming request and ensure that the response is properly encoded. This section discusses locale and encoding management for Web-tier components.

10.3.1.1 Determining HTTP Request Locale and Encoding

Runtime locale determination is simple and automatic in J2SE applications. An application developer can use J2SE internationalization APIs to set an application's locale programmatically.

Locale semantics for J2EE applications are more complex than for J2SE applications. For example, the system default locale for a Web component is the Web container's default locale. In a distributed environment, this default locale may differ among containers, making the locale dependent on the container servicing the request. Using `Locale.getDefault` in Web applications is not recommended, because the value returned represents the Web container's locale, not the client's locale.

An internationalized enterprise application's Web tier must somehow determine the encoding of incoming request parameters. As explained previously in this chapter, an encoding defines the relationship between a character set's code points and a data stream's unit size and serialization rules. Correct data interpretation requires knowing how the data are encoded. Unfortunately, there's no standard way to determine HTTP request parameter encoding. An HTML browser encodes each request using the encoding of the page that was the source of the request, but that knowledge is only useful if the original page's encoding is known.

There are several approaches to determining and tracking HTTP request locale:

- **Deduce encoding from the `Accept-language` HTTP header**—The `Accept-language` header does not unambiguously indicate request encoding, but it can provide an appropriate locale for content generation. The method `ServletRequest.getLocale` returns a preferred `Locale` that the Web container chooses based on the `Accept-language` header value. The method `ServletRequest.getLocales` returns an `Enumeration` of `Locale` objects that the client will accept, based on the contents of multiple `Accept-language` header values. A Web component can use `getLocales` to select the most appropriate locale from among the available options.

  On the other hand, however, this approach is unreliable because there is no unique relationship between the value of the `Accept-language` header and the request encoding. Most character sets may be represented in a variety of encodings. The `Accept-language` value, even if accurate, only narrows the range of possible encodings. For these reasons, relying on `Accept-language` for determining request encoding is discouraged.

  HTTP defines two other relevant `Accept-` headers. `Accept-charset` is a list of character sets the browser will accept, which can be useful in choosing a response encoding. `Accept-encoding` is a document's so-called "content coding," usually a type of data compression. Neither of these headers indicates request encoding. See RFC 2616 listed in Section 10.9 on page 345 for details.

- **Provide separate application entry points for different locales**—In the Web tier, one servlet may be mapped to several URLs, each corresponding to a particular locale. The URL might even contain the locale identifier; for example, `http://j2eeserver/j2eeapp/login/`**en_US** for United States English, and `http://j2eeserver/j2eeapp/login/`**de_CH**, for Swiss German. This approach is especially appropriate for applications that heavily use manually-localized JSP pages, because such pages are typically already separated by the URL namespace.

- **Define an application-wide encoding**—If every Web component in an application transmits all of its pages in the same encoding, then requests from those pages will always be in that encoding. This approach simplifies design, but has the drawback that any component that does not set the encoding correctly will not work properly. This drawback can be eliminated using a servlet filter; see the next section for a description. As described previously in this chapter, UTF-8 encoding unifies ASCII with Unicode. Standardizing on UTF-8 is the recommended approach because it provides the broadest coverage of character sets.

The method `ServletRequest.setCharacterEncoding` (Java Servlet specification version 2.3 and above only) overrides a servlet request's default encoding with a given encoding, which thereafter is used to interpret request parameters. This method must be called before any data is retrieved from the request object.

In summary, the BluePrints recommendation is to standardize on a single encoding, preferably UTF-8, to provide consistent request encoding, efficient data transmission, broad character set coverage, and wide browser support. When a consistent encoding cannot be used (because of noncompliant browsers, for example), consider storing locale and encoding in session state, or use separate URLs for each locale or encoding as described in the next section.

10.3.1.2 Storing Locale and Encoding at Runtime

Instead of determining locale and encoding for each request, locale can be stored for use by subsequent requests. There are several ways to accomplish this:

- **Store locale and encoding in hidden variables or parameters**—The encoding of a page could be stored in hidden variables in forms or query string parameters, so every request would contain an indication of the request parameter encoding. This approach suffers from a few problems. Additional parameters and hidden form variables complicate page creation. Accurately changing the encoding of a page implies changing all of the parameters or form variables, which complicates maintenance. Parameters or hidden form variables are appropriate to indicate request encoding only when both the application cannot be standardized on a single encoding, and it doesn't use stateful components.

- **Store encoding as session state**—A stateful server-side component (a session bean or servlet using `HttpSession`) can maintain the encoding of generated content in a session attribute. This approach is recommended for applications that must use both multiple encodings and stateful components.

- **Store the locale and encoding as a user preference**—Most enterprise applications store some user profile information—sometimes only a password. User profile parameters can be used to localize all requests following login. User preference information may be kept in a client-side cookie, stored in a database and accessed with JDBC, stored in Web-tier session state, or accessed as a user profile entity bean.

10.3.1.3 Setting HTTP Response Locale and Encoding

Response encoding of JSP pages and servlets determines both the format of characters in the response and the request encoding of any subsequent request from the served page.

An HTTP server indicates content encoding using part of the `Content-type` HTTP header. This header's value is either `TYPE` or `TYPE;charset=CHARSET` where `TYPE` is the content type (RFC 1049) and `CHARSET` is the name of the encoding as registered with the Internet Assigned Names Authority (IANA). The default value for `TYPE` is `text/html`; the default value for `CHARSET` is `ISO-8859-1`. A reference to the IANA registry of values for `charset` is listed in Section 10.9 on page 345.

There are two ways to set encoding of a servlet's HTTP response:

- **Use `ServletResponse.setContentType`**—Use this method to manually set the entire `Content-type` header. Include the encoding as the value of `charset`; for example:

```
response.setContentType("text/html;charset=Shift_JIS");
```

- **Use `ServletResponse.setLocale`**—Use this method to set HTTP headers appropriate for the given locale, including the `charset=` portion of the `Content-type` header.

Set the locale or content type before calling `Servlet.getWriter` to ensure that the resulting `Writer` is configured for the correct encoding.

Two attributes of a JSP page's `page` directive can control encoding:

- **Use the `contentType` attribute**—Use content type and `charset`, as for `ServletResponse.setContentType`.

- **Use the `pageEncoding` attribute**—(JSP pages version 1.2 and above only) Use just the value of `charset`.

A JSP container may issue a runtime error if the encoding for the page is inappropriate for the content type. It may produce a translation-time error when a JSP page specifies an unsupported encoding.

The content type and encoding of a JSP page is fixed at page translation time when they are set using a directive. Use either a custom tag or a servlet to set encoding at runtime.

An application can use a servlet filter to set response encoding to a single value *before* a servlet or JSP page receives the request. This technique provides a single point of control for enforcing standardized encoding and ensures that encoding is correct before a servlet uses its response object. The sample application enforces response encoding with a servlet filter. The servlet filter can also serve as a guard, logging an error message if any client makes a request using an unsupported encoding.

Automatic selection of language, character set, and encoding selection make things easy for users. But it's important always to provide a way for users to change languages manually as well. Page headers or footers are a good place for hyperlinks or dropdown boxes for manual language selection. When you offer users a choice of languages, the name of each language should be in the language to be chosen, rather than the language of the current page.

10.3.2 Presentation Component Design

Internationalization and localization are important concerns when designing presentation components such as JSP pages, JavaBeans helper components, and custom tags. Examples of localizable Web-tier components include:

- JSP page fragments included dynamically in a response based on locale

- Helper JavaBeans components that customize their behavior to a locale

- Custom tags that order lists of data using a collating sequence appropriate for a locale

- Custom tags that customize database requests to a specified locale

- Custom tags that use locale to format numbers, dates, currency, percentages, and so on

All of these components may use the J2SE internationalization APIs. Remember always to consider internationalization when designing presentation components.

10.3.2.3.1 Example

This example from the sample application presents a localizable custom tag that displays currency values in a format appropriate for a locale.

The sample application includes a presentation component called a `list` tag, which formats a list of items from a `java.util.Iterator`. The `list` tag evaluates and outputs its body text for each value the iterator returns. Each value is a JavaBeans component that exposes its values as get and set property accessors.

The example presentation component, a `listItem` tag, formats and displays the current item within a `list` tag's body text. A sample usage of this tag looks like this:

```
<waf:listItem property="unitCost" formatText="currency"
locale="ja_JP" precision="0"/>
```

The tag's attributes control its behavior in the following ways:

- The tag's `property` attribute identifies the JavaBeans property to format from the current iterator value. The `listItem` tag retrieves the value to display by calling the current item's `getUnitCost` method. This method is the get property accessor as defined by the JavaBeans naming convention.

- The `listItem` tag's `formatText` attribute indicates how to format the item. In the example above, the tag formats the value as currency; it can also format decimals and percentages.

- The `precision` attribute indicates how many zeroes appear after the decimal. In this case, the currency is Yen, which requires no decimal part, so there are `0` digits after the decimal point.

- Finally, the tag formats the item according to the value of the `locale` attribute. The locale name follows the standard convention described in Section 10.1.1.1 on page 313; in the example, the locale is `ja_JP`, meaning Japanese (ja) in Japan (JP). The tag handler code maps this string to the corresponding `Locale` object. The tag handler code uses the standard J2SE class `CurrencyFormat` to format the value, complete with Yen sign.

Another example usage of the `listItem` tag might look like this:

```
<waf:listItem property="unitCost" formatText="currency"
locale="en_US" precision="2"/>
```

The locale in this example is `en_US`, so the `CurrencyFormatter` will use appropriate localization for United States English. Because this currency amount is in dollars, the `precision` is two (to display cents).

Note that this tag does not actually convert currency between Yen and dollars. Rather, it simply formats the value that `getUnitCost` returns for the specified locale.

Components other than custom tags can also be internationalized. For example, `unitCost` in the above example is a property of a JavaBean component, which itself could be localized. The component could return one price, in Yen, for locale `ja_JP`, and a different price, in dollars, for locale `en_US`. In such a case, the Java-Beans component (part of the application MVC model) would *produce* a unit cost appropriate to the locale, while the presentation tag (part of the application MVC view) would *format* the value in a way appropriate for the locale. (This scenario is hypothetical, as the sample application does not provide this functionality in quite this way.)

The sample application contains other examples of locale-aware presentation components. Localizable presentation components greatly simplify internationalization.

10.3.3 Internationalizing and Localizing JSP Pages

Because locale is primarily about how to present data, localization is most appropriately implemented in MVC views. In the Web tier, MVC views are usually JSP pages. J2EE Web applications should localize content in the Web tier with JSP pages.

Two common approaches exist for localizing JSP pages: creating JSP pages that can be localized with resource bundles or maintaining separate JSP pages for each locale. Each approach has strengths and drawbacks. The next two sections discuss the tradeoffs between these two options.

Use separate JSP pages for each locale when content structure and display logic differ greatly between locales or when messages depend on the target locale. Resource bundles are recommended for error and logging messages (see Section 10.7 on page 341), and when content varies between locales only in data values and not in structure.

10.3.3.4 Localizing JSP Pages with Resource Bundles

A common way to localize JSP pages is to assemble chunks of localized text using locale-aware custom tags. Each time the page is served, the custom tags select text from a resource bundle for the current locale.

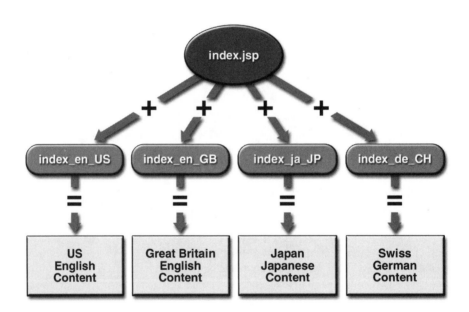

Figure 10.2 Localizing JSP Pages with Resource Bundles

Figure 10.2 shows a single internationalized JSP page that is localized with resource bundles for several locales. Benefits of this approach include:

- **Easier maintenance**—A single JSP page is the source file for a particular screen in all locales. A modification to the JSP page changes the dynamic content generated for all locales.

- **Consistent page structure**—Because the source code for a screen is shared between locales, the page maintains the same structure in all locales, changing only in data values, message text, and language displayed.

- **Easy extensibility**—A new locale can be added by simply defining a new resource bundle for the locale.

The consistency provided by this approach is also a major drawback. While changing the content of this page is easy, customizing its structure to locales is harder, because one JSP page produces content for all locales.

This approach shares a single JSP page across locales, so the page encoding must be compatible with the encodings of all application character sets. The JSP directive `setContentType` specifies the content type and the encoding for the page at page translation time, so all pages produced using this directive must use the same encoding. For reasons explained earlier in this chapter, standardizing on UTF-8 encoding is recommended.

The recommended way to implement a single JSP page customized to multiple locales is to use resource bundles. Access resource bundles from custom tags in the pages instead of using resource bundles from scriptlet or expression code. Custom tags improve the readability and maintainability of JSP pages, and reduce duplicated code.

10.3.3.5 Locale-Specific JSP Pages

Another approach to localizing JSP pages is to provide a separate JSP page for each locale.

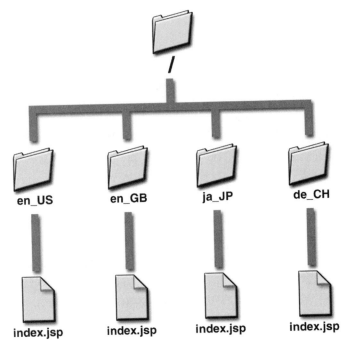

Figure 10.3 Localizing by Creating Separate JSP Pages for Each Locale

Figure 10.3 shows a directory tree of an internationalized JSP page, `index.jsp`. There are actually four separate versions of the file, each in a separate directory in the server's namespace. In this approach, a servlet or servlet filter forwards each request for a JSP page to the appropriate file based on the requesting client's locale. The names of the directories that separate the different file versions use the standard resource bundle suffix naming convention. An alternative is to use file naming conventions instead of directories. For example, the name of a file for the default locale is `index.jsp`, the Japan Japanese localized JSP file would be called `index_ja_JP.jsp`, the Swiss German file would be `index_de_CH.jsp`, and so on. While this approach will work, applications with a large number of files and locales might easily become difficult to manage.

Grouping JSP pages, static pages, and other resources such as graphics files in one directory per locale is a BluePrints best practice. Note that JSP pages can be localized selectively with this scheme. The logic for determining which file to forward to is in a dispatching servlet or servlet filter, which can implement the same naming convention scheme as do resource bundles. The forwarding component can always choose the most specific file available and use a default file (with no localization suffix) as a fallback.

The page-per-locale approach has the following benefits:

- **Greater customizability**—Using resource bundles to customize a single JSP page results in pages whose structure is essentially the same for all locales. Using one JSP page per locale provides maximum customizability of the content for a locale, because customizations are not limited to the contents of a resource bundle. As a result, the page-per-locale approach is prefereable when content differs substantially between locales.

- **Source clarity**—All of the content for a locale appears in a single file (the JSP file for the locale) instead of being separated between a JSP page file with some structural tags, and a properties file or resource bundle class containing named strings.

At the same time, this approach has some drawbacks. Maintaining a consistent look-and-feel between locales is more difficult with separate JSP pages than with resource bundles. Separate files must be created and maintained consistently for several locales. This means more maintenance than does the resource bundle approach.

The Web-tier framework and tools you select for creating your application may influence your decision in how to support internationalized content.

The sample application uses a templating mechanism, providing both structural consistency between locales and the flexibility of page-per-locale localization. The templating mechanism uses an XML "screen definitions file" for each locale to assemble localized JSP pages into a single page. The screen definitions file for a locale specifies a template file, and maps localized JSP pages to symbolic names such as "header," "footer," and so on. The template file defines the overall structure for a page, and uses custom tags to include localized JSP pages, which it references by symbolic name. Because the screen definitions file specifies the template, both page layout and "look and feel" can be unified across locales (by using a single template) or customized for particular locales (by using separate templates).

Regardless of which option you choose, setting the JSP page response encoding correctly is crucial. The sample application standardizes all page encoding to UTF-8, and enforces this encoding with a servlet filter for all JSP pages it serves.

10.4   EIS Tier Internationalization

Because data in an enterprise information system can vary by locale, localization issues can reach all the way into the EIS tier. This section discusses some issues regarding persistent data and schema in databases.

10.4.1 Persistent Localized Data

A J2EE application requires internationalization support in its persistence layer as well as in component source code. Persistence layer design should always address internationalization concerns.

Both container-managed persistence and bean-managed persistence require that an application's JDBC driver and back-end data store support all character sets and all encodings used to represent persistent data. UTF-8 encoding is advised because it is widely supported by JDBC drivers and databases, and supports many character sets.

10.4.1.0.1 Value Conversion, Value Representation, and Information Loss

Uniform value representations in a database simplify database access and application code, but improper localization can cause subtle flaws in application logic. Value representations in a database should be as independent of locale as possible, if the conversion from the original representation can be performed *without information loss*. Where such a conversion cannot be performed, a data value should include a locale and unit designator. The key distinction to make is between the data value, which usually should not be modified, and the way that the value is represented, which usually should be uniform for all database records.

The following examples illustrate the difference between a data value and the way the value is represented:

- **Fixed decimal numbers**—English-speaking countries often format decimal numbers as 1,234.56, whereas people in many other countries format the same number as 1.234,56. Rather than maintain the original punctuation, a database attribute for such a value should be a coded decimal type that can later be presented in any format or encoding. Where there is a business reason to do so, a locale should be stored along with the data value.

- **Strings**—The sequence of characters in a string, not the string's encoding, determines the string's value: For example, any number of different byte sequences can represent the string abc. Saving strings in a database in a variety of encodings, even if the encoding is stored with the value, can complicate processing the strings. The recommended approach for persisting strings received in multiple encodings is to use a universal encoding such as UTF-8 as the database attribute type, and convert from the received encoding to the database encoding before storing the value. The string can later be converted to other encodings for display.

  Where there is a business reason to do so, store a string along with its original encoding and/or locale, so that the original string can be recovered by encoding conversion. For example, a multilingual Customer Relationship Management (CRM) application might use a stored locale to route each customer request to a service representative who speaks that customer's language. The application could use the stored encoding to encode the response to the customer.

- **Currency**—It is impossible to overemphasize the importance of properly handling currency values. Your organization's business rules, not the user's locale, determine the values of quantities such as prices in a catalog. If your application quotes a price in Yen to a Japanese customer, for example, the application should persist the value in Yen, not a value converted to U.S. dollars. (If business rules mandate conversion to dollars at the time of the quote, then the value should be displayed in dollars to avoid misleading the customer.) The application must always record currency values denominated in the currency mandated by business rules. When currency is converted, an audit trail often also requires storing the conversion rate and the value and denomination before conversion. An application's handling of currency values should always be checked by someone who understands the business's accounting rules. Extensive testing with audits can also uncover currency conversion errors. The J2SE platform version 1.4 class `java.util.Currency` represents ISO 4217 currency codes, and can be used for currency formatting; see the J2SE javadoc documentation for details.

- **Physical properties and dimensions**—Some value conversions for physical properties can cause information loss, others do not. For example, the conversion formula from degrees Fahrenheit to degrees Celsius

$$^\circ C = \frac{5(^\circ F - 32)}{9}$$

can introduce rounding errors that may or may not be significant for your application. Whether to store the original value with a dimension or to store a converted value with an implied dimension depends on the application's precision requirements.

- **Time and date**—Some global distributed applications standardize on a universal time coordinate (UTC) for all representations of dates and times, plus (optionally) an indication of time zone. Because UTC can be determined from local date and time for any geographic point, no data is lost in the conversion. As with currency, this determination depends on the organization's business rules.

There are many more situations where data value and data representation may vary by locale. Uniform value representation in a database simplifies application coding, but should never cause information loss.

10.4.2 Internationalizing Database Schema

The effect of internationalization on an application's data model is one of the more important reasons to consider internationalization in an application's design phase. Many internationalized data sets cannot be represented reasonably as resource bundles or as static JSP pages, either because the data set is too large or the data change too fast, or both. Such data sets are usually stored in and accessed from databases.

Data model entities often include locale-dependent attributes such as descriptive text, images, or resource references. In an internationalized application, an entity has a one-to-many relationship with these items. For example, each item in a non-internationalized catalog has a single descriptive text string, whereas an internationalized catalog item requires a descriptive text string for each supported locale.

Consider the example of internationalizing the description of a catalog item. Three alternative ways to model an internationalized attribute appear in Figure 10.4.

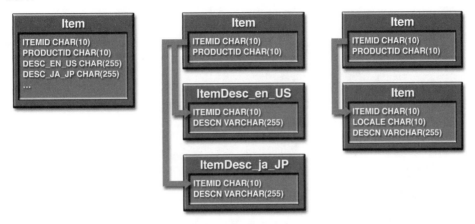

Figure 10.4 Internationalized Attribute Modeling Alternatives

One way to internationalize an attribute is to add a new attribute to the entity for every supported locale. The leftmost example in Figure 10.4 shows an item table with a description column for each locale. But that approach would require both code changes and the addition of a column to every internationalized table each time a new locale is added.

Another approach is to place the attribute in a separate entity for each locale. The middle example in Figure 10.4 shows an item table that has no descriptive text but joins to a separate catalog description table for each locale. But this approach still requires schema and code modifications to add a locale to the application.

The third option (recommended) is to include locale in the data model, making it part of the identity of the entity representing the localized resource. The rightmost example in Figure 10.4 shows an `Item` table that joins with an `ItemDetails` table. The primary key of the `ItemDetails` table includes both the ID of the item being described and the locale for the description and other resources. The application code for this approach contains no hard-coded locale information, so adding a new locale is as simple as adding localized data to the table.

The sample application models internationalize data in exactly this way. Figure 10.5 shows a part of the sample application's data model. It contains a hierarchical categorization of items by product, and products by category. The category, product, and item tables each have an associated detail table that contains locale-specific data. Application code retrieves localized resources from this table, looking up descriptive text, images, names, and so on, by both locale and ID.

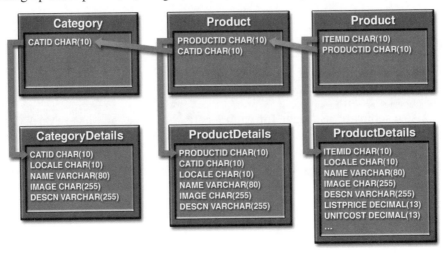

Figure 10.5 Internationalized Catalog Schema

Note that, in these tables, details tables contain all localized data. The primary key (that is, the identity) of all details tables is the locale and an ID. A properly-designed schema will support future language additions with no changes to either code or database schema. Adding a new locale in this design is as simple as adding new localized data to the details tables. An internationalized database schema requires more up-front design work, but provides a great deal of flexibility for supporting localized content later on.

10.5   Internationalized Application Design

Previous sections discussed internationalization issues by tier. This section covers some design techniques that are useful across tiers in internationalized, distributed applications.

10.6   Internationalizing Applications with XML

There are a variety of ways to internationalize J2EE applications:

- **Use resource bundles in code**—for programmatic control of internationalization; see Section 10.2.1 on page 316.

- **Use custom tags**—for JSP pages that vary by locale only in data values; see Section 10.3.3.4 on page 328.

- **Use a separate JSP page for each locale**—for pages that have a different structure for each locale; see Section 10.3.3.5 on page 330.

- **Transform XML with XSLT**—to internationalize XML content.

An application may use any or all of these techniques. This section covers the final option, using XML and XSLT to localize and communicate locale within and between applications.

10.6.1 Generating Localized Dynamic Content with XSLT

One flexible way to create internationalized content is to use locale-specific XSLT stylesheets to style model data that are represented as XML. For example, an enterprise bean might use JMS to asynchronously send localized XHTML to a user by email.

XSL stylesheets are very effective for creating customized, dynamic structured content in any application tier. The application component (JSP page, servlet, or enterprise bean) can create XML that represents localized model data that are the results of a service request. An XSL styling component can then produce localized content, inserting and styling model data from the XML document. The name of the stylesheet that performs the localization is based on the requested locale, which is encoded in the XML itself. Localizations for new locales can be created by simply generating model data for the new locale, and then styling that data with a new XSL stylesheet. This approach cleanly separates business logic (the XML data) from presentation (the template text in the stylesheets).

An example of this approach, including a description of a way to communicate locale among decoupled application components, appears in Section 10.6.3 on page 338).

10.6.2 Communicating Locale within an Application

The Java programming language represents values of type `String`, `StringBuffer`, and `Character` as Unicode. As a result, enterprise bean methods that use these types consistently preserve international character values, including method invocations through EJB local and remote interfaces.

Enterprise bean business method signatures may include locale information when business logic depends on locale or where the data returned by a bean method is localized. Examples of enterprise beans whose behavior may be locale-dependent include components for tax calculation or shipping, or components that deal directly with external systems such as Web services or clients. A catalog enterprise bean might include method signatures with locale to indicate the language for viewing the catalog's entries.

Placing locale in session state can greatly simplify code localization. Instead of including a `Locale` argument in every business method signature, consider placing the current `Locale` in session state, either as an `HttpSession` attribute (for Web-only applications) or by using a stateful session bean (for applications using enterprise beans). A `Locale` stored in session state can be determined once, early in the session, and then used by all components for the remainder of the session.

10.6.3 Communicating Locale among Applications

Most large organizations have not one, but several mission-critical business applications. Seldom are these applications integrated "out of the box." The art of integrating disparate enterprise applications to work together as a whole is called Enterprise Application Integration (EAI).

A currently-popular EAI strategy uses messaging to link together coarse-grained, loosely-coupled applications. For example, Web services use Internet protocols and data formats (often HTTP and XML) to send and receive messages that are formatted as XML documents.

When one internationalized enterprise application requests a service from another application, the requesting application must somehow indicate the locale of the request, so that the data encoded in the request can be properly interpreted. J2EE applications often communicate among themselves and with other IT systems using XML message passing. In particular, EJB components may communicate with external applications using JMS to send and receive payloads of XML messages. Web-tier components may provide XML Web services via HTTP to end users or to other information systems. Each of these scenarios requires a way to indicate locale.

Applications that send XML messages should encode the locale of the request, the requested locale of the response, or both, as strings in an element of the XML message. The naming conventions used for resource bundles provide a useful and widely-understood way to represent a locale as a string.

Code Example 10.1 shows a sample XML message representing an invoice localized for the United States English locale. As in this case, the locale of the request and the response are usually the same, so only a single `locale` element is necessary.

```xml
<?xml version="1.0" encoding="UTF-8"?>
<invoice>
    <orderid>1234</orderid>
    <locale>en_US</locale>
</invoice>
```

Code Example 10.1   Sample XML Message with United States English Locale

The same message with a Japanese locale appears in Code Example 10.2 below.

```xml
<?xml version="1.0" encoding="UTF-8"?>
<invoice>
    <orderid>1234</orderid>
    <locale>ja_JP</locale>
</invoice>
```

Code Example 10.2   An XML Message with Japanese Locale

Note that the string used to represent the locale follows the naming convention for resource bundle class name suffixes. Choose a universal encoding such as

UTF-8 for all such XML messages, and be sure to include the document encoding in the XML declaration, as the code examples show.

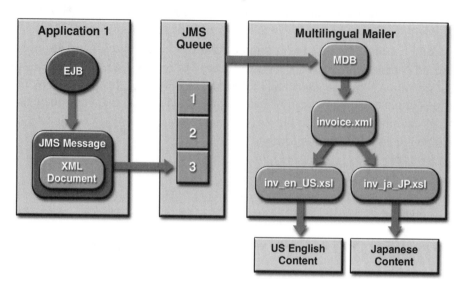

Figure 10.6   Communicating Localized Content

A message receiver may use the locale encoded in the request to localize the content of an XML message it receives. The sample application contains a multilingual mailer application that transforms XML messages into localized emails to customers. A sample scenario appears in Figure 10.6 above. In this diagram, an EJB component in Application 1 sends an XML message via JMS to a multilingual mailer application. The mailer application receives JMS messages (using a message-driven bean), localizes the message contents, and sends the localized contents as emails to users.

The message-driven bean in the mailer application receives and merges the XML payload (invoice.xml) of each JMS message with a stylesheet containing template text. The bean selects an XSL stylesheet based on the incoming message type (inv in this case) and the requested locale. The stylesheet contains XSL template rules that create email body text by inserting values from the XML document into localized template text. The result of the XSL transformation is an email message localized to the locale requested by the incoming message.

This flexible solution provides a simple way to extend the mailer application for new locales. To add a new locale, a developer need only generate localized values from the model (as XML), create an XSL stylesheet for the new locale, and follow the stylesheet naming convention. The mailer application will correctly style incoming messages for the new locale.

Notice that this design maintains MVC separation: The data sent in the XML message is model data, the XSL stylesheet generates the view (the "view" is the email being sent to the customer), and the bean acts as a controller that selects and assembles the view. The stylesheet in this design acts much like a JSP page, outputting template text with dynamic data values matched from the XML document. Yet this example does not use the Web tier at all: It occurs entirely in the EJB tier and in message-oriented middleware.

MVC separation is especially important for enterprise application integration, because enterprise applications communicate most effectively at the level of data and application model. Legacy interface engines that rely on "screen scraping" exist solely to simulate an application model by interacting with a view. The legacy interface layer would be entirely unnecessary if the model were available directly as a service.

The example presented above shows just one way that locale that is communicated between applications may be used to produce localized content.

10.7   Localizing Error and Logging Messages

Error messages provide both users and system administrators with information about exceptional conditions. Localizing error messages and logging messages is an important part of localizing an application.

10.7.1 Client Messages and Application Exceptions

An application's presentation layer should localize messages to clients. Subclasses of `java.lang.Exception` are recommended for communicating errors between tiers. In a distributed environment, such exception classes must be serializable so that they can move across tier boundaries.

In general, exception classes should not contain localized messages; instead, they should contain information detailing the error. The presentation tier can use the error information to create an error message suitable for the client. JSP pages are a useful mechanism for formatting error messages for Web tier clients. For example, consider a message that creation of a new user account failed because the user ID already exists. A JSP page could deliver content appropriate to the user locale, getting only the user identifier from the exception object.

This section explains existing mechanisms for Web-tier error reporting, and then provides general guidelines for using them in an internationalized design.

10.7.1.0.1 JSP Pages Error Mechanism

JSP pages have defined behavior for handling request-time errors. Server behavior for errors that occur at page compilation or deployment time is not specified, and is therefore implementation dependent.

Uncaught JSP page exceptions are forwarded to the JSP page's error page, if one is defined. An error page informs the user that an error has occurred. JSP page errorPage defines the URL for the page to display when a JSP page produces errors; for example:

```
<%@ page language="java" errorPage="errorPages/userExists.jsp" %>
```

When the JSP page catches an unchecked exception, it creates a new ServletRequest parameter called javax.servlet.jsp.jspException, which contains the exception object. The error page may use this request parameter to format an error message.

The error page must include an isErrorPage directive, like this:

```
<%@ page language="java" isErrorPage="true" %>
```

The isErrorPage directive causes the implicit scripting variable exception to be initialized to the exception object thrown by the original JSP page. The page may then format the message using the data encoded in the exception. An error page that could potentially receive more than one type of exception would need to include some sort of logic, best implemented in a custom tag, to deliver the correct error message.

10.7.1.0.2 Servlet Error Mechanism

A servlet may indicate an error either by throwing an exception, or by calling ServletResponse.sendError with an HTTP error code argument. The servlet container's default behavior for either case is to serve an implementation-specific error page. Application assemblers or deployers can use servlet deployment descriptor entry <error-page> to specify custom error pages. Errors may be classified either by fully-specified exception class name or by HTTP error code. Servlets should throw only exceptions that are subclasses of RuntimeException, ServletException, or IOException, none of which should be used for application-level exceptions from EJB components. The servlet container error page mechanism should be used only for reporting Web-tier application exceptions.

10.7.1.0.3 Localizing Error Messages

Localization is primarily about presentation, not business logic. The BluePrints recommendation is to localize error messages in the code that generates a response to a client. For example, JSP pages and servlets in the Web tier can generate localized dynamic error messages for HTML browsers or XML-based rich clients. Application clients can localize data on the server or the client, but in either case, localization should occur in presentation code.

An internationalized MVC controller can easily localize error messages. The controller can catch all exceptions thrown from the Web tier and route them to the appropriate error page based on the name of the exception class. The controller looks up the error page URL in an XML-based exception map, which maps exception class type to error pages by locale. Application component providers, assemblers, or deployers would use the exception map to define localized error pages for application exceptions. Code Example 10.1 below provides a hypothetical example of how such a map might look.

```
<ExceptionMap>
  <Exception type="EjbAppExceptions.UserExistsException">
    <ErrorPage locale="en">/jsp/UserExists.jsp</ErrorPage>
    <ErrorPage locale="sp">/jsp/sp/UserExists.jsp</ErrorPage>
    <!-- Add pages for other locales here -->
  </Exception>
  <!-- Add additional exception mappings -->
</ExceptionMap>
```

Code Example 10.1 Sample Localizing Exception Map for Web-Tier Controller

A locale-aware Web controller would catch application exceptions from the application's business layer (often implemented by the EJB tier), get the class name of the thrown exception (using `getClass.getName`), look up the error JSP page in the exception map, and forward the request to the corresponding page (using `RequestDispatcher.forward`). As described above, the servlet container already offers a way to forward requests to error pages based on uncaught exceptions. The approach presented here also provides localization and handles error messages for business-layer application exceptions.

Looking again at Code Example 10.1, note that the controller forwards an exception's contents to an error page corresponding to the user's locale. An individual error JSP page in this example formats the contents of one application exception for a particular locale. The data in the exception are *not* localized: The localization is handled by the JSP page formatting the message. In the example shown, `UserExistsException` reports that the given user name already exists in the system, and the exception object contains the user name that caused the error. The exception does not contain localized messages, because the localization is handled by the JSP page for the locale. The English page (`/jsp/UserExists.jsp`) contains a line something like this:

```
User <app:exception property="userName"/> already exists.
```

while the Spanish page (`/jsp/sp/UserExists.jsp`) contains a line like this:

```
El usuario <app:exception property="userName"/> ya existe.
```

Note that the JSP pages follow the BluePrints recommendation to use a custom tag, rather than a scriptlet or an expression, to retrieve the user name from the application exception.

10.7.2 System Exceptions and Message Logging

System exceptions are intended for a system administrator, so they need to be readable by those maintaining the runtime system. System exceptions and log messages need localization, but using the application presentation layer is too complex for this purpose. Instead, the BluePrints recommendation is to use resource bundles to localize system exceptions and log messages. System exception and log messages are typically for one locale only. The simplest way to determine a locale for system messages is to use the system default locale. If the application default locale differs from server to server, the system message locale may be indicated in a deployment descriptor environment entry for the component that produces the message.

Large system messages are localizable using XSLT (as described in Section 10.6.1 on page 337).

System exceptions should always be subclasses of `java.lang.RuntimeException`. Typically, the message of a `RuntimeException` explains the error condition. In an internationalized design, the exception message should contain the resource bundle key of the system message, not the message itself. The component that writes the log can use resource bundles and class `MessageFormat` to localize the exception message.

10.8   Summary

An application must be properly internationalized before it can be localized. The J2SE platform APIs provide many useful tools that enable the developer to internationalize a J2EE application. J2EE applications can be localized by creating parameterized pages or by using separate pages for each locale. J2EE applications require proper treatment of locale and encodings when accepting input, communicating data between tiers, processing data in EJB components, and modeling database schemas. Localization of J2EE applications can also be done within each page or at an application level using separate JSP pages for each locale. Finally, J2EE applications should report system errors in all tiers in a language appropriate for system administrators.

10.9   References and Resources

- A guide to J2SE 1.4 internationalization:
  `<http://java.sun.com/j2se/1.4/docs/guide/intl>`

- *The Java^{TM} Tutorial Continued: The Rest of the JDK^{TM}*. M. Campione, K. Walrath, A. Huml, Tutorial Team. Copyright 1998, Addison-Wesley.
  `<http://java.sun.com/docs/books/tutorial/i18n/index.html>`

- *Java^{TM} Internationalization*. A. Deitsch, D. Czarnecki. Copyright 2001. O'Reilly & Associates.

- *The Java^{TM} Servlet Programming*. J. Hunter, W. Crawford. Copyright 2001, O'Reilly & Associates.

- Standard IANA names for encoded character sets:
  `<http://www.iana.org/assignments/character-sets>`

- RFC-1049, *A Content-Type Header Field for Internet Messages*
  `<http://www.ietf.org/rfc/rfc1049.txt>`

- RFC-1766, *Tags for the Identification of Languages*
  `<http://www.ietf.org/rfc/rfc1766.txt>`

- RFC-2045, *Multipurpose Internet Mail Extensions, Part 1: Format of Internet Message Bodies.* `<http://ds.internic.net/rfc/rfc2045.txt>`

- RFC-2616, *Hypertext Transport Protocol—HTTP 1.1*
  `<http://www.w3.org/Protocols/rfc2616/rfc2616.html>`

- The IETF Internet-Draft *"Character Set" Considered Harmful* clarifies internationalization terminology:
  `<http://www.w3.org/MarkUp/html-spec/charset-harmful.html>`

- Unicode Technical Report 10, *Unicode Collation Algorithm.* M. Davis, K. Whistler. `<http://www.unicode.org/unicode/reports/tr10>`

- Unicode Technical Report 17, *Character Encoding.* K. Whistler, M. Davis. `<http://www.unicode.org/unicode/reports/tr17>`

- The Java Standard Tag Libraries project can be found at:
  `<http://java.sun.com/products/jsp/taglibraries.html>`

- Resources about ISO 639, 2-character language name abbreviations:
  `<http://xml.coverpages.org/languageIdentifiers.html#iso639>`

- Resources about ISO 3166, 2-character country name abbreviations:
  `<http://xml.coverpages.org/country3166.html>`

Architecture of the Sample Application

by Sean Brydon

$\mathbf{A}$T this point, you should have a good understanding not only of the J2EE platform and its technologies but also how best to apply these technologies in your application. This chapter pulls it all together to show recommended approaches to designing an entire application.

This chapter presents the high-level architecture for the sample Java Pet Store application and demonstrates the approach to designing some key aspects of this application. The focus is on common enterprise application architectural issues and solutions using J2EE technology, especially as implemented in the sample application. You should view this as a guideline to good design for applications built for the J2EE platform environment. Keep in mind that these are guidelines and suggested approaches. You may find that some aspects work well for you and some are not as applicable.

The chapter begins with a description of some of the J2EE architectural approaches and the J2EE design patterns. It also examines the design issues common to all J2EE applications. These architectural concepts form the basis for the design of the sample application. After covering these concepts, the chapter presents an overview of the sample application. Then, it examines the key design approaches used in the sample application itself.

11.1   J2EE Architecture Approaches

Before delving into the design and architecture of the sample application, it is important to understand some commonly used J2EE architectural approaches. J2EE applications that are interactive benefit from using the Model-View-Controller (MVC) architecture. MVC is particularly well-suited for interactive Web applications—applications where a Web user interacts with a Web site, with multiple iterations of screen page displays and multiple round-trips of requesting and displaying data.

In contrast, a workflow architecture is more suitable for applications that focus on process control and have fewer interactive features. Such applications may use asynchronous messaging, implemented with message-driven beans and JMS, so that different processing steps in the workflow can communicate.

In addition to the architecture, J2EE design patterns help to determine well-formed application designs.

11.1.1 Model-View-Controller Architecture

The Model-View-Controller architecture is a widely-used architectural approach for interactive applications. It divides functionality among objects involved in maintaining and presenting data to minimize the degree of coupling between the objects. The architecture maps traditional application tasks—input, processing, and output—to the graphical user interaction model. They also map into the domain of multitier Web-based enterprise applications.

The MVC architecture divides applications into three layers—model, view, and controller—and decouples their respective responsibilities. Each layer handles specific tasks and has specific responsibilities to the other areas.

- A model represents business data and business logic or operations that govern access and modification of this business data. Often the model serves as a software approximation to real-world functionality. The model notifies views when it changes and provides the ability for the view to query the model about its state. It also provides the ability for the controller to access application functionality encapsulated by the model.

- A view renders the contents of a model. It accesses data from the model and specifies how that data should be presented. It updates data presentation when the model changes. A view also forwards user input to a controller.

- A controller defines application behavior. It dispatches user requests and selects views for presentation. It interprets user inputs and maps them into actions to be performed by the model. In a stand-alone GUI client, user inputs include button clicks and menu selections. In a Web application, they are HTTP GET and POST requests to the Web tier. A controller selects the next view to display based on the user interactions and the outcome of the model operations. An application typically has one controller for each set of related functionality. Some applications use a separate controller for each client type, because view interaction and selection often vary between client types.

Figure 11.1 depicts the relationships between the model, view, and controller layers of an MVC application.

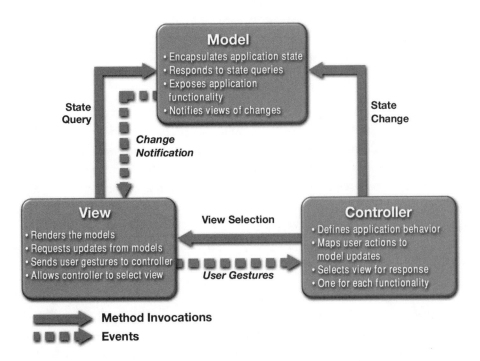

Figure 11.1 The Model-View-Controller Architecture

Separating responsibilities among model, view, and controller objects reduces code duplication and makes applications easier to maintain. It also makes handling data easier, whether adding new data sources or changing data presentation, because business logic is kept separate from data. It is easier to support new client types, because it is not necessary to change the business logic with the addition of each new type of client.

11.1.2 J2EE Design Patterns

A design pattern describes a proven solution to a recurring design problem. Design patterns leverage the knowledge and insights of other developers. They are reusable solutions for common problems. Design patterns address individual problems, but they can be combined in different ways to achieve a solution for an entire system. Because design patterns can be named, they become part of the architect's vocabulary for describing a solution.

There are a common set of design patterns for the J2EE platform. This section briefly mentions those J2EE design patterns that apply to the sample application. Later, you will see how these patterns are combined and used in the application architecture. Refer to Section 11.6 on page 383 for references to sources of more information on patterns. In particular, you should refer to *Core J2EE Patterns*, by Alur, Crupi, and Malks, as that book gives a complete description of all the J2EE patterns.

- **Intercepting filter**—This pattern applies to request pre- and post-processing. It applies additional services needed to process a request. For example, an intercepting filter such as a servlet filter may handle all incoming requests to the Web site and provide a central mechanism for authorization.

- **View helper**—A view helper encapsulates the presentation and data access logic portions of a view, thus refining the view and keeping it simpler. Presentation logic concerns formatting data for display on a page, while data access logic involves retrieving data. View helpers are often JSP tags for rendering or representing data and JavaBeans for retrieving data.

- **Composite view**—This pattern makes view presentation more manageable by creating a template to handle common page elements for a view. Often, Web pages contain a combination of dynamic content and static elements, such as a header, footer, logo, background, and so forth. The dynamic portion is particular to a page, but the static elements are the same on every page. The composite view template captures the common features.

- **Front controller**—This pattern provides a centralized controller for managing requests. A front controller receives all incoming client requests, forwards each request to an appropriate request handler, and presents an appropriate response to the client.

- **Value object**—This pattern facilitates data exchange between tiers (usually the Web and EJB tiers) by reducing the cost of distributed communication. In one remote call, a single value object can be used to retrieve a set of related data, which then is available locally to the client. See Chapter 5 for more information on value objects.

- **Session facade**—This pattern coordinates operations between cooperating business objects, unifying application functions into a single, simplified interface for presentation to the calling code. It encapsulates and hides the complexity of classes that must cooperate in specific, possibly complex ways, and isolates its callers from business object implementation changes. A session facade, usually implemented as a session bean, hides the interactions of underlying enterprise beans.

- **Business delegate**—This pattern intervenes between a remote business object and its client, adapting the business object's interface to a friendlier interface for the client. It decouples the Web tier presentation logic from the EJB tier by providing a facade or proxy to the EJB tier services. The delegate takes care of lower-level details, such as looking up remote objects and handling remote exceptions, and may perform performance optimizations, such as caching data retrieved from remote objects to reduce the number of remote calls.

- **Data access object**—This pattern abstracts data access logic to specific resources. It separates the interfaces to a systems resource from the underlying strategy used to access that resource. By encapsulating data access calls, data access objects facilitate adapting data access to different schemas or database types. See Chapters 5 and 6 for more information on data access objects.

When deciding on a pattern to use, keep in mind that certain patterns are more applicable to a particular application tier. For example, patterns related to views and presentation are applied in the Web tier. Good examples of Web tier patterns are composite view and view helper. Other patterns are more concerned with controlling business logic, and they are more useful in the EJB tier. Session facade is a good example of an EJB tier pattern. Other patterns focus on retrieving data or delegating operations, and they are best applied between tiers. The value object and business delegate patterns fall into this category.

11.2   Sample Application Overview

The sample application is a typical e-commerce application: an online pet store enterprise that sells products—animals—to customers. The application has a Web site through which it presents an interface to customers. Administrators and external businesses such as suppliers use other application interfaces to maintain inventory and perform managerial tasks. Each class of users has access to specific categories of functionality, and each interacts with the application through a specific user interface mechanism.

While the application handles most tasks automatically, some tasks must be done manually, such as managing inventory and shipping orders.

You can consider the entire sample application as the Pet Store enterprise. Figure 11.2 provides a high-level view of the business or real-world problem that the application is intended to solve.

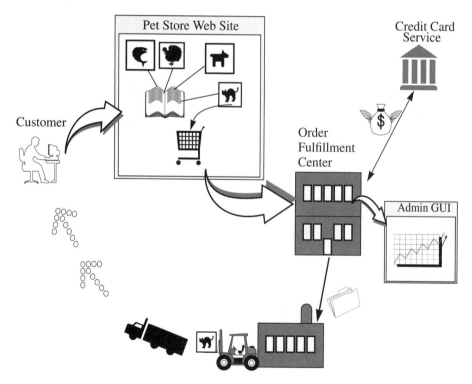

Figure 11.2   Real-World Business

Conceptually, the business divides into these functional units:

- The Web site presents an online pet store interface to the customer. The customer shops and places orders through this interface. When a customer completes an order, the interface sends the order to the order fulfillment center. Because the Web site functional unit drives further business processing when it sends a purchase order to the fulfillment center, it can be thought of as the front end.

- The fulfillment center fulfills customer orders. It has an order fulfillment component and a supplier component. The fulfillment center processes orders based on the enterprise's business rules, manages financial transactions, and arranges for products to ship to customers. Because not all products are in stock at any given moment, order processing may occur over a period of time. Administrators and other suppliers may interact with the fulfillment center. This portion of the business is referred to as the back end, because its processing is triggered by placing an order, an action that occurs in the Web site portion. Although the supplier component is part of the sample application, it could just as easily be a service external to the application.

11.3   Designing the Sample Application

Designing an application starts with assessing functional requirements and then determining an optimal software implementation to meet those requirements. There are numerous analysis tools for gathering and assessing application requirements. Use case analysis is one such tool. Use case analysis identifies the actors in a system and the operations they may perform.

The pet store application is a typical e-commerce site. The customer selects items from a catalog, places them in a shopping cart, and, when ready, purchases the shopping cart contents. Prior to a purchase, the sample application displays the order: the selected items, quantity and price for each item, and the total cost. The customer can revise or update the order. To complete the purchase, the customer provides a shipping address and a credit card number.

Figure 11.3 shows a high-level use case diagram for the sample application. It shows the potential system actors and their actions:

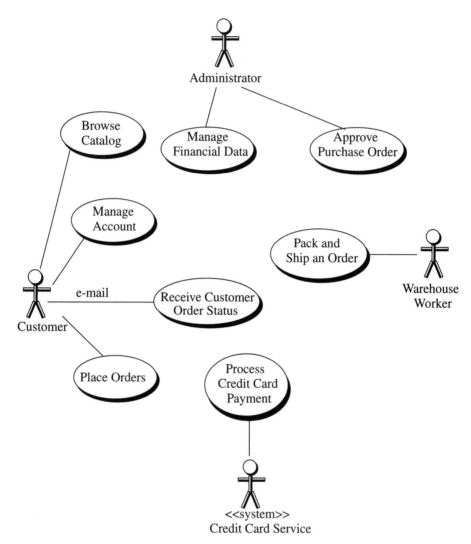

Figure 11.3 Sample Application Use Case Diagram

- A customer shops, places orders, manages her user account, and receives e-mail.

- An administration manager reviews enterprise financial data.

- A bank system processes credit cards.

- A warehouse worker packs and ships orders.

Once you have determined the system's requirements, you can begin designing the application. We have designed the sample application using two different architecture models. The Model-View-Controller architecture works well for the interactive Web site unit, such as the pet store Web site. Because the fulfillment center is not an interactive application, its design is based on a process-oriented architecture.

11.3.1 Choosing Application Tiers

One important design step is to decide the tiers that the application uses. The J2EE platform is designed for multitier applications, and it offers flexibility in distributing application functionality across the tiers. Certain tiers are always present in a Web-enabled application such as the sample application, including:

- The client tier provided by the browser

- The Web tier provided by the server

- The EJB tier provided by the server

- The enterprise information system or database tier holding persistent application data

It is important to choose whether a Web tier component accesses the enterprise information system resources directly or through an EJB tier. The decision depends on the application's functionality, complexity, and scalability requirements. Good design takes into account the possibility for change and builds in the facility to easily migrate to an EJB-centric approach. The EJB tier offers advantages to its components, such as automatically handling security, transactions, distributed processing, and so forth. By using EJB components, developers can reduce the level of systems programming required for the application and instead can concentrate on the application's business logic.

Next, decide how to distribute application functionality across these tiers. Such distribution follows the application's division into objects and should be undertaken carefully.

In a Web-centric design, Web tier components using container services such as the JDBC API can communicate directly with the enterprise information system resources that hold application data. In this approach, Web tier components are responsible for almost all of the application functionality. They handle dynamic content generation, content presentation, and user requests. They must implement core application functionality, such as order processing and enforcing the application's business rules. Finally, the Web tier components must also manage transactions, such as by using JTA, and connection pooling for data access. Because it must handle so many functions, Web-centric application software can easily become monolithic. As a result, unless special efforts are taken, it does not scale well with increasing software complexity.

In an EJB-centric design, enterprise beans running on EJB servers encapsulate the enterprise information system resources and the core application logic. Web tier components communicate with EJB tier components instead of directly accessing the enterprise information system resources. This approach moves most of the core application functionality to EJB tier components, using the Web tier components only as a front end for receiving client Web requests and for presenting HTML responses to the client.

The principal advantage of an EJB-centric approach is that enterprise beans have access to a broad set of enterprise-level services. These services make it easier to manage transaction and security aspects of the application. The EJB container handles system-level details and provides a managed environment for its components, allowing a developer to focus entirely on the application domain issues. These standardized container-provided services translate into better software reliability. They also make it easier for an application to support multiple client types. The EJB architecture supports a programming paradigm that promotes encapsulation and use of components, resulting in software that stays manageable as applications grow more complex.

There is a trade-off between the two approaches. The Web-centric approach can enable a quick start for small applications with few transactional needs, while the EJB-centric approach is better for building a large-scale enterprise application where code and performance scalability are prime factors. The Web-centric approach, while more prevalent, has limitations for building large-scale, complex applications. Applications built with a Web-centric approach can rapidly become too complex and difficult to maintain.

There are strengths to both approaches, and good design requires selecting the right balance for each application. The sample application demonstrates an approach designed for growth. This design can be considered an EJB-centric architecture. While all of the application's modules use an EJB-centric design, in theory a Web-centric model could have been used in at least one case for the module that reads the catalog.

11.3.2 Choosing Local or Distributed Architecture

Most enterprise applications are distributed across a network, because client and data store resources are usually located on different machines from the application itself. An EJB-centric approach, with the business logic residing on the middle tier, gives architects the flexibility to design the application as a distributed or a local application. (Distributed applications are those that interact through remote communication mechanisms.)

The J2EE platform provides facilities to help create distributed applications, but it also lets application developers apply a local model to their application. A developer needs to weigh the advantages and disadvantages of local and remote architecture models, and balance these against the requirements of the application.

11.3.2.1 Comparison of Local and Distributed Architectures

A key consideration for developers is whether to use enterprise beans with a local client view or a remote client view. With careful thought, developers can use enterprise beans with both local and remote client views.

Applications implemented with a local architecture model have their components reside in the same Java Virtual Machine (JVM). Because their co-location in the same address space is guaranteed, these components can communicate with each other without the overhead of remote network calls, thus permitting more efficient fine-grained access among them. As a result, these applications usually exhibit better performance.

A distributed architecture is one in which the application is potentially implemented across multiple JVMs, though a distributed application may be deployed on a single JVM. A distributed architecture is more complex because of additional system-level issues, such as remote communication, security, and so forth. At the same time, it may be more modular, maintainable, and reusable because there is less dependency among individual components. While this approach offers greater flexibility to the application, it usually results in decreased performance because access to a remote component involves significant network overhead. Such overhead includes the cost of serialization and deserialization, along with parameter marshalling and demarshalling. (Although much of this overhead may be optimized away if the application is deployed on a single JVM, some overhead still remains.) Applications in a distributed architecture must pass parameters by value, which often necessitates excessive data copying.

A distributed architecture is also typically more scalable than a local application design. Despite the higher performance of a local application architecture, its components must reside in the same address space, so it cannot scale beyond a single machine. While it is possible to partition the clients of a local application to separate instances running the same application, this becomes harder to achieve since they often need to access and update shared data. A distributed system is generally more scalable than a local application since the components are designed from the ground up to run in a different address space.

Distributed applications are generally more highly available than local applications. Since a distributed component does not know or depend on a particular JVM, it is easier to migrate the distributed enterprise bean component to a different JVM in the event of a hardware failure.

11.3.2.2 J2EE Platform Distributed and Local Options

Often, a distributed application is designed to consist of multiple local applications or components. The local components are used for the portions of the application that require a high level of data passing and fine-grained access, while the remote components allow for greater scalability and network access.

Enterprise beans, which offer local and remote client views, give applications the ability to use a local or a distributed architecture. Enterprise beans within the same JVM can access one another using a local client view and thus take advantage of the local architectural model. Web components residing in the same VM may optionally have access to an enterprise bean's local client view and take advantage of the same benefits from EJB container services. Using an enterprise bean's remote client view gives the application the advantages of a distributed architecture model.

Applications that require a distributed architecture can be designed to reduce the complexity and performance implications of accessing remote objects. The details of locating remote business objects can be encapsulated in a service locator object, thus hiding these details from the rest of an application, whereas accessing business objects can be encapsulated in a business delegate. Fine-grained data access to distributed objects can be reduced by using a single value object to retrieve a set of related data in one remote call. After the value object retrieves its data, it is available locally for an application, which can then access its individual items.

11.4   Architecture of the Sample Application

With an understanding of these basic architectural considerations, you are ready to examine the architecture of the sample application in detail. Recall that the application is divided into two units: a Web site that serves as a front end to the user and an order fulfillment center on the back end. The Web site follows the Model-View-Controller architecture. Its architecture also combines a number of the J2EE design patterns. The fulfillment center follows a process workflow architecture.

Figure 11.4 provides a high-level view of the major modules of the sample application and the application's relationship to its key participants.

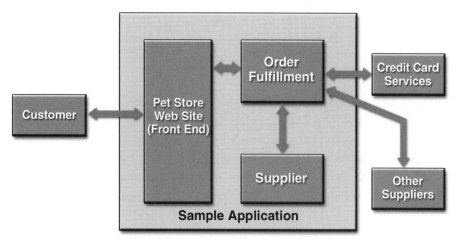

Figure 11.4   Sample Application Architecture and Participants

This discussion does not cover every detail of these architectures; instead, it illustrates several salient points of the design. You should also refer to the Java BluePrints Web site for more detailed information on the sample application architecture and design documents, along with the latest source code.

11.4.1 Application Web Site Architecture

Developing an overall application architecture involves subdividing the application into objects or components and assigning these components to tiers, a process called object decomposition. While most components are consigned to one tier or another, some serve to connect the tiers and need to span tiers, and they must be designed accordingly.

Object design becomes important as applications grow more complex. Large scale development of object-oriented software requires frameworks that define how objects interact. The framework must enable software designs and code to be easily reused. It must also identify the responsibility of each component; that is, the division into components must ensure the unambiguous identity of what the component represents and what it must accomplish.

Additionally, for multitier enterprise applications, it is important to:

- Separate stable code from code that changes more frequently. Usually the presentation and user interface change more often than business rules and database schemas. The overall architecture should separate stable portions of the application from the more volatile parts.

- Divide development effort along skill lines. The people that comprise an enterprise development team typically represent a very diverse set of skills. There are Web page designers who do HTML layout and graphics, programmers, application domain experts, and enterprise information system resource access specialists, among others. The decomposition should result in a set of objects that can be assigned to various subteams based on their particular skills. This division of labor allows work on each object to proceed in parallel.

The MVC architecture works well for the sample application. At the highest level, the application divides into three logical categories of layers—layers that deal with presentation aspects of the application, those that deal with the business rules and data, and those that accept and interpret user requests and control the business objects to fulfill these requests.

Generally, the look and feel of the application interface changes often, its behavior changes less frequently, and business data and rules are relatively stable. Thus, objects responsible for control are often more stable than presentation objects, while business rules and data are generally the most stable of all.

Web page designers, HTML and JSP technology experts, and application administrators handle implementing presentation objects after the application has been deployed. Application developers implement control-related objects. Developers, domain experts, and database experts implement business rules and data objects.

As discussed previously, the sample application's Web site handles customer interactions. (See Section 11.2 on page 352.) The Web site presents the application's data—the product catalog—to the user in response to the user's requests. The Web site's primary responsibilities include handling user requests, retrieving and displaying product catalog data to a user's browser, and allowing users to select and purchase products.

The next phase of the design process is to partition the application into modules and objects that address the different functional requirements. The partitioning process includes deciding how to apportion the application across the different tiers of the J2EE platform, which portions of the application need to be distributed, and which should be implemented for local interaction.

The discussion begins with the functional specification for the user interface to the pet store Web site. See Figure 11.5.

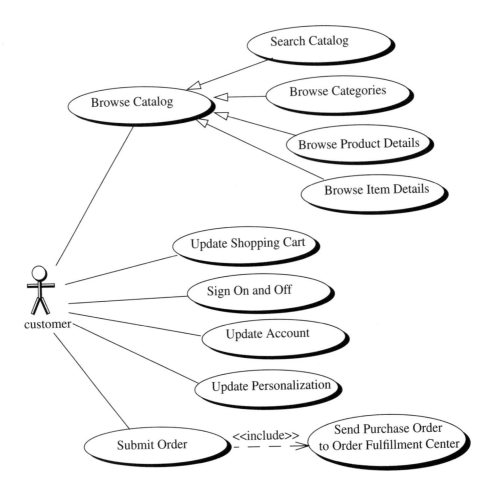

Figure 11.5   Use Cases between Customer and Web Site

A customer accessing the Web site expects to see:

- Links or navigation bars to common navigational tasks
- A catalog providing an organized view of the site's contents
- A search mechanism
- A master view of catalog items

- A detail view that describes the details of a particular item

- A shopping cart view that lets customers review and modify the contents of their shopping cart

- A checkout view that displays the total order cost and allows the customer to enter billing and shipping information

- A receipt view to provide confirmation of the purchase

In addition to these user interface requirements, the application must also support some security requirements, such as allowing only properly signed-on users to access certain features while allowing all users free access to other areas of the site.

Once the functional requirements are identified, the application can be divided into modules based on functionality. Such separation reduces the dependency between modules and allows them to be developed independently. In addition, identifying interfaces between modules enables modules to be developed by third-party component providers.

In this view, the application is divided into these modules:

- A control module to create and maintain user account information, which includes a user identifier, billing, and contact information. This information is maintained in a database. The control module also creates and manages the user's shopping cart and controls the interactions with the user.

- A sign-on module to handle the user log-in process and security, such as verifying a user identifier and password

- A product catalog module that returns product information from the catalog based on a user's search criteria

- A customer module that manages a user's purchasing process and maintains account records for a customer

- A messaging module that enables the application to send and receive asynchronous messages containing purchase orders

Figure 11.6 shows how the modules in the sample application Web site relate to each other.

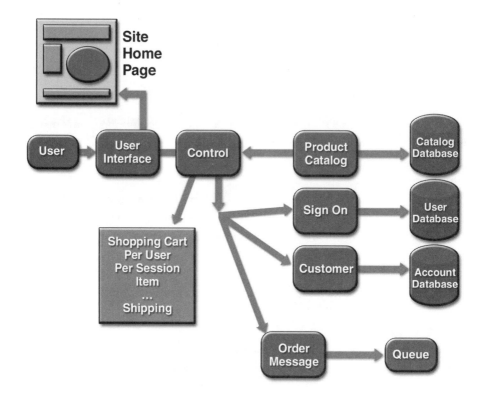

Figure 11.6   Functional Modules for the Sample Application Web Site

Once the application is partitioned into functional modules, the next step is to identify units of business logic, data, and presentation logic and model them as software objects. This starts with identifying the options at the highest level, then working down.

The overall design and organization of the Web site follows the Model-View-Controller architecture, while the internal design of some of its individual components follow the J2EE patterns. The application uses the MVC architecture because it provides a structure for handling complex, presentation-oriented applications.

In classic MVC architecture, views register themselves with the model for change notifications. When the model changes, it notifies a view of what changed. In the application's Web site, the nature of HTTP requires the client view to use a request-response paradigm to interact with the model on the EJB tier. Rather than using notification, model changes are reported as a response to the client view.

The sample application's Web site is a complex application. It has numerous views and pages displayed to the customer in potentially different languages, plus content may be personalized. Customers can make an array of different requests, each of which the application interprets and services, with data coming from multiple sources. The application dynamically determines the sequence of views to display to the customer.

Applying the Model-View-Controller architecture to the sample application reduces its complexity and makes it more manageable. The architecture enhances the degree to which the application can be maintained and extended. By separating business and control logic from data presentation, the architecture provides the flexibility to handle such application complexity.

In the design of the Web site application, it is first partitioned into model-view-controller layers. The application divides roughly as shown in Figure 11.7. Keep in mind that these are not clear boundaries between model, view, and controller. Application functions typically straddle these layers.

The next few sections examine the operations that are performed within and across each Model-View-Controller architecture section and their design issues. They also suggest the appropriate J2EE technologies and design patterns to handle these issues.

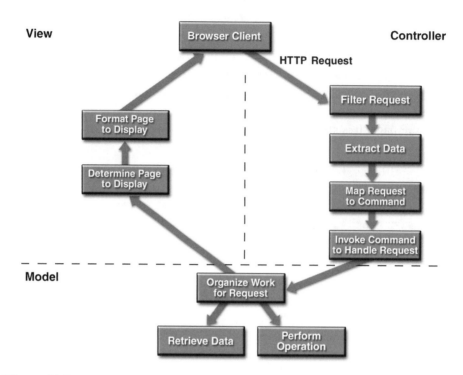

Figure 11.7   Model-View-Controller Architecture in Sample Application

11.4.1.1 View Layer of the Application Architecture

The sample application uses the J2EE platform technologies (servlets, JSP pages, and XML) for handling user views. In general, the application uses JSP pages for presentations where the presentation data changes rather than the structure of the presentation. The application could use servlets for graphics and other binary data representations or when it appears that data structure frequently changes. If the data already exists in XML or if it must be viewed in multiple ways, this could be handled using XML combined with XSLT.

When designing the application views, consider these key issues:

- Separate presentation logic from business and control logic.

  View components should focus on presentation. It is important when designing the view portion of an application to keep logic for presenting a view separate from logic that implements business rules and logic that controls process flow.

In addition, it is best to keep presentation logic modular by using view templates and helper objects to structure and build page content.

JSPs are an excellent technology for creating views for Web applications. However, it is important to use JSP pages effectively. The sample application uses JSPs for the Web site so that the JSP logic focuses on rendering the view. The application's JSP pages do not contain control logic. (A controller handles control logic.) This makes it easier to reuse the presentation logic portion of the JSP page. It is also important to avoid putting logic in embedded scriptlets.

The application uses a view helper pattern. It also encapsulates presentation logic in JSP custom tags and uses JavaBeans to hold data. Presentation logic implemented in custom tags or JavaBeans is separate from data and it is modular and reusable—it is defined in one place and used referentially from different JSPs.

- Manage page layout.

Applications usually strive for a common look and feel, and keeping page layouts similar within an application is important to establishing such a look and feel. The pages for the sample application all have the same structure: a banner across the top, a navigation menu down the left side, and a footer at the bottom. Page content appears to the right of the navigation menu, between the banner and the footer. The content of each segment is independent of the others.

Figure 11.8 shows two pages from the sample application. Notice the layout similarity between these pages: the Java Pet Store banner across the top, menu selections on the left side, and the same footer information across the bottom. Page content appears to the right of the menu. However, the content of the two pages is very different

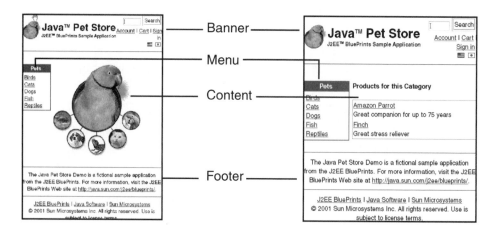

Figure 11.8   Two Sample Application Pages

A templating mechanism, such as a composite view design pattern used by the sample application, helps to keep page layout consistent. A template determines how to assemble view components into a single view. It consolidates page layout in one location, making it easy to change page layout in one place and have all pages remain consistent. In addition, a template, such as composite view, separates layout from content.

- Separate developer roles.

The MVC architecture provides the means to separate the work of developers who have different skill sets. For the most part, Web page authors primarily have visual design skills. They usually are graphic artists or content editors, and may not be programmers. On the other hand, programmers who know the business model, work flow, and application requirements develop the model and controller components. Separating developer roles minimizes interference among developers and lets them work independently. The application uses the view helper pattern to separate data presentation from business logic. This separation enables the Web page author to change view presentation without fear of corrupting programming logic. Likewise, programmers can implement application logic without affecting the page layout.

11.4.1.2 Model Layer of the Application Architecture

The model portion of the MVC architecture encapsulates the business objects and API for the application's functionality. The sample application uses enterprise beans to implement its business logic. Enterprise beans (and the EJB tier) are the recommended J2EE technology for implementing these business objects. Enterprise beans are preferred because of the services provided by the EJB container, particularly for applications that are transactional, distributed, and potentially scalable, and where security is important. Simpler applications with fewer needs may be able to provide their own services and may consider implementing their model as Java objects.

The design of the model portion of the application considers these issues:

- Keep the functional interface manageable.

  The model for most applications consists of many cooperating business objects. As the number of business objects increases, developers have more difficulty understanding how they interact. Developers can be overwhelmed by the number of APIs exposed by these object interfaces.

  A complex API can be simplified using two mechanisms—a facade class and a command pattern. A facade coordinates operations between cooperating classes. It presents a single interface to the business objects representing the application model or functionality. A facade encapsulates and hides the complexity of these business objects from clients. In addition, because their implementation details are kept hidden by a facade, the objects can change without affecting the clients. The sample application uses a session facade session bean as a single interface to other enterprise bean business objects.

  A facade's effectiveness is limited, since complex applications can cause the facade's API to grow too large. This is the case with the sample application. Rather than continuing to add methods to the session facade class, the sample application implements a command pattern on top of the facade. A command pattern encapsulates each application function in a separate class. Each command instance represents a single request for an application service along with data necessary to perform the service.

- Develop code as components to promote reuse.

  Application development is enhanced when developers design code to be modular, reusable components, or promote using off-the-shelf frameworks and components. Modular components are designed to be independent from other components; they are only loosely-coupled to other components. With loose coupling, changes to components have little or no impact on other components. Also, modular components are designed to do only a single function. Single-function components can be easily reused and they have no extra overhead. Off-the-shelf frameworks can serve as a backbone to which other components plug in. Both off-the-shelf frameworks and components let developers leverage the expertise of others.

- Manage data access for portability.

The sample application uses business data stored in several databases. Data could also be stored in legacy systems. Each type of data repository may have its own API. It is best if the application's business objects are not tightly coupled to a specific data persistence mechanism, because changing the underlying data store or database requires changing the data access logic in the business objects. The application uses enterprise beans with container-managed persistence because, with container-managed persistence, the EJB container handles the data access details. This decouples access to persistent data from the data's particular storage mechanism. When the application uses enterprise beans with bean-managed persistence, which it must do in certain situations, it then implements a data access object to achieve the same decoupling. A data access object encapsulates data access mechanism details so that these details are kept separate from business logic.

- Locate objects.

Enterprise beans and other components in a distributed system routinely use the Java Naming and Directory Interface (JNDI) to locate other resources and components. Lookup procedures can be complex. The application uses a service locator object to handle all the lookup details for finding distributed objects. A business object can make one call to the service locator rather than including this lookup logic itself, thus letting it focus on business logic.

- Separate developer roles.

As with view development, business component development is most effective when developer roles are separated. For example, by using container-managed persistence or having database developers implement data access objects, the application shields business logic developers from the implementation details of database access calls.

11.4.1.3 Controller Layer of the Application Architecture

The controller section of the MVC architecture controls the flow of the application and serves as the glue between the model and view—it executes business logic in the model in response to user requests and helps select the next view for display. The controller decouples data presentation from business data and logic.

It is possible to implement a controller in the client, Web, or EJB tier, or in a combination of these tiers. A client presenting only views is considered a thin client. A rich client implements views and a controller. Generally, a Web-tier controller handles HTTP requests, passing requests to an EJB-tier controller, which in turn invokes the business logic processing. A Web-tier controller also selects view components for presentation by a thin Web client.

The sample application divides controller functionality between its Web and EJB tiers, and control crosses tier boundaries. The controller receives and handles requests between the Web and EJB tiers. The application also combines a controller with a command pattern. A Web-tier front controller, implemented as a servlet, receives HTTP requests and performs functions specific to the Web tier, such as changing output encoding. All user requests flow through the front controller. The front controller, using the data in the request, extracts the type of request and converts it to the appropriate type of event object. It then passes the event to the EJB-tier controller, implemented as a session bean, which matches the event to the proper command. Ultimately, the command invokes the appropriate action on a session facade, which executes the business logic.

The application selects the next view to display entirely in the Web tier, using the screen flow manager for this task. While selection of the next view can be done in either tier, it usually is done in the Web tier.

A front controller is a good design approach because it provides a single point of contact for all application requests. It interprets requests, executes business logic, and handles security, error handling, and view selection. Centralizing application control provides a natural point for implementing application-wide services and reduces code redundancy.

Implementing a controller with a command pattern not only simplifies a session facade interface (see Section 11.4.1.2 on page 369), it also keeps the controller implementation cleaner by encapsulating event- and request-handling tasks into smaller objects. It also enables Java platform events to be used as the bridge between Web- and EJB-tier controllers.

The application's controller section includes a request intercepting filter. This servlet provides application-wide security services. The request intercepting filter handles all incoming user requests and checks that users are properly logged in. Centralizing application-wide services in one place makes it is easy to add and remove services.

11.4.1.4 Applying MVC Architecture to Web Application

The architecture for the sample application's Web site consists of a set of components divided into model, view, and controller layers. The components in the controller layer handle client requests—they receive client requests and start the process of providing the appropriate response. The controller layer components are Request Intercepting Filter, Event Controller, Event Factory, Event, EJB Tier Controller, and Command Factory.

The model layer contains the components that handle business logic: Session Facade, Business Object, and Data Access Object. They extract and formulate the data required to handle a client request. The Command Handler component straddles the controller and model layer, and serves as a bridge between them. The view layer contains the components whose job is to format and present a response to the client. It consists of the following components: Screen View, Composite View, Screen Flow Manager, and View Helper. Three additional components— Service Locator, Value Object, and Business Delegate—apply the MVC approach in a distributed setting. They handle the issues that arise in a distributed architecture.

Let's examine the architecture of the application in more detail by following a user request received by the Web site. This section shows how the model, view, and controller portions of the Web site handle the request and how different objects or components are designed to handle the application's functionality. Whenever possible, these components follow J2EE design patterns. Figure 11.9 shows how the sample application architecture decomposes into components.

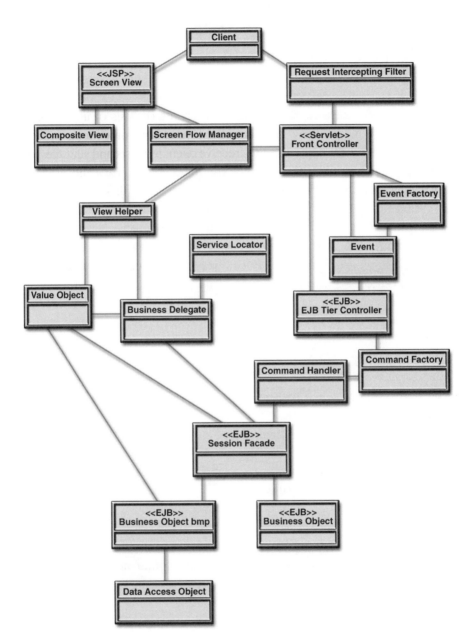

Figure 11.9 Class Diagram Showing Sample Application Architectural Components

A client interacts with different views presented in the browser and eventually submits an HTTP request. The request goes to the controller section where it is handled by a Request Intercepting Filter. This servlet filter receives the request and does the necessary security checks. It then passes the request to the Front Controller servlet. The Front Controller's job is to pull out data from the request form and create an event object with that data. It uses an event factory to create the right type of event and then passes the event to an EJB Tier Controller session bean. This session bean maps the event to a command using the services of a Command Factory and a Command Handler object. A Command Handler object simplifies a session facade by determining the action to perform.

To handle the request, the Command Handler object invokes the correct action on a Session Facade, which is a session bean in the model section. The Session Facade organizes the work that needs to be done. It invokes operations on other session and entity beans, referred to as business objects, that carry out the details of the application's business logic. Entity beans may access the database if it's necessary to retrieve data. If the entity bean uses container-managed persistence, the EJB container handles the data access logic. Otherwise, if the entity bean uses bean-managed persistence, there may be an additional Data Access Object to hold the access logic.

The sample application includes an EJB Tier Controller that relies on a command handler object. The EJB Tier Controller provides a single method, handleEvent, through which requests from the Front Controller pass as events. The handleEvent method includes an event argument that encapsulates the requested operation and any required data. Based on the event type, the EJB Tier Controller uses the Command Factory to get the proper Command Handler. The Command Handler orchestrates updates to model data contained in EJB components. By using the command pattern, the EJB Tier Controller delegates the execution of business functionality to the Command Handler.

For example, the application centralizes business logic in a PlaceOrder command handler. The PlaceOrder command handler orchestrates the details of business operations in one object. The PlaceOrder command handler bean calls four different enterprise beans (both entity and session beans) to carry out its operations, such as requesting database information, preparing orders, formulating response information, building and sending XML messages, and so forth.

To present a page to the user, the application must retrieve data and then format it properly. Not only must the application build the presentation page, it must also know the correct page to display within the sequence of pages. At the data retrieval level, the application uses a Service Locator object to perform look up functions. It also uses a Business Delegate to bridge the EJB and Web tiers, particularly if its entity beans are implemented with a remote client view. The Business Delegate is an object that hides the data retrieval details, such as remote exceptions. A Value Object may be used to limit the number of remote access calls.

Other components take care of the presentation of the retrieved data. The Screen View is a JSP page that builds the next screen to display to the user. It relies on a Composite View, which is a template containing the page structure (header, footer, and so forth). It also relies on a View Helper, either a JavaBean component or a helper object, that extracts the dynamic content for the page from the retrieved data. The Screen Flow Manager object keeps track of the next page in the sequence of pages.

Figure 11.9 reflects a remote view architecture. In actuality, the sample application Web site uses a local architecture approach. While this approach limits distribution to one VM, it does provide increased performance and the ability to have fine-grained method access. It also enables the application to leverage all the container-managed persistence capabilities offered by the EJB container.

Using a local or a remote architecture affects the design of the application and its deployment strategy. Figure 11.9 would have fewer layers had it reflected this local client view design. With a local client view, the design can include finer granularity between components. Local method calls do not have the overhead of remote method calls. Because there are few layers and tiers are co-located, it is not necessary to use value objects or business delegates. Value objects are not necessary for entity beans implemented with a local client view.

Deployment is also affected by use of a local or remote architecture. An application implementing a local architecture must be deployed in one unit. Applications with a remote architecture may be deployed as separate units or as one unit. For example, you can deploy the Web tier separate from the EJB tier, or even deploy EJB components separately.

11.4.2 Fulfillment Center Architecture

The order fulfillment center fulfills customer orders and manages the business's financial transactions. Processing starts in this back end of the system when a customer's purchase order is received from the Web site. Processing an order from start to finish may take a few days.

Three modules comprise the fulfillment center—the order process coordinator, administrator, and supplier modules. There are submodules within each module, such as the customer relations submodule. Each module of the fulfillment center can be packaged in a separate EAR file. Packaging modules separately makes it easier to add and change modules. For example, the supplier currently is internal to the system environment, but the design allows the application assembler to easily add other, external suppliers.

Figure 11.10 shows the modules of the order fulfillment center and their relationships to each other.

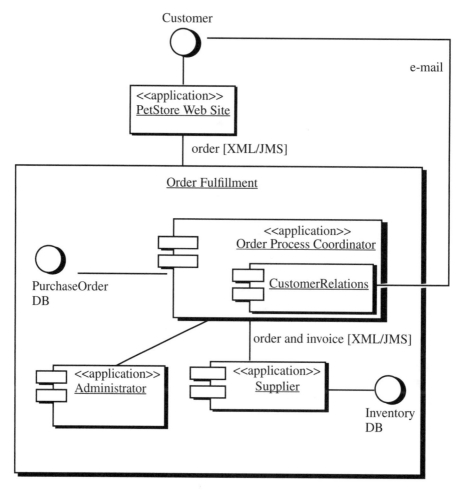

Figure 11.10 Order Fulfillment Center Architecture

- The order processing module receives the purchase order and verifies the customer's credit status. The order processing module acts as the processing coordinator or workflow manager, and maintains a global view of the entire order processing flow. When it receives an order from the Web site, it assigns it an identifier and stores it in the database. It communicates with the administrator module if an order requires financial verification.

- The administrator module handles any special financial verification or processing, such as for large orders, and obtains credit card approvals.

- A customer relation submodule within the order processing module notifies the customer that the order has been accepted.

- The order processing module passes the order to the supplier.

- The supplier fills as much of the order as it can from inventory. The supplier maintains the inventory data in a database. It also invoices the order processing module for the portion of the order it is filling and ships this amount.

- The order processing module updates its purchase order records based on information from the supplier and the customer relations submodule notifies the customer of order shipments. This process continues until the order is completely filled.

Figure 11.11 shows the flow of work in the order fulfillment center.

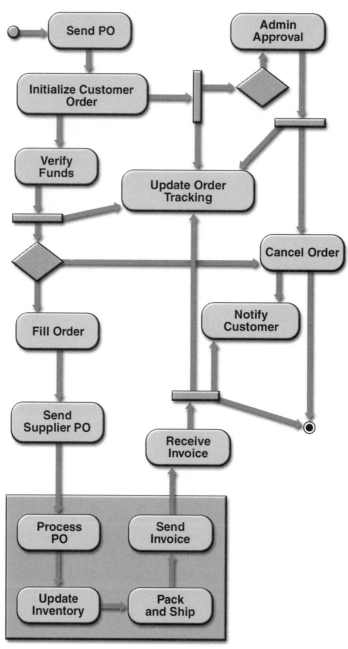

Figure 11.11 Fulfillment Center Workflow

How is this implemented in the application software? The order fulfillment center is process-oriented, its process driven by the receipt of an order from the Web site. It typically performs the same sequence of activities for each order, and this process usually lasts for longer than a single session. Single session refers to a client's session, usually an interactive session on the Web site. A single session lasts a few minutes or it can last up to several hours at most. The order fulfillment center's activities, from start to completion, may last several days.

The software implementing the fulfillment center does not use the Model-View-Controller architecture, although it does make use of some of the J2EE design patterns. The fulfillment center uses a number of the J2EE platform technologies, including JMS API, message-driven enterprise beans, JavaMail API, and XML.

The MVC architecture, with its focus on view presentation, is better for GUI-based applications such as the Web site. It is not as well-suited for handling complex process control with potentially extended latency between activities, nor for loosely-coupled communication between participants. The transactional model for the fulfillment center is also quite different than that for the Web site. Web site actions can be rolled back, but recovery is more complex in the fulfillment workflow.

The fulfillment center GUIs are designed following the MVC architecture. In addition, design strategies such as the session facade pattern used in the Web site may apply in the fulfillment center. When a session facade is used in the fulfillment center, it is used selectively and only for coordinating components within a model. A session facade is not designed to coordinate an entire ongoing process such as that of the fulfillment center. A session facade, because it is a session bean, is better for storing state for the duration of a single session. The entire fulfillment process lasts longer than a single session and its state cannot be held in a session bean. Instead, the fulfillment center maintains its state in persistent storage, using entity beans to store and retrieve this state.

This discussion focuses on the architecture of the order processing module, because this module coordinates all the pieces of the fulfillment center application and ensures that customer orders are processed and filled. It uses the JMS API and message-driven beans to accomplish its tasks. Conceptually, the order processing module divides into three pieces:

- A workflow manager coordinates the activities in the fulfillment center. It knows the overall process and the sequence of activity steps.

- Each activity handles its portion of the business logic. For example, one activity notifies the customer of the order status while a different activity prepares invoices for shipped products.

- Transition delegates handle the details of transitioning to the next activity. They prepare messages and send them to JMS destinations.

The order processing module implements a persistent message model that ensures that message state is saved. The order processing module sends messages to JMS destinations, some of which are queues and others are topics. A queue saves message state until the message is received. A topic is used to distribute a message to multiple recipients who have subscribed to the topic. The fulfillment center uses durable topic subscriptions so that message state is saved until all recipients receive the message.

The fulfillment center separates the implementation of process control from business logic. A process manager is responsible for the entire workflow process. It knows the sequence of steps and the rules for following these steps. It ensures that the appropriate module or activity is invoked at the right point to carry out an operation. If necessary, it saves process state in persistent storage so that an order can be filled over multiple days. The process manager uses a persistent message model that saves message state. The activity module contains the business logic, which determines how the operation should be carried out. The business logic within a given activity may be implemented with a session facade pattern.

Messages are sent asynchronously using the JMS API between work flow activities. For example, the manage order flow activity sends an asynchronous message (through a JMS queue) to the verify credit activity so that the customer's credit is verified before completing the order. The verify credit activity sends an asynchronous message to the process manager indicating the results of the credit check. These messages are encoded in XML, making it easy for different applications to communicate. The customer relations submodule uses the JavaMail API to send e-mail notifying customers of order acceptance and shipments.

Each activity in the fulfillment center corresponds to a named JMS destination, either a queue or topic. This named destination is the endpoint that maps to a step in the workflow. Components of the system can send messages to and receive messages from these named destinations. A message-driven bean implements the boundary of the application or module responsible for each piece of the work flow. A message-driven bean enables asynchronous process control messaging, thereby removing any tight-coupling restrictions between activities. The message-driven bean receives and handles the incoming message request to the particular destination. It passes the message contents to its related work activity module, which might be the module to formulate an order addressed to the supplier or a notification message for the customer, and that module carries out the operation. The message-driven bean then invokes a transition delegate, whose responsibility is to notify the next step in the work flow. The order of steps in the work flow is determined and coded appropriately in each transition delegate. The transition delegate asynchronously sends the appropriate message to a named JMS destination, which is subscribed to by the next activity in the sequence. The delegate may also notify the order processing module so that it can maintain its global view of the work flow.

Depending on the particular point in the work flow, a transition delegate may be notifying a single activity or it may be notifying several activities. When it needs to notify a single activity, a transition delegate sends its message to a JMS queue. The message-driven bean for the activity that has subscribed to this queue receives any messages sent to the queue. The queue holds the message until it is received by the message-driven bean. When a transition delegate notifies more than one activity, it sends a message to a JMS topic that is subscribed to by the interested activities. This is a durable subscription to ensure that the topic holds the message until received by all subscribers. For example, the transition delegate for the ship order activity notifies the invoice order activity and the notify customer activity. The invoice order activity and the notify customer activity both subscribe to the same named topic to which the ship order transition delegate sends its message. They both receive the message and can act upon it.

Figure 11.12 shows how the activity workflow manager software models a portion of the process control workflow. The diagram shows the message-driven bean placed at the boundary of each activity to receive messages for that activity and the transition delegate that knows the JMS destination subscribed to by the next activity in the sequence. Messages are encoded in XML and are sent via the JMS API to a JMS destination, either a queue or topic.

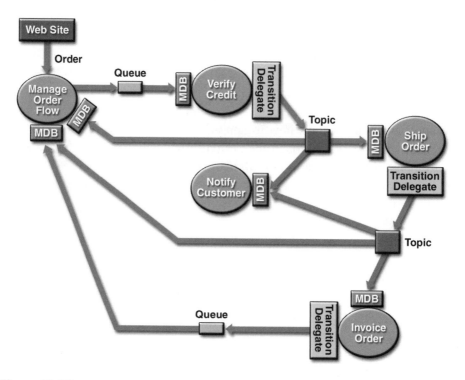

Figure 11.12 Process Work Flow of Fulfillment Center

As noted previously, the process work flow often takes longer than a single session to complete. The state of the various activities must be saved. While the process work flow diagram does not show where and when state is saved, entity beans save state when needed to the purchase order or inventory database.

11.5   Summary

This chapter examined the recommended architectures for J2EE applications and covered designing an application for the J2EE platform. It described the Model-View-Controller architecture and showed how this architecture applies to enterprise applications. It also described the more commonly used J2EE design patterns, which are useful for designing components within an application.

The architecture of the sample application partitions its functionality into modules, assigns functionality to tiers, and decomposes the modules into specific objects to represent the behavior and data of the application. The principles guiding the architecture include reuse of software designs and code, separation of stable code from volatile code, object decomposition along skill lines, and ease of migration from a Web-centric to EJB-centric model.

The sample application adapts the MVC architecture to the domain of enterprise applications and shows how to apply J2EE design patterns to application components. It takes you through the design of the sample application, starting with formulating functional specifications and high-level considerations such as choosing application tiers and deciding between a local or distributed model. It shows you how to decompose an application into objects and design and implement these objects so that they are efficient, modular, and reusable.

The J2EE platform provides system services that simplify the work that application objects need to perform. The sample application uses the J2EE support for distributed transactions across multiple JDBC databases. In addition, it uses deployment and security capabilities of the J2EE platform to support customers with different profiles.

11.6   References and Resources

The following resources are recommended for further information on design patterns in general and on particular J2EE design patterns.

- *Core J2EE Patterns*. D. Alur, J. Crupi, D. Malks. Copyright 2001, Prentice Hall PTR.

- *Design Patterns*. E. Gamma, R. Helm, R. Johnson, J. Vlissides. Copyright 1995, Addison-Wesley.

- *Refactoring: Improving the Design of Existing Code*. M. Fowler, et al. Copyright 1999, Addison-Wesley.

- *Pattern-Oriented Software Architecture, Volume 1: A System of Patterns*. F. Buschmann, et al. Copyright 1996, John Wiley & Sons.

- *Pattern-Oriented Software Architecture, Volume 2: Patterns for Concurrent and Networked Objects*. D. Schmidt, et al. Copyright 2000, John Wiley & Sons.

Afterword

THIS book has presented an overview of application design and development with the Java 2 Platform, Enterprise Edition. Its goal has been to introduce enterprise developers to the concepts and technology used in designing applications for the J2EE platform, and to give practical examples of a typical enterprise application.

While this book has explored many of the decisions that must be made in the process of designing and developing applications, it is necessarily limited in scope. We've made an effort to be concise in order to focus on high-level design considerations rather than on extensive implementation details.

While the Java BluePrints program tries to maintain this overall focus, it does provide additional resources for analyzing application design and developing effective approaches to specific problems. The goal of the program is to offer an ongoing support mechanism for developers engaged in applying Java technologies to real-world problems and to evolve a variety of best practices to apply to designing Java applications.

The Java BluePrints program includes a regularly updated Web site, articles published by developer-focused magazines and third-party Web sites, and future books in the Addison-Wesley Java Series, Enterprise Edition.

Your comments on this book, your requests for coverage of additional topics, your participation in our online surveys, and your attendance at our sessions at events such as the JavaOne^{SM} Developer Conference are all important to the success of the Java BluePrints program. Please contact us any time with your feedback:

```
javablueprints-feedback@sun.com.
```

The Java BluePrints Team

Glossary

access control The methods by which interactions with resources are limited to collections of users or programs for the purpose of enforcing integrity, confidentiality, or availability constraints.

ACID The acronym for the four properties guaranteed by transactions: atomicity, consistency, isolation, and durability.

activation The process of transferring an enterprise bean from secondary storage to memory. (See **passivation**.)

applet A component that typically executes in a Web browser, but can execute in a variety of other applications or devices that support the applet programming model.

applet container A container that includes support for the applet programming model.

Application Component Provider A vendor that provides the Java classes that implement components' methods, JSP page definitions, and any required deployment descriptors.

Application Assembler A person that combines components and modules into deployable application units.

application client A first-tier client component that executes in its own Java virtual machine. Application clients have access to some J2EE platform APIs (JNDI, JDBC, RMI-IIOP, JMS).

application client container A container that supports application client components.

application client module A software unit that consists of one or more classes and an application client deployment descriptor.

authentication The process by which an entity proves to another entity that it is acting on behalf of a specific identity. The J2EE platform requires three types of authentication: basic, form-based, and mutual, and supports digest authentication.

authorization See **access control**.

authorization constraint An authorization rule that determines who is permitted to access a Web resource collection.

basic authentication An authentication mechanism in which a Web server authenticates an entity with a user name and password obtained using the Web client's built-in authentication mechanism.

bean-managed persistence Data transfer between an entity bean's variables and a resource manager managed by the entity bean.

bean-managed transaction A transaction whose boundaries are defined by an enterprise bean.

business logic The code that implements the functionality of an application. In the Enterprise JavaBeans model, this logic is implemented by the methods of an enterprise bean.

business method A method of an enterprise bean that implements the business logic or rules of an application.

callback methods Methods in a component called by the container to notify the component of important events in its life cycle.

caller Same as **caller principal**.

caller principal The principal that identifies the invoker of the enterprise bean method.

client certificate authentication An authentication mechanism in which a client uses a X.509 certificate to establish its identity.

commit The point in a transaction when all updates to any resources involved in the transaction are made permanent.

component An application-level software unit supported by a container. Components are configurable at deployment time. The J2EE platform defines four types of components: enterprise beans, Web components, applets, and application clients.

component contract The contract between a component and its container. The contract includes life cycle management of the component, a context interface that the instance uses to obtain various information and services from its container, and a list of services that every container must provide for its components.

connection See **resource manager connection**.

connection factory See **resource manager connection factory**.

connector A standard extension mechanism for containers to provide connectivity to enterprise information systems. A connector is specific to an enterprise information system and consists of a resource adapter and application development tools for enterprise information system connectivity. The resource adapter is plugged into a container through its support for system-level contracts defined in the connector architecture.

Connector architecture An architecture for integration of J2EE products with enterprise information systems. There are two parts to this architecture: a resource adapter provided by an enterprise information system vendor and the J2EE product that allows this resource adapter to plug in. This architecture defines a set of contracts that a resource adapter has to support to plug in to a J2EE product, for example, transactions, security, and resource management.

container An entity that provides life cycle management, security, deployment, and runtime services to components. Each type of container (EJB, Web, JSP, servlet, applet, and application client) also provides component-specific services.

container-managed persistence Data transfer between an entity bean's variables and a resource manager managed by the entity bean's container.

container-managed transaction A transaction whose boundaries are defined by an EJB container. An entity bean must use container-managed transactions.

context attribute An object bound into the context associated with a servlet.

conversational state The field values of a session bean plus the transitive closure of the objects reachable from the bean's fields. The transitive closure of a bean is defined in terms of the serialization protocol for the Java programming language, that is, the fields that would be stored by serializing the bean instance.

CORBA Common Object Request Broker Architecture. A language-independent, distributed object model specified by the Object Management Group.

create method A method defined in the home interface and invoked by a client to create an enterprise bean.

credentials The information describing the security attributes of a principal.

CTS Compatibility Test Suite. A suite of compatibility tests for verifying that a J2EE product complies with the J2EE platform specification.

delegation An act whereby one principal authorizes another principal to use its identity or privileges with some restrictions.

Deployer A person who installs modules and J2EE applications into an operational environment.

deployment The process whereby software is installed into an operational environment.

deployment descriptor An XML file provided with each module and application that describes how they should be deployed. The deployment descriptor directs a deployment tool to deploy a module or application with specific container options and describes specific configuration requirements that a Deployer must resolve.

digest authentication An authentication mechanism in which a Web client authenticates to a Web server by sending the server a message digest along its HTTP request message. The digest is computed by employing a one-way hash algorithm to a concatenation of the HTTP request message and the client's password. The digest is typically much smaller than the HTTP request and doesn't contain the password.

distributed application An application made up of distinct components running in separate runtime environments, usually on different platforms connected via a network. Typical distributed applications are two-tier (client-server), three-tier (client-middleware-server), and multitier (client-multiple middleware-multiple servers).

DOM Document Object Model. A tree of objects with interfaces for traversing the tree and writing an XML version of it, as defined by the W3C specification.

DTD Document Type Definition. A description of the structure and properties of a class of XML files.

EAR file A JAR archive that contains a J2EE application.

EJB™ See **Enterprise JavaBeans**.

EJB container A container that implements the EJB component contract of the J2EE architecture. This contract specifies a runtime environment for enterprise beans that includes security, concurrency, life cycle management, transaction, deployment, naming, and other services. An EJB container is provided by an EJB or J2EE server.

EJB Container Provider A vendor that supplies an EJB container.

EJB context An object that allows an enterprise bean to invoke services provided by the container and to obtain the information about the caller of a client-invoked method.

EJB home object An object that provides the life cycle operations (create, remove, find) for an enterprise bean. The class for the EJB home object is generated by the container's deployment tools. The EJB home object implements the enterprise bean's home interface. The client references an EJB home object to perform life cycle operations on an EJB object. The client uses JNDI to locate an EJB home object.

EJB JAR file A JAR archive that contains an EJB module.

EJB module A software unit that consists of one or more enterprise beans and an EJB deployment descriptor.

EJB object An object whose class implements the enterprise bean's remote interface. A client never references an enterprise bean instance directly; a client always references an EJB object. The class of an EJB object is generated by the container's deployment tools.

EJB server Software provides services to an EJB container. For example, an EJB container typically relies on a transaction manager that is part of the EJB server to perform the two-phase commit across all the participating resource managers. The J2EE architecture assumes that an EJB container is hosted by an EJB server from the same vendor, so it does not specify the contract between these two entities. An EJB server may host one or more EJB containers.

EJB Server Provider A vendor that supplies an EJB server.

enterprise bean A component that implements a business task or business entity and resides in an EJB container; either an entity bean or a session bean.

enterprise information system The applications that comprise an enterprise's existing system for handling company-wide information. These applications provide an information infrastructure for an enterprise. An enterprise information system offers a well-defined set of services to its clients. These services are exposed to clients as local and/or remote interfaces. Examples of enterprise information systems include enterprise resource planning systems, mainframe transaction processing systems, and legacy database systems.

enterprise information system resource An entity that provides enterprise information system-specific functionality to its clients. Examples are a record or set of records in a database system, a business object in an enterprise resource planning system, and a transaction program in a transaction processing system.

Enterprise Bean Provider An application programmer who produces enterprise bean classes, remote and home interfaces, and deployment descriptor files, and packages them in an EJB .jar file.

Enterprise JavaBeans™ **(EJB**™**)** A component architecture for the development and deployment of object-oriented, distributed, enterprise-level applications. Applications written using the Enterprise JavaBeans architecture are scalable, transactional, and secure.

entity bean An enterprise bean that represents persistent data maintained in a database. An entity bean can manage its own persistence or it can delegate this function to its container. An entity bean is identified by a primary key. If the container in which an entity bean is hosted crashes, the entity bean, its primary key, and any remote references survive the crash.

finder method A method defined in the home interface and invoked by a client to locate an entity bean.

form-based authentication An authentication mechanism in which a Web container provides an application-specific form for logging in.

group A collection of principals within a given security policy domain.

handle An object that identifies an enterprise bean. A client may serialize the handle and then later deserialize it to obtain a reference to the enterprise bean.

home interface One of two interfaces for an enterprise bean. The home interface defines zero or more methods for creating and removing an enterprise bean. For session beans, the home interface defines create and remove methods, while for entity beans, the home interface defines create, finder, and remove methods.

home handle An object that can be used to obtain a reference of the home interface. A home handle can be serialized and written to stable storage and deserialized to obtain the reference.

HTML HyperText Markup Language. A markup language for hypertext documents on the Internet. HTML enables the embedding of images, sounds, video streams, form fields, references to other objects with URLs and basic text formatting.

HTTP HyperText Transfer Protocol. The Internet protocol used to fetch hypertext objects from remote hosts. HTTP messages consist of requests from client to server and responses from server to client.

HTTPS HTTP layered over the SSL protocol.

impersonation An act whereby one entity assumes the identity and privileges of another entity without restrictions and without any indication visible to the recipients of the impersonator's calls that delegation has taken place. Impersonation is a case of simple delegation.

IDL Interface Definition Language. A language used to define interfaces to remote CORBA objects. The interfaces are independent of operating systems and programming languages.

IIOP Internet Inter-ORB Protocol. A protocol used for communication between CORBA object request brokers.

initialization parameter A parameter that initializes the context associated with a servlet.

ISV Independent Software Vendor.

J2EE™ Java 2, Enterprise Edition.

J2ME™ Java 2, Micro Edition.

J2SE™ Java 2, Standard Edition.

J2EE application Any deployable unit of J2EE functionality. This can be a single module or a group of modules packaged into an `.ear` file with a J2EE application deployment descriptor. J2EE applications are typically engineered to be distributed across multiple computing tiers.

J2EE product An implementation that conforms to the J2EE platform specification.

J2EE Product Provider A vendor that supplies a J2EE product.

J2EE server The runtime portion of a J2EE product. A J2EE server provides Web and/or EJB containers.

JAR Java ARchive A platform-independent file format that permits many files to be aggregated into one file.

Java™ 2 Platform, Standard Edition (J2SE platform) The core Java technology platform.

Java™ 2 Platform, Enterprise Edition (J2EE platform) An environment for developing and deploying enterprise applications. The J2EE platform consists of a set of services, application programming interfaces (APIs), and protocols that provide the functionality for developing multitiered, Web-based applications.

Java™ 2 SDK, Enterprise Edition (J2EE SDK) Sun's implementation of the J2EE platform. This implementation provides an operational definition of the J2EE platform.

Java™ Message Service (JMS) An API for using enterprise messaging systems such as IBM MQ Series, TIBCO Rendezvous, and so on.

Java Naming and Directory Interface™ (JNDI) An API that provides naming and directory functionality.

Java™ Transaction API (JTA) An API that allows applications and J2EE servers to access transactions.

Java™ Transaction Service (JTS) Specifies the implementation of a transaction manager that supports JTA and implements the Java mapping of the OMG Object Transaction Service (OTS) 1.1 specification at the level below the API.

JavaBeans™ component A Java class that can be manipulated in a visual builder tool and composed into applications. A JavaBeans component must adhere to certain property and event interface conventions.

Java IDL A technology that provides CORBA interoperability and connectivity capabilities for the J2EE platform. These capabilities enable J2EE applications to invoke operations on remote network services using the OMG IDL and IIOP.

JavaMail™ An API for sending and receiving e-mail.

JavaServer Pages™ (JSP) An extensible Web technology that uses template data, custom elements, scripting languages, and server-side Java objects to return dynamic content to a client. Typically the template data is HTML or XML elements, and in many cases the client is a Web browser.

JDBC™ An API for database-independent connectivity between the J2EE platform and a wide range of data sources.

JMS See **Java Message Service**.

JNDI See **Java Naming and Directory Interface**.

JSP See **JavaServer Pages**.

JSP action A JSP element that can act on implicit objects and other server-side objects or can define new scripting variables. Actions follow the XML syntax for elements with a start tag, a body, and an end tag; if the body is empty it can also use the empty tag syntax. The tag must use a prefix.

JSP action, custom An action described in a portable manner by a tag library descriptor and a collection of Java classes and imported into a JSP page by a `taglib` directive. A custom action is invoked when a JSP page uses a *custom tag*.

JSP action, standard An action that is defined in the JSP specification and is always available to a JSP file without being imported.

JSP application A stand-alone Web application, written using the JavaServer Pages technology, that can contain JSP pages, servlets, HTML files, images, applets, and JavaBeans components.

JSP container A container that provides the same services as a servlet container and an engine that interprets and processes JSP pages into a servlet.

JSP container, distributed A JSP container that can run a Web application that is tagged as distributable and is spread across multiple Java virtual machines that might be running on different hosts.

JSP declaration A JSP scripting element that declares methods, variables, or both in a JSP file.

JSP directive A JSP element that gives an instruction to the JSP container and is interpreted at translation time.

JSP element A portion of a JSP page that is recognized by a JSP translator. An element can be a directive, an action, or a scripting element.

JSP expression A scripting element that contains a valid scripting language expression that is evaluated, converted to a String, and placed into the implicit out object.

JSP file A file that contains a JSP page. In the Servlet 2.2 specification, a JSP file must have a .jsp extension.

JSP page A text-based document using fixed template data and JSP elements that describes how to process a request to create a response.

JSP scripting element A JSP declaration, scriptlet, or expression whose tag syntax is defined by the JSP specification and whose content is written according to the scripting language used in the JSP page. The JSP specification describes the syntax and semantics for the case where the language page attribute is "java."

JSP scriptlet A JSP scripting element containing any code fragment that is valid in the scripting language used in the JSP page. The JSP specification describes what is a valid scriptlet for the case where the language page attribute is "java."

JSP tag A piece of text between a left angle bracket and a right angle bracket that is used in a JSP file as part of a JSP element. The tag is distinguishable as markup, as opposed to data, because it is surrounded by angle brackets.

JSP tag library A collection of custom tags identifying custom actions described via a tag library descriptor and Java classes.

JTA See **Java Transaction API**.

JTS See **Java Transaction Service**.

method permission An authorization rule that determines who is permitted to execute one or more enterprise bean methods.

module A software unit that consists of one or more J2EE components of the same container type and one deployment descriptor of that type. There are three types of modules: EJB, Web, and application client. Modules can be deployed as stand-alone units or assembled into an application.

mutual authentication An authentication mechanism employed by two parties for the purpose of proving each other's identity to one another.

ORB Object Request Broker. A library than enables CORBA objects to locate and communicate with one another.

OS principal A principal native to the operating system on which the J2EE platform is executing.

OTS Object Transaction Service. A definition of the interfaces that permit CORBA objects to participate in transactions.

naming context A set of associations between distinct, atomic people-friendly identifiers and objects.

naming environment A mechanism that allows a component to be customized without the need to access or change the component's source code. A container implements the component's naming environment and provides it to the component as a JNDI naming context. Each component names and accesses its environment entries using the `java:comp/env` JNDI context. The environment entries are declaratively specified in the component's deployment descriptor.

passivation The process of transferring an enterprise bean from memory to secondary storage. (See **activation**.)

persistence The protocol for transferring the state of an entity bean between its instance variables and an underlying database.

POA Portable Object Adapter. A CORBA standard for building server-side applications that are portable across heterogeneous ORBs.

principal The identity assigned to a user as a result of authentication.

privilege A security attribute that does not have the property of uniqueness and that may be shared by many principals.

primary key An object that uniquely identifies an entity bean within a home.

realm See **security policy domain**. Also, a string, passed as part of an HTTP request during basic authentication, that defines a protection space. The protected resources on a server can be partitioned into a set of protection spaces, each with its own authentication scheme and/or authorization database.

re-entrant entity bean An entity bean that can handle multiple simultaneous, interleaved, or nested invocations that will not interfere with each other.

Reference Implementation See **Java 2 SDK, Enterprise Edition**.

remote interface One of two interfaces for an enterprise bean. The remote interface defines the business methods callable by a client.

remove method Method defined in the home interface and invoked by a client to destroy an enterprise bean.

resource adapter A system-level software driver that is used by an EJB container or an application client to connect to an enterprise information system. A resource adapter is typically specific to an enterprise information system. It is available as a library and is used within the address space of the server or client using it. A resource adapter plugs into a container. The application components deployed on the container then use the client API (exposed by adapter) or tool generated high-level abstractions to access the underlying enterprise information system. The resource adapter and EJB container collaborate to provide the underlying mechanisms—transactions, security, and connection pooling—for connectivity to the enterprise information system.

resource manager Provides access to a set of shared resources. A resource manager participates in transactions that are externally controlled and coordinated by a transaction manager. A resource manager is typically in a different address space or on a different machine from the clients that access it. Note: An enterprise information system is referred to as resource manager when it is mentioned in the context of resource and transaction management.

resource manager connection An object that represents a session with a resource manager.

resource manager connection factory An object used for creating a resource manager connection.

RMI Remote Method Invocation. A technology that allows an object running in one Java virtual machine to invoke methods on an object running in a different Java virtual machine.

RMI-IIOP A version of RMI implemented to use the CORBA IIOP protocol. RMI over IIOP provides interoperability with CORBA objects implemented in any language if all the remote interfaces are originally defined as RMI interfaces.

role (development) The function performed by a party in the development and deployment phases of an application developed using J2EE technology. The roles are: Application Component Provider, Application Assembler, Deployer, J2EE Product Provider, EJB Container Provider, EJB Server Provider, Web Container Provider, Web Server Provider, Tool Provider, and System Administrator.

role (security) An abstract logical grouping of users that is defined by the Application Assembler. When an application is deployed, the roles are mapped to security identities, such as principals or groups, in the operational environment.

role mapping The process of associating the groups and/or principals recognized by the container to security roles specified in the deployment descriptor. Security roles have to be mapped by the Deployer before the component is installed in the server.

rollback The point in a transaction when all updates to any resources involved in the transaction are reversed.

SAX Simple API for XML. An event-driven, serial-access mechanism for accessing XML documents.

screen scraping A technique for accessing a legacy information system by simulating user interaction with the legacy system's user interface.

security attributes A set of properties associated with a principal. Security attributes can be associated with a principal by an authentication protocol and/or by a J2EE Product Provider.

security constraint A declarative way to annotate the intended protection of Web content. A security constraint consists of a Web resource collection, an authorization constraint, and a user data constraint.

security context An object that encapsulates the shared-state information regarding security between two entities.

security permission A mechanism, defined by J2SE, used by the J2EE platform to express the programming restrictions imposed on Application Component Providers.

security permission set The minimum set of security permissions that a J2EE Product Provider must provide for the execution of each component type.

security policy domain A scope over which security policies are defined and enforced by a security administrator. A security policy domain has a collection of users (or principals), uses a well defined authentication protocol(s) for authenticating users (or principals), and may have groups to simplify the setting of security policies.

security role See **role (security)**.

security technology domain A scope over which the same security mechanism is used to enforce a security policy. Multiple security policy domains can exist within a single technology domain.

security view The set of security roles defined by the Application Assembler.

server principal The OS principal that the server is executing as.

servlet A Java program that extends the functionality of a Web server, generating dynamic content and interacting with Web clients using a request-response paradigm.

servlet container A container that provides the network services over which requests and responses are sent, decodes requests, and formats responses. All servlet containers must support HTTP as a protocol for requests and responses, but may also support additional request-response protocols, such as HTTPS.

servlet container, distributed A servlet container that can run a Web application that is tagged as distributable and that executes across multiple Java virtual machines running on the same host or on different hosts.

servlet context An object that contains a servlet's view of the Web application within which the servlet is running. Using the context, a servlet can log events, obtain URL references to resources, and set and store attributes that other servlets in the context can use.

servlet mapping Defines an association between a URL pattern and a servlet. The mapping is used to map requests to servlets.

session An object used by a servlet to track a user's interaction with a Web application across multiple HTTP requests.

session bean An enterprise bean that is created by a client and that usually exists only for the duration of a single client-server session. A session bean performs operations, such as calculations or accessing a database, for the client. While a session bean may be transactional, it is not recoverable should a system crash occur. Session bean objects either can be stateless or can maintain conversational state across methods and transactions. If a session bean maintains state, then the EJB container manages this state if the object must be removed from memory. However, the session bean object itself must manage its own persistent data.

SSL Secure Socket Layer. A security protocol that provides privacy over the Internet. The protocol allows client-server applications to communicate in a way that cannot be eavesdropped or tampered with. Servers are always authenticated and clients are optionally authenticated.

SQL Structured Query Language. The standardized relational database language for defining database objects and manipulating data.

SQL/J A set of standards that includes specifications for embedding SQL statements in methods in the Java programming language and specifications for calling Java static methods as SQL stored procedures and user-defined functions. An SQL checker can detect errors in static SQL statements at program development time, rather than at execution time as with a JDBC driver.

stateful session bean A session bean with a conversational state.

stateless session bean A session bean with no conversational state. All instances of a stateless session bean are identical.

System Administrator The person responsible for configuring and administering the enterprise's computers, networks, and software systems.

transaction An atomic unit of work that modifies data. A transaction encloses one or more program statements, all of which either complete or roll back. Transactions enable multiple users to access the same data concurrently.

transaction attribute A value specified in an enterprise bean's deployment descriptor that is used by the EJB container to control the transaction scope when the enterprise bean's methods are invoked. A transaction attribute can have the following values: `Required`, `RequiresNew`, `Supports`, `NotSupported`, `Mandatory`, `Never`.

transaction isolation level The degree to which the intermediate state of the data being modified by a transaction is visible to other concurrent transactions and data being modified by other transactions is visible to it.

transaction manager Provides the services and management functions required to support transaction demarcation, transactional resource management, synchronization, and transaction context propagation.

Tool Provider An organization or software vendor that provides tools used for the development, packaging, and deployment of J2EE applications.

URI Uniform Resource Identifier. A compact string of characters for identifying an abstract or physical resource. A URI is either a URL or a URN. URLs and URNs are concrete entities that actually exist; A URI is an abstract superclass.

URL Uniform Resource Locator. A standard for writing a textual reference to an arbitrary piece of data in the World Wide Web. A URL looks like "protocol:// host/localinfo" where "protocol" specifies a protocol for fetching the object (such as HTTP or FTP), "host" specifies the Internet name of the targeted host, and "localinfo" is a string (often a file name) passed to the protocol handler on the remote host.

URL path The URL passed by a HTTP request to invoke a servlet. The URL consists of the Context Path + Servlet Path + PathInfo, where Context Path is the path prefix associated with a servlet context of which this servlet is a part. If this context is the default context rooted at the base of the Web server's URL namespace, the path prefix will be an empty string. Otherwise, the path prefix starts with a / character but does not end with a / character. Servlet Path is the path section that directly corresponds to the mapping that activated this request. This path starts with a / character. PathInfo is the part of the request path that follows the Servlet Path but precedes the query string.

Index

X

The Java™ Series

 The Java Web Services Tutorial
ISBN 0-201-63456-2

 The Java Programming Language Third Edition
ISBN 0-201-70433-1

 Effective Java Programming Language Guide
ISBN 0-201-31005-8

 The J2EE Tutorial
ISBN 0-201-79168-4

 The Java Tutorial, Third Edition
A Short Course on the Basics
ISBN 0-201-70393-9

 The Java Tutorial Continued
The Rest of the JDK
ISBN 0-201-48558-3

 J2EE Technology in Practice
ISBN 0-201-74622-0

 The Java Developers ALMANAC 1.4, Volume 1
ISBN 0-201-75280-8

 The Java Developers ALMANAC 1.4, Volume 2
ISBN 0-201-76810-0

 The Java Class Libraries Second Edition, Volume 1
ISBN 0-201-31002-3

 The Java Class Libraries Second Edition, Volume 2
ISBN 0-201-31003-1

 The Java Class Libraries Second Edition, Volume 1
Supplement for the Java 2 Platform
ISBN 0-201-48552-4

 Programming Open Service Gateways with Java Embedded Server Technology
ISBN 0-201-71102-8

 Java Card Technology for Smart Cards
ISBN 0-201-70329-7

 JavaSpaces Principles, Patterns, and Practice
ISBN 0-201-30955-6

 Inside Java 2 Platform Security
ISBN 0-201-31000-7

 The Java Language Specification Second Edition
ISBN 0-201-31008-2

 Java Message Service API Tutorial and Reference
ISBN 0-201-78472-6

 Concurrent Programming in Java Second Edition
Design Principles and Patterns
ISBN 0-201-31009-0

 JNDI API Tutorial and Reference
ISBN 0-201-70502-8

 The Java Native Interface
ISBN 0-201-32577-2

 The Java Virtual Machine Specification Second Edition
ISBN 0-201-43294-3

 Applying Enterprise JavaBeans
ISBN 0-201-70267-3

 Programming Wireless Devices with the Java 2 Platform, Micro Edition
ISBN 0-201-74627-1

 Java 2 Platform, Enterprise Edition
Platform and Component Specifications
ISBN 0-201-70456-0

 J2EE Connector Architecture and Enterprise Application Integration
ISBN 0-201-77580-8

 Designing Enterprise Applications with the J2EE Platform, Second Edition
ISBN 0-201-78790-3

 The Java 3D API Specification, Second Edition
ISBN 0-201-71041-2

 Java Look and Feel Design Guidelines: Advanced Topics
ISBN 0-201-77582-4

 The JFC Swing Tutorial
A Guide to Constructing GUIs
ISBN 0-201-43321-4

 JDBC API Tutorial and Reference, Second Edition
Universal Data Access for the Java 2 Platform
ISBN 0-201-43328-1

 Java Platform Performance
Strategies and Tactics
ISBN 0-201-70969-4

 The Jini Specifications Second Edition
ISBN 0-201-72617-3

Please see our web site (http://www.awl.com/cseng/javaseries)
for more information on these titles.